NOBLE FAMILIES OF PORTUGAL

ABREU

Felgueiras Gaio

Translated and Edited by Luís Pontes

CLEARFIELD

Printed for
Clearfield Company by
Genealogical Publishing Co.
Baltimore, Maryland
2009

ISBN-13: 978-0-8063-5407-1

Made in the United States of America

PREFACE

Manoel José da Costa FELGUEIRAS GAIO (1750-1831) born in Barcelos, in the northern Portuguese Province of Minho, is one of the most important genealogists of all time in Portugal, and certainly the best-known. A member of the nobility, he was a also a landowner, a judge and a benefactor of the Santa Casa de Misericórdia of Barcelos (a public hospital), to which he willed his monumental *Nobiliário de Famílias de Portugal* which is composed of 33 books and encompasses more than 500 families. To write this work, Gaio spent many decades of his life (working until his very last years) in a continuous and painstaking activity of genealogical research and data organization, based on an enormous number and diversity of bibliographical references and documental sources, many of them no longer in existence.

In spite of this importance, the *Nobiliário* remained unpublished for over a century after Gaio's death. Its first printing dates from 1938-1941, when it was edited and published in Braga by Agostinho de Azevedo Meirelles and Domingos de Araújo Affonso. However, even after its publication, the *Nobiliário* remained available only to those who could find a copy of it (its first printing had only 250 copies) and, above all, to the very few able to overcome the enormous difficulties posed by its text, written in old-fashioned Portugese and filled with abbreviations, ambiguities, obscure passages, historical allusions, etc., which make it difficult to understand even for the average native Portugese speaker.

The edition we begin to present in an English version is based on this first publication. Our aim in this translation has been twofold: to keep the information content as close as possible to the original text, and at the same time to adopt a fluent modern style, enabling the English reader to overcome the above-mentioned difficulties. In order to achieve our goal, we have had to make several additions and modifications to the original, such as providing cultural and historical background information, changing the numbering of sections and subsections (which was frequently incorrect in the original text and, because of that, greatly differs from this translation in many passages), commenting on contradictions and ambiguities, suppressing repeated information, etc. Also the division of the work has been modified, and we have opted to break the compendium into smaller parts; for instance, this first volume is only about the Abreu family.

We hope our work will help anyone with interest in Portugese and Spanish genealogy, though not proficient in the Portugese language, to have direct contact with this major source of reference. And in doing so, we also hope to be helping descendants of the "Portuguese diaspora," dispersed across the world, to find and know more about their Iberian roots.

Luís Pontes
Juiz de Fora, August 25th, 2007

PORTUGUESE RANKS OF NOBILITY*

KNIGHT-*FIDALGO* VS. *FIDALGO*-KNIGHT: WHEN ORDER MATTERS

In Portugal, a usual means of nobilitation was linked to the *affiliations* in the Royal Household, by which a man was declared to be a noble and was given a rank in a category system encompassing three classes, each of them with three ranks, as follows (with the original Portuguese titles in parentheses and categories decreasing top-bottom):

1st Class:
1) Knight-*Fidalgo* (*Fidalgo Cavaleiro*)
2) Squire-*Fidalgo* (*Fidalgo Escudeiro*)
3) Page-*Fidalgo* (*Moço Fidalgo*)

2nd Class:
1) *Fidalgo*-Knight (*Cavaleiro Fidalgo*)
2) *Fidalgo*-Squire (*Escudeiro Fidalgo*)
3) Chamber Valet (*Moço da Câmera*)

3rd Class:
1) Knight (*Cavaleiro*)
2) Squire (*Escudeiro*)
3) Messenger (*Reposteiro*)

For all these ranks there was also a division between numerary, supranumerary and extranumerary members. Numerary members, who ranked first, were entitled to stipends and had their names properly recorded in the Court to which they were admitted. Supranumerary members, who ranked second, were also admitted to the Court and enjoyed the same privileges as the numerary, except for the stipends. And the extranumerary members were not registered members of the Court, and did not enjoy all the privileges that the numerary and supranumerary members had.

Among the two top ranks of the two top classes, there is a curious and meaningful distinction (for instance, between a *Knight-Fidalgo* and a *Fidalgo-Knight*). A Knight-Fidalgo (and something similar was true of a Squire-Fidalgo), was first of all a noble, and then a knight. On the other hand, a Fidalgo-Knight was first of all a knight, and then a noble. This was a way of dealing with two classes of nobility, the *old* and the *new* (also known as hereditary nobility and civil nobility, respectively). In the first class were ranked those who acquired their nobility naturally by birth, whereas in the second class, their nobility was acquired through the offices they held.

*Luís Pontes, based on Gaio's essay Da Nobreza (On Nobility). Both these texts deal exclusively with low nobility titles; high nobility titles in Portugal are similar to those in the rest of Europe: Duque (Duke), Marquês (Marquis), Conde (Count/Earl), Visconde(Viscount) and Barão (Baron), and are not discussed here.

This rigorous criterion, though, did not last too long, especially when the King's need of sailors, warriors and settlers grew after the Portuguese Empire began expanding over new colonies in Africa, Asia and America. Granting nobility was a common and inexpensive currency for the King to pay his subjects' relevant works of colonization, and commoners began receiving the highest ranks in compensation for pioneering the conquered territory.

It was possible for a noble in this system to climb a number of steps in the hierarchy. For instance, a Page-Fidalgo could be advanced to Squire-Fidalgo, and then to Knight-Fidalgo. This promotion usually also depended on the services rendered by the recipient, who had to prove his ancestry and deeds by testimonies and other means before a Royal Board.

There is a caveat about this system: Before 1572, the year in which King Sebastian changed the ranking rules, *the opposite was true*, *i. e.*, a Fidalgo-Knight was superior to a Knight-Fidalgo, and a Fidalgo-Squire was superior to a Squire-Fidalgo.

THE STRUCTURING OF INFORMATION IN GAIO'S WORK

Chapters. In Gaio's *Noble Families of Portugal*, each family is dealt with in a separate chapter, whose length may vary from a few lines to several hundred pages. This first volume is composed of two chapters, the Abreus of Regalados and the Abreus of Grade, so named after the places where these families originally come from.

There are many cross-references among the chapters, which are indicated by "NFP [Family Name]". For instance, "NFP Almeida" refers to the Chapter about the Almeida family (of Gaio's Noble Families of Portugal — NFP).

Sections §. Chapters are divided into sections, the number of which may vary from one or two to a few hundred, depending on the size of the chapter. For instance, in this volume, in the chapter of the Abreus of Regalados there are 144 sections, whereas in the chapter of the Abreus of Grade there are 31 sections.

Each section gives the descendance (sometimes encompassing 5, 6 or more generations) of the first person mentioned in it. For instance, in the chapter of Abreu of Regalados, section §5 begins with Lopo Gomes de Abreu and mentions his descendants until the fourth generation.

It is important to note that *sections are generally independent of each other, so the numerical succession of sections does not necessarily indicate chronological succession of generations (although this can incidentally happen sometimes).* For instance, whereas in §9 the first name mentioned is Vasco Gomes de Abreu, in the next section (§10) the first name given does not refer to Vasco's descendants, but to Vasco's brother Antão Gomes de Abreu. In some cases, there may even be no connection between two successive sections (for instance, §124 is about Ruy Gomes de Abreu, whereas §125 refers to Francisco de Abreu, whose parentage is not even mentioned).

Subsections N. As the term indicates, a subsection is a subdivision of a section and, like the latter, it describes the descendancy of the first person mentioned in it (whose name is written in upper case, to distinguish it from the other names of the same subsection, which are all written in lower case). However, differently to section counting, the order of subsections (N1, N2, …, etc.) *does establish a succession of generations (within a given stem).* For instance, in the above-mentioned example in §5, Lopo Gomes de Abreu (written as LOPO GOMES DE ABREU, because he is the first person mentioned in his subsection) is ranked N10 (because his father was N9), and all Lopo's three children — Isabel Montenegro, Maria Sotomayor and Francisco Gomes de Abreu — are ranked N11, etc.[i] So in this system, people with the same distance in generations from a common stem (referred to as N1) are given the same subsection number. In this fashion, for instance, numbers are the same among brothers, first cousins, and so on.

---

[i] In the convention we have adopted, this would be given as "NFP Abreu of Regalados §5 N10 Sub11" or, briefly, "§5 N10 Sub11." (T. N.)

SPELLING AND RESTORATION OF NAMES

In order to provide the reader with a more reliable database, *we have opted to keep the original spelling of all the names of people mentioned in the original* (1938) *Portuguese edition.* (Exceptions to this rule are the historical figures (v. g., kings and queens), whose names are written in their English forms). This has led us to write, for instance, the name "Thereja" (as it originally appeared) instead of changing it to the modern form "Teresa." In the same fashion, we have kept "Affonço" instead of writing "Afonso," and so on.

One aspect of the first edition which makes its reading particularly cumbersome is the extensive use of abbreviations (v. g., "Mª Rz" and "Ant.º Per.ª") for people's names. In cases like these, we have opted to restore the original name, writing it out with the full original spelling, and using a dot ['] to indicate this reconstruction: so we have written the above-mentioned names as "Maria˙ Rodrigues'" and "Antonio˙ Pereira˙." In some special cases we have opted to suppress the original spelling because it deviates too much from the modern version, so keeping the original form would be rather clumsy. For instance, we have preferred to write "Sampayo'" instead of the original form "S. Payo."

LIST OF ABBREVIATIONS

b. = born
B. = bastard
d. = deceased; died
D. = *Dom, Dona*
dsp = *decessit sine prole* (died without issue)
f. = fought
fn. = footnote
lf. = leaf
lit. = literally
m. = married
NFP = *Noble Families of Portugal/ Nobiliário de Famílias de Portugal*

p. = page
PC = Pedigree Chart(s)
Port. = Portuguese
pp. = pages
r. = reigned
Ref. = Reference
rev. = reverse
Rev. = Reverend
s. = sheet
sp = *sine prole* (without issue)
T = Tome
T.N. = Translator's note

FOOTNOTES

There are two types of footnotes in this text:
a) Original first edition footnotes, numbered in arabic numbers in a single increasing sequence (1, 2, 3, ...) through the end of the book.
b) Translator´s notes, numbered in roman numbers and starting from *i* at each page in which they appear.

NOBLE FAMILIES OF PORTUGAL

ABREU

The Abreus of Regalados
The Abreus of Grade

ABREU

THE ABREUS OF REGALADOS

§1

N1   GONÇALO MARTINS˙ DE ABREU, or *Evreu* came from the city of Évreux, in Normandy, France, to Portugal. He was descended through a male line from the Counts of Évreux – an ancient princely house of Normandy, which was a branch of the ruling house of Denmark –, who in turn were distant descendants of Edward the Elder, King of England, whose line extended downward for six generations from this sovereign until Amaury V, who eventually vested the county of Évreux in the French crown[i]. This is the family of the counts of Évreux to which the Portuguese chronicler D. Antonio˙ de Lima and other reputable authors trace the Abreus. This connection should not be confused with the second line of the counts of the same name, deriving from

---

[i] In the original text, the last Count of Évreux of the first line is called *Américo* V, which is a mistake, for his name was *Amaury V de Monfort*. As to the fact that the first Counts of Évreux were descendants of King Edward the Elder, we have not found this link, although it is well known that there is a connection between these counts and Aethelwulf, King of the West Saxons in England and Edward the Elder's uncle. The information by which "Americo" (Amaury) was a sixth-generation descendant of King Edward the Elder is ambiguous in the original: "*[os] Condes de Evreus (...) tiverão principio em Eduardo 1.º o velho, e subsestirão athe Américo 5 seu 5.º neto*". It is not clear if this counting of generations begins in the English sovereign or in the first Count of Évreux; by guesswork we have opted for the first version, although, as far as we are concerned and as we have said above, this fact has yet to be confirmed. (More details about the Counts of Évreux are given in the foldout at the back of this book.) (T. N.)

Philip III the Bold, King of France (sic)[i], a mistake committed by Gándara [Chap. 17, p. 14], Chief Chronicler of Castile[ii], and also by the author of *Estrangeiros no Lima* [Vol. 1, p. 340][iii], though not endorsed by many ancient genealogical works and serious authors, who favor the connection with the first Évreux line. Some have also claimed the Abreus descend from the family of Arcão dos Cotos justifying this hypothesis by the weak argument of the presence of wings in the arms of the Abreus[iv], though this claim has not been accepted by the consensus of opinion. Gándara [*s*. 148] mentions the high nobility of this family; Alvaro de Vera [*Notas ao Conde D. Pedro, s.* 224, pp. 644-645] states that the family of Abreu has left descendants in nearly all titled houses of Portugal and many of Castile, its members accounting for over 70 peerages (dukedoms, marquessates and countships). From the same Counts of Évreux descend the house of Évreux and the Earls of Essex in England.

Ancient genealogical chronicles greatly differ over the identity of the children, grandchildren and great grandchildren of Gonçallo Martins˙ de Evreus, whose name has been corrupted into *Abreus* (sic). We abide by the opinion in this matter of the most eminent researchers on this family, whose great antiquity has yet very little documentation able to settle these controversies.

Gonçallo Martins˙ de Evreus, later *Abreu*, was a companion to Count Henry of Burgundy, Chief Steward to the Count's wife, Queen Theresa and their son, King Afonso Henriques, and *rico homem*[v], as is recorded in a charter of donation made by the Queen in 1112 and kept at the Abbey of Saint Dominic in Lisbon. Gonçallo Martins˙ was a general in the battle of Veiga da Matança, so named after the great slaughter suffered by the Castilians in Veiga, near Arcos de Valdevez[vi], in

Count Henry of Burgundy [b. 1066, d. 1112] was the fourth son of Duke Henry of Burgundy. This male line of ascent continues with Robert, first Duke of Burgundy; Robert II, the Pious, King of France, and Hugh Capet, King of France. Count Henry went to Spain and fought in the wars of the Reconquest (moved by Christians against the Moors who had seized the Iberic Peninsula in the 8th century), where he sided with Alfonsus VI, King of Leon, and married D. Theresa, the Spanish King's illegitimate daughter. He received in dowry the County of Portucale, cradle of the Kingdom of Portugal which would eventually be founded by his legitimate son D. Afonso Henriques [b. ~1110, d. 1185]. Henry of Burgundy is therefore the stem of the Dynasty of Burgundy, the first of Portugal.

---

[i] Actually, the second or Capetian line of the Counts of Évreux does not begin in Philip III the Bold, King of France, but in his brother Louis of France, to whom King Philip granted the said county. In spite of this, it is still valid Gaio´s remark that it is a mistake to connect the Abreus to this branch of the Royal Household of France . (More details about the Counts of Évreux are given in the foldout at the back of this book.) (T. N.)

[ii] Felipe de la Gándara, Spanish chronicler of the 17th century, who was appointed Chronicler of Leon and Galicia by the King. (T. N.)

[iii] *Estrangeiros no Lima* (2 Vols.) was written by Manuel Gomes de Lima Bezerra and published for the first time in 1785-1791 in Coimbra. (T. N.)

[iv] Cotos: *lit. Port. old-fash.* wings. (T. N.)

[v] *Rico homem* (*lit.* rich man) was a title used by the members of the greater aristocracy in medieval Portugal, who had the right to attend the King's court. (T. N.)

[vi] Veiga da Matança (lit.: Slaughter Crop Field) was a battle fought in 1143 on a plain in northern Portugal (near Arcos de Valdevez) between the forces of King Afonso Henriques of Portugal and those of his cousin, King Afonso VII of Leon, allegedly caused by the refusal of the Portuguese King to pay vassalage to the Spanish Emperor. Legend has it that the Vez River, on whose banks the battle was fought, had its waters temporarily turned red by the blood of the many wounded and dead. In spite of this belief, some say this encounter was more a challenge between the two sovereigns' knights than a real battle. (T. N.)

which the victory was won for the Portuguese forces by the said ancestor of the Abreus, who shrewdly ordered his men to dig pits on the battlefield, covered with grating, into which the enemies fell. El Rei[i] bestowed upon him the tower and the house of Grade[ii], and he settled in the parish of São Pedro de Morufe, in the territory of Monção, where he founded the tower of Abreu, as well as a manor and a fief in the village of Morufe, with its seat in Pica de Regalados, all these estates belonging to his family. He had over one hundred and sixty thousand vassals in his villages and other places, such as São Fins, Lapela, Barbeita, Regalados and others. His wife's name is unknown. He is said to have had the following children:

> 2 Lourenço Gonçalves˙ de Abreu
> 2 Gomes de Abreu N3 (son of Gonçallo Martins˙ N1, according to some authors)

N2   LOURENÇO GONÇALVES˙ DE ABREU, son of Gonçallo Martins˙ N1, inherited his father's house and built the Tower of Lapela, of which he was governor. A very distinguished nobleman, he took part with his father in the battle of Veiga da Matança in Arcos de Valdevez. His wife's name is unknown

> 3 Gomes Lourenço de Abreu
> 3 Alvaro Lourenço de Abreu

For this battle, see footnote vi on the previous page

N3   GOMES LOURENÇO DE ABREU, called by some Gomes de Abreu, son of Lourenço Gonçalves˙ de Abreu N2. According to others, he was the son of Gonçallo Martins˙ N1, whom we prefer to consider his grandfather. There are records about him in the Monastery of Longos Vales. He was a very distinguished nobleman in the time of King Sancho I. Nothing is known about his wife

> 4 Ruy Gomes de Abreu

King Sancho I r. 1185–1211

N4   RUY GOMES DE ABREU, son of Gomes Lourenço N3, was the lord of the house of Abreu and a very distinguished nobleman in the time of King Sancho I and King Afonso II. His wife's name is unknown

> 5 Lourenço Rodrigues˙ de Abreu
> 5 Gonçallo Rodrigues˙ de Abreu §3
> 5 Maria Gomes, wife of Garcia Paes

King Sancho I r. 1185–1211
King Afonso II r. 1211–1223

---

[i] El Rei: Certainly Afonso Henriques, first King of Portugal, who *r.* 1139-1185. (T. N.)

[ii] *Grade*: Port. grating. (T. N.)

King Sancho II r. 1223–1248
King Afonso III r. 1248–1279

N5   LOURENÇO RODRIGUES˙ DE ABREU, son of Ruy de Abreu N4, was the lord of Regalados and of the manor-house of Abreu, and lived in the time of King Sancho II and King Afonso III

   6 Gomes Lourenço de Abreu

King Afonso III r. 1248–1279
King Dinis r. 1279–1325

N6   GOMES LOURENÇO DE ABREU, son of Lourenço Rodrigues˙ de Abreu N5, inherited his father's house and the fief of Regalados, and was a very distinguished nobleman in the time of King Afonso III and King Dinis. He was also the lord of Valladares by his wife, D. Guiomar Lourenço de Valladares, daughter of Lourenço Soares de Valladares [NFP Valadares §2 N4]. When El Rei Dinis wished to bestow the municipality of Melgaço upon another nobleman, Gomes Lourenço opposed this and received a favourable sentence on July 1, 1317

   7 Lourenço Gomes de Abreu §2
   7 Domingos˙ Gomes de Abreu, upon whom in 1371 El Rei bestowed the lordship of Bayão
   7 D. Beringeira Gomes de Abreu, wife of Vasco Affonço˙ de Lira [NFP Lira, Introduction N8]
   7 Gomes Lourenço de Abreu §64
   7 D. Mecia Gomes de Abreu, who is said by some to have married Garcia Vaz˙ Aranha, with which we do not agree
   7 D. Beatris de Abreu, wife of João Vicente de Vallena
   7 B. Gomes Lourenço Villarinho, lord of the manor of Villaboa, entailer of the Chapel of São Bras in São João de Longos Vales and son of Gomes Lourenço de Abreu according to some
    8 Affonço˙ Lourenço Villarinho, who married Ignes Affonço˙ Bacellar and is the ancestor of the family of Villarinho

§2

N1   LOURENÇO GOMES DE ABREU[1], son of Gomes Lourenço de Abreu §1 N6. He is the ancestor of the Abreus about whom there are fewer uncertainties,

---

[1] The father of Lourenço Gomes is not originally mentioned in the *Livro das Linhagens* of Count D. Pedro, but rather in the addition to D. Pedro's work, made by Lavanha, according to Alvaro Ferreira de Vera. In *Corografia Portuguesa,* Tome 3, p. 367, it is stated that this Lourenço de Abreu was the son of Gomes Lourenço de Abreu and D. Guiomar Lourenço de Valladares [§1 N6] and the grandson of Gonçallo˙ Rodrigues˙ de Abreu and D. Mecia Rodrigues˙ Fafes [§3 N 5].

though his own pedigree is the object of controversies[i]. Some say his parents were the same mentioned in §1 N6, but some also argue he was the grandson of Gonçallo Rodrigues˙ de Abreu [§1 N4 Sub5], with which we disagree. This Lourenço Gomes de Abreu was the lord of the fiefs of Regalados[2], Barbeita and Valladares, the last of which came to him through his mother. He also had the castles of Lapela, Melgaço, and was the most distinguished nobleman of Entre Douro e Minho Province, having been appointed representative of the nobility of this province in the time of King Dinis [Ref.: D. Antonio˙ de Lima, *Livro das Linhagens*]. He was also appointed Ambassador of King Afonso IV of Portugal to King James II of Aragon, and afterwards to King Afonso II of Castile to negotiate peace between Portugal and Castile [Ref.: *Chronicle of King Afonso IV*[ii]]. He married D. Theresa Correa˙ de Azevedo˙, daughter of Estevão Paes de Azevedo and his wife D. Guiomar Rodrigues˙ de Vasconcellos˙ [Ref.: NFP Azevedo §6 N13; Count D. Pedro, *Livro de Linhagens*, title 39 N9, p. 21 (which text also features additions on this matter made by Lavanha, p. 47, and by Alvaro Ferreira de Vera, p. 218 and p. 643); Zurita, Part 1, Book 6, Ch. 68]

> 2 Diogo Gomes de Abreu §492
> 2 Gomes Gonçalves˙ de Abreu §99, from whom the family of Falcão is descended
> 2 Vasco Gomes de Abreu[3]
> 2 D. Constança Lourenço de Abreu, wife of Affonso˙ Rodrigues˙ Villarinho [NFP Vilarinho §1 N3]. Others say she was the daughter of Gomes Lourenço (de Abreu) §64 N1, with which we disagree
> 2 D. Guiomar Lourenço de Abreu, wife of Soeiro Affonso˙ Soares Tangil
> 2 D. Beatris Gomes de Abreu §22

N2   VASCO GOMES DE ABREU, son of Lourenço de Abreu §2 N1, was a very distinguished nobleman, whose kinship to Queen Leonor Telles led him to

---

[i] Perhaps this is the reason why the author decided to identify this Lourenço Gomes de Abreu by N1, and not N7 (which he ought to receive, in case of being the son of Gomes Lourenço de Abreu N6). This numeration change also happens to his brother, Gomes Lourenço de Abreu (initially mentioned in §1 N6, and whose descendency is detailed in §64). (T. N.)

[2] Regalados was afterwards granted by King John I to the Count of Barcellos, perhaps when this monarch took the lands of his son. The Count of Barcellos in his turn bestowed these lands upon Nuno Viegas, the Younger, as is written in NFP Rego §1 N4 and in this chapter N3 below.

[ii] Written by Rui de Pina (~1440 - ~1522). (T. N.)

[3] Alvaro Ferreira˙ de Vera (in his additions to Count D. Pedro's *Livro das Linhagens*, s. 218) mentions only two sons of Lourenço Gomes: Diogo Gomes and Vasco Gomes (referred to in N2), and says they were related to Queen Leonor Telles by Guiomar Rodrigues˙ de Vasconcellos˙, their maternal grandmother.

side with Castile against Portugal. He is mentioned in the *Chronicle of King Ferdinand*[i], Ch. 141, in the following terms:

He inherited the house of his father and, by grant of King Ferdinand was the lord of Valladares, Lapela, Melgaço, and Honor of Abreu, which had belonged to his great grandfather Lourenço Rodrigues˙ de Abreu [§1 N5], having been mentioned in the records of King Afonso IV, King Peter I and King Ferdinand. Vasco Gomes de Abreu was with other counsellors a witness to the solemn oath taken by King Peter I, by which this monarch declared that D. Ignes de Castro was his legitimate wife. As this nobleman sided with the forces of Queen Leonor Telles, King John I confiscated all his lands in the district of Frazão and bestowed them upon Lourenço Figueira.

The *Historia Genealogica da Casa Real* (*Genealogical History of the Royal Household of Portugal*, Tome 12, p. 428) in a passage about Gaspar Alvares˙ Lousada, says this Vasco Gomes de Abreu requested a licence from King Ferdinand to rebuild his tower, which was wasted by time and war, in order to preserve the memory of his ancestors in the land of Abreu. The licence to rebuild the tower, then named Stronghold, was indeed granted to him, and can be found in Fernão Lopes's *Chronicle of King Ferdinand*, Vol. 2, p. 9, which says: *"We El Rei Ferdinand etc. grant the licence to build a house in the place called Abreu, with the same height it had in former times, along with surrounding gateways and walls as well as battlements, parapets, and front entrance as it had been erected˙before"*, from which the antiquity of this family becomes apparent. This ancient building stood in the land of Riba Douro over the Monastery of São João de Longos Vales, and eventually passed from the house of Abreu to that of Gontomil.

According to some genealogists, this Vasco Gomes de Abreu married Mayor Annes Portocarreiro, daughter of Fernão Annes Portocarreiro and his wife Maria Vasques Rezende, being this Fernão the brother of (...), lord of Vila Real [NFP Azevedo §114 N15][ii]. Yet others state that D. Mayor Annes was the daughter of João Rodrigues˙ Portocarreiro, and the granddaughter of this Fernão Annes, which opinion we do not agree with

  3 Diogo Gomes de Abreu

  3 Mecia Gomes de Abreu, who according to some was married to Garcia Vaz˙ Aranha, from whom the Abreus of Grade are descended, with which we do not agree

  3 Tereja Gomes de Abreu §24, who married Lopo Gomes de Lira [with issue in NFP Lira §1 N2]

King Afonso IV r. 1325–1357
King Peter I r. 1357–1367
King Ferdinand r. 1367–1383
King John I r. 1385–1433
(For more details about the historical events mentioned here, see box the next page)

---

[i] Written by Fernão Lopes (~1380 - 1460). (T. N.)

[ii] In NFP Azevedo §114 N15, D. Mayor Annes Portocarreiro's mother is given as Maria˙ Vasques *de Azevedo˙* (and not Maria Vasques Rezende). In the same passage D. Mayor Annes is also said to have married *Diogo* Gomes de Abreu, and not Vasco Gomes de Abreu, with the first version seeming to be a mistake. (T. N.)

QUEEN IGNES DE CASTRO

The affair of King Peter I and Ignes de Castro is one of the most celebrated romances in Portuguese history and literature. Ignes de Castro, who was the illegitimate daughter of a Castilian nobleman of royal ancestry, arrived in Portugal as a lady-in-waiting to D. Constanza, when this lady married Prince Peter (the future King Peter I, who was to reign from 1357 to 1367), son of King Afonso IV. Prince Peter fell deeply in love with Ignes de Castro, with whom he started an affair and by whom he had four children, in spite of his marriage to D. Constanza. However, King Afonso's top advisers feared the growing influence exerted by this Castilian lady on the future King of Portugal, and decided to eliminate her. In fact, with the king's approval, on January 7th, 1355, in Coimbra, Ignes de Castro was stabbed to death by three members of the nobility. This murder triggered a civil war between the Portuguese heir and his royal father, which devasted the country. Upon Afonso's death, Peter became king and savagely executed two of Ignes's murderers (the third managed to seek refuge in the papal territory of Avignon, France), this being the reason why he was given the byname of Peter the Cruel. In 1360, he made a solemn statement by which he declared that, after D. Constanza's death, he had secretly married Ignes de Castro, thereby legitimating the children he had by her (this was the oath witnessed by Vasco Gomes de Abreu §2 N2 and other noblemen). So, curiously, Ignes de Castro became Queen of Portugal after her death. Legend says (although this story is most probably untrue), that King Peter had Ignes's body crowned and her hands kissed by the courtiers.

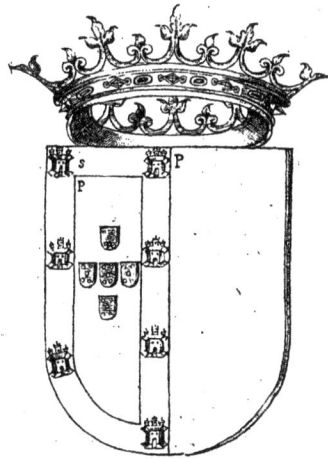

Arms of the Queens of Portugal

QUEEN LEONOR TELLES DE MENEZES

After the troubling episodes involving Ignes de Castro and King Peter I, the latter's son, King Ferdinand (r. 1367-1383) also plunged Portugal into a serious political crisis when he fell in love with Leonor Telles de Menezes, a lady and member of the lesser Castilian nobility, wife of a Portuguese nobleman called João Lourenço da Cunha. King Ferdinand obtained the annulment of Leonor's marriage on alleged grounds of consanguinity in order to marry her (which he did secretly), and had by her a daughter, Beatriz, who was his sole legitimate child and who would later become the wife of King John I of Castile. Upon King Ferdinand's death in 1383, his widow Queen Leonor became the first woman to rule over Portugal whilst the succession to the throne remained in abeyance. She wished to bestow the reign upon her daughter and her son-in-law the Castilian King, a decision supported by a significant part of the upper Portuguese clergy and nobility (including Vasco Gomes de Abreu and his son Diogo Gomes de Abreu, referred to in §2 N2 and N3). However, these plans were opposed by the bourgeoisie, the members of the lower nobility and the common people, who favored the coronation of John, the Master of the Chivalric Order of Aviz, an illegitimate half-brother of King Ferdinand. Aided by his champion, Nuno Alvares Pereira (who was later to become the Constable of Portugal), the Master of Aviz led his partisans to a resounding victory over an invading Castilian army in the battle of Aljubarrota (August 14, 1385), which consolidated the independence of Portugal over Castile's ambitions (at least temporarily) and marked the end of the dynasty of Burgundy (of which King Ferdinand was the last representative) and the beginning of the dynasty of Aviz (of which John I was the first sovereign).

3 João Gomes de Abreu §23

3 Elena Gomes de Abreu (according to some a bastard daughter), wife of Vasco Gil Bacellar, lord of the manor-house of Bacelar [NFP Bacelar §1 N7]

3 Alvaro Vaz de Abreu, considered by some the ancestor of the Abreus of Grade [an opinion we also support, as is written in NFP Abreu of Grade, §1 N1]. He married D. Maria˙ Rodrigues˙ Pacheco and had

    4 João de Abreu, a distinguished nobleman in Caminha, who married Ignes Dias de Sousa, daughter of D. Lopo Dias de Sousa, Master of the Order of Christ. João de Abreu was the father of

    5 Alvaro de Abreu, from whom the Abreus of Grade are descended

For more details about this conflict, see box on the previous page.

King John I r. 1385–1433
King Ferdinand r. 1367–1383

N3   DIOGO GOMES DE ABREU, son of Vasco Gomes de Abreu N2, was the lord of the fief of Abreu, Valadares, Regalados, and other estates. He is mentioned in *Livro Velho* [N. 162, *s.* 589][i], in which it is stated that he accompanied his father when the latter sided with Castile, a deed which prevented him from enjoying his lands in Portugal. Notwithstanding, he regained royal favor when he accompanied King John I of Portugal. He possessed the royal rights of Vila Boa by a former grant of El Rei Ferdinand, and was appointed Chief Alcaide of Melgaço and Castro Laboreiro. He married his first wife D. Violante Affonso Telles de Menezes, aunt to the Queen of Castile, but had no issue by her. Later he married D. Leonor Viegas, daughter of Nuno Viegas, the Younger, Law Officer of Tras-os-Montes and lord of Calvos Dara, Aldea Nova, Cabeceiras de Basto, Arco de Baulhe, Aguiar de Neiva, Roças and Villa Boa da Roda. (It seems that this second marriage conveyed the advowson of Roças into Diogo de Abreu's family). Nuno Viegas, Diogo de Abreu's second father-in-law, was married to Ignes Dias do Rego, daughter of Ruy Dias do Rego. We have learned in a chronicle that Nuno Viegas and his wife made in 1433 an enfeoffment of their lands of Couceiro and the house of Regalados (the latter estate being an inheritance of the Abreu family), and that in 1423 King John I bestowed upon him the fief of Regalados, which had previously belonged to the Count of Barcelos [NFP Lago §1 N4 and NFP Rego §1 N5]

    4 Pedro Gomes de Abreu

    4 Vasco Gomes de Abreu §9

    4 Antao Gomes de Abreu §10

    4 João Gomes de Abreu §16

    4 Alvaro Gomes de Abreu

    4 D. Leonor de Abreu, who married D. Duarte da Cunha, son of Viscount D. Leonel de Lima

---

[i] *Livro Velho das Linhagens* (*lit*.: Ancient Book of Lineage), a Portuguese genealogical compendium written by an anonymous monk of the 13th century and published by Antonio Caetano de Sousa in 1727. (T. N.)

4 Affonço Gomes de Abreu

4 Duarte Gomes de Abreu (these last two names appear in a justification instrument possessed by the lords of the house of Avelar)

King Afonso V r. 1438–1481

N4 PEDRO GOMES DE ABREU, son of Diogo Gomes de Abreu N3, was the lord of the fief and house of Abreu in Valladares, as well as Roças and its advowsons, Villa Boa da Roda, and owned the royal rights of Monção, Aguiar de Neiva, Pena and other lands. He was the Governor of Lapela, a councillor to King Afonso V and the lord of Regalados, being mentioned in Book 1195 (sic). His Majesty returned to him part of his father's possessions according to a peace deal made with Castile. As said above, he enjoyed the royal rights of Monção, the manor and advowson of Roças and the manors of Couceiro and Corutelo, which had been enfeoffed by his grandfather Nuno Viegas. Pedro Gomes de Abreu married Aldonça de Sousa, bastard daughter of Lopo Dias de Sousa, who was appointed Master of the Order of Christ by El Rei Ferdinand at Queen

For this conclict and Queen Leonor Teles de Menezes, see box on p. 9

Leonor Teles de Menezes's request, his aunt, for the Queen was the sister of his mother D. Maria˙ de Menezes, wife of his father Alvaro Dias de Sousa [NFP Sousa §4 N17 and N(...) (sic)]

5 Lopo Gomes de Abreu[4]

5 João Gomes de Sousa §28

5 Mendo Gomes de Abreu §73

5 Vasco Gomes de Abreu

5 Ruy Gomes de Abreu §124

5 Nuno Gomes de Abreu

5 Luis Gomes de Abreu

5 D. Brites de Sousa, wife of Martim Affonso˙ de Mello, lord of Mello [with issue in NFP Mello §1 N10]

5 Diogo Gomes de Abreu

Besides the above issue, mentioned in the partition instrument (see fn. 4), Pedro de Abreu is said by others to have had other children, probably illegitimate for they do not appear in his will:

5 Elena Gomes de Abreu §22

5 D. Aldonça de Sousa. In NFP Araujo §2 N20 this lady also appears

---

[4] Lopo Gomes de Abreu and his siblings are mentioned in a partition document of the estates of Diogo Gomes and his wife Leonor Viegas [mentioned above in N3], signed by Alvaro Pires Vieira, Royal Corregidor in the time of King Afonso V, and written on March 15, 1458 in Torres Vedras by João Villa Real, whose copy or original was in the possession of Jacinto de Magalhães˙ e Menezes, lord of the house of Cardoso and the couple's grandson.

as the wife of Payo Rodrigues˙ de Araujo˙, lord of Barbudo, with issue

    5 B. Ruy Rodrigo Gomes de Abreu §52

N5   LOPO GOMES DE ABREU, son of Pedro Gomes N4, was the Aldaide General of Lapela. He had a legal dispute over the fief of Abreu with his uncle, which was judged in his favor in 1459[5]. He was the lord of Regalados, Abreu, Valadares, Roças, Vila Boa de Roda, Land of Pena and Aguiar da Neiva. He married D. Ignes de Lima, daughter of D. Leonel de Lima, first Viscount of Vila Nova de Cerveira, and his wife D. Felipa da Cunha, e Mello [NFP Lima §1 N11], who was the daughter of Alvaro da Cunha, lord of Pombeiro, and his wife D. Brites de Mello[6]

    6 Pedro Gomes de Abreu

    6 Duarte de Abreu, sp

    6 D. Brites de Lima, wife of João de Brito, brother of Luis de Brito, lord of the entail of São Lourenço [NFP Brito §6 N8][i]

    6 D. Felipa, wife of Baltasar˙ de Sequeira˙, lord of Prado. Afterwards she married Fernão de Sousa, called "o da Batalha" (*lit.* "the one who was in the battle")

N6   PEDRO GOMES DE ABREU, son of Lopo Gomes de Abreu N5. He succeeded to his father's house, was the lord of Regalados, Alcaide General of Lapela and Commendatory of the Order of Christ in Morufe. Due to the many crimes he commited he had to sell the manor of Corutelo in order to pay his legal expenses. He married D. Genebra de Magalhães˙, daughter of Fernando de Magalhães˙, the Elder, and his wife Brites de Mesquita, daughter of Martim Gonçalves˙ Pimentel. This Fernando de Magalhães˙ was the lord of the manor of Briteiros, which he bought from the Countess of Faro [NFP Magalhães §18 N6][ii]

    7 Leonel de Abreu

    7 Duarte de Abreu, who had illegitimate children

    7 Gomes Gonçalves˙ de Abreu, who married Catarina˙ Annes Golias [with issue in NFP Golias §1 N2]

---

[5] Faria, *Epitome da Historia Portuguesa*, Part 3, Ch. 3, p. 492.

[6] D. Ignes de Lima, wife of this Lopo Gomes de Abreu N5, was the sister of D. Rodrigo de Mello e Lima, Commander of Refoios and father of Joanna de Mello e Lima, who married her relative João Gomes de Sousa [§28 N 5].

[i] In NFP Brito §6 N8, João de Brito's (second) wife's name is Brites *da Silva*, and not Brites de Lima (T. N.)

[ii] Notwithstanding that, in NFP Magalhães §18 N6 Sub7, Genebra de Magalhães is said to have been the wife of *Francisco˙ de Magalhães* and that this couple did not have issue. (T. N.)

Infante João (1349-1387), Duke of Valencia de Campos, was the son of King Peter I of Portugal and Ignes de Castro (see also box on p. 9 and chart on p. 28)

7 Antonio Fernandes˙ de Abreu, who married his niece Agueda Golias [with issue in NFP Golias §7 N3], his descendancy being also mentioned in *Corographia Portuguesa*, Tome 3, p. 368[i]

Pedro Gomes de Abreu had bastard children by Catarina˙ de Eça, Abbess of Lorvão, daughter of D. Fernando de Eça and granddaughter of Infante *Dom* João, son of King Peter I and D. Ignes de Castro [NFP Eça §1 N2 and §6 N3]. The abbess made a sepulchre for her father in the Convent of Espirito Santo of Gouvea, upon which she put an epitaph mentioning his ancestry, to which her father's body was moved on January 25th, 1479

> 7 B. Antonio˙ de Abreu §51[ii]
> 7 B. Jorge de Abreu §7
> 7 B. Pedro Gomes de Abreu
> 7 B. Ruy Gomes de Abreu [§52], who married Ignes Brandão, daughter of Fernão Brandão, in Vianna
>> 8 Antonio˙ de Abreu
>> 8 Diogo Gomes
>> 8 Jorge de Abreu
>> 8 D. Brites
>> 8 D. Margarida˙
> 7 B. D. Catarina˙ de Abreu, wife of Pedro Marinho of Monção [with issue in NFP Marinho §2 N13][iii]
> 7 B. Diogo Gomes de Abreu, who went to India in 1546
> 7 B. João Gomes de Abreu, who some confuse with a namesake and ancestor of the house of Anquião, who is mentioned in §28

N7　LEONEL DE ABREU, son of Pedro Gomes de Abreu N6, inherited the house and lordships of his father and was the Alcaide General of Lapela, an office he exchanged for 100.000 *reis* with the Marquis of Villa Real. He married Maria˙ da Silva, daughter of Pedro Ribeiro˙ de Sousa (Alcaide General of Pombal and Commendatory of the Order of Christ) and Joanna de Lemos [NFP Vasconcelos §45 N16][iv]

> 8 Fernão de Lima, who was slain by the Moors in Tangier, sp
> 8 Pedro Gomes de Abreu, who was slain by the Moors in Mazagan, sp

---

[i] *Corographia Portuguesa* (3 vols.), written by Father Antonio Carvalho da Costa (1650-1715) and published for the first time between 1706 and 1712. (T. N.)

[ii] In §51, he is called Antonio de Abreu *Lima*. (T. N.)

[iii] In NFP Marinho §2 N13, Pedro Marinho's wife is called Catarina˙ *de Eça* and not Catarina de Abreu. (T. N.)

[iv] In NFP Vasconcelos §45 N16 Sub17, Leonel de Abreu's wife is called Maria˙ *de Meneses* and not Maria˙ da Silva. (T. N.)

8 D. Margarida de Abreu, wife of Manoel de Magalhães˙, lord of Ponte da Barca [NFP Magalhães §1 N9][i]

8 D. Catarina˙, a nun in the convent of Monchique

8 D. Isabel, a nun in Monchique

8 João Gomes de Abreu, who served the King, sp

8 Francisco, a clergyman

8 Pedro, a clergyman

8 D. Felipa, a nun in Monchique

8 D. Maria˙, a nun in Monchique

8 D. Isabel, a nun in the convent of Remedios, Braga

Leonel de Abreu's second wife was D. Maria˙ de Noronha, daughter of Francisco˙ de Lima, third Viscount of Vila Nova de Cerveira and Isabel de Almeida, daughter of D. João de Almeida, second Count of Abrantes

8 Francisco˙ de Abreu

8 João Gomes de Abreu, who served in India and was the captain of Bocaim

8 Pedro Gomes de Abreu, who had bastard issue

9 Manoel˙ de Abreu, who was married in Macarellos to (...), daughter of Antão Thome

8 Lopo Gomes de Abreu §54

8 Jorge de Abreu de Noronha

8 B. D. Felipa de Abreu, wife of Alvaro de Abreu Soares, bastard son of Affonço de Abreu [NFP Abreu of Grade §11 N6]

8 B. Pedro Gomes de Abreu, who went to India

8 B. Leonel de Abreu, who studied in Coimbra

For details about Portuguese ranks of nobility, see p. v

N 8 FRANCISCO˙ DE ABREU, son of Leonel de Abreu N7, was a Page-*Fidalgo* of the King's Household (by virtue of which he was entitled to a 12500-real stipend) and inherited the house and lordships of his father. He married Francisca˙ da Silva˙, daughter of Manoel˙ Machado (lord of Entre Homem and Cavado, and Commendatory of the Order of Christ in Sousel) and Joanna de Sousa˙ [NFP Machado §53 N19][ii]

9 João Gomes de Abreu, who was killed by his cousin Francisco˙ de Sousa in the yard of the Church of Saint Dominic, sp

9 Leonel de Abreu

9 D. Manoel˙ de Lima §25

9 Antonio˙ de Abreu Lima, who went to India and was married to D. Brites Velho, daughter of Fernão Velho, Tutor to Duke Theodosius

[i] In NFP Magalhães §1 N9, Margarida de Abreu is called Margarida *da Silva*. (T. N.)

[ii] Yet in NFP Machado §53 N19, Francisca da Silva's mother is called Joanna *da Silva˙*, and not Joanna de Sousa. (T.N.)

9 D. Maria˙ de Noronha, wife of Ayres Coelho, lord of Felgueiras [NFP Coelho §(...) (sic)]

9 D. Joana, sp

9 D. Guiomar, sp

N9   LEONEL DE ABREU, son of Francisco˙ de Abreu N8, owned the house of his father and the lordship of Regalados. He married Ignes Pereira˙ or Ignes de Lima, daughter of Francisco˙ Pereira˙, lord of Bertiandos, and D. Ana de Lima [NFP Pereira §63 N18]

> 10 Pedro Gomes de Abreu
>
> 10 Leonel de Abreu §4
>
> 10 D. Isabel da Silva, wife of Belchior Pinto, lord of Bom Jardim [with issue in NFP Pinto §8 N12]*ⁱ*
>
> 10 João Gomes de Abreu §144
>
> 10 D. Catarina˙ de Noronha, wife of Baltazar˙ Pereira˙, lord of the entail of Bertiandos, sp
>
> 10 Lopes Gomes de Abreu §5
>
> 10 D. Maria˙ de Abreu, who died mad. She married Domingos Dias and had issue about which we do not have further details available
>
> 10 Antonio˙ de Abreu Lima §29
>
> 10 B. Antonio˙ de Abreu Lima. As an illegitimate son he was granted the title of Squire-*Fidalgo* of the King's Household in 1621, by which he was entitled to a stipend of 583 (...) and 2 *seitis*. Upon his departure to India he was advanced to Knight-Fidalgo of the King's Household with a 300-*real* stipend. He married Joana Marinho Falcão, with issue

For details about Portuguese ranks of nobility, see p. v

N10   PEDRO GOMES DE ABREU, son of Leonel de Abreu N9, succeeded to his father's house and was the lord of Regalados. He moved to Castile in the time of King John IV, where he was created Count of Regalados. He married Anna de Brito, daughter of Gaspar de Araujo˙, lord of Pesqueiras [NFP Araujo §123 N23]

King John IV r. 1640–1656

> 11 Leonel de Abreu, second Count of Regalados and Knight of Avis, sp
>
> 11 Francisco˙ de Abreu, third Count of Regalados, who married Maria˙ Gomes Sandoval, daughter of Diogo Gomes Sandoval, Count of Infantado
>
> > 12 Pedro Gomes de Abreu, fourth Count of Regalados, sp

ⁱ In NFP Pinto §8 N12, Belchior Pinto's (second) wife's name is Izabel *de Lima*, and not Isabel da Silva. (T. N.)

11 Lopo Gomes de Abreu, Knight of Calatrava, sp

11 Pedro Gomes de Abreu, Knight of Santiago and a heavy cavalry captain, sp

11 Manoel˙ de Abreu Lima, Knight of Santiago and a heavy cavalry captain, sp

11 Antonio˙ de Abreu Lima, Knight of the Order of Calatrava

11 Gaspar Gomes de Abreu, fifth Count of Regalados, who married D. Maria˙ Cortes, by whom he had:

> 12 D. Affonço Gomes de Abreu, who married D. Maria˙ Viegas, sister of Francisco˙ Viegas, a dean in Coimbra
>
> 12 D. Isabel
>
> 12 D. Francisca˙, no further details

11 João Gomes de Abreu

11 D. Ignes Maria˙ de Abreu §8 [7]

Pedro Gomes de Abreu had bastard issue by (...):

11 B. D. Antonio˙ de Abreu Lima §6

11 B. Jorge de Abreu §7

N11   JOÃO GOMES DE ABREU, son of Pedro Gomes, N10, was the sixth Count of Regalados and married his niece Ignes Maria˙ de Abreu, daughter of Ignes Maria˙ de Abreu and D. Jorge Villaragude [§8 N11]

> 12 João Gomes de Abreu, sp.
>
> 12 D. Maria˙
>
> 12 D. Ignes
>
> 12 D. Anna, sp.

§3

N5   GONÇALLO RODRIGUES˙ DE ABREU, son of Ruy Gomes de Abreu §1 N4, was the lord of Barbeita. Some say he was the son of Lourenço Gonçalves˙ de Abreu §1 N2 and the paternal grandson of Gonçallo Martins˙ de Abreu §1 N1, who fought in the battle of Matança. Others say he inherited the honor and manor-house of his father, and was Chief Steward to King Sancho I and King Afonso II. He took part in the battle of Elvas in 1225 and the civil battle of Oporto in 1245[i],

King Sancho I r. 1185–1211
King Afonso II r. 1211–1223

---

[7] Alvaro Ferreira de Vera (s. 218) mentions the ancestors of this family until Gomes Lourenço de Abreu §1 N6.

[i] This was certainly one of the conflicts related to the troubled final years of the reign of Sancho II, who confronted the bourgeosie, the Church, and eventually lost the Portuguese crown to his brother Afonso III. If this Gonçallo de Abreu participated in these events, it is certainly a mistake the claim mentioned a few lines above in the text, by which he also took part in the battle of Veiga da Matança, for this battle was fought three generations before (see footnote *vi* on p. 4). (T. N.)

in which he saved the life of Ruy Fafes by giving him his own horse [Ref: *Monarquia Lusitana*, Tome 4, Book 14, *s.* 153][i]. For this deed he was held in high esteem by the said Ruy Fafes, whose daughter, D. Mecia Rodrigues*, he eventually married. Ruy Fafes's wife, D. Thereza Pires Alcoforado, was the daughter of Pedro Martins* Alcoforado and D. Thereza Soares [NFP Alcoforado §1 N3]. Ruy Fafes was the son of Fafes Godins and Sancha Giraldes, daughter of Giral Nunes and his wife Sancha Paes [Ref.: Count D. Pedro, title 39, *s.* 217]

> 6 Gomes Lourenço de Abreu, who is said by some to be the Gomes Lourenço de Abreu referred to in §1 N6
> 6 Nuno Gonçalves* de Abreu §82
> 6 Lopo Gonçalves* de Abreu §83
> 6 Garcia de Abreu §130
> 6 Ruy Gomes de Abreu

N6 RUY GOMES DE ABREU, said by some to be the son of Gonçallo Rodrigues* N5[ii], was the lord of the manor-house of Abreu and the father of

> 7 Lourenço Rodrigues* de Abreu, who had
>> 8 Gomes Lourenço §1 N6

§4

N10 LEONEL DE ABREU, son of Leonel de Abreu §2 N9, married D. Ignes Pita, daughter of Bras Rodrigues* Pita (a Knight of the Order of Christ of Avalle de Monção) and his mistress Ignes Vaz* de Antas [NFP Antas §8 N10 Sub11][iii]

> 11 D. Joana de Abreu de Lima
> 11 D. Isabel , a nun in the Convent of Monção
> 11 D. Maria*, a nun in Monção

---

[i] *Monarchia Lusitana* is an extensive collection of historical works written by a succession of Portuguese monks in the 17th century. (T. N.)

[ii] This information contradicts what is said in §1, which states that this Ruy Gomes de Abreu — also referred to in §1 N4, and who was the father of Lourenço Rodrigues de Abreu §1 N5 (and §1 N6 Sub7) and the grandfather of Gomes Lourenço (de Abreu) §1 N6 (and §1 N6 Sub8) — was the son of Gomes Lourenço de Abreu §1 N3. There is also a contradiction between what is stated in §3 N6 — according to which Gomes Lourenço §3 N6 Sub8 is the son of Lourenço Rodrigues de Abreu §3 N6 Sub7; the grandson of Ruy Gomes de Abreu §3 N6 and the great grandson of Gonçallo Rodrigues de Abreu §3 N5 — and what is stated in *Corografia Portuguesa*, which connects Gomes Lourenço (§3 N6 Sub8 and §1 N6) directly to Gonçallo* Rodrigues* de Abreu §3 N5. (T. N.)

[iii] In NFP Antas §8 N10, Ignes Pita is said to be the daughter of Bras Rodrigues* Pita and *Isabel Mendes* de Antas, and not Ignes Vaz* de Antas. (T. N.)

Leonel de Abreu married as his second wife D. Ignes Pereira*, daughter of Giraldo de Brito of Braga and D. Francisca* Pereira*, sp. Later he married as his third wife D. Maria* de Abreu, daughter of Pedro Gomes de Abreu of Briteiros [§71 N9], sp. He also had by Isabel Pereira* de Castro

    11 B. D. Catarina* de Abreu, who had issue by Antonio* de Abreu, Abbot of Moreira §29

    11 B. Simão de Abreu §55

N11   D. JOANA DE ABREU LIMA, daughter of Leonel* de Abreu N10, married Antonio* de Magalhães* de Menezes, son of Alexandre de Magalhães* de Menezes and his wife D. Isabel de Castro [NFP Magalhães §2 N11]

§5

N10   LOPO GOMES DE ABREU, son of Leonel de Abreu §2 N9[i]. For the services performed by his brothers Pedro Gomes and João Gomes, he was appointed Captain General of the Fleet of India, and commanded the rescue of Bayona and Redondela in 1587 and 1589 until the British Fleet rounded Cape Finisterre. He obtained grants on August 20, 1590, recorded in King Philip II's Book 21, s. 362. He married D. Tereja Soares, daughter of Payo Serre de Montenegro, a Galician nobleman, and his wife D. Maria* Sotomayor*, daughter of Alvaro de Oca and D. Thereza Soares*, lords of the house of Sotomayor

    11 D. Isabel Montenegro, unmarried

    11 D. Maria* Sotomayor

A pedigree chart which we have seen states that this Lopo Gomes was the abbot of Roças (with which we disagree) and had by Apolonia de Toris

    11 Francisco* Gomes de Abreu, who married D. Maria* de Brito Cação, by whom he had:

    12 D. Clara Maria* de Abreu Lima, who married Appellate Judge Thomas Feleciano de Albernos and had

        13 Thomas Feleciano de Albernos, a Knight of the Order of Christ and a Second Lieutenant in Brazil

        13 D. Maria* Feliciana, a nun in the Convent of Salvador, who cancelled her vows to marry Antonio* Mascarenhas de Mello, Stableman of Infante D. Manoel, a change she would eventually regret on her deathbed. She had

        14 Jose de Mascarenhas*, sp.

        14 D.

          D.

          D. (*sic*)

King Philip II of Spain r. 1556–1598; as Philip I of Portugal r. 1580–1598

---

[i] In §1 N9, Lopo Gomes de Abreu is called *Lopes* Gomes de Abreu. (T. N.)

N11   MARIA˙SOTOMAYOR, daughter of Lopo Gomes de Abreu N10, married her cousin D. Fernando Sotomayor, son of D. Pedro Sotomayor, Chief Justice in the Kingdom of Naples, and D. Maria˙ de Esquizo, as recorded in a dowry charter written on October 27, 1603 by notary public Gaspar Lobato of Monção

      12 D. Francisca˙ de Sotomayor

N12   FRANCISCA˙ DE SOTOMAYOR, daughter of D. Maria˙ de Sotomayor N11, was the Marchioness of Tenorio and in 1639 married D. João de Lima, son of D. Lourenço de Lima, Viscount of Vila Nova and D. Luiza de Tavora [NFP Lima §6 N18]

         13 D. Fernão Alvares˙ Sotomayor e Lima, Marquis of Tenorio
         13 D. Patornilha de Chaves

§6

N11   ANTONIO˙ DE ABREU LIMA, bastard son of Pedro Gomes de Abreu §2 N10. He traveled twice to India according to records dated June 19, 1534 in the Archives of King Sebastian [s. 41]. He married D. Maria Quaresma, sp. He married as his second wife D. Brites Velho Barreto, daughter of Fernão Velho Barreto, Servant to the Duke of Bragança, and his wife Genebra de Barros [NFP Barreto Velho of Viana do Minho §106 N2, NFP Barros §9 N6 and NFP Abreu §51 N7][i]

§7

N7   JORGE DE ABREU, bastard son of Pedro Gomes de Abreu §2 N6 (others say this Jorge de Abreu was the son of Pedro Gomes §2 N10, which we do not uphold). He married Brites da Silva, daughter of Gonçallo Rodrigues˙ de Magalhães˙ and his wife Briolanja de Azevedo. This Gonçallo Rodrigues de Magalhães˙ was the fourth son of Fernão de Magalhães˙, lord of the manor of Briteiros, and Brites de Mesquita˙ [NFP Magalhães §22 N7]

      8 Pedro Gomes de Abreu, who married Anna de Barros, daughter of
         Lopo de Barros, brother of the first Bishop of Leiria [NFP Barros
         §47 N6]
      8 Lopo Gomes de Abreu §71

---

[i] In NFP Barreto Velho of Viana do Minho §106 N2, Genebra de Barros's husband is called Fernão Velho *de Araujo*, and not Fernão Velho Barreto. In Abreu §51 N7, there is an Antonio de Abreu Lima who is said by the author to be distinct from his "namesake" presented here. However, it is quite a strange piece of information, for it is hard to believe that they were different persons if they had the same name and the same wife. (T. N.)

Safim is a Moroccan city which was conquered by the Portuguese in 1500

For details about Portuguese ranks of nobility, see p. v

8 Francisco˙ de Abreu Lima, who took part in the conquest of Safim and had bastard issue

    9 Jorge de Abreu, who went to India

8 Martim Coelho de Abreu §72

8 Diogo Gomes de Abreu, who went to India and had bastard issue

    9 João Gomes de Abreu, who went to India in 1562 with an appointment of Page-*Fidalgo*

8 D. Felipa, a nun in Braga like her sisters below:

8 D. Maria˙

8 D. Guiomar

8 D. Briolanja

Some also claim to be descendants of Jorge de Abreu by the following line:

    8 Jorge Annes de Abreu Lima, who married Susana de Sá, and had:

        9 Salvador de Abreu Lima, who married Brites de Mascarenhas, daughter of Simão de Mascarenhas and Ignes Henriques˙ [NFP Mascarenhas §26 N4]*[i]*

            10 Maria˙ de Abreu de Noronha, lady of the entail of Souto Mendinho, who married Jeronimo Fernandes˙ Carneiro Tinoco [with issue in NFP Tinoco §9 N3] though the only source for this information is a chronicle possessed by his alleged descendants

N8   PEDRO GOMES DE ABREU, son of Jorge de Abreu N7, was the lord of the manor of Briteiros and a Fidalgo of the King's Household, as stated in his dowry document. He married (on March 3, 1548) D. Anna de Barros, daughter of D. Beatris Bravo de Araujo˙, lady of the house of Real in Braga, and her husband Lopo de Barros, a Fidalgo of the King's Household, as recorded in the said document dated March 2, 1549 at the manor of Real by notary public Jose de Freitas Peixoto, by which the said Pedro Gomes de Abreu received the manor of Pousada, in which estate he was enfeoffed [NFP Barros §47 N6]

    9 D. Antonia˙ de Abreu

    9 Jorge de Abreu, who had bastard issue by Maria˙ de Abreu, bastard daughter of Martim Coelho §72 N8

        10 B. Pedro Gomes de Abreu, who went to India in 1622, sp

    9 D. Maria˙ de Abreu, wife of Baltazar˙ Alvares˙ Vieira Barroso

    9 Lopo Gomes de Abreu, who was a bastard son according to some, and had bastard issue

        10 Pedro Gomes de Abreu

---

*[i]*In Mascarenhas §26 N4, Simão de Mascarenhas is called Simão *Vaz* Mascarenhas, and his wife is called *Izabel* Henriques˙, and not Ignes Henriques˙. (T. N.)

N9   ANTONIA˙ DE ABREU, was the daughter of Pedro Gomes de Abreu N8 and the lady of the entail of Pousada. She married Alvaro Coelho da Silva, son of Baltazar˙ Coelho and his wife Antonia˙ de Sousa [NFP Magalhães §18 N8][i]

    10 Pedro Coelho da Silva˙
    10 Baltazar Coelho da Silva §53[ii]
    10 Luis da Silva, a Knight of Malta

N10   PEDRO COELHO DA SILVA, son of D. Antonia˙ de Abreu N9, married during his mother's lifetime D. Margarida do Rego Sarmento˙, daughter of Antonio˙ Soeiro and Justa do Rego [NFP Alpoim §3 N21][iii]. Upon his mother's decease his lands were taken up by his brother Baltazar˙ Coelho

        11 D. Maria˙ da Silva, who had a legal dispute over the entail of Pousada with Baltazar˙ Coelho da Silva, her father's brother. She married João de Alpoim da Silva [NFP Alpoim §3 N21]. Her ancestry until Pedro Gomes de Abreu N8 is recorded in the sentence she obtained against the said Baltazar˙ Coelho, written on February 12, 1658 in the city of Oporto by João de Alpoim, a copy of which can be found in Francisco˙ Xavier˙ de Alpoim's file in the office of notary public Francisco˙ Jose de Faria Vieira of Barcelos, a document which we have had the opportunity to examine

        11 D. Luiza da Silva, wife of of her uncle Baltazar˙ Coelho, a Fidalgo of the King's Household, also mentioned in §53 N10, sp

§8

N11   D. IGNES MARIA˙ DE ABREU, daughter of Pedro Gomes de Abreu §2 N10, was a lady-in-waiting to the Empress[iv] and married D. Jorge Vilaragude, Count of Holocao and Marquis of Canera in Aragon

      12 Ignes Maria˙ de Abreu, married her uncle João Gomes de Abreu §1 N11

---

[i] In Magalhães §18 N8, the name of Alvaro Coelho da Silva's mother and Baltazar˙ Coelho's wife was *Brites* de Sousa, and not Antonia˙ de Sousa. (T. N.)

[ii] In §53, it is said that Baltazar Coelho, Alvaro Coelho da Silva's son, was a Fidalgo of the King's Household like his father, from which we presume the latter was granted this title as well. (T. N.)

[iii] In Alpoim §3 N21 it is stated that Pedro Coelho da Silva's wife's name was Margarida *Prego* (and not Margarida do Rego Sarmento˙), and that she was the daughter of Antonio˙ Soeiro and Justa *Prego* (and not Justa do Rego). (T. N.)

[iv] Possibly Queen Maria Anna, daughter of the Holy Roman Emperor Ferdinand III and second wife of King Philip IV, who ruled over Spain between 1621-1665 and over Portugal (as Philip III) between 1621-1640. (T. N.)

§9

N4   VASCO GOMES DE ABREU, son of Diogo Gomes de Abreu §2 N3, married Brites or Mayor Portocarreiro, daughter of Gomes de Sá of the town of Santarém, son of Pedro de Sá and his wife Isabel de Villa Lobos, daughter of Vasco Queimado, manager of the House of India; the said Gomes de Sá was married to Theresa da Silva˙, daughter of D. Rodrigo de Lima, Prior of Refoios [NFP Sá §25 N4]*i*

> 5 D. Leonor de Abreu, whose first husband was D. Duarte da Cunha, son of Viscount D. Leonel de Lima [NFP Lima §14 N12). D. Leonor married as her second husband Mizem Vasco de Gouvea, by whom she was slain [as described in NFP Gouvea §(...) (sic)]

§10

N4 ANTÃO GOMES DE ABREU, son of Diogo Gomes de Abreu §2 N3, married D. Isabel de Mello de Albergaria, daughter of Fernão Soares de Albergaria, lord of Prado and his wife D. Isabel de Mello, daughter of Estevão Soares de Mello, lord of Mello [NFP Mello §1 N9 and NFP Soares de Albergaria §4 N6]

> 5 Vasco Gomes de Abreu
> 5 João Gomes de Abreu, author of *Trovas* (Ballads); he was highly esteemed by King Manuel I, and died on a trip to India on the Island of São Lourenço
> 5 Lopo Gomes de Abreu, Protonotary Apostolic and Canon of Viseu
> 5 Lourenço Soares de Abreu §12
> 5 Pedro Gomes de Abreu §13
> 5 D. Thereja, wife of João de Sousa, lord of the lands of Roças
> 5 Diogo Gomes
> 5 Gonçallo Gomes, who went to India, sp.

N5 VASCO GOMES DE ABREU, son of Antão Gomes de Abreu N4, was the captain of a vessel called São Gabriel which sailed to India in 1505, and also the captain of a fleet which got lost on Christmas Day, 1507. He did not marry, though he had issue by D. Joanna de Eça, daughter of D. Branca de Eça and her second husband João Rodrigues˙ de Azevedo˙ [NFP Eça §10 N3)

> 6 B. Diogo Soares N6, below
> 6 B. Felipa da Cunha or Felipa de Abreu, mistress of Xisto da Cunha

King Manuel I r. 1495–1521. São Lourenço is an ancient Portuguese name for the Isle of Madagascar

---

i In NFP Sá §25 N4, Gomes de Sá is said to have married a different woman: Brites Portocarreiro, daughter of João Tello de Menezes, Count of Viana. (T. N.)

[with issue in NFP Cunha §32 N13], by whom she had

    7 B. Luiz

    7 B. Duarte

    7 B. Estevão da Cunha[i]

  6 B. Fernão Vasques de Abreu §27

Vasco Gomes de Abreu also had by D. Francisca˙ de Eça:

  6 B. Jorge de Mello, unmarried

  6 B. Cristovão de Mello §11

N6 DIOGO SOARES, son of Vasco Gomes de Abreu N5, called *Rodavalho*, was the Commendatory of Bugalhal and Baldigem in the Order of Christ, and was legitimated by King Manuel I in 1507. He married D. Isabel Coutinho, daughter of Pedro Lopes de Azevedo and his wife D. Maria˙ Ribeiro˙ [NFP Azevedo §19 N20]

    7 Vasco Gomes de Abreu, who died unmarried in Africa, slain by the Moors together with captain Luis Loureiro

    7 Lourenço Soares de Abreu

    7 João Soares, who was slain by the Moors in India

    7 Fernão Coutinho

    7 Diogo Soares de Abreu, sp

    7 Manoel˙ de Mello de Abreu §56

    7 D. Anna de Vilhena, wife of Manoel˙ Godinho de Castello Branco[ii]

N7 LOURENÇO SOARES DE ABREU, son of Diogo Soares N6, married D. Maria˙ de Cisneiros, daughter of Gaspar de Cisneiros, Fishing Standards Inspector of the Duke of Bragança and Lord Treasurer of Catana

    8 Gaspar de Azevedo˙ Coutinho

    8 D. Maria˙ Coutinho, wife of Leonel de Moura Rolim, with issue

    8 Antão de Mello, who went to India

    8 Fernão Soares, who went to India with his brother

    8 D. Catarina˙ Coutinho, wife of Fernão Tavares de Brito

    8 D. Isabel de Eça, wife of her cousin Diogo de Mello [in §11 N7]

    8 B. Lourenço de Mello de Eça, who served in India and was captain of Goa

---

[i] In NFP Cunha §32 N13, Estevão da Cunha is said to have been the son of Xisto da Cunha and Maria de Araujo˙, by whom Xisto had many other bastard children. (T. N.)

[ii] In N7 and N8, it is informed that this Anna de Vilhena (married to Manoel Godinho de Castello Branco) had a niece and a grandniece of the same name, whose husbands were respectively Manoel Godinho and Manoel Godinho de Castello Branco (the latter with exactly the same name of the first Anna de Vilhena's husband). Either this is a great coincidence or the author has made a mistake. (T. N.)

8 B. D. Margarida Coutinho, who married in India

8 B. D. Anna de Vilhena, wife of Manoel Godinho of Lisbon[i]

N8 MARIA COUTINHO˙, daughter of Lourenço Soares N7, married Leonel de Moura Rolim

    9 Francisco˙ de Moura, Commendatory of the Order of Christ and Captain of Chaul, sp

    9 D. Catarina˙ de Vilhena, wife of Antonio˙ de Brito Tavares

    9 D. Anna de Vilhena, wife of de Manoel˙ Godinho de Castello Branco, a Knight of the Order of Christ and a Clerk of the Writs[ii]

Chaul is a territory located about 40 miles south of Bombay in India, and was a Portuguese colony from 1521 to 1740

§11

N6 CRISTOVÃO DE MELLO, son of Vasco Gomes de Abreu §10 N5, married D. Guiomar, daughter of Dr. João Pires

    7 Diogo de Mello Soares

    7 Vasco Gomes de Abreu, married (...), daughter of Torraval, who erected the Belem cross, and had

        8 Cristovão Soares de Mello

        8 D. Guiomar de Eça

N7 DIOGO DE MELLO SOARES, son of Cristovão de Mello N6, married D. Isabel de Eça, daughter of his cousin Lourenço Soares de Abreu [in §10 N7]

§12

N5 LOURENÇO SOARES DE ABREU, son of Antão Gomes de Abreu, §10 N4, was Inspector General of the Household of Cardinal-Infante Henry. He married D. Isabel Vilhegas, daughter of D. Diogo Vilhegas, Bishop of Ceuta and afterwards of Viseu, born in Calsadilha, near Lorena in the land of Campos, Castile, being called Calsadilha for this reason, [NFP Ortis Vilhegas §1 N1]

Cardinal-Infante Henry, who became Cardinal-King and r. 1578-1580

    6 Diogo Soares de Albergaria

    6 Gomes Soares de Albergaria, Commendatory of the Order of Christ; he had a bastard daughter who became a nun

    6 Vasco Gomes, who was slain by the Moors in Tangier

    6 D. Maria˙, wife of Luis Brandão, Commendatory of Santo Estevão, son of Dr. Antonio˙ Sanches Brandão [NFP Brandão §11 N10][iii]

---

[i] See footnote *ii* on the previous page. (T. N.)

[ii] See footnote *ii* on the previous page. (T. N.)

[iii] In NFP Brandão §11 N10, the father of D. Maria˙ (Luis Brandão's wife) is called Lourenço Soares de *Albergaria*, and not Lourenço Soares de Abreu. (T. N.).

6 D. Catarina or Joanna, wife of Tristão da Silva˙

6 D. Guiomar, who was possibly a nun

6 B. Gaspar de Azevedo˙, who followed his brother into Africa

6 B. Diogo Soares, *ditto*

6 B. Vasco Gomes, *ditto*

Cardinal-Infante Henry,
who became Cardinal-King
and r. 1578-1580

N6 DIOGO SOARES DE ALBERGARIA, son of Lourenço Soares N5, inherited his father's office of Overseer of Cardinal–Infante Henry, and upon the latter's decease was granted the office of Overseer of Infanta Maria, daughter of King Manuel I. He died as captain of Mina, having been married to Catarina˙ de Thoar or Catarina˙ de Roxas, daughter of D. Fernando de Toar or D. Fernando de Roxas (lord of Segum and Main Guard to Queen Joanna, wife of Emperor Charles V (sic))[i] and his wife D. Isabel Annes

    7 Lourenço Soares de Abreu, who married D. Ignes de la Barrera, daughter of Diogo de Laboreira, a Castilian merchant, by whom he had

        8 D. Catarina˙ de Roxas, who died in infancy

        8 Lourenço de Mello, who went to India

        8 D. Maria˙ de Roxas, wife of Francisco˙ Figueira de Azevedo [with issue in NFP Figueira §11 N6][ii]

    7 Lopo Soares de Albergaria, Choirmaster of the See of Viseu, elected Bishop of Portalegre

§13

N5 PEDRO GOMES DE ABREU, son of Antão Gomes de Abreu §10 N4. A clergyman and Canon of Viseu, he received other grants and was made Chaplain-Fidalgo. He had bastard issue by several women, though some say he had most of his children by Brites Paes Pereira˙, daughter of Luis Mendes de Vasconcellos

    6 B. Antão Gomes de Abreu §14

    6 B. Antonio de Abreu

    6 B. Diogo Soares de Mello §15

---

[i] This information is a mistake. The Queen Joana mentioned here is possibly Holy Roman Emperor Charles V's daughter, who became the Crown Princess of Portugal by her marriage to Prince John, son of King John III. Charles V's wife was Queen Elisabeth (also a daughter of King John III of Portugal). (T. N.)

[ii] In NFP Figueira §11 N6, Francisco˙ Figueira de Azevedo's wife is called Maria˙ *da Silva* and not Maria de Roxas, and her father is called Lourenço Soares *de Albergaria*, and not Lourenço Soares de Abreu. (T. N.)

For details about Portuguese ranks of nobility, see p. v

6 B. Pedro Gomes de Abreu, who had

> 7 João Gomes de Abreu, who was granted a charter of Fidalgo-Knight of the King's Household upon a voyage to India

6 B. João Gomes de Abreu §76

6 B. D. Anna Soares, wife of Heytor Homem, sp

6 B. D. Joanna or D. Jeronima, wife of Roque de Abreu [in §26 N6]

6 B. D. Joanna Soares

N6 ANTONIO˙ DE ABREU, bastard son of Pedro Gomes de Abreu N5, who distinguished himself for his valor and was slain in front of his house in Viseu. He fathered a daughter by Anna de Vasconcellos, who upon his death proved that she was contracted to marry him, which caused her daughter inherit his house. Anna de Vasconcellos was the daughter of Diogo Mendes de Vasconcellos and his wife Eulalia Vaz de Castello Branco, though others state her parents were Antonio˙ Rodrigues˙ de Castello Branco and D. Clara Soares

> 7 B. D. Maria˙ de Abreu inherited her father's house by her mother's justification. She married (in the city of Viseu) Manoel˙ de Abreu, son of Luis Loureiro of Roma, Village of Besteiros (sic) and Anna de Abreu Lima [NFP Loureiro §3 N8][i]

§14

N6 ANTAO GOMES DE ABREU, bastard son of Pedro Gomes de Abreu §13 N5. He had by D. Olaya Mascarenhas, whom he married just before his death

> 7 Vasco Gomes, who married Isabel do Amaral, daughter of João Paes do Amaral and Maria Loureiro, sp

> 7 João Gomes de Abreu, who married D. Maria˙ de Mello, daughter of Ruy Gomes de Abreu §57 N7

§15

N6 DIOGO SOARES DE MELLO, bastard son of Pedro Gomes de Abreu §13 N5, lived in Viseu and was married twice, the first time to D. Felicia Gomes

> 7 Vasco de Abreu, Governor of Mazagan

> 7 (...), a Bernardine monk

Diogo Soares de Mello's second wife was Jeronima Cardoso (daughter of Antonio˙, or Antão Cardoso of Viseu), by whom he had

> 7 D. Elena de Abreu

Mazagan is a city founded by the Portuguese on the Moroccan coast in 1513, which remained under Portuguese control (in spite of several attempts by the Muslims to conquer it) until 1759, the year in which the Marquis of Pombal, King Joseph I's Prime Minister, decided to end the Portuguese presence in that region, whereupon he ordered the evacuation of the city and sent its population to northern Brazil, where the settlers founded the city of New Mazagan

---

[i] In NFP Loureiro §3 N8 and N7, Manuel de Abreu is mentioned as Manuel˙ de Abreu *Castelo Branco˙*, and his wife is called Maria˙ *Soares de Mello* and not Maria de Abreu. (T. N.)

N7 D. ELENA DE ABREU, daughter of Diogo Soares de Mello N6 (and his second wife). Like her father, she owned the entail of Santo Estevão and the house of Cadea in the town of Viseu, where she married Alvaro Carvalho de Vasconcellos, son of Francisco˙ Monteiro˙ and Joanna de Barros de Carvalho˙ of Viseu, and grandson of João Rodrigues˙ Monteiro

> 8 D. Anna de Mello de Carvalho, who married Theobaldo de Lemos de Campos, second son of Henrique de Lemos de Campos and his wife D. Briolanja de Lemos, heiress and lady of the entail of Alvelos and daughter of Theobaldo de Lemos do Amaral, who litigated the said entail with D. Maria Cardoso. Henrique de Lemos was the son of Antonio˙ de Lemos (lord of the entail of Moure, in the territory of Viseu) and his wife D. Elena de Campos [NFP Lemos §15 N6][i]

§16

N4 JOÃO GOMES DE ABREU, son of Diogo Gomes de Abreu §2 N3. He was called D. João because he had been the Bishop of Viseu[8]. Before he became Bishop he had issue by Brites de Eça, daughter of D. Fernando de Eça and paternal granddaughter of *Infante* D. João and his first wife D. Maria˙ Telles de Menezes [NFP Eça §1 N2]. Also before his nomination, D. João Gomes de Abreu was the Commendatory of São João de Longos Vales. He died on February 16, 1482

Infante João (1349-1387), Duke of Valencia de Campos, was the son of King Peter I of Portugal and Ignes de Castro (see also box on p. 9 and chart on the next page)

> 5 B. Pedro Gomes de Abreu, who was born before his father's election as bishop
>
> 5 B. Diogo Gomes de Abreu §19
>
> 5 B. Luis de Abreu, who married D. Felipa, daughter of Diogo Affonso˙, Treasurer of Prince D. Affonso, son of King John II, with issue

João Gomes de Abreu had a son by a single woman called Maria Vaz˙, as recorded in a legitimate deed dated 1552 requested by Gaspar Rabello de Abreu, Treasury Clerk of King John III, from the manor of Couceiro, in the territory of Regalados[9]

> 5 B. Fernão Gomes or Rodrigues˙ de Abreu §80

---

[i] In NFP Lemos §15 N6, it is stated that Theobaldo de Lemos' first wife's name is Anna de *Vasconcellos˙ e Mello*, and not Anna de Mello de Carvalho, though her parentage is the same as we give here. (T.N.)

[8] Fray Manoel˙ da Esperança, in the history of his order (*Historia Sarafica.*, Part 2, Book 11, Ch. 8 N2, p. 536).

[9] According to the Choirmaster of Evora, this deed was made in 1562 and written by notary public Thome Fernandes˙ in Regalados.

ROYAL LINES IN THE PORTUGUESE FAMILY OF ABREU

In the 15th century, two members of the family of Abreu (Pedro Gomes de Abreu §2 N6 and his cousin João Gomes de Abreu §16 N4 Sub5) had illegitimate issue by two sisters of royal ancestry: Catarina de Eça and Brites de Eça respectively, who were the daughters of Fernando, Lord of Eça, and the paternal granddaughters of Infante João (1349-1387), son of King Peter I of Portugal and Ignes de Castro (more details about the latter can be seen on p. 9).

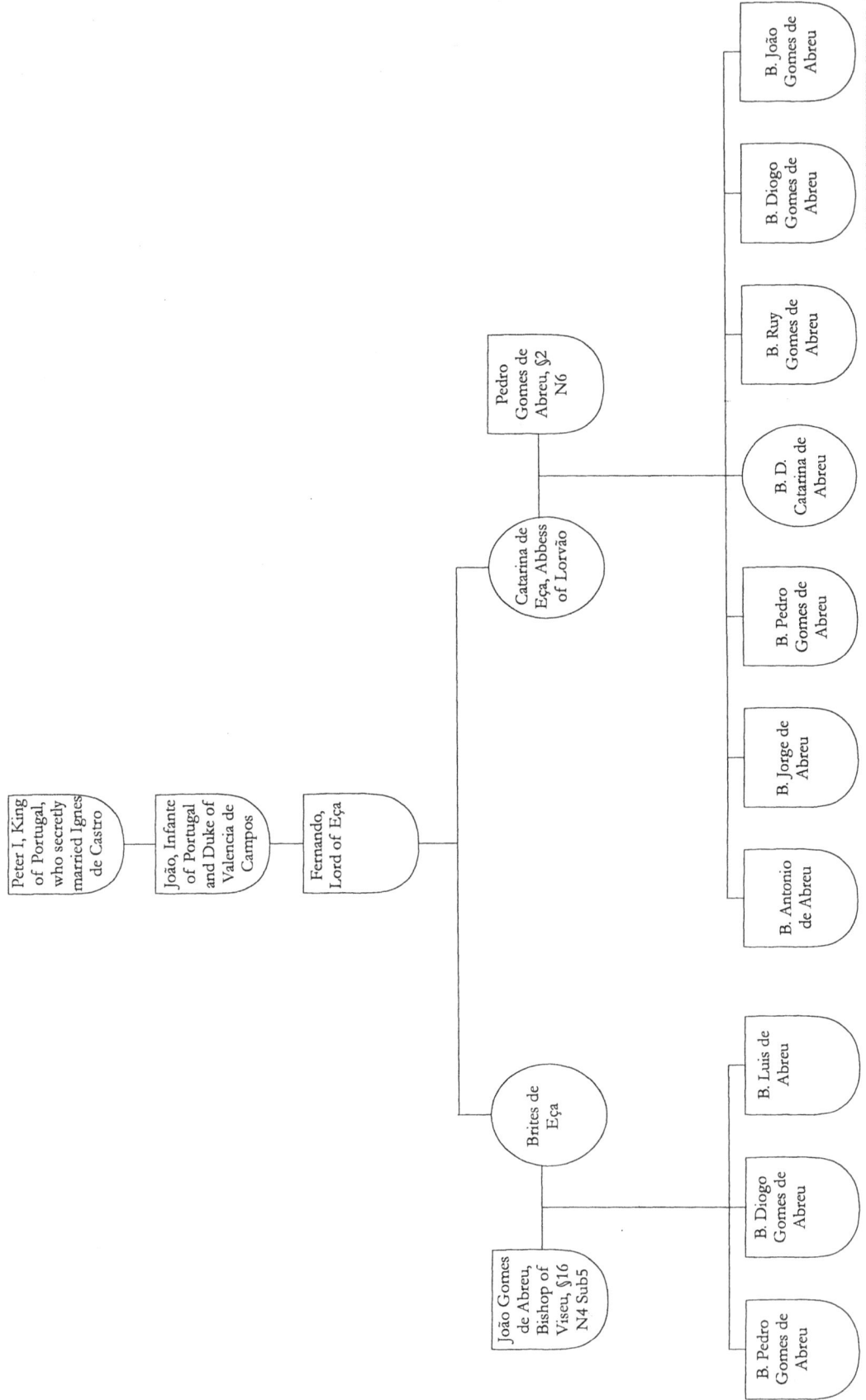

João Gomes de Abreu had by Isabel Gonçalves˙, a single woman

> 5 B. Jorge de Abreu (legitimated by El Rei Afonso V in 1479 and 1481)
>
> 5 B. Leonor de Abreu (legitimated by El Rei Afonso V in 1479 and 1481)

He also had by D. Isabel (daughter of the Count of Caminha D. Pedro Alvares˙ Sotomayor), whom he wished to marry [NFP Sotomaior §1 N10]

> 5 B. Gil Fernandes de Abreu §40

N5 PEDRO GOMES DE ABREU, son of D. João Gomes de Abreu N4, born before his father's election as Bishop. His legitimation by King Afonso V was recorded on March 8, 1479 in Book 2 of Legitimations, *s. 227*. He married Mecia da Cunha, who, in a dispute, had lost the entail of Taboa, which her great grandfather Vasco Martins˙ da Cunha, known as "Donkey Tail", had previously taken from his elder brother Estevão Soares. D. Mecia de Cunha was the daughter of Alvaro da Cunha and his wife D. Ignes de Goes [NFP Cunha §12 N12]. The said Pedro Gomes de Abreu possessed the entail of Taboa by his wife, but eventually lost it to one of his wife's grandnephews

> 6 João Gomes da Cunha
>
> 6 Martim Vaz˙ da Cunha, Prior of Tabua
>
> 6 Gaspar da Cunha §66
>
> 6 Pedro Gomes da Cunha §21
>
> 6 Roque de Abreu §26, who married his relative Joanna, daughter of another Pedro Gomes de Abreu [in §13 N5]
>
> 6 Diogo Gomes da Cunha §20
>
> 6 Domingos de Abreu, of Povolide §18
>
> 6 Luis de Abreu §79
>
> 6 Isabel or Leonor da Cunha, lady-in-waiting to Queen Leonor, married João Rodrigues˙ Homem, son of Royal Corregidor Dr. Rodrigo Homem and grandson of Diogo Homem, a distinguished nobleman, and his wife D. Violante de Pina, daughter of Fernão de Pina, Commendatory of Vimioso [NFP Homem §28 N4][i]
>
> 6 Matheus da Cunha, from whom the Cunhas of Alvoroninha are descended

---

[i] In NFP Homem §28 N4, João Rodrigues˙ Homem's wife (and Pedro Gomes de Abreu's daughter) is called *Izabel da Cunha de Eça*, and not Isabel or Leonor da Cunha. (T. N.)

For details about Portuguese ranks of nobility, see p. v

King John II r. 1481–1495

Dio, or Diu, an Indian town which was conquered by Portugal in 1535 and remained as a Portuguese colony until 1961

For details about Portuguese ranks of nobility, see p. v

N6 JOÃO GOMES DA CUNHA, son of Pedro Gomes da Cunha N5, who was granted the title of Page-Fidalgo in Tomar in 1507, which entitled him to a 100-*real* allowance. He married D. Cecilia, daughter of Dr. Rodrigo Homem (Judge of the Appeal Court and Trial Judge of the estates of Queen Leonor, wife of King John II) and his wife Felipa de Andrade. Cecilia was the paternal granddaughter of Diogo Homem, a distinguished nobleman, and his wife Violante de Pina, daughter of Fernão de Pina, Commendatory of Vimioso [NFP Homem §28 N3]

    7 Gaspar da Cunha
    7 Baltazar· da Cunha, who died in the conquest of Dio, sp
    7 Belchior da Cunha, a clergyman
    7 Gonçallo Gomes da Cunha §17
    7 Aleixo da Cunha, sp
    7 D. Mecia da Cunha, wife of Dr. Antonio· de Macedo, a chancellor of the Appeal Court §50
    7 Francisco· Vaz da Cunha §44
    7 Roque de Abreu
    7 Diogo Gomes de Abreu
    7 D. Felipa de Abreu, wife of Manoel· Fernandes· de Sampaio·

N7 GASPAR DA CUNHA, son of João Gomes da Cunha N6. He was made Page-Fidalgo in 1512 and advanced to Squire-Fidalgo by a charter dated March 7th 1535. He married D. Francisca· de Macedo, daughter of his brother-in-law Antonio· de Macedo and Antonio's first wife Antonia· Nunes, by which marriage Gaspar entered into possession of the entail of Taboa, which he obtained through a dispute. After his death, his widow Francisca· married Antonio de Povoas, Commendatory of Ervedal [§50 N7 and NFP Macedo §28 N2][i]

    8 Jose da Cunha, who married Isabel de Serpa, daughter of Jorge de Serpa, a resident of Covilhão
        9 Lourenço da Cunha who according to some was married to his cousin Catarina· de Eça, daughter of Manoel· da Cunha [N8 below]
            10 D. Anna da Cunha, daughter of Francisco· Pereira· de Miranda, lord of Carvalhais, sp
    8 Manoel· da Cunha
    8 D. Joanna, a nun

---

[i] In NFP Macedo §28 N2, Antonio· de Macedo's first wife is called Antonia· *de Magalhães·*, and not Antonia· Nunes; and in §50 N7 it is also stated that Francisca de Macedo, Gaspar da Cunha's wife, was the daughter of his sister Mecia da Cunha. (T. N.)

N8 MANOEL˙ DA CUNHA, son of Gaspar da Cunha N7, was the lord of the entail of Taboa. He married Joanna Pessoa, daughter of João Homem Pessoa and Joanna de Mello, paternal granddaughter of Baltazar˙ Pessoa, Governor of India. Manoel˙ da Cunha was granted the title of Squire-Fidalgo of the King's Household by a charter dated August 26, 1605 [NFP Pessoa §2 N4]

For details about Portuguese ranks of nobility, see p. v

    9 Nazareno da Cunha, who went to India, sp
    9 Luis Vaz˙ da Cunha, who died young
    9 Sebastião da Cunha, *ditto*
    9 D. Maria˙ da Cunha
    9 D. Catarina˙ da Cunha, who married her cousin Lourenço da Cunha
       N7 Sub8 Sub9 above, sp
    9 D. Isabel, unmarried

N9 D. MARIA˙ DA CUNHA, daughter of Manoel˙ da Cunha N8. She had a dispute with her brother over the entail of Taboa, which she claimed to be hers. She married Simão da Costa, Captain General of Taboa, son of (...) and his wife Brites Vasques Mascarenhas

    10 Anna da Cunha

N10 D. ANNA DA CUNHA, daughter of D. Maria˙ da Cunha N9, inherited her parents' house and the entail of Taboa, and married her relative Luis Pessoa de Mello, with whom she lived in her manor of Santa Eufemia, near Anobra, in the municipality of Coimbra. Her husband was the son of Sebastião Pessoa Homem and the grandson of João Homem Pessoa and Anna de Mello, and also the grandson of Baltazar˙ Pessoa, Governor of India [as mentioned by Barros, *Decade* 3, Book 6, Ch. 5 and Book 7, Ch. 9[i]; NFP Pessoa §2 N4]. (In NFP Pessoa §2 N5 it is stated that Sebastião Pessoa Homem was the son of João Pessoa Homem and Catarina˙ Ferreira˙, and the grandson of another João Homem Pessoa and Anna de Mello)[ii]

    11 Manoel˙ Vasques da Cunha, who married Paulla de Vasconcellos˙
       of Verride, sp
    11 Luis Vasques da Cunha
    11 Vasco Martins da Cunha
    11 Alexandre de Mello
    11 João de Mello

---

[i] João de Barros (~1496-1570), considered by some the most important historian of Portugal, author of *Decades of Asia* (4 vols., the last of which was completed by Lavanha), describing the Portuguese conquest of India. (T. N.)

[ii] In the original text, it is relatively common to find the order of the surnames inverted when they appear more than once. For instance, João Homem Pessoa appears in this passage and is called João *Pessoa Homem* a few lines below. (T. N.)

11 D. Eufemia
11 D. Damasia
11 D. Marianna

N11 LUIS VASQUES DA CUNHA, son of D. Anna da Cunha N10, succeeded his brother in the entail of Taboa. He married Maria˙ Coutinho˙ de Eça e Bulhões˙, daughter of Antonio˙ Coutinho˙ Feyo and Leonor Travaços de Eça, daughter of Francisco˙ Travaços de Faria and Luisa de Bulhões˙, who was the daughter of Cosme Denis Freire de Carvoeiros and his wife Pascoella de Bulhões.
12 Bernardo da Cunha, e Mello

N12 BERNARDO DA CUNHA, E MELLO, son of Luis Vasques N11. He succeded to the entail of Passos of Taboa, and married D. Maria Vitoria de Figueiredo˙ Couceiro da Silva, daughter of Bernardo de Figueiredo˙ and his wife D. Marianna Couceiro da Silva, of Pereira
13 Luis Anastacio da Cunha, with issue in Tentugal
13 D. Anna da Cunha
13 D. Antonia˙ da Cunha, sp

N13 D. ANNA DA CUNHA, E MELLO, daughter of Bernardo da Cunha N12, succeeded to the house of Passos of Taboa, which she obtained from her brother in a partition of their house's entails, following the lack of definition over the succession to these estates due the fire in the house of Tentugal and the consequent destruction of the documents stored there. She married Antonio Pedro˙ de Gamboa Vasconcellos of the manor of Barrosa, who at the time of this marriage was a widower and had a son. She had by her husband
14 D. Custodia Gamboa, sp
14 Jose Maria Gamboa, sp
14 Antonio˙ Pedro Gamboa, still alive, sp[i]
14 D. Julliana Gamboa da Cunha, who married Francisco˙ Xavier˙ de Gamboa of Lousã, with issue, both still alive
14 D. Maria˙ Candida

N14 D. MARIA˙ CANDIDA, daughter of Anna da Cunha N13, married Jose Carlos Juzarte da Silva˙ Corte Real, a Fidalgo of the King's Household and lord of the manor of Rojão. Afterwards this Jose Carlos Jusarte married D. Joanna Arraes de Mendonça, who has been appointed the heiress of the entail of Pevolide [NFP Perestrelo §2 N14]
15 Jose Carlos Jusarte da Cunha Corte Real, born in 1801
15 Antonio˙ Xavier˙ Jusarte da Cunha, born in 1802

---

[i] *Still alive*: Of course, at the time this work was written (~1790-1831). (T.N.)

§17

N7 GONÇALLO GOMES DA CUNHA, son of João Gomes da Cunha §16 N6, a Fidalgo of the King's Household, a lawyer resident in Coimbra and Probate Court Judge in Covilhão. He married Antonia˙ da Costa, daughter of Manoel˙ Martins Botelho

> 8 Leonardo da Cunha, Travelling Judge of Alenquer and Corregidor in the Azores, with issue
>
> 8 D. Maria˙ de Mello, who retired to the convent of Semide. She had issue by her first cousin Gaspar da Fonseca, Commendatory of the Order of Malta. This D. Maria˙ de Mello is also said to have married Diogo Pessoa da Costa [with issue in NFP Homem §39 N6]

N8 LEONARDO DA CUNHA, son of Gonçallo Gomes da Cunha N7, studied humanities, was a Page-Fidalgo of the King's Household and Corregidor in the Azores. He was married (in the town of Botão) to (...) Bravo

> 9 Manoel˙ Gomes da Cunha

N9 MANOEL˙ GOMES DA CUNHA, son of Leonardo da Cunha N8, married Angella Figueira Boto, daughter and heiress of Francisco˙ Figueira Boto, Commendatory of the Order of Christ and his wife D. Jacinta de Mendonça. Angella Figueira Boto was the paternal granddaughter of João Mendes de Carvalho˙ and Cecilia Figueira, and the maternal granddaughter of Rodrigo Lopes de Almeida and Anna de Lemos

> 10 Maria˙ Alvares˙ da Cunha, who married Luis da Costa Cabreira, son of Luisa Monis Marmeleiro and João Cabreira de Mendonça [with issue in NFP Marmeleiro §2 N5]*i*
>
> > 11 João Cabreira da Costa, who married his aunt (his mother's sister) Anna da Cunha [NFP Marmeleiro §2 N6]

§18

N6 DOMINGOS DE ABREU, son of Pedro Gomes de Abreu §16 N5, lived in Pevolide and married Isabel (...), daughter of Gonçallo Vaz˙ de Mello, lord of Pevolide, son of Pedro Lourenço Ferreira˙, known as *Mata Judeus* (*lit.* Killer of Jews) [NFP Mello §42 N11]

---

i In NFP Marmeleiro §2 N5, Luis da Costa Cabreira's wife (and Manoel˙ Gomes da Cunha's daughter) is called Maria˙ *Gonçalves˙* da Cunha, and not Maria˙ Alvares˙ da Cunha. (T. N.)

For details about Portuguese ranks of nobility, see p. v

7 Antonio˙ de Abreu, Prior of Pevolide, who had bastard children
7 Gaspar de Mello de Abreu
7 Pedro de Mello, who married Joanna, sp
7 Theresa de Abreu, wife of Francisco˙ Jose de Mello, with issue

N7 GASPAR DE MELLO DE ABREU, son of Domingos˙ de Abreu N6, married Isabel de Magalhães˙, daughter of Dr. Pedro or Diogo Barbosa of Lisbon – Judge of the Appeal Court, who also held the office of General Trial Judge in India –, brother of Fernão de Magalhães˙, Royal Appellate Judge and Chief Chancellor, both being the children of Pedro de Barros and Brites de Magalhães˙.
> 8 Ignacio de Abreu, who died unmarried
> 8 Pedro Gomes de Abreu
> 8 Lourenço da Cunha, sp
> 8 Isabel de Abreu

N8 PEDRO GOMES DE ABREU, son of Gaspar de Mello N7, married Maria˙ de Castro, daughter of João Gomes Pessoa, (brother of Manoel˙ Feyo de Mello, lord of Monte Redondo [NFP Feyo §2 N4 and N5]) and Anna de Mello[i]
> 9 Gaspar de Mello, who died in India, sp
> 9 Andre de Mello
> 9 Manoel˙ Feyo, a Bernardine monk
> 9 João de Mello, an Augustinian monk
> 9 D. Joanna, a nun in the convent of Cellas
> 9 D. Paulla
> 9 D. Isabel, in Vinhó

N9 ALEXANDRE DE MELLO (sic)[ii], son of Pedro Gomes de Abreu N8. He was the lord of the entail of Villar near Viseu and married Maria˙ Brandão, daughter of Domingos˙, or Pedro Alves˙ Brandão (brother of João Alves˙ Brandão, Inquisitor of the Council Board in Lisbon) and his wife Maria Paes, daughter of Domingos˙ Rodrigues˙, Appellate Judge in Oporto
> 10 João de Mello de Abreu

N10 JOÃO DE MELLO DE ABREU, son of Alexandre de Mello N9, married Maria˙ Botelho, daughter of Fernão de Horta Botelho and Maria˙ Brandão [NFP Aranha §84 N4][iii]

---

[i] In NFP Feyo §2 N4, Manoel˙ Feyo de Mello is not said to have had a brother called João Gomes Pessoa, but one called João *de Mello Feyo*. (T. N.)

[ii] A few line above (in N8) he is called *Andre* de Mello (and not Alexandre de Mello), and we do not know which version is right. (T. N.)

[iii] In NFP Aranha §84 N4, Maria˙ Brandão is said to have married *Francisco˙* Botelho, and not Fernão de Horta Botelho. (T. N.)

11 D. Joana de Abreu, wife of D. Francisco˙ Jose de Mello, son of D. Pedro de Mello and D. Maria˙ Margarida de Mendonça [NFP Mello §65 N18]

11 B. Antonio˙ de Mello, Prior of the Monastery-Fief of Santa Maria in Trancoso

§19

King Manuel I r. 1495-1521

N5 DIOGO GOMES DE ABREU, bastard son of Bishop D. João Gomes §16 N4. He was legitimated by King Manuel I, was granted the command of several orders and married Theresa, daughter of Diogo de Azevedo˙, brother of Martim Lopes de Azevedo. He did not have issue by this marriage, but had bastard children

6 B. Pedro Gomes de Abreu

6 B. D. (...)

N6 PEDRO GOMES DE ABREU, son of Diogo Gomes N5, married Maria˙ Pessoa de Mello, daughter of João Homem Pessoa and D. Anna de Mello

§20

N6 DIOGO GOMES DA CUNHA, son of Pedro Gomes de Abreu §16 N5 and Maria Fernandes[i], went to India in 1538. It seems that shortly before dying he married his mistress Jeronima Cardoso of Viseu, by whom he had

7 Pedro Gomes de Abreu, who went to India in 1576

Chaul is a territory located about 40 miles south of Bombay in India, and was a Portuguese colony from 1521 to 1740

7 Manoel˙ da Cunha, who was the Captain of Chaul and went to India several times, the last time in 1608

§21

N6 PEDRO GOMES DA CUNHA, son of Pedro Gomes de Abreu §16 N5[ii] (according to some he was an illegitimate son), lived in the manor of Consiguem[iiii] near Viseu. He married D. Francisca˙ de Castro, daughter of Diogo Borges de

---

[i] In §16 N5, it is stated that Pedro Gomes de Abreu married Mecia da Cunha and it is implicitly understood that he had his children (including Diogo da Cunha) by his wife; in that passage there is no mention about Maria Fernandes, who is here said to be the mother of Diogo Gomes da Cunha. (T. N.)

[ii] In the original text, in this passage it is stated that Pedro Gomes da Cunha was the son of (another) Pedro Gomes da Cunha, which seems to be a mistake, for in §16 N5 Pedro Gomes da Cunha N6 is said to be the son of Pedro Gomes *de Abreu* (husband of Mecia da Cunha), a version which we have preferred to adopt. (T.N.)

[iii] This manor is called Contiguem in N6, Consiguem or Conseguere in N7 and Consigem in N8; it is most probably a sole estate, though we do not know which name is the right one. (T. N.)

Castro and D. Catarina˙ Fogaça (Chief lady-in-waiting to D. Joanna de Eça), who lived in their manor in Capela, where they were buried [see also NFP Borges §1 N9]

      7 Diogo Borges de Castro

      7 Simão da Cunha, who died unmarried

      7 Gil de Castro, who married D. Brites (...), daughter of (...), brother of Gaspar Borges de Azevedo˙. Their children had issue [see NFP Borges §4 N9]

      7 Pedro Borges de Castro [with issue in NFP Borges §20]

      7 D. Catarina˙ de Castro

      7 D. Elena da Cunha, who married her nephew Pedro Borges [NFP Borges §20 N9]

      7 D. Maria˙ de Castro, who married Antonio˙ de Almada of Louriçal, sp

N7 DIOGO BORGES DE CASTRO, son of Pedro Gomes N6. He succeeded to the manor of Continguem or Conseguere[i] [NFP Borges §4 N8] and his father's house. He married D. Maria˙ de Barros of Ruidades

      8 Pedro Borges de Castro

      8 Catarina˙ Borges, no further details

N8 PEDRO BORGES DE CASTRO, son of Diogo Borges N7, inherited the house of Continguem[ii] and married D. Maria˙ de Moraes

      9 Pedro Borges de Castro, who married D. Elena de Eça, daughter of Gil de Castro, above, sp

      9 D. Catarina˙ de Castro

Pedro Borges de Castro married as his second wife D. Catarina˙

      9 Diogo Borges de Castro, lord of Silva and Captain of Viseu

N9 D. CATARINA˙ BORGES DE CASTRO, daughter of Pedro Borges N8, married Theotonio de Figueiredo˙ de Moraes

      10 Antonio˙ de Figueiredo˙

      10 Diogo Borges de Castro, who lived in the manor of Silva near Viseu

N10 ANTONIO˙ DE FIGUEIREDO˙, son of Catarina˙ de Castro N9, married Antonia˙ da Fonseca˙

      11 Felipa de Castro, wife of Appellate Judge Luis Gomes Loureiro of Coimbra, with issue

---

[i] See footnote *iii* on the previous page. (T. N.)

[ii] See footnote *iii* on the previous page. (T. N.)

§22

N2 BEATRIZ GOMES DE ABREU, daughter of Lourenço Gomes §2 N1, married João Vicente de Valencia

    3 D. Maria˙ Garcia˙, wife of Gonçallo Annes da Cunha

§23

N3 JOÃO GOMES DE ABREU, son of Vasco Gomes de Abreu §2 N2 [Ref.: *Corographia Portuguesa*, Part I, Chap. 63][i] who, according to Annes Amado, was Alcaide General of Tomar and Torres Vedras in the time of King John I. He almost lost his life for having refused to open the gate of Santarem to Queen Leonor, who had taken possession of that village. He married Ignes Dias de Sousa, bastard daughter of Lopo Dias de Sousa, Master of the Order of Christ

    4 Alvaro de Abreu

N4 ALVARO DE ABREU, son of João Gomes de Abreu N3, married Leonor Pereira˙ de Castro

    5 Ruy de Abreu, of Monção, with issue

§24

N3 TEREJA GOMES DE ABREU, daughter of Vasco Gomes de Abreu §2 N2, married Lopo Gomes de Lira, a Galician nobleman and Alcaide General of Braga and Ponte de Lima [NFP Lira §1 N2]

§25

N9 D. MANOEL˙ DE LIMA, son of Francisco˙ de Abreu §2 N8, was a Page-Fidalgo of the King's Household and Abbot of Rocas, though did not receive holy orders because he had committed murder. He had bastard issue by Maria de Barros

    10 B. Leonel de Abreu Lima, who married Anna Pereira˙ de Castro, lady of the house of Juste, daughter and heiress of Maria˙ Pereira˙ de Lira [NFP Araujo §347 N25][ii]. Leonel de Abreu served in India with the nobility charter granted to his father

King John I r. 1385-1433. For details about the dispute between King John I and Queen Leonor over the Kingdom of Portugal, see box on p. 9

For details about Portuguese ranks of nobility, see p. v

---

[i] *Corographia Portuguesa* (3 vols.), written by Father Antonio Carvalho da Costa (1650-1715) and published for the first time between 1706 and 1712. (T. N.)

[ii] In NFP Araujo §347 N25, Leonel de Abreu Lima's wife (and Maria˙ Pereira˙ de Lira's daughter) is called *Joanna* Pereira˙ de Castro, and not Anna Pereira˙ de Castro. (T. N.)

For details about Portuguese ranks of nobility, see p. v

10 B. Antonio˙ de Lima de Noronha

10 B. Manoel˙ de Lima, who got married, sp

10 B. Antonio˙ de Abreu, sp

10 B. Francisco˙ de Abreu, sp

10 B. D. Francisca˙ de Abreu, sp

10 B. D. Guiomar, sp

10 B. D. Margarida

Manoel de Lima also had by Isabel de Araujo˙ of Coucieiro

10 B. Lopo Gomes de Abreu §63

10 B. Cosme de Abreu Lima §139

N10 ANTONIO˙ DE LIMA E NORONHA, son of Manoel˙ de Lima N9, was a Page-Fidalgo of the King's Household and Captain General of Cabeceiras de Basto. He married Elena de Meireles, lady of the manor of Villar, daughter and heiress of Isabel Teixeira de Meireles and her husband Dr. Domingos˙ Correa˙ da Costa [NFP Meireles §5 N11][i]

> 11 D. Maria˙ de Noronha, wife of Baltazar˙ Pereira˙ da Silva˙, son of Antonio˙ Peixoto Pereira˙ of the entail of Olaria, Council of Riveira de Pena, and his wife Francisca˙ dos Guimaraens˙ Teixeira˙. She had
>> 12 D. Maria Pereira˙ da Silva˙, wife of Amaro da Rocha Pita de Antas, a resident of Coura
> 11 D. Isabel da Silva de Noronha

N11 D. ISABEL DA SILVA DE NORONHA, daughter of Antonio de Lima de Noronha N10. She became heiress due to the break of succession in her sister's line. She married Bento Rabello Lobo, Captain General of Cabeceiras de Basto and lord of the manor of Bouças, son of Sebastião Rabello Leite Lobo and his wife D. Luisa de Sousa, e Castro, paternal grandson of Miguel Rabello Leite and his wife (...), and maternal grandson of Antonio˙ de Sousa Lobo [NFP Meireles §12 N13][ii]. Some say Bento Rabello held the office of Clerk of the Writs in Cabeceiras de Basto

> 12 Manoel˙ de Lima, who died young
> 12 Nuno de Lima de Noronha
> 12 D. Luisa
> 12 D. Josefa
> 12 D. Doroteia
> 12 D. Maria˙

---

[i] In NFP Meireles §5 N11, Isabel Teixeira˙ de Meireles´s husband is called Domingos˙ Correa˙ *de Abreu* and not Domingos Correa˙ da Costa. (T. N.)

[ii] In NFP Meireles §12 N12 and N13, Sebastião Rabello Leite and his wife D. Luiza de Sousa are said to be the parents of *Antonio*˙ Rabello Lobo (and not Bento Rabello Lobo), who is said to have been the husband of Isabel da Silva *e Lima* (and not Isabel da Silva de Noronha), daughter of Antonio˙ Lima e Noronha. (T. N.)

N12 NUNO DE LIMA, son of Isabel da Silva˙ N11, was the Captain General of Basto and inherited the manors of Villar and Bouças, as well as his father's house. He married his cousin Maria˙ Josefa de Noronha, daughter of Pedro da Cunha de Abreu (Knight of the Order of Christ and Infantry Captain, son of Pedro da Costa de Abreu, Knight of the Order of Christ, and Violante Velho) and his wife Maria˙ Pereira˙ de Abreu Lima (heiress and daughter of Leonel de Abreu Lima and his wife Anna Pereira˙ de Castro) [NFP Costa §137 N8]*i*

     13 Manoel˙ Baltazar˙ de Noronha

     13 B. João de Lima Abreu of Tuia, who died in 1760

N13 MANOEL˙ BALTAZAR˙ DE NORONHA, son of Nuno de Lima N12, was the Captain General of Basto. He married Theresa Luisa Teixeira˙ de Moura, daughter of Bento Teixeira˙ Mendes (Captain General of Arões and brother of Antonio Teixeira, a Royal Appellate Judge) and his wife Senhorinha de Moura, paternal granddaughter of Antonio˙ Teixeira˙ and Catarina˙ Alvares, and maternal granddaughter of Simão Alvares˙ de Azevedo˙, a university graduate, and his wife Maria˙ Martins [see NFP Pedigree Charts, Vol. 1, N149 and NFP Cunha §78 N7]*ii*

     14 Nuno de Lima de Abreu, who married (in Braga) Clara de Brito
         Leite [NFP Costa §(...) N(...) (sic)], sp

     14 Antonio˙ de Lima, e Abreu

     14 Jose de Lima

     14 Francisco˙

     14 Luis

     14 D. Marianna

     14 D. (...)

N14 ANTONIO DE LIMA DE NORONHA E ABREU, son of Manoel˙ Baltazar˙ de Noronha N13. As heir to his father's house he married D. Anna de Alpoim e Menezes, daughter of Francisco˙ Xavier˙ de Alpoim, a Fidalgo of the King's Household and lord of the house of Mareces and Pousada, and his wife Jeronima Thereza de Carvalho, e Menezes [NFP Felgueiras §16 N8 and NFP Costa §13 N12]*iii*

     15 D. (...), heiress

---

i In NFP Costa §137 N7 and N8, Pedro da Cunha de Abreu's father is called Pedro *Lobato* de Abreu, and not Pedro da Costa de Abreu. (T. N.)

ii In NFP Cunha §78 N7, it is stated that Thereza Luiza Teixeira˙ was the daughter of Bento Teixeira˙ *Alvares* (and not Bento Teixeira Mendes) and Senhorinha de Moura Coutinho, who was the daughter of Simão Alvares˙ de Moura de Azevedo and his wife Maria˙ *Rodrigues˙ da Rocha* (and not Maria Martins). (T. N.)

iii The names of Anna de Alpoim e Menezes and her mother Jeronima Thereza de Carvalho, e Menezes were ommited in the original text, so we have retrieved them from the cross-reference in NFP Felgueiras §16 N8. However, in NFP Costa §13 N12, it is not stated that Francisco˙ Xavier˙ de Alpoim had the daughter and the son-in-law mentioned here. Besides that, his wife is called Jeronima Thereza de Carvalho˙ e *Souza*, and not Jeronima Thereza de Carvalho, e Menezes. (T. N.)

§26

N6 ROQUE DE ABREU, son of Pedro Gomes de Abreu §16 N5 (others say this Roque de Abreu was the son of João Gomes de Abreu §16 N6 and his wife, with which we do not agree, for we consider both Roque and João the children of Pedro Gomes de Abreu §16 N5)[i]. He married his relative Joanna Soares, daughter of Pedro Gomes de Abreu, Canon of Viseu [§13 N5], and lived with her in the municipality of Penalva

> 7 Lourenço Soares, a clergyman, though one author says he married and had
>> 8 Cristovão de Abreu, who was in India in 1591
> 7 Thome Soares, who died unmarried
> 7 Brites da Cunha §78
> 7 Ignacio de Abreu Soares
> 7 Violante de Abreu, second wife of Martim de Mello Soares [with issue in NFP Mello §29 N13]
> 7 Juliana de Abreu, who married Manoel˙ de Sousa, e Mello, son of Fernão de Mello [NFP Mello §29 N12 Sub13], sp
> 7 Roque Fernandes de Abreu, who is said by some to have been the son of Luis de Abreu §79 N6

N7 IGNACIO SOARES DE ABREU[ii], son of Roque de Abreu N6, married (in Bouzella) Antonia˙ de Sá, daughter of Lopo Cardoso Rabello and Isabel de Sá

> 8 Luis da Silva˙ da Cunha §102
> 8 Manoel˙ de Sousa da Silva˙, who went to India
> 8 Alexandre da Cunha
> 8 Ignacio de Abreu, who died unmarried

N8 ALEXANDRE DA CUNHA, son of Ignacio Soares N7, was a Fidalgo of the King's Household and the Captain General of Lafões. He owned the royal estates of Varoso by his wife Simoa de Azevedo (who inherited her father's lands and lived in Bousela), daughter of Simão de Azevedo Cabral and his wife Felipa de Sá de Moura, paternal granddaughter of Gonçallo Fernandes˙ Cabral and his wife Maria˙ de Azevedo˙. Gonçallo Fernandes˙ was the son of Gil Gonçalves˙ of Celorico de Basto and the maternal grandson of Luis de Sá, lord of the royal estates of Barroso, a descendant of the Sás of Penaguião

> 9 Roque da Cunha, e Mello §77
> 9 D. Felipa de Sá, e Mello

---

[i] In §16 N5 it is stated that Roque de Abreu had a brother called João Gomes *da Cunha*, and not João Gomes de Abreu. (T. N.)

[ii] A few lines above in the text the order of his surnames is inverted: Ignacio *de Abreu Soares*. (T. N.)

9 Luis da Cunha, e Mello, who married Antonia Rabello or Isabel Rabello, daughter of Domingos˙ Dias Homem and Maria˙ de Campos. He had

10 Antonia˙ de Mello, wife of her relative Jose de Abreu de Mello [§78 N9]

N9 FELIPA DE SÁ DE MELLO, daughter of Alexandre da Cunha N8, married Diogo de Barros, son of Lucas de Barros de Azevedo˙ of São Pedro do Sul, near Viseu and D. Feliciana Barbosa

10 Felipa de Mello, who married Vasco Pereira˙ Marinho of Braga [NFP Marinho §30 N18][i]

§27

THE ABREUS OF QUINTÃO

N6 FERNÃO VASQUES DE ABREU, bastard son of Vasco Gomes de Abreu §10 N5, was a Fidalgo of the King's Household and lord of Sarnache dos Alhos. He married Francisca˙ Dias Cabral, daughter of Jorge Dias Cabral, Commendatory of Ancede and his mistress Maria˙ de Macedo, daughter of Gonçallo Maldonado, a distinguished Castilian nobleman, and Brites de Sousa, daughter of Diogo Gonçalves˙ de Macedo (Chief Chamberlain to King John I, lord of Melgaço, São Seriz, Pindelo and other estates) and his wife Mor Fernandes de Sousa, daughter of D. Fernando Affonso˙ de Sousa, Chief Steward to the King. Diogo Gonçalves˙ de Macedo was the son of Martim Gonçalves˙ de Macedo, who displayed great valor at the battle of Aljubarrota, in which he dismounted to recover King John I's mace, which had been snatched by D. Alvaro de Sandoval. Upon receiving the mace back from Martim Gonçalves, the King wished personally to discharge it on the said Sandoval, but found him already dead. For this valiant action Martim Gonçalves received the name of *Macedo* [see NFP Macedo §1 N8][ii].

King John I r. 1385–1433

The battle of Aljubarrota was f. August 14, 1385 (for more details, see box on p. 9)

---

[i] In NFP Marinho §30 N18, it is stated that Vasco Pereira˙ Marinho Falcão married Felipa de Mello da Cunha, daughter of Diogo de Barros de Azevedo˙ and his wife Felipa *da Cunha*, e Melo (and not Felipa de Sá e Mello). (T. N.)

[ii] According to this version, the name *Macedo* derives from *maça*, Port. for mace. In NFP Macedo §1 N8, it is stated that Martim Gonçalves˙ also killed D. Alvaro de Sandoval. In the same reference, though, it is informed that this Martim Gonçalves˙ de Macedo was the son of Gonçallo Annes de Macedo, the paternal grandson of João Gonçalves˙ de Macedo and the great grandson of Affonço Gonçalves˙ de Macedo, who was the first to bear the name of Macedo, which he took from the place of Maceda, in Trás-os-Montes Province, where he was probably from, and this information seems to invalidate the version by which the origin of the name Macedo derives from the episody of the King's mace in the battle of Aljubarrota. (T. N.)

Gonçallo Maldonado was the son of Alvaro Maldonado, a Castilian nobleman who in the time of King Afonso V came to Portugal, where he married Maria de Gouvea. Jorge Dias Cabral was the son of Diogo Fernandes Cabral, Prior of Povos and Dean of the Royal Chapel, who was held in high esteem by King John II. When this sovereign deceased, Diogo Fernandes Cabral and other noblemen attended him at his death in Caldas de Alvaro [see NFP Queirós §3 N12, NFP Cabral §7 N9 and NFP Maldonado §1 N2]*i*

> 7 Diogo de Abreu, though some authors do not mention him amongst Fernão de Abreu's children
> 7 Ruy de Abreu, who was a Fidalgo of the King's Household and lived in Lisbon
> 7 Francisca˙ de Abreu, wife of Alvaro Mendes of the entail of Fontellas [with issue in NFP Vasconcelos §12 N16]*ii*

N7 DIOGO DE ABREU, son of Fernão Vasques de Abreu N6, married Maria˙ da Cunha, daughter of Ruy Lourenço de Carvalho˙ and Tereja Coutinho˙*iii* [NFP Cunha §6 N12 and N13][10]

---

i In NFP Queirós §3 N12 and NFP Cabral §7 N9, it is informed that Jorge Dias Cabral was the son of Diogo *Dias* Cabral, and not Diogo Fernandes˙ Cabral, though this latter version also appears in NFP Maldonado §1 N2. (T. N.)

ii In NFP Vasconcelos §12 N16, Francisca˙ de Abreu's husband is given as Alvaro Mendes *de Vasconcellos*.(T. N.)

iii In the original version, it is stated in this passage that Maria˙ da Cunha was the daughter of Fernão da Cunha, Alcaide General of Basto, and his wife Maria˙ de Carvalho. Yet in NFP Cunha §6 N12 and N13, this latter parentage is explicitly considered to be a mistake, for Maria da Cunha is said to be the daughter of Theresa Coutinho (Fernão da Cunha's sister) and her husband Ruy Lourenço de Carvalho˙, which is also in accordance with the author's next footnote. (T. N.)

[10] In a charter dated February 21, 1608, by which Gaspar da Cunha, son of Simão de Carvalho˙ [NFP Carvalho §30 N19]*iv*, was granted the right to bear a coat of arms, it is stated that Gaspar was a fourth-generation descendant of Ruy Lourenço de Carvalho˙ and Tereja Coutinho˙. Also according to this record, Maria˙ da Cunha, wife of Diogo de Abreu N7, was not the daughter of Fernão da Cunha, but of the said Ruy Lourenço and D. Theresa.

In Monchique, where Pedro da Cunha had a fief, he enfeoffed his niece Maria˙ da Cunha in the manor of Borba for her to marry Diogo de Abreu of Quintão. Yet when Pedro da Cunha called upon Diogo de Abreu to accompany him in the campaign of Azamor and manage his household, the latter refused to go because he was newly wed. Chafed by this refusal, Pedro da Cunha, upon his return to Basto, took away the manor he had bestowed upon the couple, which made D. Maria write a letter to her uncle saying: "*It was you who wanted me to marry Diogo de Abreu and not I. You also granted me the estates and the title of your niece. As you now take away from me the estates, leaving me only the title, I deem it better to return to you the title as well, for it is no longer good for me to bear it*", and afterwards she stopped considering herself his niece.

iv In NFP Carvalho §30, there is not a paragraph N19, though in NFP Carvalho §30 N11 Sub12, it is stated that a Simão Affonso˙ de Carvalho˙ was the son of Anna de Carvalho and had bastard issue whose descendency became extinct. Yet we do not know with certainty whether this Simão Affonso de Carvalho is the same Simão de Carvalho mentioned above in this footnote. (T. N.)

8 Isabel de Abreu, who married Gregorio Lopes do Rego [in §30]

8 Violante de Abreu, who had issueless children

8 Manoel˙ de Abreu, who married Anna Dias de Quiro [NFP Vasconcellos §71 N18]

8 Branca de Abreu

8 Francisca˙ de Abreu, who married Gregorio˙ Dias, son of Catarina˙ de Quiro [NFP Vasconcellos §72 N18]

King Afonso V r. 1438–1481
King John II r. 1481–1495

N8 BRANCA DE ABREU, daughter of Diogo de Abreu N7, married Francisco˙ de Macedo, who held the office of Clerk of the Writs in Celorico de Basto and lived in his manor of Macarote, in the parish of Villa Garcia, municipality of Basto. Branca and her husband were the lords of the manor of Tuia in the parish of Freixo. Francisco˙ de Macedo presented on February 3, 1554 a justification of his noble ancestry, stating that he was the son of Pedro de Macedo and Ignes de Sequeira˙, daughter of Martim or João Teixeira˙ de Antas and his wife Catarina˙ Ferreira˙, or Violante de Barros. Pedro de Macedo was the son of Vasco Annes de Moraes (Valet de Chambre to King Afonso V and King John II) and his wife Marianna Teixeira˙, daughter of Pedro Teixeira˙ and Joanna Martins de Macedo [NFP Teixeira §36 N14][i]

9 Guiomar de Macedo

9 Isabel de Macedo, who married (in Faia) Francisco˙ Ribeiro˙ [NFP Vasconcellos §160 N18]

9 Manoel˙ de Abreu, who married Anna Dias Soutello

9 Pedro de Macedo

9 Gonçallo de Macedo

9 Paullo de Macedo

9 Miguel de Macedo

9 Anna de Macedo, wife of Gonçallo de Abreu

9 D. Ignes de Macedo, wife of Sebastião Dias

N9 GUIOMAR DE MACEDO, daughter of Branca de Abreu N8, married João Gonçalves˙ of Masacorte

10 Guiomar de Macedo

10 Francisca˙ de Macedo §31

10 Maria˙ da Cunha

10 Isabel de Macedo, wife of Simão Ribeiro˙ of Santa Clara, son of Francisco˙ Correa˙ and Isabel Ribeiro˙ [in §43][ii]

10 Branca de Abreu

10 Magdalena de Macedo

---

[i] In NFP Teixeira §36 N13, Vasco Annes de Moraes's wife (and Pedro Teixeira˙'s daughter) is called *Izabel de Macedo* Teixeira˙ (or *Izabel* Teixeira˙ *de Macedo*) and not Marianna Teixeira˙ (T. N.)

[ii] In §43, Isabel de Macedo's husband is called Simão Ribeiro˙ *de Sousa*. (T. N.)

N10 MAGDALENA DE MACEDO, daughter of Guiomar de Macedo N9, married her first husband, Francisco˙ Peixoto, son of Gonçallo Peixoto and Felipa Pereira˙ [NFP Peixoto §4 N8][i]

    11 Francisco˙ de Macedo

    11 Baltazar Peixoto, unmarried

    11 Gaspar de Macedo, whose first marriage, on September 17, 1625 in Amarante, was to Isabel de Abreu, daughter of Antonio˙ Cerqueira˙ and his wife Maria˙ da Cunha

Magdalena de Macedo's second marriage, on February 2, 1665[ii], was to João da Cunha, son of Manoel˙ Ferreira˙ and Maria˙ da Cunha, with issue

N11 FRANCISCO˙ DE MACEDO, son of Magdalena de Macedo N10. He married (on June 29, 1636, in Amarante) Angela de Sequeira˙, daughter of João de Sequeira˙, probate court officer in Amarante, and his wife Catarina˙ do Couto. Angela de Sequeira was the paternal granddaughter of Baltazar˙ Gomes and Catarina˙ Lopes, and the maternal granddaughter of Manoel˙ Alvares and Francisca˙ do Couto

    12 Gonçallo de Macedo

    12 Luisa de Macedo

    12 Maria˙ da Cunha, wife of Pedro Mendes, son of Sebastião Navarro and Clara da Fonseca˙ [NFP Queiros §21 N17]

    12 Isabel de Sequeira˙, wife of João de Magalhães˙ §37

N12 LUISA DE MACEDO, daughter of Francisco˙ de Macedo N11, married (on April 26, 1674) Pedro de Magalhães˙ of Reguengo, son of Jose de Magalhães˙ and Elena Cerqueira˙ [NFP Magalhães §45 N12]

    13 Francisco˙ de Magalhães˙, no further details

§28

N5 JOÃO GOMES DE ABREU, son of Pedro Gomes de Abreu §2 N4. João Gomes de Abreu (who had earlier assumed the name of Sousa)[iii] was a Page-Fidalgo to King John II and King Manuel I. He had also been a captain in India in the time of King Afonso V, as recorded in a charter belonging to the lords of the house of Anquião, dated January 15, 1500, of which the lords of the house of Outeiro, his

For details about Portuguese ranks of nobility, see p. v.
King Afonso V r. 1438-1481
King John II r. 1481–1495
King Manuel I r. 1495–1521

---

[i] In NFP Peixoto §4 N8, Francisco˙ Peixoto's wife is called *Margarida* de Macedo and not Magdalena de Macedo. (T. N.)

[ii] This year of 1665 for Magdalena de Macedo's second marriage is most probably a mistake, for in the same passage it is informed that the children of her first marriage married four decades before that (in 1625 and 1636). (T. N.)

[iii] Actually, in §2 N4, this son of Pedro Gomes de Abreu is called João Gomes de *Sousa*, and not João Gomes de Abreu. (T. N.)

descendants in Ponte de Lima, have a copy, which we have had the opportunity to see. He married (on June 3, 1487) Joanna de Mello, lady of the house of Anquião, which he acquired through his marriage, as recorded in a charter written on the same date by notary public Alvaro Dias in Ponte de Lima, in which João Gomes de Abreu's parents' names are recorded. D. Joanna de Mello was the bastard daughter of D. Rodrigo de Mello e Lima, Commendatory of Refoios, and was legitimated by King John II by a charter written on June 27, 1433[i] in Santarém (although another chronicle states this legitimation occurred in 1487). Besides the manor of Anquião, she received as a dowry two thousand gold sovereigns. The manor of Anquião had been inherited by the said D. Rodrigo in the partition of the estates of his father, the Viscount, upon his death. D. Rodrigo de Mello was the advowee of the Chapel of Our Lady of the Rosary in the Convent of Saint Anthony of Ponte de Lima (founded by the Viscount his father, where the mausoleum of the lords of Anquião is located) and also of the Church of Outeiro in Ponte de Lima [NFP Lima §2 N12]. The names of his children are mentioned in his wife D. Joanna's will dated January 14th, 1549

> 6 Diogo Gomes de Abreu
>
> 6 Jorge de Abreu Lima
>
> 6 Felipa de Lima, who married Francisco˙ de Caldas [NFP Caldas §4 N4], when she was already the widow of Francisco˙ Barbosa, son of Francisco˙ Barbosa Aranha; others say her name was Brites
>
> 6 Catarina˙, who was a nun in the convent of Vitorinho like her three sisters below
>
> 6 Isabel
>
> 6 Cecilia
>
> 6 Brites

For details about Portuguese ranks of nobility, see p. v.

N6 DIOGO GOMES DE ABREU, son of João Gomes de Abreu N5, was the second lord of Anquião. He was a Page-*Fidalgo*, being later advanced to Squire-Fidalgo and then to Knight-Fidalgo, by charters dated January 1st, 1512 and October, 21, 1521. He served in India in 1533, and was granted a 1200-real allowance in 1548. He died in Lisbon upon his return from India. He was married to Ignacia Pereira˙, daughter of Diogo Borges Pacheco, last Abbot of Facha and his mistress Leonor Pereira˙ [NFP Araujo §177 N20]. The said Ignacia Pereira˙ was buried in her family's mausoleum in the Chapel of Our Lady of the Rosary, on whose tomb is written: "Here lies D. Ignacia Pereira˙ wife of Diogo Gomes de Abreu Page-Fidalgo of El Rei". According to his will, dated April 29, 1592 and his inventory, dated 1593, he had the following children:

---

[i] This year is certainly a mistake, for King John II reigned between 1481 and 1495. Perhaps the author meant 1483, and not 1433. (T. N.)

7 Antonio˙ de Abreu Lima

7 João Gomes, who died in infancy

7 Ruy Gomes de Abreu §57

7 Pedro Gomes de Abreu, who went to India

7 Manoel˙ de Mello, *ditto*

7 Nicolao de Mello Lima §58

7 João de Abreu, who went to India

7 D. Joanna, a nun in the convent of Vitorinho

7 D. Catarina˙ de Lima, who some say was a bastard daughter. Her first husband was Vasco Marinho, a Galician knight, and her second husband was Francisco˙ Soares, sp

7 Felipa de Lima, also a bastard daughter according to others, married Damião do Valle Peixoto [with issue in NFP Araujo §195 N23][i]

7 Jorge de Abreu, also a bastard son according to some, sp

N7 ANTONIO˙ DE ABREU LIMA, son of Diogo Gomes de Abreu N6, was the lord of the house of Anquião. He was created Fidalgo of the King's Household with a 2400-real housing allowance by a charter dated May 12, 1609, having also been granted a command by a charter dated January 8 of the same year. He married Anna de Magalhães˙, daughter of Antonio de Magalhães˙, lord of Mato Bom and his wife Beatriz de Amorim [NFP Amorim §25 N5][ii]

8 Pedro Gomes de Abreu

8 Ruy Gomes de Abreu §104

8 João Gomes de Abreu, Rector of Fornelos

8 D. Brites, a nun in the convent of Salvador in Braga

N8 PEDRO GOMES DE ABREU, son of Antonio˙ de Abreu Lima N7, was the lord of Anquião and a Fidalgo of the King's Household. He married Antonia˙ de Barros de Magalhães˙, daughter of João Antunes de Magalhães˙, advowee of Toris, and his wife Briolanja de Barros[iii], paternal granddaughter of Antonio˙ Pires de Magalhães˙, and maternal granddaughter of Gonçallo˙ Esteves de Barros, advowee of Toris, and his wife Isabel de Barros, this latter being the daughter of Diogo de Barros, advowee of Toris [NFP Barros §52 N4; NFP Amorim §56 N6][iv]

---

[i] In NFP Araujo §195 N23, Damião do Valle Peixoto's wife (and Diogo Gomes de Abreu's daughter) is called Felipa de Lima *e Mello*. (T. N.)

[ii] In NFP Amorim §25 N5, Anna de Magalhães''s mother is called Beatriz *da Morim*. (T. N.)

[iii] In NFP Barros §52 N4, João Antunes de Magalhães''s wife is called Briolanja *Velho* de Barros. (T. N.)

[iv] In the original text, in this passage there is also a reference to NFP Gavião §1 Sub. N2, though in this reference it is simply impossible to find any names mentioned in this paragraph. Yet in NFP Gavião §1 N8, it is mentioned that Antonio˙ Barreto Gavião was the husband of Maria˙ de Barros, daughter of João Antunes de Magalhães˙ and Briolanja Velho de Barros, i. e., this Maria de Barros was the sister of Antónia˙ de Barros de Magalhães˙, Pedro Gomes de Abreu's wife. (T. N.)

9 Antonio˙ de Abreu, who married Bernardina Pacheco, sp
9 João Gomes de Abreu
9 D. Marinha, a nun in the convent of Vale de Pereiras
9 D. Anna, a nun in the convent of Salvador in Braga

N9 JOÃO GOMES DE ABREU, son of Pedro Gomes de Abreu N8, was a Fidalgo of the King's Household and the lord of the house of Anquião. He married as his first wife Joanna Pimenta, daughter of Francisco˙ Cordeiro Malheiro and his wife Ignes Pimenta, paternal granddaughter of Alvaro Felgueiras˙ and his wife Maria Malheiro. Ignes Pimenta was, according to some, the daughter of João Pimenta Pereira˙ and his wife Maria˙ Lobato de Sousa, this latter being the daughter of João Pereira˙ de Araujo˙ and Brites Lobato. João Pimenta was the son of Alvaro Felgueiras˙ and Maria Malheiro, though according to another (and more reliable) version, João Pimenta's mother was Ignes Pimenta [NFP Felgueiras §41 N2 and N3][i]

10 Antonio˙ de Abreu Lima
10 D. Jacinta, a nun in the Convent of Valle de Pereira

---

[i] The chapters of Abreu and Felgueiras have many differences as regards the names of some members of this family. Though we do not have elements to verify which version is right, in some cases the author gives clues about what information he thinks more likely to be correct. These differences can be summarized in the table below.

Person	NAME IN NFP ABREU §28 N9	NAME IN NFP FELGUEIRAS §41 N2-N4
João Gomes de Abreu's wife	Joanna Pimenta	Joanna Pimenta*
João Gomes de Abreu's father-in-law	Francisco˙ Cordeiro Malheiro	Francisco• Cardozo Malheiro
João Pimenta Pereira's wife	Maria• Lobato de Souza	Maria• Lobato de Souza**
João Pimenta Pereira's mother (and Alvaro Felgueiras' wife)	Maria• Malheiro or Ignez Pimenta***	Maria• Malheiro and/or Ignez Pimenta ****
João Pereira de Araújo's wife	Brites Lobato	Brites Lobo

* This information can be found in NFP Felgueiras §41 N4 Sub5. Yet in NFP Felgueiras §41 N2 Sub3 Sub4, the author mentions a version by which João Gomes de Abreu's wife's name is *Ignez* Pimenta˙, with which he disagrees.

**This information can be found in NFP Felgueiras §41 N3. Yet in NFP Felgueiras §41 N2 Sub3, João Pimenta Pereira's wife's name is *Joanna de Castro*, though the author seems to disagree with this latter opinion.

*** The author states that the latter name seems to be more probable.

**** The author mentions a version according to which Alvaro Felgueira was married to Maria Malheiro and had by her Francisco Cardoso Malheiro. This last filiation is also mentioned in NFP Abreu §28 N9 (though in this chapter Maria Malheiro's son is called Francisco *Cordeiro* Malheiro, as already shown in the table above. (T. N.)

João Gomes de Abreu married as his second wife Leonor de Mello (or Antonia˙ de Mello), daughter of Paullo de Mello Sampaio˙ and Francisca˙ de Almeida [NFP Sampaio §2 N9][i]

    10 João Gomes, who served in India

    10 Pedro Gomes, *ditto*

    10 D. Maria˙

    10 D. Francisca˙

    10 D. Pascoa, unmarried

N10 ANTONIO˙ DE ABREU LIMA, son of the first wife of João Gomes de Abreu N9, was a Fidalgo of the King's Household and the lord of the fief of Anquião. He married Antonia˙ de Mello (or Leonor de Mello), daughter of Paullo de Mello Sampaio˙ and Francisca˙ de Almeida [NFP Sampaio §2 N9][ii]

    11 Antonio˙ de Abreu Lima

    11 Luis de Abreu, sp

    11 João Gomes, sp

    11 Francisco˙ Xavier, sp

    11 D. Paullo, a priest of the Order of the Holy Cross of Coimbra

    11 D. Rosa, sp

    11 D. Thomasia, sp

    11 D. Francisca˙, sp

    11 D. Joanna, sp

    11 D. Ventura, sp

    11 D. Josefa, sp

    11 Manoel

    11 D. Theresa, sp

    11 D. Arcangella Micaela de Abreu, wife of Pedro de Barros Barbosa, Lord of Carcaveira [with issue in NFP Araujo §380 N28]. Arcangella was abducted by the said Pedro de Barros, for her parents did not approve of her marriage[iii]

---

[i] In the original text, the cross-reference for this part is NFP Costa §72 N11, though this paragraph does not even exist, nor have we been able to find these people mentioned in another part of the chapter NFP Costa. Yet they are mentioned in NFP Sampaio, though in this latter chapter it is informed [NFP Sampaio §2 N9 Sub10] that Leonor de Mello and her husband João Gomes de Abreu did not have issue, which contradicts the information presented here. (T. N.)

[ii] This information contradicts the previous footnote. As we have already said, in NFP Sampaio §2 N9, it is stated that Leonor de Mello was married to *João Gomes* de Abreu (and not Antonio de Abreu), and we do not know which information is right. (T. N.)

[iii] In NFP Araujo §380 N28, Pedro de Barros Barbosa's wife is called Arcangella *de Abreu Lima*. (T. N.)

> 11 D. Luisa de Abreu, wife of Manoel˙ Peixoto de Carvalho˙, lord of the house of Pousada [with issue in NFP Machado §16 N24]ⁱ
>
> 11 D. Josefa Francisca˙ de Mello, wife of Bento da Costa Soares of Lamego [with issue in NFP Andrade Freire §28 N10]ⁱⁱ
>
> > 12 D. Catarina˙, an heiress, wife of Diogo Lopes de Carvalho˙, lord of the entail of Poço [NFP Carvalho §(...) (sic)]

N11 ANTONIO˙ DE ABREU LIMA, son of Antonio˙ de Abreu N10, was a Fidalgo of the King's Household and the lord of the fief of Anquião. He married Antonia˙ Maria˙ Gama de Andrade˙, daughter of Lourenço da Gama de Andrade˙ (Knight of the Order of Christ and lord of the entail of Villar) and his wife Joanna da Gama Lobo [NFP Prado §4 N13]

> 12 Antonio˙ Jose de Abreu Lima
>
> 12 D. Ana, who died young
>
> 12 Jose, *ditto*
>
> 12 Lourenço da Gama, Prior of Arcos in the Bishopric of Coimbra

N12 ANTONIO˙ JOSE DE ABREU LIMA, son of Antonio˙ de Abreu Lima N11, was the lord of the house of Anquião and a *Fidalgo* of the King's Household by a charter dated 1747. He married (in Coimbra) Francisca˙ Antonia˙ Xavier de Moraes Lara, e Sousa, daughter and heiress of Francisco˙ de Moraes de Brito da Serra (lord of the house of Portalagre in Coimbra — which was granted to him by his father-in-law —, a Fidalgo of the King's Household and Knight of the Order of Christ) and his relative and wife Leonor Angelica de Lara, e Sousa, daughter and heiress of Francisco˙ de Moraes Serra, Knight of the Order of Christ and Maria˙ de Vasconcelos de Eça, the latter couple having lived in Portalegre

> > 13 Fernando Xavier˙ de Abreu, who died without issue and was buried in the family mausoleum in the Monastery of Santo Antonio da Estrela in Coimbra
> >
> > 13 Francisco˙ Joaquim˙ de Abreu Lima
> >
> > 13 D. Francisca˙ Antonia˙ Xavier˙ de Moraes Lara, e Sousa

---

ⁱ In NFP Machado §16 N24, Manoel˙ Peixoto de Carvalho˙'s wife is called Luiza de Abreu *Lima*. (T. N.)

ⁱⁱ In NFP Andrade Freire §28 N10, Bento da Costa Soares's wife is called Josefa Francisca˙ *Pereira˙* de Mello, *e Lima*. In that chapter, this couple is also said to have been the parents of D. Maria˙ Freire de Mello, besides having the daughter D. Catarina who is mentioned here. (T. N.)

N13 FRANCISCO˙ JOAQUIM˙ DE ABREU LIMA, son of Antonio˙ Jose de Abreu N12, inherited his father's house and was a *Fidalgo* of the King's Household. He married his relative Rosalia Manoela de Abreu Lima, daughter and heiress of Leonel de Abreu Lima, lord of the house of Paço Vedro and a Fidalgo of the King's Household [§104 N11]

      14 Elena de Moraes de Noronha, e Menezes
      14 Antonio˙ de Abreu Lima
      14 Leonel de Abreu, a Knight of Malta
      14 Francisco˙ de Abreu Lima, a university graduate

§29

N10 ANTONIO˙ DE ABREU, son of Leonel de Abreu §2 N9[i], was the Abbot of Moreira and had by Catarina˙ de Abreu, the daughter who Leonel de Abreu had by his first wife Ignes Pita [in §4 N10], or by his mistress Isabel Pereira˙ de Castro,

      11 B. Lopo Gomes de Abreu

He also had by a woman from Regalados called Maria˙ Lomba Cerqueira˙

      11 B. Isabel de Abreu §70, who married Antonio˙ de Brito Pimenta of Ponte de Lima [with issue in §70 N11]
      11 B. Manoel˙ da Silva Abreu, who married Catarina˙ Gamboa of Alenquer or Villa Franca, and had
      12 Manoel˙ de Abreu

N11 LOPO GOMES DE ABREU, bastard son of Antonio˙ de Abreu N10, married Felipa de Magalhães˙ da Cunha, bastard daughter of Simão de Magalhães de Barros, a canon, and Maria da Cunha Coutinho˙ [see NFP Pedigree Charts, Vol. I, N158; NFP Barros §38 N11]

      12 D. Felipa or D. Felicia Quiteria Joanna de Abreu Lima, who married João Mendes de Vasconcellos˙ [NFP Vasconcellos §9 N20]
      12 Antonio˙ de Abreu Lima, Abbot of Rocas
      12 Leonel de Abreu, Abbot of Rocas
      12 D. Maria˙ Josefa, a nun
      12 D. Cecília de Abreu, a nun

§30

N8 ISABEL DE ABREU, daughter of Diogo de Abreu §27 N7, married Gregorio Lopes do Rego and lived with him in their manor of Reguengo, in the territory of

---

[i] In §2 N9, this son of Leonel de Abreu is called Antonio de Abreu *Lima*. (T. N.)

the village of Basto. Gregorio Lopes do Rego was the son of João Lopes Mansilha and his wife Felipa da Fonseca, of Trancoso, and the grandson of Gil Affonço Mansilha, lord of the manor of Lourentim, which he fortified, in the parish of São Miguel de Lobrigos, township of Penaguião. Isabel de Abreu married Gregorio Lopes do Rego as his second wife, for he was then the widower of Isabel Francisca˙ de Quiro, daughter of the Commendatory of Freixo [NFP Vasconcellos §69 N17]

      9 Simão de Carvalho˙ da Cunha

      9 Andre Lopes de Abreu Rego §32

      9 Ignacia Lopes, from whom the family of Chapa is descended

      9 Diogo Lopes de Abreu Rego, who married Luisa de Carvalho, daughter of Fernão de Carvalho [with issue in NFP Carvalho §88 N11]

      9 Maria˙ de Abreu, wife of Baltazar˙ de Carvalho Coutinho [with issue in NFP Carvalho §84 N14][i]

N9 SIMÃO DE CARVALHO DA CUNHA, son of Isabel de Abreu N8, inherited his father's house and married Elena Esteves Rabello, the widow of Antonio˙ de Macedo. As stated in NFP Esteves de Figueiredo §1 N5, Elena Esteves Rabello was the daughter of Diogo Gonçalves˙ and his wife Brites Rabello de Figueiredo, the paternal granddaughter of Gonçallo Esteves Rabello and his wife Maria˙ Annes from the city of Oporto, and the great granddaughter of Gonçallo˙ Esteves and his wife (...) Esteves, lady-in-waiting to the Duchess of Bragança. Brites Rabello de Figueiredo˙ was the sister of João Esteves de Figueiredo˙, after whom the manor of Figueiredo was named, and who was the husband of Isabel de Queiroz, daughter of João de Queiroz and Maria˙ Marinha

      10 Gaspar da Cunha Coutinho, a university graduate. (In the coat of arms charter granted on February 21, 1608 to this Gaspar da Cunha, it is stated that his mother was Elena Esteves, which makes us believe that Simão de Carvalho˙'s wife was Elena Esteves, daughter of Antonio˙ Macedo and Elena Esteves (sic)[ii])

---

[i] Another hypothesis about this family is mentioned in NFP Cunha §6 N13, in which Maria de Abreu da Cunha was married to Fernão da Cunha Coutinho˙, according to his descendants. (T. N.)

[ii] This last piece of information is in contradiction with what is stated above in this paragraph, by which Elena Esteves's parents were Diogo Gonçalves˙ and his wife Brites Rabello de Figueiredo. There is also a mistake about Antonio de Macedo, who at first is said to be Elena Esteves's deceased husband, though later is said to be her father. (T. N.).

N10 GASPAR DA CUNHA COUTINHO˙, a university graduate, son of Simão Carvalho˙ da Cunha N9, inherited the house of his father and married Maria˙ Carneiro, daughter of Ayres da Mota and his wife Antonia˙ Carneiro [NFP Mota §12 N19]. He was also known as Gaspar da Cunha Coutinho˙ of Amarante

> 11 Baptista da Cunha
> 11 Rozaria da Cunha, wife of João Esteves de Basto [with issue in §33]
> 11 Elena da Cunha, wife of Gaspar de Macedo [with issue in §34]
> 11 Ayres da Cunha
> 11 Paullo da Cunha
> 11 Guiomar da Cunha
> 11 João da Cunha

N11 BAPTISTA DA CUNHA, son of Gaspar da Cunha N10, inherited his father's house and married Clara Carvalho or Clara Teixeira˙ , daughter of Manoel˙ Carvalho and his wife Paulla de Freitas. Manoel˙ Carvalho was the Captain General of Gouvea, as recorded in a charter possessed by his descendants, and through his wife he acquired the manor of Agrochão upon Tamega

> 12 Luis da Cunha Coutinho˙
> 12 B. Maria˙ da Cunha, wife of Antonio˙ Pereira˙; had issueless children
> 12 B. Paulla Vieira, wife of Manoel˙ da Fonseca˙; had issueless children

LORDS OF THE HOUSE OF ALIVIADA

N12 LUIS DA CUNHA COUTINHO˙, son of Baptista da Cunha N11, inherited his father's house and married Elena de Vasconcellos˙, daughter of João de Moura Camelo of Belas, a university graduate, and his wife Maria˙ de Vasconcellos, paternal granddaughter of Francisco˙ de Moura and his wife Joanna Campello

> 13 Luis da Cunha Coutinho˙
> 13 Maria˙ da Cunha, unmarried
> 13 Clara da Cunha, unmarried

N13 LUIS DA CUNHA COUTINHO˙, son of Luis da Cunha N12, inherited his father's house and was married twice, the first time to Joanna Theresa de Vasconcellos˙ Mourão, daughter of Jeronimo Monteiro (Knight of the Order of Christ and a Fidalgo of the King's Household, which title was granted to him by intervention of his brother-in-law, Royal Appellate Judge Fernando Pires Mourão) and his wife Anna Mourão of Vila Real [NFP Vasconcellos §131 N22]

> 14 Maria˙ da Cunha, unmarried, sp
> 14 Theresa da Cunha, who married Domingos˙ Vieira de Mello, grantee of the entail of Ribeiro, who is reported to have killed her, sp

Luis da Cunha Coutinho married (in April, 1761) his second wife D. Maria˙ de Mello of São Tomé de Covelas, of the township of Ferreiros de Tendains, daughter of Jose Machado Pereira˙ and his wife D. Isabel Maria˙ de Mello. Jose Machado was the lord of the house of Lage in São Tomé de Covelas, township of Baião, and son of Antonio˙ Machado Pereira˙, lord of the said house, and D. Luisa de Azevedo˙ Machado of São Martinho de Sande. Jose Machado's wife, D. Isabel Maria˙ de Mello, was the daughter of Manoel˙ Pereira˙ de Vasconcellos˙, lord of the manor of Alagoa in São Lourenço de Douro, and D. Paulla Brandão, paternal granddaughter of Manoel˙ Godinho de Vasconcellos˙, lord of the manor of Alagoa and D. Maria˙ de Corte Real, and maternal granddaughter of Captain Antonio˙ Brandão, lord of the manor of Sobreira, in Melres

> 14 Caetano
> 14 D. Ignes
> 14 Luis da Cunha Coutinho˙ §138
> 14 D. Isabel
> 14 D. Victoria, second wife of Gonçallo˙ Pinto de Magalhães˙, son of Diogo Pinto de Magalhães˙, lord of the house of Capella in Fregim, near Amarante [NFP Magalhães §89 N18]. She had
>> 15 D. (...), by whom her uncle[i] in §(...) had a son

§31

N10 FRANCISCA˙ DE MACEDO, daughter of Guiomar de Macedo §27 N9, though others say she was the daughter of Branca de Abreu in §27 N8. She married João Regadas, who lived in Covello de Amarante and held the office of notary public in the township of (...), and was the son of Pedro Annes Barriga and his wife Leonor Alvares˙, and the paternal grandson of Estevão Regadas and his wife Theresa Pimentel of Villa Real [see NFP Machado §79 sub N2]. Leonor Alvares˙ was the daughter of Ignes Alvares˙, daughter of João Alvares˙, lord of the manor of Vinhaes in Travanca, in the township of Basto (...) [NFP Regadas §1 N2]

> 11 Paulla Regadas da Cunha
> 11 Maria˙ da Cunha, wife of Cristovão Garcia, son of D. Alvaro Garcia and Catarina˙ de Novaes. This information can be found in the memoirs of Alvaro de Sousa, nicknamed "Mesa", in which he mentions Maria da Cunha's dowry charter dated 1559, without further information, §42

---

[i] In NFP Magalhães §89 N18, he is called Luiz da Cunha Coutinho˙, son of another Luiz da Cunha Coutinho˙ and his wife Maria˙ de Mello. (T. N.)

11 Antonia˙ Regadas §41
11 Miguel Regadas, in India
11 Ignes de Sequeira˙, wife of Manoel˙ Teixeira˙ Pinto of Mesão Frio, sp

N11 PAULLA REGADAS DA CUNHA, daughter of Francisca˙ de Macedo N10, married Gaspar de Quiro, bastard son of Gonçallo de Quiro and his mistress Francisca˙ Nunes [NFP Vasconcellos § 101 N17]
12 Cristovão da Cunha, in Brazil, sp
12 João Regadas da Cunha
12 Salvador da Cunha
12 Jeronima da Cunha, wife of Manoel˙ Pacheco of the parish of Barrosas, in Guimarães, son of Manoel˙ Pacheco and his wife Clara Moreira, who resided in the manor of Ladesma [in §67][i]

N12 JOÃO REGADAS DA CUNHA, son of Paulla Regadas da Cunha N11, married Damazia Ferreira˙, daughter of Simão Ferreira˙ Lagarto, of the township of Felgueiras, and his wife Branca Saraiva
13 Joana da Cunha, who married and had issueless children
13 Gaspar da Cunha Coutinho, a university graduate, below
13 Gonçallo de Macedo Coutinho˙, sp
13 Lucas de Abreu de Macedo, Governor of Castro Laboreiro, who died in poverty and left bastard children
13 Simão Ferreira˙, sp

N13 GASPAR DA CUNHA COUTINHO˙, a university graduate, son of João Regadas da Cunha N12, was Corregidor in Viseu and married Isabel de Mena of Pinhel
14 Miguel da Cunha
14 Maria˙ da Cunha, deceased
14 Catarina˙ da Cunha
14 Luiza da Cunha, wife of Manoel˙ de Lemos Coutinho˙ of Pinhel

N14 MIGUEL DA CUNHA, son of Gaspar da Cunha N13, was Travelling Judge of Freixo de Espada à Cinta, and afterwards of Torre de Moncorvo, and held the office of Auditor-General at he time of his death. He married Joanna Felicia de Castello˙ Branco, daughter of Henrique Correa˙ da Costa of Beira Baixa and his wife Maria˙ de Macedo de Eça of Covilhã Village
15 Gaspar da Cunha
15 D. Theresa da Cunha

---

[i] In §67, Jeronima da Cunha's husband is called Manoel Pacheco *Pereira*. (T. N.)

15 D. Isabel da Cunha, wife of Theodosio Velloso de Figueiredo˙, sp
15 D. Marianna

§32

N9 ANDRE LOPES DE ABREU REGO, son of Isabel de Abreu N8 in §30. He married Felipa Teixeira˙, daughter and heiress of Ayres Teixeira˙ of the parish of Tolões in Covilhã, territory of Basto, and his wife Anna Mendes, who according to Fray Reymundo, was a descendant of the Mendes of Fontelas. Felipa Teixeira was the paternal granddaughter of Duarte Vaz Teixeira˙, a resident in Covilhã, and his wife Brites Pinto [NFP Vasconcelos §77 N16][i]

    10 Ayres Teixeira˙

N10 AYRES TEIXEIRA˙, son of Andre Lopes N9, inherited his father's house and married Ignes Campello, bastard daughter of Francisco˙ Alvares˙, Abbot of Touguinho, and his mistress Maria˙ Gonçalves˙, called Mosqueira, of the parish of Tolões

    11 Manoel˙ Teixeira˙ de Queiroz

N11 MANOEL˙ TEIXEIRA˙ DE QUEIROZ, son of Ayres Teixeira˙ N10, inherited his father's house and married Gracia de Queiroz, the third daughter of Martim Mendes de Vasconcellos, who held the entail of Fontellas, and his wife Ignes de Sequeira˙ [NFP Vasconcelos N39]

§33

N11 ROZARIA DA CUNHA, daughter of Gaspar da Cunha §30 N10, married João Esteves de Basto, a physician, son of Thome de Basto and his wife Guiomar Rebello, daughter of Domingos˙ Gonçalves˙ and Brites Rebello de Figueiredo [see this pedigree in NFP Queiroz §31 N20 and Esteves de Figueiredo §2 N6]

    12 Antonio˙ da Mota Cunha
    12 Thome de Basto da Cunha, Appellate Judge in the Oporto region, Trial Judge for Civil Affairs and Judge of Petitions in the State of India
    12 Margarida da Cunha, who married Marcos Ferreira˙ de Sousa, son of Marcos Ferreira˙ and his wife Maria˙ de Macedo [referred to in NFP Queiroz §31 N2]
    12 Gaspar da Cunha, a priest of the Order of Saint John the Evangelist
    12 Angella, a Bernardine nun

---

[i] In NFP Vasconcellos §77 N16, Felipa Teixeira's mother is called Anna Mendes *de Vasconcellos˙*, and is said to have married *João*, or Ayres Teixeira˙. (T. N.)

12 Guiomar, a nun

12 Maria˙ Carneiro, unmarried

N12 ANTONIO˙ DA MOTA DA CUNHA, son of Rozaria da Cunha N11, inherited his father's house and married (in the manor of Crasto de Caramos in Felgueiras) Maria˙ Coelho da Silva˙, daughter and heiress of Pedro Coelho da Silva˙ (a *Fidalgo* of the King's Household of the manor of Crasto) and his wife Margarida Nogueira˙ de Sampaio˙. Maria Coelho da Silva was the paternal granddaughter of another Pedro Coelho da Silva˙, a Fidalgo of the King's Household and his wife Barbara de Basto. This Barbara de Basto was the full sister of Gonçallo˙ de Basto, a *Fidalgo*-Knight and Chief Courier of Évora (who proved in his nobility charter that the Bastos were akin to all the Magalhães of Amarante, for Lady Maria de Basto was the wife of João de Magalhães˙, the legitimate son of Ruy Pires de Magalhães˙, full brother of Gil de Magalhães˙ e Menezes, lord of Ponte da Barca [NFP Magalhães §34 N 7 and N F P B asto §4 N 4 and B asto §3 N 3])[i]

For details about Portuguese ranks of nobility, see p. v

13 Father Thome de Basto da Cunha §36

13 Antonio˙ da Mota da Cunha

13 Father Manoel˙, a priest of the Order of Saint John the Evangelist

13 D. Dionizio, a priest of the Order of the Holy Cross of Coimbra

13 Guiomar Rebello

13 Barbara da Silva˙

13 Brother João, a Franciscan monk

13 Rosaria da Cunha

13 Maria˙ da Cunha

13 Theresa Nogueira˙ de Sampaio˙

N13 ANTONIO˙ DA MOTA DA CUNHA, son of Antonio˙ da Mota da Cunha §33 N12, inherited his father's house and married as his first wife Clara Teixeira˙ of the township of Felgueiras, daughter of Paullo Teixeira˙ de Carvalho˙, brother of Antonio˙ Teixeira˙ de Carvalho˙, a subcanon in the See of Lamego.

14 Antonio˙ Caetano da Mota, e Cunha

Antonio da Mota da Cunha married as his second wife D. Paulla da Silva, daughter of Amaro da Silva, Trial Judge of Barcelos and Auditor of Beira, and his wife D. Bernarda Machado, a couple who lived in Guimarães

---

[i] In NFP Magalhães §34 N7, it is stated that João de Magalhães˙ was the bastard (not the legitimate) son of Ruy Pires de Magalhães˙. In Basto §3 N3, it is not said that Barbara de Basto had a brother called Gonçallo de Basto, but that she had two brothers called Gaspar de Basto and Manoel˙ de Basto. Perhaps the author confused the names Gaspar and Gonçallo. (T. N.)

14 Gonçallo Antonio˙ da Cunha Coelho, who married in Oporto of his own will, sp. This Gonçallo lost the manor of Castro to his nephew

14 Pedro Coelho, a university graduate who became reduced to poverty and moved to Lisbon, without further information

N14 ANTONIO˙ CAETANO DA MOTA, son of the first wife of Antonio˙ da Mota da Cunha N13, did not marry but had (in Venda da Serra) a bastard son by his mistress Maria˙ de Freitas, nicknamed Arela, from Vila Nova dos Infantes

15 Agostinho Jose da Mota, who took the manor of Crasto from his uncle, without further information

§34

N11 ELENA DA CUNHA, daughter of Gaspar da Cunha Coutinho˙ §30 N10. She married Gaspar de Macedo, a university graduate, son of Manoel˙ Cerqueira˙ and his wife Camilla de Macedo, having been granted as her dowry part of the estate of Quintão, which belonged to her father. The couple lived in the manor of Amarante [see more details in NFP Macedo §10 N13 and Macedo §10 N14]

12 Gaspar de Macedo da Cunha

N12 GASPAR DE MACEDO DA CUNHA, son of Elena da Cunha N11, was an appellate judge in the region of Oporto and married D. Gracia de Queiros, daughter of Manoel˙ Teixeira˙ da Cunha and his wife Gracia de Queiros [NFP Macedo §10 N15][i]

13 Luis de Macedo da Cunha, who married (in Guimarães) D. Maria˙ Pereira˙, daughter of Francisco˙ Peixoto Pereira˙, sp

13 D. Maria˙ Elena, who married Jacinto Teixeira˙, sp

Gaspar had bastard children by Maria˙ Pessoa

13 B. Joanna de Macedo, who married Pedro de Oliveira˙ of Fregim, with issue

13 B. Leonor de Macedo, who married Manoel˙ Pereira˙ Salgado

N13 LEONOR DE MACEDO, bastard daughter of Gaspar de Macedo N12 and Maria Pessoa, who was the daughter of Francisco˙ Campello and Anna Pessoa, and the paternal granddaughter of João Campello, a clergyman, and his mistress Joanna Felipa from the parish of São Simão. Anna Pessoa was the daughter of

---

[i] In NFP Macedo in §10 N15, Gaspar de Macedo da Cunha's wife is called Gracia de Queiros e *Vasconcellos.* (T. N.)

Baltazar˙ Pessoa and Margarida do Ferreiro, and the granddaughter of Antonio˙ Fernandes˙ and his wife Maria˙ Gonçalves˙. Leonor de Macedo had by her husband Manoel˙ Pereira˙ Salgado

      14 Hipolito de Macedo, a university graduate

N14 Dr. HIPOLITO DE MACEDO, son of Leonor de Macedo N13, was a physician in the city of Oporto and married Theodosia de Macedo Pereira˙, daughter of Pantalião dos Reys Pereira˙ and his wife Joanna dos Reys

      15 Vicente de Macedo da Cunha
      15 Jose Pinto de Macedo §35
      15 Brother Francisco, a Dominican monk
      15 D. Leonor
      15 D. Ursulla, who was unmarried in 1768
      15 Luis Gaspar, absent
      15 Fernando, absent

N15 VICENTE˙ DE MACEDO DA CUNHA, son of Dr. Hipolito de Macedo N14, is a Knight of the Order of Christ and became the lord of his grandparents' house because his uncle had no heirs. He married twice, the first time (in the City of Oporto) to D. Joanna de Almeida, sister of Dr. Gervasio de Almeida, who was Travelling Judge of Ponte de Lima and nowadays holds the office of Auditor in a Regiment in Elvas[i]

      16 D. Josefa de Almeida

Vicente de Macedo's second marriage was to D. Anna Luisa Mendes, daughter of Manoel˙ Mendes Paraiso, a businessman, and his wife Maria˙ Francisca˙

      16 D. Maria˙
      16 D. Margarida
      16 D. Rosa
      16 D. Joanna
      16 D. Anna
      16 Jose
      16 Joaquim˙
      16 João

§35

N15 JOSE PINTO DE MACEDO, son of Dr. Hipolito de Macedo §34 N14, married of his own will

---

[i] Nowadays: of course, at the time this work was written (~1790-1831). (T. N.)

§36

N13 Father THOME DE BASTO DA CUNHA, eldest son of Antonio˙ da Mota da Cunha §33 N12. He had bastard children by his mistress Maria˙ de Campos Pereira˙, daughter of Antonio˙ Pereira˙ and Joanna de Campos of Vila Cais

14 Maria˙ da Cunha

14 Antonio˙ da Mota, who died in India

14 João Rebello, who married in Lisbon and holds the rank of major, living in America (Brazil) in the Captaincy of Piauí[i]

N14 MARIA˙ DA CUNHA bastard daughter of Father Thome de Basto N13, married Alvaro de Sousa, a law officer and an accountant in the township of Gouvea, son of Francisco˙ Pinheiro de Vasconcellos˙ and his wife Maria˙ de Sousa [NFP Pinheiro §38 N13][ii]

15 Leopoldo Luis de Sousa

N15 LEOPOLDO LUIS DE SOUSA, son of Maria˙ da Cunha N14. He held the same positions as his father, and was probate court judge in the township of Gouvea. He married Theresa (…), daughter of João Soares, bastard son of Bernardo Soares of Castanheira, who became a notary public in Amarante, an office previously held by his father. João Soares married Maria˙ Pinto, daughter of Domingos˙ Pinto, a notary public in the township of Gouvea, and his wife Maria Pinto

16 Anna Leonor

16 Pedro

16 Maria˙ Clara

16 Rosa Maria˙

16 Maria˙ Ignacia

16 Margarida Josefa

§37

N12 ISABEL DE SEQUEIRA, daughter of Francisco˙ de Macedo §27 N11, married João de Magalhães˙, son of Francisco˙ do Couto de Magalhães˙ and his wife Maria˙ Ramalho, daughter of Gonçallo Ribeiro˙ of Real [referred to in NFP Magalhães §51 N13][iii]

---

[i] The author uses here the present tense probably because João Rebello was alive at the time this work was written (~1790-1831). (T. N.)

[ii] In NFP Pinheiro §38 N13, Maria da Cunha's husband is called Alvaro de Sousa *e Vasconcellos*. (T. N.)

[iii] In NFP Magalhães §51 N13, Francisco do Couto de Magalhães's wife is called *Margarida* Ramalho, and not Maria Ramalho. (T. N.)

§38

N1 PEDRO NUNES DE ABREU, who lived in Galites, in the village of Travanquinha, district of Guarda, Bishopric of Coimbra, according to an instrument dated 1642 which is part of the records of a court case mentioned below. He lived around 1540 in the time of El Rei John III, was amongst the most important people of that region and was granted a Fidalgo charter. There are no records proving that he was married, though he fathered

     2 Francisco˙ Nunes Colaço

     2 Antonio˙ Nunes de Abreu §39

N2 FRANCISCO˙ NUNES COLACO, son of Pedro Nunes N1, married in the city of Portalegre, where he lived

     3 Antonio˙ Nunes Portalegre, who married and widowed sp. He entailed the many estates he possessed in the village of Moura in Alentejo, imposing on the grantees the condition that they would celebrate 24 sung masses for his soul in the Monastery of St. Francis in the same village, and would thereupon bear the name of Portalegre

     3 Catarina˙ Alvares˙ de Abreu

N3 CATARINA˙ ALVARES˙ DE ABREU, daughter of Francisco˙ Nunes N2, married (...) Ferreira˙ do Aguiar

     4 Father Matheus Ferreira˙ de Aguiar, who was the first grantee of his uncle Antonio Nunes Portalegre's entail

     4 Francisco˙ Ferreira˙ de Aguiar, who married (in the village of Moura) Leonor Gonçalves˙ Calva, sp. He was the second grantee of his uncle's entails, having in turn appointed D. Francisca˙ de Payva §39 N4 Sub5 as his grantee after his death

     4 Leonor Ferreira˙, who was excluded from succession by the entail institutor

     4 Brites Ferreira˙, *ditto*

§39

N3 ANTONIO˙ NUNES DE ABREU, son of Francisco˙ Nunes Colaco §38 N2, lived in the village of Travanquinha. There is no information about whom he married

     4 Pedro Nunes de Abreu, sp, who lived in the house of Administrator Manoel˙ de Vasconcellos˙

     4 Francisco˙ de Gouvea, unmarried, who lived in the house of Count Meirinho Mor[i]

     4 Simão Nunes de Abreu, a university graduate

---

[i] Probably the second Count of Sabugal, Francisco de Castelo Branco, who was the Royal Law Officer of Portugal. (T. N.)

N4 SIMÃO NUNES DE ABREU, a university graduate, son of Antonio˙ Nunes N3, lived in the village of Travanquinha, where he was born, and married (in Gouvea) D. Luisa de Payva

King Philip IV of Spain r. 1621–1665; as Philip III of Portugal r. 1621–1640. For details about Portuguese ranks of nobility, see p. v.

    5 Francisco˙ de Payva, e Abreu
    5 Simão de Payva, e Abreu, who presented the proofs of his ancestry in 1642

N5 FRANCISCO˙ DE PAYVA DE ABREU, son of Simão Nunes de Abreu N4, a university graduate, was a Royal Law Officer and a Knight of King Philip IV's Household. He married D. Antonia˙ de Andrade˙ Figueiredo˙, daughter of Manoel˙ Leitão de Andrade˙, a *Fidalgo*-Squire, and his wife Maria˙ de Andrade˙ [in NFP Leitão §26 N11]

    6 D. Francisca˙ de Payva, e Andrade˙, who inherited her father's house and was the lady of the lands enfeoffed by Antonio˙ Nunes Portalegre. She married Miguel de Coimbra de Macedo, son of Felipe de Coimbra and his wife Isabel Vieira, lord of the entail of the Coimbras in Braga [NFP Coimbra §1 N4][i]

§40

N5 GIL FERNANDES˙ DE ABREU, bastard son of João Gomes de Abreu §16 N4, lived in Souto Street in Braga, where he was a local councillor in 1493, and whose mother was D. Isabel, daughter of the Count of Caminha D. Pedro Alvares˙ Sotomayor. Yet others say he was the son of Fernão Gomes de Abreu §80 N5 and his wife Mecia Cardoso, and the grandson of the man we consider to be his father, which opinion we do not agree with. Gil Fernandes˙ married Isabel Annes de Bouro, daughter of João Affonso˙ de Bouro (who held the office of Judge in Braga in 1445) and granddaughter of Affonso˙ Martins Bouro and Catarina˙ Annes

    6 Duarte Gil Bouro
    6 Fernão Gil de Abreu, who married D. Genebra de Sousa, daughter of Fernão de Sousa [with issue in NFP Magalhães˙ §29 N8]
    6 Antonio˙ de Abreu

N6 DUARTE GIL BOURO DE ABREU, son of Gil Fernandes˙ de Abreu N5, was the lord of the manor of Sol and lived in Braga around 1499 and 1528 (sic). He married D. Isabel Toscano Raposo, daughter of Rodrigo Annes Gravel and his wife D. Leonor Martins Toscano, who was the sister of Gomes Martins Toscano, Commendatory of the Order of Christ in Merlim; D. Leonor Martins Toscano

---

[i] In NFP Coimbra §1 N3, Miguel de Coimbra de Macedo's mother is called Isabel Vieira *de Andrade*. (T. N.)

and her brother were the children of João Rodrigues˙ Beina, a Galician nobleman, and his wife D. Leonor Rodrigues Toscano, from Alentejo. Leonor Rodrigues Toscano was the daughter of Ruy Martins Toscano (a Galician nobleman, Alcaide General of Portel and vassal of King Peter I) and Theresa Gonçalves˙ Vianna, and was the granddaughter of Giraldo Rodrigues˙ Toscano and Aldonça Rodrigues˙ Pestana. [NFP Toscano §1 N4]*i*. Notwithstanding this information about Duarte de Abreu's wife's parentage, Father Marcelino Pereira˙ claims that D. Leonor Martins Toscano was the daughter of Gomes Martins˙ Toscano and D. Leonor Annes Baena

> 7 Fernão Gil Toscano
> 7 Miguel Toscano, sp
> 7 Gil Fernandes˙ de Abreu §133*ii*
> 7 Antonio˙ Gil Toscano

N7 FERNÃO GIL TOSCANO, son of Duarte Gil N6. He was the governor of the Archbishopric of Braga before Infante Edward came of age, and an Appellate Judge and Purveyor in the same city. He lived in Souto Street and was buried in the mausoleum of his house in the Chapel of Santa Luzia in the See of Braga. He owned the manor of Sol, and was a local councillor in 1532 in Braga, where he married Guiomar de Lima or D. Ignes Lourenço de Lima, bastard daughter of Dr. Fernão Lourenço de Lima, Appellate Judge in Braga and son of Bartolomeu˙ Lourenço de Lima, Commendatory of São Tirso and Abbot of Cabreiros, for whom the abbeystead of Refoios and other places was legally reserved, bastard son of D. Leonel de Lima, 1st Viscount of Vila Nova de Cerveira [NFP Lima §4 N12; see also this chapter of Abreu §133 N7]*iii*

> 8 Simão Toscano de Abreu
> 8 Pedro de Lima, who lived in Monção and presented on February 12, 1548, a petition to Dr. Antonio˙ Monteiro, Corregidor of Viana and (...) Sebastião˙ de Avall, by means of which he proved that he was the grandson of Bartolomeu˙ Lourenço
> 8 B. Henrique Toscano, who went to India
> 8 B. Jeronima Toscano
> 8 B. Ignes de São Thiago
> 8 B. Maria˙ da Trindade
> these last two daughters being nuns in the convent of Murça

Edward of Portugal (1521-1543), an illegitimate son of King John III, was appointed Archbishop of Braga by his father

---

i In NFP Toscano §1 N4, Giraldo Rodrigues˙ Toscano's wife is called Aldonça *Martins* Pestana and not Aldonça Rodrigues˙ Pestana. (T. N.)

ii In this passage of the original text, the author mentions the names of Gil Fernandes˙ de Abreu's wife and father-in-law, and says he had a daughter, called Maria Lourenço de Lima. In §133, he repeats all this information, besides giving the names of five other children of the said Gil Fernandes˙ de Abreu. In order to avoid repetition, we have opted to show these details only in §133. (T. N.)

iii In NFP Lima §4 N12, it is said that Fernão Lourenço de Lima was the bastard son of Bartolomeu Lourenço de Lima, and that his daughter's name was Guiomar de Lima. (T. N.)

N8 SIMÃO TOSCANO DE ABREU, son of Fernão Gil Toscano N7, was a Fidalgo of the King's Household, Infantry Captain in Entre Douro e Minho Province and Commendatory of São Lazaro, having also served in Tangier. He entailed the lands of the manor of Sol on September 29, 1595. He had by Magdalena de Mesquita˙ (whom he married according to some), daughter of Fernão Borges de Mesquita˙, of the house of Outis

> 9 Fernão Toscano de Abreu, who married D. Maria˙ de Menezes, bastard daughter of Antonio˙ Barreto de Menezes and his mistress Camilla Ribeiro˙ [with issue in NFP Magalhães §93 N10]. Fernão Toscano also had a bastard son
>
> 10 B. Henrique Toscano, who went to India, no further details

§41

N11 ANTONIA˙ REGADAS, daughter of Francisca˙ de Macedo §31 N10, married Simão Ribeiro˙, son of João Ribeiro˙ and Magdalena Gonçalves˙. They seem to have lived in Granja, in the parish of São Verissimo de Santa Cruz

> 12 Ignacio de Macedo
> 12 Maria˙ da Cunha

N12 MARIA DA CUNHA, daughter of Antonia Regadas˙ N11, married Antonio˙ Cerqueira˙, who was the son Gervazio Cerqueira˙, notary public in the Council of Gouvea, had by Maria˙ Gonçalves˙, nicknamed Capalea

> 13 Manoel˙ da Cunha
> 13 Jeronima da Cunha
> 13 Isabel de Abreu, wife of Gonçallo˙ de Macedo, sp
> 13 Diogo de Macedo, known as *Borrado*, in India

N13 MANOEL˙ DA CUNHA, son of Maria˙ da Cunha N12, was the Vicar of São Romão de Carvalhosa, in the Council of Santa Cruz. He had by his maid Francisca˙ Gonçalves˙

> 14 Maria˙ da Cunha, wife of Andre Cerqueira˙, son of Manoel˙ Cerqueira˙, known as Ceabra, and his wife (...)

§42

N11 MARIA DA CUNHA, daughter of Francisca˙ de Macedo §31 N10, married Cristovão Garcia˙, a notary public in the Council of Gestaço, son of Alvaro Garcia˙, known as Mexa, and his wife Catarina˙ de Novaes

12 Francisca˙ de Novaes
12 Anna da Cunha
12 Branca da Cunha
12 Isabel Garcia˙
12 Maria˙ da Cunha

N12 FRANCISCA˙ DE NOVAES, daughter of Maria˙ da Cunha N11, married Belchior Cerqueira˙, a notary public in the Council of Gestaço, son of Duarte Cerqueira˙, Abbot of Chocas and Vitoria Jacome, who was born in Canavezes
> 13 Maria de Abreu, wife of Manoel˙ Velloso de Queiros, lord of the houses of Terreiro in Santa Clara de Amarante [NFP Queiros §17 N13], by whom she had children sp

§43

N10 IZABEL DE MACEDO, daughter of Guiomar de Macedo §27 N9, married Simão Ribeiro˙ de Sousa, son of Francisco˙ Correa˙ and his wife Isabel Ribeiro˙, daughter of João Ribeiro˙ and Maria˙ Gonçalves˙
> 11 Maria de Macedo

N11 MARIA DE MACEDO, daughter of Izabel Macedo N10, married Vicente Vaz˙ Campello, a university graduate and Travelling Judge of Freixo de Espada à Cinta
> 12 Joanna de Macedo

N12 JOANNA DE MACEDO, daughter of Maria de Macedo N11, married Barnabe Vieira de Barros for love, the said Barnabe being an apothecary who lived in São Gonçalo Streeet in Amarante, son of Manoel˙ Fernandes˙ and his wife Catarina˙ Vieira, daughter of Leonel de Barros
> 13 Manoel˙ Vieira de Barros
> 13 (...), a monk

N13 MANOEL˙ VIEIRA DE BARROS, son of Joanna de Macedo N12. He was nicknamed Perna de Acha (Peg-leg) and married Maria˙ Caetana Madureira, daughter of Manoel˙ Vieira Carneiro˙ and his relative and wife Catarina˙ Pinto da Fonseca˙, daughter of Manoel˙ Pinto da Fonseca˙ of Eiris
> 14 Quiteria Maria Vieira de Barros

N14 QUITERIA MARIA VIEIRA BARROS, daughter of Manoel˙ Vieira de Barros N13. She succeeded to the house of her father and married Luis Correa˙ de Almeida, graduated at Coimbra and bastard son of (...), Abbot of Campeam, who had him by (...)

15 (...)
15 (...)
15 (...)
15 (...)
(sic)

§44

N7 FRANCISCO˙ VAZ˙ DA CUNHA, son of João Gomes da Cunha §16 N6.
(We have seen in a pedigree this Francisco˙ Vaz˙ da Cunha given as the son of
Dr. Antonio˙ Vaz˙ and D. Catarina˙ da Cunha, which we do not uphold). He
married (in Coimbra) D. Luisa Perestrello˙, sister of Bento Arraes de Mendonça
and daughter of Diogo Paes da Cunha and D. Jeronima Perestrello˙ [NFP
Perestrelo §2 N7]^i, lords of the entail of Papo de Perdiz [see NFP Pedigree
Charts, Tome 2, *ff.* 136, *rev.*]^{ii}

       8 Bento da Cunha Perestrello˙

       8 Francisco˙ Vaz Perestrello˙, an Inquisition Officer, who married D.
          Catarina˙ de Paiva and had an issueless son

N8 BENTO DA CUNHA PERESTRELLO˙, son of Francisco Vaz˙ da Cunha
N7. A chronicle possessed by the lords of the entail of Papo de Perdiz states
that Bento da Cunha Perestrello˙ owned the entail of Perestrellos in Coimbra
and also the entail of Papo de Perdiz, though this latter ownership seems to be
an error. The lands of Papo de Perdiz were enfeoffed on June 6, 1423 by Rodrigo
Esteves Papo de Perdiz, Treasurer of Coimbra and owner of the chapel of São
João de Almedina in the same city. (It seems the entail of Papo de Perdiz was
granted to the line of D. Thomasia Arraes de Mendonça, or rather, was granted
to Pedro Paes Botelho, brother of the said D. Luisa Perestrello˙ above, wife of
Francisco˙ Vaz da Cunha [NFP Perestrelo §2 N8]). Bento da Cunha Perestrello˙
married (in Castelo Viegas) D. Antonia˙ de Pina Mascarenhas, daughter of Baltazar˙
de Pina da Fonseca˙, a Page-*Fidalgo*, and his wife D. Maria de Mascarenhas,
daughter of Jorge Fernandes˙ Malafaya and his wife D. Maria˙ Mascarenhas,
daughter of Nuno Mascarenhas, who died in Chacim in 1526 [NFP Pinto §275
N11 and NFP Malafaia §2 N7]^{iii}

       9 Ignacio da Cunha Perestrello˙, who married (in Monte Mor o Velho)
          D. Luisa de Pina, daughter of Manoel˙ Jusarte and D. Maria˙ de
          Pina

For details about Portuguese ranks of nobility, see p. v

---

^{i} In NFP Perestrelo §2 N7, Francisco Vaz da Cunha's wife is called Luiza Perestrello˙ *da Cunha*, and her mother is said to be Jeronima Perestrello˙ *Botelho*. (T. N.)

^{ii} In NFP Pedigree Charts, Tome 2, *ff.* 136, *rev.*, the entail is called Paço de Perdiz (Fief of Perdiz), and not Papo de Perdiz (*lit.* Port. Partridge Crop). (T. N.)

^{iii} In NFP Malafaia §2 N7, Maria˙ Mascarenhas's father is called Nuno Mascarenhas *de Freitas*. (T. N.)

9 Antonio˙ da Cunha, the Elder
9 Andre da Cunha
9 Dr. Manoel˙ da Cunha
9 Luiz da Cunha Perestrello˙ §48
9 D. Maria˙ da Cunha Perestrello˙, who was the wife of Antonio˙ Soares
    de Albergaria (in §69), and had
        10 Antonio˙ Soares da Cunha, born in Graciosa, who married D.
           Maria˙ de Carvalho˙

Perhaps this Queen was Catherine of Austria (1507-1578), wife of King John III of Portugal

N9 ANTONIO˙ DA CUNHA, the Elder, son of Bento da Cunha Perestrello˙N8. He was the lord of the manor of Mato in São Martinho de Salreo, District of Esgueira, having obtained a nobility charter in Almeirim on January 17, 1542. He married D. Maria˙ Jeronima de Azevedo˙, a native of São Pedro do Sul, upon whom the Queen of Portugal bestowed an office in the municipality of Estareja and granted the fourth part of all the income of Angeja and Albergaria region, in reward for D. Maria˙ Jeronima's having been the most eminent lady of that territory who was chosen to nurse the Queen's son who had been born while Her Majesty traveled on the road to Silho

        10 Jeronimo da Cunha Azevedo˙
        10 Rodrigo da Cunha Perestrello˙ [see Pedigree Charts, Tome 4, *ff.* 124,
           rev.]

N10 JERONIMO DA CUNHA AZEVEDO˙, son of Antonio˙ da Cunha N9, was the lord of the manor of Mato and the Hospital of Albergaria, and also owned the fourth part of the rights of the said estates. He married D. Maria˙ Gomes Loureiro

        11 Antonio˙ da Cunha de Azevedo˙, lord of the manor of Mato, married
           D. Cecilia de Mello, with issue in §68
        11 Diogo da Cunha de Azevedo˙
        11 D. Felipa da Cunha §45
        11 D. Clara da Cunha §47

N11 DIOGO DA CUNHA DE AZEVEDO˙, son of Jeronimo da Cunha N10, was a Fidalgo of the King's Household, having obtained his charter in 1639. He married (in the village of Esgueira) D. Felippa Pacheco Cardoso, daughter of Andre Coelho Cardoso

        12 D. Maria˙ da Cunha Azevedo˙
        12 D. Luisa, a nun in the Convent of Jesus in Aveiro
        12 D. Ana, a nun in the Convent of Jesus in Aveiro

N12 D. MARIA˙ DA CUNHA DE AZEVEDO˙, daughter of Diogo da Cunha N11, married Roque Varella Peixoto, son of Sebastião Pacheco Varella Durazio, who was son of Andre Pacheco Durazio and his wife D. Felipa Varella, daughter of (…) and his wife D. Isabel Cardoso Henriques, daughter of Francisco˙ Henriques and his wife D. Maria˙ Dias Cardoso from the parish of Nossa Senhora dos Martires in Lisbon

> 13 D. Marianna, a nun in the Convent of Jesus in Aveiro
> 13 D. Isabel, a nun in the Convent of Jesus in Aveiro
> 13 Sebastião Pacheco Varella, a corregidor in Pinhel, who died in Trancoso in 1708
> 13 João de Azevedo˙ Varella da Cunha
> 13 D. Felipa, a nun and Abbess in the Convent of Sá de Aveiro
> 13 D. Luiza, a nun in the same convent
> 13 Fray Diogo, a Dominican monk
> 13 D. Francisca˙ Maria da Cunha
> 13 D. Ignes Sofia Varella

§45

N11 D. FELIPA DA CUNHA DE AZEVEDO˙, daughter of Jeronimo da Cunha §44 N10, was married twice, the first time to Dr. Francisco˙ Boto, son of Antonio˙ Rodrigues˙ Boto, a Civil Corregidor in Lisbon, and the second time to João da Silva, a native of Barcelos

> 12 D. Margarida da Silva
> 12 D. Maria˙, sp
> 12 D. Antonia˙, sp
> 12 D. Theresa, sp
> 12 D. Anna, sp
> 12 Thome da Cunha §46

N12 D. MARGARIDA DA SILVA, daughter of D. Felipa da Cunha N11 and her second husband, was married twice, the first time to Diogo Valente

> 13 João da Silva, a university graduate, sp
> 13 D. Maria˙, a nun in the Convent of Sá de Aveiro

Margarida da Silva's second marriage was to João de Matos

> 13 Manoel˙ Rodrigues˙ Leitão, sp
> 13 D. Felipa de Matos, wife of João de Magalhães˙, from the village of Esgueira

§46

N12 THOME DA CUNHA, son of D. Felipa da Cunha §45 N11 and her second husband. Some say he went to India displeased for not having had a good marriage, and left his wife in the Convent of Lorvão; others say he fled to avoid embarking on a vessel, having settled in Setúbal with a false name of Domingos˙ da Silva, in which place he got married

   13 Simoa da Silva, who married in Setúbal
   13 Maria˙ da Cunha

N13 MARIA˙ DA CUNHA, daughter of Thome da Cunha N12, was born in São Martinho de Salreo and moved to Lisbon

   14 D. (...), who married in Palmela and was the mother of
    15 Manoel˙ da Cunha

§47

N11 D. CLARA DA CUNHA, daughter of Jeronimo da Cunha §44 N10, married (in the municipality of Paiva) Francisco˙ Barbosa Reymão, son of João Barbosa Reymão and Cecilia Coelho Freire

   12 João Barbosa da Cunha
   12 Fray Manoel˙, a monk of the Order of the Holy Cross of Coimbra
   12 D. Jeronimo, *ditto*

N12 JOÃO BARBOSA DA CUNHA, son of D. Clara da Cunha N11, married (in Ovar, of which village he was the captain) his cousin Guiomar Freire de Almeida, daughter of João Barbosa and his wife D. Sebastianna de Almeida˙, paternal granddaughter of João Barbosa Reimão and Cecilia Coelho Freire [in N11 above], and maternal granddaughter of Manoel˙ de Pinho, who lived in Cesar, near Oliveira de Ameis, and D. Isabel de Almeida Cabral [NFP Pedigree Charts 93, Tome 2]

   13 D. Guiomar, a nun in Arouca
   13 Francisco˙ Barbosa da Cunha
   13 D. Jeronimo, a monk of the Order of the Holy Cross of Coimbra

N13 FRANCISCO˙ BARBOSA DA CUNHA, son of João Barbosa da Cunha N12, was the Captain of Ovar and married his second cousin D. Maria˙ Clara, daughter of Jeronimo Pereira˙ de Mello, from Vila Real and his wife D. Francisca˙ Maria˙ Pereira˙ [§68 N12][i]

---

[i] In §68 N12, Jeronimo Pereira˙ de Mello's wife is called Francisca˙ Maria˙ Pereira˙ *de Castro*. (T. N.)

14 Francisco˙

14 Jose

14 Jeronimo

N14 FRANCISCO˙ BARBOSA DA CUNHA DE AZEVEDO, son of Francisco˙ Barbosa da Cunha N13, was the Captain General of Ovar and a Knight of the Order of Christ. He married D. Arcangella Micaella Josefa de Amaral, daughter of João Rabello de Almeida, lord of the manor of Baçar, who lived in Salreo, and his wife D. Marianna Nogueira˙ de Pinho. D. Arcangella was the paternal granddaughter of Antonio˙ de Almeida˙ and D. Paulla Rabello do Amaral, and the maternal granddaughter of Antonio Nogueira˙ and Antonia˙ de Pinho. D. Paulla Rabello above was the daughter of Francisco˙ de Fonseca˙ do Amaral (son of Diogo da Fonseca˙) and his wife D. Paulla Rabello, daughter of Manoel˙ de Pinho and D. Catarina˙ Rabello

15 Jose Manoel˙ Barbosa da Cunha, e Mello

15 D. Maria˙ Clara Barbosa da Cunha, e Mello §141

N15 JOSE MANOEL˙ BARBOSA DA CUNHA, E MELLO, son of Francisco˙ Barbosa N14, married D. Joaquina Rosa Sarmento˙ Osorio, daughter of Manoel˙ Correa˙ de Mello, lord of the entail and manor of Pedregal in Paiva, and D. Angelica Bernarda, of the house of Almeidinha [see NFP Pedigree Charts, Tome 4, _ff._ 167-167 _rev._; Tome 4, _ff._ 120 _rev._; Tome 3, _ff._ 113 _rev._]

16 Francisco˙ Barbosa, a Lieutenant Colonel of the Militia in Vila Real

16 D. Arcangella

16 D. Eugenia

16 D. Maria˙ Henriqueta

§48

LORDS OF THE ENTAIL OF SUBRIVAS IN COIMBRA AND ENTAIL OF THE ABREUS AND ALMADAS IN VEIROS

N9 LUIS DA CUNHA PERESTRELLO˙, son of Bento da Cunha Perestrello˙ §44 N8. He did not marry but had bastard issue by Paschoa de Lemos da Silva, daughter of Martim de Matos and Francisca˙ de Lemos, a native of Lisbon

10 Antonia˙ Perestrello

N10 ANTONIA˙ PERESTRELLO˙, bastard daughter of Luis da Cunha N9, married Salvador de Abreu de Almada, son of B. Belchior˙ Mendes de Abreu

(Chief Accountant of the Mastership of Avis and Knight of the Order of Christ) and his wife D. Anna Ferreira˙ de Abreu, daughter of Francisco˙ Ferreira˙, a Fidalgo of the King's Household. Salvador de Abreu de Almada was the paternal grandson of Bartolomeu˙ Mendes de Abreu, Commendatory of the Order of Avis and a Fidalgo of the King's Household, husband of Margarida Fernandes˙, daughter of Luis Fernandes˙, who became Vicar of Veiros after his wife died. Margarida Fernandes and her husband Bartolomeu Mendes de Abreu – who is presumably the same mentioned in §74 and whose ancestors appear in §73 N9[i] – enfeoffed their lands in the village of Veiros in 1603 (to which he added several estates) in Belchior˙ Mendes, bastard son of the said Bartolomeu˙

> 11 Luis de Abreu da Cunha
>
> 11 D. Angelica, a nun in the convent of Tentugal

N11 LUIS DE ABREU DA CUNHA, son of Antonio˙ Perestrello˙ N10 [see NFP Pedigree Charts, Tome 2, ff. 136 rev.] He married D. Brites, daughter of Agostinho Barbosa de Novaes, Knight of the Order of Christ and Captain of Ancão, and his wife D. Brites de Novaes, a native of Penacova, or D. Elena de Moraes do Rego, from the village of Penacova

> 12 Jeronimo da Cunha Perestrello˙, about whom the only details available were that he had by Serafina de Almeida, a single woman from Eiras, a son whom he legitimated
>
> 13 Antonio˙ Carlos de Abreu de Almada Perestrello˙, who married three times, but died without issue. For this reason the lands enfeoffed by Bartolomeu Mendes de Abreu were devolved upon the mother of Antonio˙ Jusarte Lobo of Estremoz, who was a fourth generation descendant of Sebastião Gomes de Abreu, nephew of the said institutor. His cousin Manoel˙ Arraes de Mendonça Perestrello˙ in turn inherited the entails of the Perestrellos, as stated in NFP Perestrello §2 N12

§49

N2 DIOGO GOMES DE ABREU, son of Lourenço Gomes de Abreu §2 N1, was Ambassador to Castile, Alcaide General of Monção and a member of the council of King Peter I, who granted to him the lordship of Godinhaços and Duas Igrejas, as well as some smaller estates in Ponte de Lima. He was also a vassal of King Ferdinand, who appointed him Law Officer of Tras-os-Montes Province, and in 1372 granted to him the royal rights of Vilas Boas in the territory of Villa Flor.

King Peter I r. 1357–1367

King Ferdinand r. 1367–1383

---

[i] In §74, there are two people called Bartolomeu Mendes de Abreu: N10 and his grandson N11 Sub12. It seems that this reference is about the younger, for the elder's wife is *Paulla da Fonseca* (and not Margarida Fernandes), and in §74 N10 it is not informed that Bartolomeu Mendes de Abreu (the Elder) had a son called Belchior˙ Mendes de Abreu, whether bastard or legitimate. (T. N.)

Diogo Gomes was also the lord of Rio Maior, and there were records about him in the Monastery of Grijo[i]. He married Violante Affonço, lady-in-waiting to Queen D. Brites and daughter of Affonço Geraldes de Abreu, upon whom King Ferdinand bestowed the Royal Estates of Toxar in Lisbon on August 17, 1379. Violante Affonço˙ was the lady of the fief of Barbeita [mentioned in §130 N8 Sub9; see Alvaro Ferreira˙ de Vera or Count D. Pedro, *ff.* 218]. After D. Violante became a widow, King Ferdinand granted in 1374 to her children and descendants the manor of Quintella in the territory of Valadares and also the Royal Estates of Toxar and Rio Maior[ii], which had belonged to her husband, besides confirming her the fief of Barbeita, which had belonged to her father Affonço˙ Geraldes. D. Violante was a lady-in-waiting to Queen D. Brites, wife of John I, King of Castile, whom she followed to the said Kingdom. Because of that, King John I of Portugal granted the fief of Barbeita to Gomes Lourenço da Feira, and afterwards to Gonçallo˙ Lourenço Gomes, who passed them on to his children

King John I of Portugal r. 1385–1433. For Queen D. Brites and these historical events, see box on p. 9

For Constable Nuno Alvares Pereira and King John I, see also box on p. 9

> 2 Alvaro Gomes de Abreu

N3 ALVARO GOMES DE ABREU, son of Diogo Gomes de Abreu N2, was the Alcaide General of the Castle of Neiva, and was slain by Constable D. Nuno Alvares Pereira, as recorded in the *Chronicle of El Rei John I* by Fernão Lopes, and in the *Life of the Constable, Book 3, p. 243 N15*, by Fray Domingos˙ Teixeira˙, though his name is not mentioned in the text. Alvaro Gomes de Abreu married D. Isabel Lopes de Lira, daughter of Lopo Gomes de Lira (Alcaide General of Braga and Ponte de Lima) and his wife D. Theresa Gomes de Abreu [NFP Lira §1 N2]

> 4 Diogo Alvares˙ de Abreu
> 4 Aldonça Alvares˙ de Lira
> 4 Lourenço Gomes de Abreu
> 4 Vasco Gomes de Abreu
> 4 Theresa Alvares˙, wife of Fernão Gomes Pereira˙, Alcaide General of Monção

N4 ALDONÇA ALVARES˙ DE LIRA, daughter of Alvaro Gomes de Abreu N3, married Ruy Lobato, son of D. Lourenço Lobato, lord of the fief of Melão in Galicia, and his wife D. Maria˙ Tarraca or Maria˙ Surraca, and paternal grandson of D. Vasco Lobato, also lord of the fief of Melão, which he had to leave after having burned down a Bernardine convent

---

[i] Obscure fragment in the original text: "*tinha recão no Monastério de Grijo*", which has been translated largely by guesswork. (T. N.)

[ii] Obscure fragment: "*Reguengo de Toxar pello de Rio Mayor*", which has been translated largely by guesswork on the assumption that there was an error in the original text. (T. N.)

5 D. Isabel Lobato de Lira, wife of Pedro Vaz˙ de Abreu, son of another Pedro Vaz˙ de Abreu and his wife Leonor Rodrigues˙ Bacellar, with issue in §64 N3[i]

5 D. Constança Vaz˙, wife of Afonso de Castro

5 D. Guiomar Martins˙ Lobato, who married Gomes Rodrigues˙ de Caldas, lord of the honor and manor of Campoza

§50

N7 D. MECIA DA CUNHA, daughter of João Gomes da Cunha §16 N6, married Dr. Antonio˙ de Macedo, Chief Chancellor of the Appeal Court, son of João de Macedo and D. Brites de Magalhães˙ [NFP Macedo §28 N1]

8 João Gomes da Cunha

8 D. Francisca˙ de Macedo, who married her cousin Gaspar da Cunha, with issue in §16 N7

8 D. Maria˙ da Cunha, who married João Freire de Andrade, lord of Sosa

N8 JOÃO GOMES DA CUNHA, son of D. Mecia da Cunha N7, was Prior of Tábua

9 Matheus da Cunha de Eça

N9 MATHEUS DA CUNHA DE EÇA, son of João Gomes da Cunha N8, whose second marriage was to D. Francisca˙ de Figueiredo˙

10 D. Cecilia de Leça e Castro, who married Francisco˙ de Andrade, with issue

§51

N7 ANTONIO˙ DE ABREU LIMA, bastard son of Pedro Gomes de Abreu §2 N6 (some say this Antonio de Abreu was the son of Pedro Gomes de Abreu, referred to in §2 N10, though we hold a different opinion). Antonio˙ de Abreu was a Page-*Fidalgo* and a man of great valor, according to Damião de Goes in his *Chronicle of King Manoel*, Part 3. He was the lord of the manors of Atains, Mouro and Mos. His first wife was D. Maria˙ Quaresma, by whom he had no issue. Afterwards he married and had issue by D. Brites Velho, daughter of Genebra de Barros and Fernão Velho Barreto, tutor to the second Duke of Bragança [in NFP Barros §9 N6]. He also had bastard children

8 João Gomes de Abreu, Abbot of Perre §61

8 Fernão de Lima, Ambassador to Persia, who died in Tangier

For details about Portuguese ranks of nobility, see p. v

[i] In §64 N3, Pedro Vaz˙ de Abreu the Younger's wife is called Isabel *Lopes Lobato*, and not Isabel Lobato de Lira. (T. N.)

8 B. Leonel de Abreu Lima, a bastard son according to some

8 B. Pedro Gomes de Abreu, who married D. Leonor Salgado, sp; a bastard son according to some, like his brothers below

8 B. Antonio˙ de Abreu, who was the captain of a ship to India

8 B. Miguel de Abreu, who died in India

For details about Portuguese ranks of nobility, see p. v

N8 LEONEL DE ABREU LIMA, son of Antonio˙ de Abreu Lima N7 above; some say he was illegitimate. He was a Page-*Fidalgo* and was the lord of the manors of Ameal, Passo de Atains and Mos, the latter estates having been separated from Regalados in the time of his father. He lived in Viana, where he married D. Maria˙ Carneiro Jacome, daughter of (...) and his wife Angela de Medeiros of Oporto [see NFP Jacome §38 N6 and N7]*[i]*

9 Antonio˙ de Lima de Abreu

9 Miguel de Abreu Lima §59

9 Baptista de Lima e Abreu §60

9 João Gomes de Abreu, Abbot of Perre

9 Pedro Gomes de Abreu, Governor of Daman in India, where he married; father of

10 Leonel de Abreu, who served in India

9 Francisco˙, who served in India

9 Jeronimo, who served in India, sp

9 D. Brites, a nun in the Convent of Salvador

9 D. Maria˙, a nun in the Convent of Santa Ana

Daman, an Indian town on the coast of the Arabian Sea, was taken by the Portuguese in the 16th century, and remained under Portuguese rule until 1961, when it was taken over by India

For details about Portuguese ranks of nobility, see p. v

N9 ANTONIO˙ DE LIMA DE ABREU, son of Leonel de Abreu Lima N8, was a Page-*Fidalgo* of the King's Household by an instrument dated July 6, 1610 [recorded in the *Matricula* Book, *lf.* 78) and lord of the house of Atains. He married (in Viana) D. Joanna de Mello, daughter of Baltazar˙ da Cunha, e Mello, and his wife D. Isabel Drago, daughter of João Fernandes˙ Drago and his wife Victoria de Amorim [NFP Melo §45 N15]*[ii]*. In a chronicle written by Francisco˙ Velho of Marrancos, it is stated that the said D. Joanna de Mello was the daughter of Pedro de Mello e Alvim and his wife D. Catarina˙ Pinto [NFP Melo §45 N16], with which we do not agree

10 Leonel de Abreu Lima, who married D. Anna Quaresma, by whom he had no issue, though he had bastard issue

11 B. João de Lima, e Abreu, no further details

10 Pedro Gomes de Abreu

---

[i] In §38 N7, Maria Carneiro Jacome's mother is called *Genebra* Carneiro Jacome and not Maria˙ Carneiro Jacome. (T. N.)

[ii] In NFP Melo §45 N15, Antonio de Lima de Abreu's wife is called *Maria*˙ de Mello (and not Joanna de Mello); her mother (Baltazar da Cunha, e Mello's wife) is called Izabel de Grado (and not Isabel Drago), and this Izabel is said to be the daughter of João Fernandes˙ *do Grado* (instead of João Fernandes Drago). (T. N.)

10 Manoel˙ de Lima, who died in Flanders, sp

10 Agostinho, sp

10 Antonio˙ de Lima, sp

10 João Gomes, sp

10 D. Carlos, a priest of the Order of the Holy Cross of Coimbra

N10 PEDRO GOMES DE ABREU, son of Antonio˙ de Lima, e Abreu N9, was Abbot of Perre and a Fidalgo of the King's Household by a charter dated November 14, 1620 (recorded in the Matricula Book, *ff.* 29) and became the lord of the entails of Atains upon the decease of his brothers. He had issue by Catarina˙ Cerqueira, nicknamed Quiqua, from Regalados

> 11 Antonio˙ de Lima de Abreu, a Fidalgo of the King's Household and lord of the entails of Atains. In 1666, in Vila Franca, Viana, he married D. Maria˙ de Mello, e Lima, daughter of Manoel˙ de Lima e Mello and his wife Maria˙ Fagundes [with issue in NFP Costa §181 N8][i]
>
> Antonio˙ de Lima e Abreu had previously married D. Anna da Rocha Portocarreiro, daughter of Diogo da Rocha Portocarreiro and his wife D. Anna Torres de Seixas, by whom he had
>
> > 12 D. Joanna da Rocha Portocarreiro, who married Lourenço Ferreira˙ Brandão, son of Domingos˙ Ferreira˙ Villas Boas and his wife D. Marianna Brandão [with issue in NFP Vilas Boas §25 N15]

§52

N7 RUY, or RODRIGO GOMES DE ABREU, bastard son of Pedro Gomes de Abreu §2 N6, married (in Viana) D. Ignes Brandão, daughter of Fernão Brandão Sanches, Commendatory of Afife and Catanas, and Maria˙ Fagundes [NFP Brandão §14 N9][ii]

> 8 Diogo Gomes de Abreu
>
> 8 Antonio˙ de Abreu Lima, Abbot of Moreira
>
> 8 Jorge de Abreu Lima
>
> 8 Fernão de Abreu, sp, who was the last Commendatory of Cabanas
>
> 8 Vasco Gomes de Abreu, who served in India
>
> 8 D. Margarida
>
> 8 D. Brites
>
> the last two daughters were nuns in the Convent of St. Anne in Viana

---

[i] In NFP Costa §180 N7, Manoel˙ de Lima e Mello's wife is called Maria˙ *da Rocha* Fagundes. (T. N.)

[ii] In NFP Brandão §14 N9, Fernão Brandão Sanches's wife is called *Catarina* Fagundes, and not Maria˙ Fagundes. (T. N.)

N8 DIOGO GOMES DE ABREU, son of Ruy Gomes de Abreu N7, served in India, was a Knight of the Order of Christ and a Fidalgo of the King's Household. In a chronicle about the Isle of Majorca, Diogo Gomes is said to have married as his first wife D. Maria Jacome, daughter of João Maciel and Genebra Jacome, though others say Diogo Gomes married Catarina˙ Malheiro, daughter of João Maciel Finandinhos and Perpetua Nunes [NFP Jacome §23 N6 and N7]ᶦ, which seems to us to be more accurate

> 9 João Gomes de Abreu
> 9 Ruy de Abreu de Lima §62

N9 JOÃO GOMES DE ABREU, son of Diogo Gomes de Abreu N8, was a Fidalgo of the King's Household. He married (in Viana) D. Angela Aranha, daughter of a ship's pilot in Brazil called Sebastião Burgueira Aranha or João Burgueira Aranha, and his wife Maria˙ Villarinho

> 10 Diogo Gomes de Abreu, Travelling Judge in Ponte de Lima, who married D. Anna de Castro, daughter of Garcia˙ Lopes Calheiros, lord of the house of Calheiros, and his wife Genebra Jacome [with issue in NFP Barbosa §142 N27]ᶦᶦ
> 10 Rafael de Abreu Lima
> 10 Antonio˙ de Lima, sp
> 10 D. Maria˙, a nun in the convent of St. Benedict in Viana
> 10 D. Catarina˙, *ditto*
> 10 Gaspar de Abreu Lima, who went to India

N10 RAFAEL DE ABREU LIMA, son of João Gomes de Abreu N9, was a Fidalgo of the King's Household and married his cousin D. Serafina de Lima, e Vasconcellos, daughter of D. Duarte de Lima, lord of the manor and entail of Ponte Nova, and his wife D. Maria˙ de Araujo˙ e Vasconcellos, and paternal granddaughter of D. Francisco˙ de Lima and his wife D. Maria˙ de Barros [NFP Araujo §281 N27]

> 11 João Gomes de Abreu sp
> 11 Francisco˙ de Abreu Lima
> 11 Manoel˙ de Abreu Lima, Abbot of Oliveira
> 11 D. Duarte dos Serafins, priest of the Order of the Holy Cross of Coimbra
> 11 D. Angela Luiza, who married Luiz Gomes de Abreu, sp
> 11 D. Prudencia
> 11 D. Jeronima, a nun in the convent of St. Anne in Viana
> 11 D. Maria˙
> 11 D. Theresa, a nun in the convent of St. Anne in Viana

ᶦ In NFP Jacome §23 N6 and N7, João Maciel Finandinhos's wife is called Perpetua Nunes *Boto*. (T. N.)

ᶦᶦ In NFP Barbosa §142 N27, Diogo Gomes de Abreu's wife is called Anna *Lopes* de Castro. (T. N.)

§53

N10 BALTAZAR˙ COELHO DA SILVA, son of D. Antonia˙ de Abreu §7 N9, was a Fidalgo of the King's Household like his father, and married his niece D. Luiza da Silva, daughter of his brother Pedro Coelho da Silva [NFP §7 N10 Sub11]. He had no issue by his wife, whom he slew without just cause, but he had bastard children

> 11 B. João Coelho da Silva
> 11 B. D. Luiza da Silva §65

N11 JOÃO COELHO DA SILVA, bastard son of Baltazar˙ Coelho da Silva N10, married (in Felgueiras) D. Maria˙ de Sousa, daughter of Antonio˙ Alvares˙, Rector of Santo Estevão das Regadas

> 12 Baltazar˙ Coelho da Silva˙, a priest
> 12 Nuno Coelho da Silva
> 12 Luis da Silva Coelho
> 12 Antonio˙ da Silva Coelho
> 12 Alvaro Coelho da Silva
> 12 Gaspar de Amorim Coelho
> 12 D. Anna da Silva Coelha

§54

N8 LOPO GOMES DE ABREU, son of Leonel de Abreu Lima §2 N7, was Captain of the Fleet of India, lord of the manors of Agra and Torre de Gil Barbedo, and Commendatory of Seixas and Canelas. He also owned the advowsons of Troviscoso and São Tiago de Pias in Monção, and enjoyed the privileges of the Church of Rosas, alternating with his brother Francisco˙ de Abreu. He married D. Theresa Montenegro, daughter of Payo Sorede Montenegro (a Galician nobleman and lord of Moronte) and his wife D. Maria˙ de Oya Sotomayor [NFP Montenegro §1 N4][i]

> 9 D. Maria˙ de Abreu de Noronha

Lopo Gomes's second wife was D. Maria˙ de Mello, daughter of Ruy Gomes de Abreu in §57 N7, sp

N9 D. MARIA˙ DE ABREU DE NORONHA, daughter of Lopo Gomes de Abreu N8, married D. Fernando Annes Sotomayor, son of D. Pedro Sotomayor, a Knight of the Order of Santiago, and his wife D. Maria˙ de Orquico. D. Fernando was the lord of Crecente, Sotomayor and Fornelos in Galicia and was created Count of Crecente by King Philip IV

*King Philip IV of Spain
r. 1621–1665;
as Philip III of Portugal
r. 1621–1640*

---

[i] In NFP Montenegro §1 N4, Lopo Gomes de Abreu's wife is called Theresa *Sotomayor* Montenegro, and her parents' names are given as Payo *Sorrede* Montenegro and Maria *de Doca* Sotomayor. (T. N.)

10 Pedro Sotomayor, sp

10 D. Antonia˙ Sotomayor, who inherited the estates and married D. Antonio˙ Sarmento˙ Sotomayor, son of D. Diogo Sarmento˙, first Count of Gondumar, sp

10 D. Theresa Sotomayor, who succeeded her sister and married D. Bernardo Sarmento˙ de Mendonça, e Covos, first Count of Riba de Avia, Marquis of Camaraça, Frontier Governor of Galicia and Viceroy of Valencia

10 D. Francisca˙ de Sotomayor

10 D. Benita Sotomayor, who married D. Affonso˙ Henriques, sp, and afterwards married Antonio Vidão, with issue, with no further details

King Philip IV of Spain r. 1621–1665; as Philip III of Portugal r. 1621–1640

N10 D. FRANCISCA˙ SOTOMAYOR, daughter of D. Maria˙ de Abreu N9, succeeded to the house of Sotomayor upon the death of her sisters and was the Countess of Crecente. She married D. João Fernandes˙ de Lima, who was created Marquis of Tenorio by King Philip IV and was the son of D. Lourenço de Brito Nogueira˙, 7th Viscount of Vila Nova de Cerveira, and his wife D. Luisa de Tavora

11 D. Fernando Annes Sotomayor

11 D. Maria˙ Mazones, who married D. Felix Manfeni, e Nim, and had

12 D. Fernando Marones, who married D. Laura de Trillar, and had

13 (...)

13 (...) (sic)

N11 D. FERNANDO ANNES SOTOMAYOR, son of D. Francisca˙ de Sotomayor N10, inherited the house of his father. He married D. Patornilha de Chaves Mendonça Sotomayor, daughter of (...)

§55

N11 SIMÃO DE ABREU, bastard son of Leonel de Abreu §4 N10, lived in Briteiros and had by Isabel Correa˙, daughter of João Correa˙

12 Domingos Correa˙ de Abreu, an appellate judge in Braga, who married (in Basto) Isabel Teixeira˙ de Meireles, daughter of Alvaro de Meyreles de Andrade˙, lord of the manor of Vilar, and his wife Elena de Mesquita˙ [NFP Meireles §5 N10]

12 D. Anna de Abreu, no further details

§56

N7 MANOEL DE MELLO DE ABREU, son of Diogo Soares de Abreu §10 N6, married Ambrosia de Vasconcellos, daughter of Tristão Fernandes˙ Homem, who lived near Viseu, and his wife D. Isabel de Almeida, e Vasconcellos

> 8 Luis de Mello Coutinho˙
> 8 Lourenço Soares de Mello
> 8 Jeronimo Coutinho˙ de Eça, who went to India
> 8 Vasco Gomes de Mello, who died in India
> 8 D. Ignes Coutinho, who married Damião de Almeida, e Vasconcellos

§57

N7 RUY GOMES DE ABREU, son of Diogo Gomes de Abreu §28 N6, served in India and married (in Daman, India) D. Placida Pereira˙, daughter of Andre Pereira˙ from the Azores

> 8 D. Ignacia Pereira˙, who married Gonçallo Pereira˙ de Sousa
> 8 D. Maria˙ de Mello, whose first husband was Lopo Gomes de Abreu [§54 N8], sp
> D. Maria de Mello's second husband was João Gomes de Mello, e Abreu, son of Antonio˙ Gomes de Abreu [NFP §14 N6][i]

It is stated in a chronicle that Ruy Gomes de Abreu was married to D. Paulla Pereira˙, daughter of D. Antonio Pereira˙ [NFP Pereira §89 N19]

> 8 Sebastião˙ de Abreu Pereira˙

N8 SEBASTIÃO˙ DE ABREU PEREIRA˙, son of Ruy Gomes de Abreu N7, married D. Maria˙ de Aguiar, daughter of Martim Affonso˙ de Mello, and his wife D. Joanna de Aguillar, paternal granddaughter of João de Mello and his wife D. Felipa de Abreu

> 9 Andre de Abreu Pereira˙

N9 ANDRE DE ABREU PEREIRA˙, son of Sebastião˙ de Abreu N8, married D. Mecia Henriques, daughter of João de Sousa and D. Maria˙ Perestrello˙ [NFP Sousa §460 N23]. According to the *Historia Genealófica da Casa Real*, Tome 12, *lf.* 921 N14], D. Mecia Henriques˙ had married Henrique˙ de Sousa, and her marriage to Andre de Abreu is not mentioned

> 10 Alvaro de Abreu Pereira˙

Daman, an Indian town on the coast of the Arabian Sea, was taken by the Portuguese in the 16th century, and remained under Portuguese rule until 1961, when it was taken over by India.

---

[i] In NFP §14 N6, João Gomes de Mello, e Abreu's father is called *Antao* Gomes de Abreu, and not Antonio˙ Gomes de Abreu. (T. N.)

N10 ALVARO˙ PEREIRA˙ DE ABREU (sic)[i], son of Andre de Abreu Pereira˙ N9, married D. Joanna de Castro, daughter of D. Felipe de Castro and D. Joanna de Mello [Castro §120 N24]

> 11 D. Anna de Abreu Pereira˙, who married her cousin D. Salvador de Castro, son of D. Alvaro de Castro, her mother's brother [NFP Castro §120 N26]

§58

N7 NICOLAO DE MELLO, E LIMA, son of Diogo Gomes de Abreu §28 N6, married (in Vianna) D. Ignes da Rocha, daughter and heiress of Garcia˙ do Valle, and widow of D. Pedro˙ de Lima

> 8 D. Maria˙, who married (below her station) (...)
> 8 B. Manoel˙ de Abreu Lima

§59

N9 MIGUEL˙ DE ABREU LIMA, son of Leonel de Abreu Lima §51 N8, was a Fidalgo of the King's Household. He did not marry, but had by Francisca˙ Fagundes of Santar, in the parish of Vilar (as recorded in his legitimation process written on June 5, 1624 by notary public Miguel Barbosa Lomba)

> 10 B. João Gomes de Abreu

N10 JOÃO GOMES DE ABREU, bastard son of Miguel˙ de Abreu Lima N9, was a Fidalgo of the King's Household and the lord of the house and entail of Mouro. According to the records of the parish of São João (ff. 220), he married (in 1634 in Braga) D. Angela Pereira˙ Santarem, daughter of Maria˙ Vaz˙ Machado and her husband Gonçallo˙ Ferreira˙ Santarem, or Manoel˙ Ferreira˙ Santarem

> 11 D. Maria˙ de Abreu Lima

N11 D. MARIA˙ DE ABREU LIMA, daughter of João Gomes de Abreu N10, inherited her father's house and married (in the parish of São João in 1654) Gonçallo de Araujo˙ Brito, lord of the manor of Guilhades, son of Jacome de Araujo˙ e Brito and his wife Margarida Marinho Malheiro [NFP Araujo §91 N26]

---

[i] In the original text, it is relatively common to find the order of the surnames inverted when they appear more than once. In this case, Alvaro de Abreu Pereira˙ [in N9 Sub10] is called Alvaro Pereira˙ de Abreu soon after [in N10]. (T. N.)

12 Antonio˙ de Araujo˙ de Abreu, lord of the manors of Mouro and Guilhades, who married D. Anna Maria˙ Pereira˙ Gayo, daughter of Jacome Pereira˙ Gayo and his wife Paschoa de Araujo [NFP Gaio §11 N9]ⁱ, as recorded in the archives of the parish of São João do Souto in 1688, *ff.* 86

§60

N9 BAPTISTA DE LIMA DE ABREU, son of Leonel de Abreu Lima §51 N8, was an Infantry Captain and the lord of the manor of Mos, and married (in Vianna) D. Antonia˙ da Silva, sp. Out of wedlock he fathered a child by Maria Lomba of Vilarinho, daughter of João da Lomba and his wife Antonia˙ Gomes, as recorded in his legitimation process probated on September 26, 1632 in the office of notary public Miguel Barbosa

      10 Leonel de Lima de Abreu

Baptista de Lima de Abreu also had by Maria˙ Gomes of Mós

      10 João Gomes de Abreu

N10 LEONEL DE LIMA DE ABREU, son of Baptista de Lima N9, was a Fidalgo of the King's Household, lord of the manor of Mos, and married (in Braga) D. Mariana da Rocha Tinoco, sister of Canon João Tinoco, both being the children of Francisco˙ Gonçalves˙ da Rocha and his wife Elena Lopes Tinoco [NFP Tinoco §2 N3]

      11 Antonio˙ de Lima de Abreu, a Fidalgo of the King's Household, lord of the manor of Mos, who married D. Maria˙ de Mello, e Lima, daughter of Antonio˙ de Lima de Abreu and his wife D. Maria˙ de Mello e Lima [with issue in NFP Costa §182 N9]

      11 Manoel˙ de Lima, who became a Canon upon the resignation of his uncle, who in turn had been invested in the same office upon the resignation of Canon Francisco˙ Alvares˙ Tinoco, on September 21, 1692

§61

N8 JOÃO GOMES DE ABREU, son of Antonio˙ de Abreu Lima §51 N7, was the Abbot of Perre, a Fidalgo of the King's Household, and inherited the entails of Atains upon the death of his brothers. He had by Catarina˙ Cerqueira˙ da Cunha, known as Guicoa

---

ⁱ In NFP Gaio §11 N9, Antonio˙ de Araujo˙ de Abreu is called Antonio˙ de Araujo˙ *de Brito*; his wife is said to be Anna Maria˙ *de Araujo* Gayo (and not Anna Maria˙ Pereira˙ Gayo), and his mother-in-law is called Paschoa de Araujo *de Brito*. (T. N.)

9 Antonio˙ de Lima de Abreu
9 Margarida de Abreu, see below

N9 MARGARIDA LIMA DE ABREU, daughter of João Gomes de Abreu N8, married (in Vianna) Manoel˙ Rabello Velloso of São Miguel de Prado, son of Pedro Velloso and his wife Maria˙ Rabello
      10 Catarina˙ de Abreu Lima
      10 Belchior˙ de Abreu, sp
      10 Jeronimo Abreu, sp
      10 Pedro de Abreu, sp
      10 Maria˙, sp

N10 CATARINA˙ DE ABREU LIMA, daughter of Margarida de Lima N9, married Miguel Borges Pereira˙, son of Payo Borges
      11 Thome de Abreu
      11 Paulla de Abreu, who married Domingos˙ Pimenta, sp

N11 THOME DE ABREU, son of Catarina˙ de Abreu N10, married as his first wife Catarina˙ de Antas, daughter of Francisco˙ de Araujo˙ and Elena de Antas
      12 João Gomes de Abreu, a beneficiary
Afterwards Thome married Felipa de Alvim, daughter of Belchior˙ de Abreu Folgueira and Maria˙ de Barros de Alvim [NFP Araujo §200 N26][i]
      12 Captain Leonel de Abreu Lima

§62

N9 RUY DE ABREU LIMA, son of Diogo Gomes de Abreu §52 N8, married (in Vianna) D. Angela de Castro, daughter of Fernando Carmona de Castro, and his wife Isabel Alvares˙ Prego
      10 Ruy Gomes de Abreu, Abbot of Bustello
      10 D. Natalia deLima, second wife of Simão de Tavora, Commendatory of the Order of Christ, sp

§63[ii]

N10 LOPO GOMES DE ABREU, bastard son of Manoel de Lima §25 N9,

---

[i] In NFP Araujo §200 N26, Felipa de Alvim is calles Felipa de Alvim *e Souza*. (T. N.)

[ii] In the original text, this section (§63) about Lopo Gomes de Abreu and his children and grandchildren is repeated (seemingly by mistake) in §138. In order to avoid repetition, we have opted to suppress this second reference. The names are the same in the two parts, with the following exceptions: (1) In §138 of the original text, Lopo Gomes de Abreu's wife is called *Maria˙* Teixeira˙, and not Marianna Teixeira. (2) The father-in-law of João de Abreu Lima N10 is called *Belchior˙* Cerqueira˙ *da Costa*, and not Domingos Cerqueira. (3) In §63 Isabel da Costa Velloso's father is called Antonio˙ *Tescaro* de Lima, whereas in §138 he is called Antonio˙ *Toscano* Lima, a version we have preferred to adopt, for we consider Toscano a more plausible name than Tescaro. (T. N.)

married (in Braga) D. Marianna Teixeira˙, daughter of Alvaro Meirelles de Basto and his wife Elena Sobrinho˙ de Mesquita˙, sp. He had bastard issue by Maria˙ Francisca˙ of Roças

§64

LORDS OF BARBEITA

N1 GOMES LOURENÇO DE ABREU, son of (another) Gomes Lourenço de Abreu §1 N6[i]; he was the lord of the house of Vilarinhos in the manor of Vila Boa in Valadares, and the fief of Barbeita, and married D. Maria Soares, daughter of (...)

> 2 Pedro Vaz de Abreu
> 2 Affonço˙ Lourenço˙ de Abreu, lord of the Fief of Vila Boa
> 2 D. Constança˙ Lourenço˙, wife of Affonço˙ Rodrigues˙ Villarinho [see NFP Vilarinho §1 N3]; others say D. Constança was the daughter of Lourenço Gomes [§2 N1]
> 2 D. Elena Gomes, who is said by some to have married Vasco Gil Bacellar

N2 PEDRO VAZ˙ DE ABREU, son of Gomes Lourenço˙ de Abreu N1, married Leonor Rodrigues˙ Bacellar, daughter of Vasco Gil Bacellar, lord of the manor of Bacelar, and his wife Elena Gomes [NFP Bacelar §1 N7][ii]

> 3 Pedro Vaz de Abreu, known as the "Mal Degolado" ("Chipped Neck")[iii]

N3 PEDRO VAZ˙ DE ABREU, son of Pedro Vaz˙ de Abreu N2, married Isabel Lopes Lobato, daughter of Ruy Lobato and D. Aldonça Alvares˙ de Lira [§49 N4], though we have also found this Isabel Lopes married Pedro Garcia˙ de Lançós˙, or Lanções˙ [NFP Lanções §1 N2]

> 4 Gregorio˙ Vaz˙ Lobato, lord of Barbeita, who married Branca Pereira˙, daughter of Affonso˙ Pereira˙ do Lago, a Fidalgo of King Afonso V's Household, and his wife Ignes Vaz˙ de Castro [with issue in NFP Araujo §340 N21][iv]

---

[i] The author decided to identify this Gomes Lourenço de Abreu as N1 and not N7. For details about this change, see fn. *i* on p. 7, about his brother Lourenço Gomes de Abreu §2 N1. (T. N.)

[ii] In NFP Bacelar §1 N7, Elena Gomes is called Elena Gomes *de Abreu*. (T. N.)

[iii] In NFP Bacelar §19 N9, it is said that Pedro Vaz de Abreu was given this nickname in the conquest of Tangier (1471), in which he was hit by an arrow in his throat while attempting to raise a flag on a city wall. In order to take out the arrow, those who aided him had to cut part of his throat off. (T. N.)

[iv] In NFP Araujo §340 N21, Gregorio˙ Vaz˙ Lobato is called Gregorio˙ Vaz˙ Lobato *de Abreu*, and his wife is called Branca Pereira *de Castro*. (T. N.)

4 Anna Vaz· Lobato

4 Elena Gomes, wife of Heitor de Barros [with issue in NFP Bacelar §19 N10]*i*

N4 ANNA VAZ· LOBATO, daughter of Pedro Vaz de Abreu N3, married João Franco of Moreira, son of (...)

5 Estevão Franco

N5 ESTEVÃO FRANCO, son of Anna Vaz Lobato N4, married Maria· Gonçalves· de Lima, who, according to the Records of the Noble Families of Toriz, was the daughter of Gonçallo de Torres and Maria· Rodrigues· de Lima, and the maternal granddaughter of D. Rodrigo de Lima, Commendatory of Refoios [NFP Lima §2 N12]*ii*, though this information has never been corroborated by other records

6 Antonio Franco

N6 ANTONIO· FRANCO, son of Estevão Franco N5, married Cecilia Gonçalves· de Antas, daughter of Rodrigo Alvares· de Antas, Knight of Golden Spurs*iii*

7 João Franco de Puga

N7 JOÃO FRANCO DE PUGA, son of Antonio· Franco N6, married (in Rego de Azar) D. Anna de Araujo· de Tavora

8 Gaspar Franco de Araujo·

N8 GASPAR FRANCO DE ARAUJO·, son of João Franco N7, married in Merilhões

9 Antonio· de Araujo· de Azevedo·, of Merilhões, a reputable genealogist

§65

N11 D. LUISA DA SILVA, bastard daughter of Baltazar· Coelho da Silva §53 N10, married Lourenço· de Guimarães·, son of Antonio· de Guimarães· and Maria· Ribeiro·

---

i In NFP Bacelar §19 N10, this daughter of Pedro Vaz de Abreu is said to be Elena *or* Izabel Gomes de Abreu. (T. N.)

ii In NFP Lima §2 N12, Maria· Gonçalves· de Lima's mother is called *Mecia* Rodrigues· Lima, and not Maria Rodrigues· de Lima. (T. N.)

iii The use of golden spurs was a privilege of a Knight-*Fidalgo* (for details about Portuguese ranks of nobility, see p. *v*). (T. N.)

12 Baltazar˙ Coelho da Silva

12 D. Maria˙

12 D. Leonor

12 D. Anna

§66

For details about Portuguese ranks of nobility, see p. v

N6 GASPAR DA CUNHA, son of Pedro Gomes de Abreu §16 N5, was made a Page-*Fidalgo* of the King's Household by a charter dated March 10, 1534. In the Chronicle of Santa Comba Dão[i], he is said to have married Gracia Paes Fialho, lady of the entail of Papo de Perdiz, daughter of Guiomar Paes Fialho (sister of Andre Fialho – a Colonel in India, who was a descendant of the ancient Paes of Coimbra –, Diogo Paes Fialho and Manoel˙ Fialho, with no further details), and her husband (...). Gracia Paes Fialho was the maternal granddaughter of João Vaz˙ Fialho and Guiomar Paes, as mentioned below

> 7 Diogo Paes da Cunha, who was a Royal Appellate Judge, a Fidalgo of the King's Household and the lord of the entail of Papo de Perdiz. He married D. Jeronima Perestrello˙, daughter of D. Luiza Perestrello˙ and Diogo Botelho˙ [with issue in NFP Perestrelo §2 N6][ii]

The estates of Papo de Perdiz and a chapel in São João de Almedina were jointly enfeoffed on June 2, 1423 by Rodrigo Esteves, known as Papo de Perdiz (*lit.* Partridge Crop) in Coimbra , where he was a distinguished citizen and held the office of Lord Treasurer. As he had no issue by his wife Maria˙ Domingues˙, he appointed Affonso Paes, his wife's first husband's son as first grantee, on whose behalf his mother also granted her thirds, which she added to the entail by an instrument dated February 15, 1446. This Affonso˙ Paes married his relative Brites Paes, and by her had Margarida˙ Paes (a nun in Semide) (1), Affonso˙ Paes (1) and Diogo Paes (1). As the succession rules of this entail applied to the grantee's nearest relative, regardless of sex, the successor was Margarida˙ Paes, who before entering upon a religious life bestowed the entail upon her brother Affonso˙ Paes (1), who married Isabel Rodrigues˙ and by her had Brites Paes. However, Diogo Paes (1) disputed with his niece the succession of the entail, and eventually won their possession through a confirmation charter granted by King John II. Diogo Paes (1) married F(...), by whom he had Guiomar Paes (2), wife of João Vaz˙ Fialho, who served in India, the latter being the parents of the following children: Guiomar Paes Fialho (3), who married (...) and was the mother of Gracia Paes Fialho, wife of Gaspar da Cunha N6 above; Andre Paes Fialho (3), who served in India, sp as mentioned above; Diogo Paes Fialho (3); Manoel˙ Fialho (3) (with no further details)

---

[i] Santa Comba Dão is a municipality in the District of Viseu in central Portugal. (T. N.)

[ii] In NFP Perestrelo §2 N6, Diogo Botelho˙ is called Diogo *Perestrello˙* Botelho˙. (T. N.)

§67

N12 JERONIMA DA CUNHA, daughter of Paulla da Cunha §31 N11, married Manoel˙ Pacheco Pereira˙ of Barrosas, Guimarães, son of Manoel˙ Pacheco˙ and his wife Clara Moreira [NFP Pacheco §10 N13], residents of the manor of Ladesma

> 13 Manoel˙ da Cunha, a clergyman
> 13 Francisca˙ de Macedo
> 13 Anna da Cunha
> 13 Catarina˙ da Cunha Pacheco
> 13 Paulla de Macedo
> 13 Isabel de Macedo
> 13 Clara da Cunha

N13 CATARINA˙ DA CUNHA PACHECO, daughter of Jeronima da Cunha N12, married Manoel˙ Freire

> 14 João Pacheco da Cunha

N14 JOÃO PACHECO DA CUNHA, son of Catarina˙ da Cunha N13, married Guiomar Ribeiro˙ de Mesquita˙

> 15 D. Maria˙ Pacheco de Mesquita˙

N15 D. MARIA˙ PACHECO DE MESQUITA˙, daughter of João Pacheco N14, married Frutuoso Mendes, Captain of the Fort of St. Joseph in Angola

> 16 João Nicolao Pacheco Pereira˙ de Ladesma[i]
> 16 D. Maria˙ Luisa Pacheco, sp
> 16 Bernardo Jose Pacheco, sp
> 16 Father Antonio˙ Pedro Pacheco

N16 JOÃO NICOLAO PACHECO PEREIRA˙ DE LADESMA, son of D. Maria˙ Pacheco N15, married D. Marianna Margarida˙ da Fonseca˙

> 17 Sebastião Pacheco Pereira˙ de Ladesma
> 17 D. Maria˙ do Carmo
> 17 D. Maria˙ Jose
> 17 João Simplicio Pacheco, unmarried
> 17 Jose Maria˙ Pacheco

---

[i] Though in N16 the name "de Ladesma" is mentioned as a surname (João Nicolao Pacheco Pereira˙ de Ladesma), it is also informed in this section that the great great grandparents of Maria˙ Pacheco de Mesquita˙ (João Nicolao's mother) were "Manoel˙ Pacheco˙ and his wife Clara Moreira, residents of the manor of Ladesma". We do not know if this "de Ladesma" was mistakenly interpreted by the author as a surname in N16, or if it has indeed become a surname of toponymic origin . (T. N.)

§68

N11 ANTONIO˙ DA CUNHA DE AZEVEDO˙, son of Jeronimo da Cunha de Azevedo˙ §44 N10, lived in his manor of Mato de São Martinho de Salreu, in which he was enfeoffed together with his wife D. Cecilia de Mello, daughter of Cristovão Coelho de Mello (lord of the entail of Sampaio in the parish of Moucos) and his wife D. Ignes Pereira˙ [NFP Azevedo §136 N25]

    12 Jeronimo Pereira˙ de Mello

    12 D. Ignes Pereira˙, wife of Jacinto Barbosa de Novaes, sp

    12 D. Vicencia, a nun in the convent of Tentugal

N12 JERONIMO PEREIRA˙ DE MELLO, son of Antonio˙ da Cunha de Azevedo˙ N11, married Francisca˙ Maria˙ Pereira˙ de Castro, daughter of João de Macedo Sotomayor and his wife D. Anna de Mello of Vilar de Massada, near Vila Real. He and his wife were the lords of the entail of Sampaio, near Vila Real

    13 Jose Teixeira˙ de Mello, e Castro

    13 Antonio˙, who died young

    13 João Teixeira˙ de Mello

    13 D. Maria˙ Clara da Cunha, who married her cousin Francisco˙ Barbosa da Cunha, Captain General of Ovar [§47 N13]

N13 JOSE TEIXEIRA˙ DE MELLO, E CASTRO, son of Jeronimo Pereira˙ de Mello N12, was the lord of the entail of Sampaio and manor of Mato, and married D. (...)

    14 Antonio˙ Teixeira˙ de Mello, e Castro

N14 ANTONIO˙ TEIXEIRA˙ DE MELLO, E CASTRO, son of Jose Teixeira˙ N13, married D. Josefa Pereira˙

    15 D. Anna Joaquina˙, who was the last grantee of the entail of Sampaio

§69

N9 D. MARIA˙ DA CUNHA PERESTRELLO˙, daughter of Bento da Cunha Perestrello˙ §44 N8, married Antonio˙ Soares de Albergaria, son of D. Maria˙ Soares and her husband João Dripe [NFP Soares de Albergaria §17 N13]

    10 Antonio˙ Soares da Cunha

N10 ANTONIO˙ SOARES DA CUNHA, son of D. Maria˙ da Cunha N9, married D. Maria˙ de Carvalho, daughter of Manoel˙ de Carvalho and his wife Guiomar Antunes [NFP Carvalho §136 N15]

    11 D. Maria˙ Soares da Cunha, wife of João Pinto de Almeida, son of Antonio˙ de Almeida [with issue in NFP Pinto §278 N13]

§70

LORDS OF THE HOUSE OF ABOBREIRA NEAR PONTE DE LIMA

N11 ISABEL DE ABREU, bastard daughter of Antonio˙ de Abreu Lima, Abbot of Moreira §29 N10, married Antonio˙ de Brito Pimenta, a Fidalgo of the King's Household, lord of the house of Abobreira [see §130 N10], bastard son of Francisco˙ de Brito Malheiro and Catarina˙ de Brito Pimenta, paternal grandson of Rafael Gomes do Lago and Magdalena Malheiro. Catarina˙ de Brito Pimenta was the daughter of Manoel˙ Coelho Calheiros and his wife Cecilia Pimenta, paternal granddaughter of Gaspar Coelho de Castro and Isabel Lopes Calheiros, and maternal granddaughter of Baltazar˙ Pimenta, lord of the house of Abobreira [NFP Abreu §130; NFP Calheiros §11 N15 and §16; NFP Costa §66 N10; NFP Brito §30 N8][i]

> 12 D. Eulalia Pimenta de Abreu
> 12 D. Clemencia de Abreu Lima, who married Frutuozo Pimenta de Brito, a Fidalgo of the King's Household and Knight of the Order of Christ, son of Baltazar˙ Pimenta de Brito and his wife Maria˙ de Araujo˙ [with issue in NFP Araujo §26 N27[ii]; see also NFP Pedigree Charts, Tome 3, ff. 182]
> 12 D. Catarina˙ de Abreu Lima, wife of Visente Correa˙ dos Guimarães˙ [with issue in NFP Barbosa §177 N27 and NFP Correa §73 N8][iii]

§71

N8 LOPO GOMES DE ABREU, son of Jorge de Abreu §7 N7, was a beneficiary in the church of Santa Maria de Cales and had a bastard son
> 9 B. Pedro Gomes de Abreu

N9 PEDRO GOMES DE ABREU, bastard son of Lopo Gomes de Abreu N8, was legitimated, went to India in 1576 and became the Captain of Mombasa. He married D. Pelagia Teixeira˙, sp, but had bastard issue before his marriage
> 10 B. Lopo Gomes de Abreu
> 10 B. D. Maria˙ de Abreu, third wife of Leonel de Abreu Lima §4 N10

Mombasa, an African town founded by the Arabs on the Indic Ocean coast (in nowadays Kenya), was a part of the Portuguese Empire between 1593 and 1698, and also between 1728 and 1729

---

[i] In NFP Calheiros §11 N15, Rafael Gomes do Lago's wife is called *Margarida* Malheiro *de Abreu*, and not Magdalena Malheiro. (T. N.)

[ii] In NFP Araujo §26 N27, Frutuozo Pimenta de Brito's wife is called Clemencia *Affonso˙* de Lima, and not Clemencia de Abreu Lima, and the latter's mother (António de Brito Pimenta's wife) is called Isabel de Abreu *de Lima Brito Malheiro*. (T. N.)

[iii] In NFP Barbosa §177 N27 and NFP Correa §73 N8, Catarina˙ de Abreu Lima's parents are called Antonio˙ de *Brito Pimenta* (and not Antonio˙ de Abreu Lima) and Izabel de Abreu *Lima*. (T. N.)

N10 LOPO GOMES DE ABREU, bastard son of Pedro Gomes N9, was married in India to (...)

        11 Pedro Gomes de Abreu

        11 Gonçallo Gomes de Abreu, who went to India with his brother in 1598

§72

N8 MARTIM COELHO DE ABREU, son of Jorge de Abreu §7 N7, was a clergyman, lived in the manor of Telhada in Santa Leucadia de Briteiros and had bastard children

        9 D. (...), a nun in Remedios in Braga

        9 D. Maria˙ de Abreu, wife of (...) Brochado

        This D. Maria˙ de Abreu was a paramour of her cousin Jorge de Abreu [§7 N8 sub N9], by whom she had issue

§73

N5 MENDO GOMES DE ABREU, son of Pedro Gomes de Abreu §2 N4, was very distinguished in the time of King Edward and King Afonso V. In his old age he also served King Manuel I whilst the latter was still the Duke of Beja. Annes Amado states that he married (...), daughter of Ruy de Abreu, a nobleman who lived in Beja, or Elvas

King Edward r. 1433–1438 King Afonso V r. 1438–1481. Manuel I was the Duke of Beja until 1495, when he bacame King of Portugal

        6 Luis Mendes de Abreu

        6 Alvaro Mendes de Abreu

N6 LUIS MENDES DE ABREU, son of Mendo Gomes de Abreu N5, succeeded to his father's house and married (...) in Beja

        7 Lourenço Mendes de Abreu

        7 Ruy Mendes de Abreu

N7 LOURENÇO MENDES DE ABREU, son of Luis Mendes de Abreu N6 [see NFP Pinho §6 N13 (sic)[i]], succeeded to his father's house and married Brites Fialho[11]

        8 Antão Mendes de Abreu

        8 Mendo de Abreu, sp

        8 Pedro Gomes de Abreu, sp

N8 ANTÃO MENDES DE ABREU, son of Lourenço Mendes N7, succeeded to his father's house. In Leiria, when already at an advanced age, he married Brites

---

[i] In NFP Pinho there is no passage identified by §6 N13, nor have we been able to find any mention to this family elsewhere in that chapter. (T. N.)

[11] It seems that Belchior˙ Mendes de Abreu, mentioned in §48 N10, also descends from this line.

Balieira Castello Branco, daughter of Gomes Balieiro [NFP Andrade Freire §16 N4 Sub5] (a knight who served in Africa and was Chief Steward to Infante D. Pedro) and his wife D. Maria˙ Ribeiro˙. Antão Mendes was buried at the entrance to the Main Chapel of St. Francis's Church in Leiria, and his tomb is decorated with the coat of arms of the Abreus and the images of a rapier, a spear and a banner, a clear sign that he held military offices

> 9 Lourenço Mendes de Abreu
> 9 Luis Gomes de Abreu, a priest
> 9 Garcia˙ Mendes de Abreu §132
> 9 D. Leonor de Abreu, who according to her descendants was married
> > to João Munhos, son of D. Affonso˙ Munhos [with issue in NFP
> > Munhoz of Soure §1 N2]

N9 LOURENÇO MENDES DE ABREU, son of Antão Mendes de Abreu N8, succeeded to his father's house and married (in the village of Pombal) Anna Gomes Veiga, daughter of Antão Gomes da Veiga

> 10 Matheus Pegado de Abreu §110
> 10 Antão Mendes de Abreu
> 10 Ruy Mendes de Abreu, Judge of the Appellate House, Chief
> > Chancellor of Bahia (in Brazil) and Knight of the Order of Christ.
> > He married D. Isabel de Miranda and had
> > 11 Antão, who did not have issue, like his brothers below
> > 11 Lourenço
> > 11 Pedro
> 10 Bartolomeu Mendes de Abreu §74
> 10 D. Gracia Mendes de Abreu
> 10 Garcia˙, a Bernardine monk
> 10 Pedro Gomes de Abreu §75
> 10 Felipa Mendes de Abreu §112
> 10 Miguel Mendes de Abreu §111

N10 ANTÃO MENDES DE ABREU, son of Lourenço Mendes N9, succeeded to his father's house, was Judge of the Appeal Court, and married D. Jeronima Cogominho, daughter of Diogo Colaço and his wife D. Brites Velho Tinoco, daughter of Martim Velho Tinoco and his wife Anna Martins Cogominho [NFP Velho §13 N15][i]

> 11 Lourenço Mendes, who died young, sp
> 11 Ruy Mendes de Abreu
> 11 Gracia Mendes de Abreu, sp
> 11 Pedro, a Franciscan monk in the province of Arrabida, who
> > assumed the name of Brother Diogo of the Desert

---

[i] In NFP Velho §13 N15, Antão Mendes de Abreu's wife is called Jeronima *Velho* (and not Jeronima Cogominho), and her parents are said to be *Manoel* Colaço (and not Diogo Colaço) and Brites Velho. (T. N.)

N11 RUY MENDES DE ABREU, son of Antão Mendes de Abreu N10 (though we have seen a record stating this Ruy Mendes was the son of the one we consider here as his grandfather), succeeded to his father's house, served in the Coast Guards, was a Knight of the Order of Christ and was granted the title of Fidalgo by a restitution charter as a legitimate descendant of the house of Regalados. He had by Marta Borges

  12 B. Antonia˙ de Abreu

N12 ANTONIA˙ DE ABREU, bastard daughter of Ruy Mendes N11, married (in Santarem) João Ferreira˙ Couceiro, a nobleman, son of Cristovão Couceiro and D. Leonor Barbosa de Figueiredo˙, daughter of Francisco˙ Barbosa de Figueiredo˙, Fidalgo of the King's Household and D. Leonor de Sousa das Coberturas

  13 Ruy Mendes de Abreu, who led a reckless life and was executed in Lisbon because of the many crimes he commited. He had a bastard son by a woman from Ancão

    14 João Couceiro de Abreu, who was a Criminal Justice of the Mouraria neighbourhood in Lisbon, a Knight of the Order of Christ and the Chief Guard ot the Tower of Tombo. He married D. Ignes Tenorio de Farya of Setúbal, bastard daughter of Antonio˙ de Farya Tenorio, a rich businessman, by whom he had

    15 Ruy Mendes, with issue

    15 Diogo de Abreu, a monk in the monastery of (...)

    15 Antonio˙ Couceiro de Abreu, a Fidalgo of the King's Household, who married D. Theresa Henriques˙ de Almeida, daughter of D. Henrique˙ Henriques˙ de Almeida, sp

  13 D. Joanna

N13 D. JOANNA DE ABREU, daughter of D. Antonia˙ de Abreu N12, married Luis de Sousa Falcão, son of Jose de Sousa Falcão and D. Isabel de Cisneiros [see NFP Falcão §11 N9][i]

  14 D. Antonia˙ Caetana de Sousa

  14 (...), with issue in NFP Falcão §21 (sic)[ii]

N14 D. ANTONIA˙ CAETANA DE SOUSA, daughter and heiress of D. Joanna de Abreu N13, married Antonio˙ de Abreu Rego Castello Branco˙, a Fidalgo of the King's Household, son of Pedro Vaz Soares, Fidalgo of the King's Household and Commendatory of the Order of Christ

  15 Pedro Vaz Soares Castello Branco˙, Fidalgo of the King's Household

  15 D. Joanna Luisa de Castello Branco˙

---

[i] In NFP Falcão §11 N9, Joze de Sousa Falcão's wife is called *Brites* de Cisneiros, and not Isabel de Cisneiros. (T. N.)

[ii] In NFP Falcão §21, there is no reference to anyone supposedly from this family. Besides that, in NFP Falcão §11 N10, Luiz de Souza Falcão's sole mentioned child is Antonia˙ Caetana de Souza. (T. N.)

N15 D. JOANNA LUISA DE CASTELLO BRANCO˙, daughter of D. Antonia˙ Caetana N14, was the second wife of Jose Lourenço Botelho˙

   16 Gonçallo
   16 Lourenço Botelho˙ de Castro
She married as her second husband Gonçallo Pedro de Mello
   16 Manoel˙
   16 Pedro de Mello

§74

N10 BARTOLOMEU MENDES DE ABREU, son of Lourenço Mendes de Abreu §73 N9, married D. Paulla da Fonseca˙, daughter of Perpetua Velho da Fonseca˙ and her husband Paullo Velho da Fonseca˙ [NFP Velho §9 N15]
   11 Lourenço Mendes de Abreu
   11 D. Joanna
   11 D. Anna, unmarried

N11 LOURENÇO MENDES DE ABREU, son of Bartolomeu Mendes N10, married D. Maria˙ de Abreu, daughter of Miguel˙ Mendes de Abreu and his wife D. Maria˙ da Fonseca˙, daughter of João de Azambuja [§111 N10; see also NFP Velho §9 N16][i]
   12 Bartolomeu Mendes de Abreu [see §48 above]
   12 D. Patornilha Jose de Abreu
   12 D. Paulla Maria˙ de Abreu

N12 D. PAULLA MARIA˙ DE ABREU, daughter of Lourenço Mendes N11, was the second wife of Luis Galvão de Azambuja, Captain General of Leiria, son of João de Azambuja da Fonseca˙ and his wife D. Luisa Botelho Galvão, paternal grandson of João de Azambuja (in N11 above, son of Fernão Rodrigues˙ de Azambuja) and his wife Maria˙ Ferreira˙ da Fonseca˙, and maternal grandson of Francisco˙ Botelho and Maria˙ Galvão
   13 D. Patornilha Josefa de Abreu, her parents' heiress, wife of Sebastião Soares de Sousa Evangelho [with issue in NFP Evangelho §2 N10]

---

[i] In NFP Velho §9 N16, Lourenço Mendes de Abreu's wife is called Maria˙ *da Fonseca* (and not Maria de Abreu), and she is said to be her husband's cousin. (T. N.)

§75

N10 PEDRO GOMES DE ABREU, son of Lourenço Mendes de Abreu §73 N9, married D. Catarina˙ da Fonseca˙ Cogominho, daughter of Perpetua Velho, and her husband Paullo Velho da Fonseca˙ [see NFP Velho §8 N14 and NFP Coutinho §51 N14]

        11 Paullo Gomes de Abreu

        11 Fray Antão, a Bernardine monk

        11 Andre Gomes, sp

        11 D. Antonia de Abreu, wife of Luis de Sousa de Sequeira˙, son of
          João, or Luis Rodrigues˙ de Sequeira˙

        11 D. Anna

        11 D. Marianna

        11 D. Isabel

N 11 PAULLO GOMES DE ABREU, son of Pedro Gomes N10, married D. Anna de Castro

§76

For Anthony, the Prior of Crato, see box on the next page

N6 JOÃO GOMES DE ABREU, son of Pedro Gomes de Abreu §13 N5, supported the cause of Anthony˙, the Prior of Crato, for which he suffered many adversities. He married Brites de Mello and had

        7 Francisco˙ de Abreu de Mello

        7 Jorge de Abreu, who was the Governor of Alfaites for 18 years

        7 Sebastião de Abreu, Governor of Ceylon

        7 Vasco Gomes de Abreu, Governor of Salvaterra

        7 Jeronimo Soares de Mello, who married Francisca˙, or Maria˙ de
          Mello and had

         8 Antonio˙ de Mello, a Jesuit

         8 Manoel˙ de Abreu de Mello

        7 D. Maria˙ de Abreu de Mello

        7 D. Francisca˙ de Mello

N7 D. MARIA˙ DE ABREU DE MELLO, daughter of João Gomes de Abreu N6, married Estevão de Correa de Araujo˙, e Sousa

        8 Manoel˙ de Abreu de Mello

Arms of the Princes of Portugal

Anthony, the Prior of Crato

Anthony, the Prior of Crato (1531-1595), was the bastard son of Prince Louis, King John III's son, who had him by a new Christian (i.e. a Jewess). He was the first cousin of King Sebastian, and accompanied this sovereign in the African campaign which ended with the disastrous defeat at Alcazarquivir (August 4th, 1578). In that battle, in which King Sebastian was killed, Antonio was made a prisoner by the Moors, but later managed to return to Portugal.

King Sebastian's decease (at twenty-four years of age, leaving no descendants and no brothers and sisters) triggered a dynastic crisis in Portugal, in which Anthony disputed the kingdom with some of his cousins. He was supported by nationalist groups, particularly the bourgeoisie and the common people, who opposed the claim of the powerful Philip II, King of Spain, who was also a grandson of King John III by the latter's daughter Isabella of Portugal.

Yet Philip II was supported by the upper nobility and clergy of Portugal, who saw in him the opportunity of keeping their privileges in the vacuum of power created upon the disaster in Morocco. Philip II was indeed crowned King of Portugal in 1580 (then becoming Philip I of Portugal), thereby promoting the Iberian Union (i. e., the union of the Spanish and the Portuguese under the same sovereign), a situation which lasted until the reign of his grandson Philip IV (Philip III of Portugal), who lost the Portuguese kingdom through a revolution that gave it to John, the Duke of Bragança (also a descendant of King John III), who then became King John IV of Portugal (1640), the first sovereign of the dynasty of Bragança, which was to reign in Portugal until 1910, the year in which the monarchy was overthrown by a republican coup d'état.

N8 MANOEL˙ DE ABREU DE MELLO, son of D. Maria˙ de Abreu N7, lived in Parada, in the municipality of São João de Areias, district of Viseu. He married D. Francisca˙ Moniz Cabral, daughter of Manoel˙ Henrique de Almeida and Guiomar Moniz Barradas, daughter of Theotonio de Escovar and Catarina˙ Barradas da Silva. Manoel˙ Henrique was the son of Antonio˙ Cabral and the grandson of Pedro Alvares˙ Cabral, lord of Belmonte[i]

> 9 Alexandre de Mello de Eça
> 9 Vasco de Mello de Eça, who married in Cabernais near Viseu in 1705, and had issue
> 9 João de Mello Eça

N9 JOÃO DE MELLO DE EÇA, son of Manoel˙ de Abreu de Mello N8. Like his father, he lived in Parada, in the municipality of São João de Areias. He got married (in the village of Póvoa de Santa Cristina, near Tentugal) to (...), daughter of Agostinho Negrão, Prior of São Silvestre in the plain of Coimbra, a descendant of the noble family of Cerveira

---

[i] In NFP Cabral §3 N8, it is said that Pedro Alvares˙ Cabral (the lord of Belmonte and the Admiral who discovered Brazil in 1500) had a son called Antonio˙ Cabral, about whom the only information provided is that he did not marry. There were other members of this family with the name Pedro Alvares Cabral, but none of them is said to have had the descendancy mentioned here. (T. N.)

For details about Portuguese ranks of nobility, see p. v

10 D. Constança de Mello, who married (with issue) Manoel˙ Borges Chichorro of Montemor-o-Velho, son of Thome de Freitas and his wife Maria Borges

§77

N9 ROQUE DA CUNHA, e MELLO, son of Alexandre da Cunha §26 N8, was a Squire-*Fidalgo* and married his cousin D. Maria˙ de Almeida, daughter of Gonçallo de Azevedo Cabral and his wife D. Felipa de Almeida, paternal granddaughter of Simão de Azevedo Cabral and his wife D. Felipa de Sá, e Moura, mentioned in §26 N8

    10 Alexandre da Cunha, e Mello
    10 Gonçallo da Silva˙, Abbot of Bordonhos

N10 ALEXANDRE DA CUNHA, E MELLO, son of Roque da Cunha N9, succeeded to his father's house, married D. Theresa de Mello, daughter of Bras de Figueiredo˙ Castello Branco, lord of the entail of Gondomar, and his wife D. Isabel Soares de Mello [NFP Loureiro §13 N9]

    11 Roque, who died young
    11 Xavier, who died young
    11 Bras da Cunha de Figueiredo˙
    11 D. Felipa de Almeida, a nun in Arouca

N11 BRAS DA CUNHA DE FIGUEIREDO˙, son of Alexandre da Cunha N10. He succeeded to the house of his grandfather and father by the same nobility charter which had been granted to them, though he did not inherit the royal estates of Varoso, which were taken from him by Paullo Carneiro˙ de Araujo˙ in a dispute before the Crown. He married (in São Pedro do Sul) D. Antonia˙ Theresa de Mesquita, daughter of Pedro de Mesquita˙ Loureiro

    12 Luis Fradique da Cunha, e Mello

N12 LUIS FRADIQUE DA CUNHA, E MELLO, son of Bras da Cunha N11. He was the Captain General of Lafões, was granted the charter and house of his father, lived in São Pedro do Sul and married D. Maria˙ Felicianna da Rocha, daughter of João Homem da Rocha, lord of the manor of Freixo, and his wife D. Maria˙ Barreiro, of Nespereira, parish of Villa Maior, in the municipality of Lafões

    13 Alexandre da Cunha, e Mello
    13 D. Margarida Ignes de Castro
    13 D. Francisca˙ Joanna de Abreu, wife of Bento de Mello Falcão, Knight of the Order of Christ, with issue
    13 D. Dionizia
    13 D. Felipa

13 D. Maria˙

13 Manoel˙, who died young

13 Brother Jose Francisco˙

N13 ALEXANDRE DA CUNHA, e MELLO DE ABREU, son of Luis Fradique da Cunha N12, married (in Oporto) D. Rosa

    14 Antonio˙ de Mello da Cunha, who married but did not have issue

    14 Jose de Mello, Abbot of Santa Eulália, in the foothills of the Arouca Mountains

§78

N7 D. BRITES DA CUNHA, daughter of Roque de Abreu §26 N6, married Pedro Lourenço de Oliveira˙, a native of Oliveira de Frades, son of João Lourenço, grandson of Pedro Lourenço and great grandson of Gonçallo˙

King Afonso IV r. 1325–1357 Lourenço, lord of Alcofra. By grant of King Afonso IV, Pedro Lourenço de Oliveira˙ inherited from these ancestors the fief, the entail and the advowson of Alcofra

    8 Jorge de Abreu de Mello

    8 D. Joanna da Silva˙ e Eça, who was the wife of Manoel˙ Tenreiro de Andrade˙ [NFP Tenreiro §1 N2] and had

        9 João Tenreiro da Silva, who married D. Maria˙ de Mello, daughter of D. Joanna de Mello and her husband Sebastião de Figueiredo˙ [with issue in NFP Melo §59 N15][i]

N8 JORGE DE ABREU DE MELLO, son of D. Brites da Cunha N7, married D. Sebastianna de Almeida, daughter of Fernão de Almeida de Novaes and D. Catarina˙ Coelho de Carvalho˙

    9 Jose de Abreu de Mello

    9 Antonio˙ de Abreu, sp

N9 JOSE DE ABREU DE MELLO, son of Jorge de Abreu N8, succeeded to his father's house and was the lord of the manor of Pareciras, in the municipality of Lafões. He married (in Viseu) D. Antonia˙ de Mello, his niece, daughter of Luis da Cunha, e Mello, a Fidalgo of the King's Household, and his wife D. Isabel Rabello [§26 N8 Sub9]

---

[i] In NFP Melo §59 N15, it is informed that João Tenreiro da Silva was a Fidalgo of the King's Household. (T. N.)

10 Jose de Abreu de Mello

10 Fray Luis, a Bernardine monk

10 Manoel˙ de Mello, a major in Angola

10 D. Sebastianna, a nun in the convent of Lorvão

10 D. Simoa, *ditto*

10 D. Eufemia, who retired to the same convent

10 D. Marianna

10 D. Isabel

N10 JOSE DE ABREU DE MELLO, son of Jorge de Abreu N9, succeeded to his father's house and married his relative D. Theresa Bernarda de Magalhães˙, daughter of João Rabello de Magalhães˙ (a resident of the parish of Cortiçô in the municipality of Algodres) and his wife D. Bernarda Teixeira˙ da Silva [NFP Pedigree Charts, Tome 4, *ff.* 114]. Jose de Abreu de Mello was the lord of the house of Pereiras in the municipality of Lafões; he was also an Inquisition Officer, coadvowee of the churches of St. James of Carvalhais and Santa Cruz da Trapa and advowee of the chapter of St. Anthony in Viseu

11 Antonio˙ de Mello da Cunha de Abreu

11 João de Magalhães˙ de Abreu, a canon in Viseu

N11 ANTONIO˙ DE MELLO DA CUNHA, E ABREU, son of Jose de Abreu de Mello N10, had bastard issue

12 Bernardo de Mello da Cunha, e Abreu

§79

N6 LUIS DE ABREU, whom we consider the legitimate son of Pedro Gomes de Abreu §16 N5, though this is denied by some, who consider him the bastard son of Roque de Abreu §26 N6. In a chronicle which we have seen, it is stated that he married Agueda Fernandes de Figueiredo˙

7 Roque Fernandes˙ de Abreu

7 Antonio˙ Fernandes˙ de Abreu §128

N7 ROQUE FERNANDES˙ DE ABREU, son of Luis de Abreu N6, though some consider him the bastard son of Roque de Abreu §26 N6, was granted nobility privileges and married Isabel Nunes

8 Roque Fernandes˙ de Abreu

8 Dr. Miguel Nunes de Abreu, Vicar-General and Governor of the Bishopric of Coimbra, an office he held together with the Priorship of Elvas on the occasion of his death. As requested in his will, he was buried near the cross of the church of his priory, where his distinguished tomb lies

8 Antonio˙ Fernandes˙ de Abreu, who married Agueda Gomes Golias [NFP Golias §7 N3]

8 Agueda de Abreu, wife of Pedro Castanheda de Moura [NFP Moura §16 N14, according to Jose Correa˙ de Mello's *Castanhedas de Sinde*][i]

N8 ROQUE FERNANDES˙ DE ABREU, son of Roque Fernandes˙ de Abreu N7, succeeded to his father's house and also inherited the lands of his brother Manoel˙ Nunes. He married Isabel Francisca˙ de Figueiredo˙, daughter of Pedro Affonso de Figueiredo˙ [NFP Figueiredo §21 N8]

9 Dr. Luis de Abreu, dsp

9 Isabel Nunes de Abreu

9 Anna de Abreu §119

9 Elena Madeira, wife of Dr. Pedro Moreira, §122[ii]

10 Francisca˙ de Abreu, wife of Manoel˙ Sequeira˙ de Abreu

10 Catarina˙ de Sena, a nun in the convent of Saint Anne in Coimbra

10 Theodozia, *ditto*

N9 ISABEL NUNES DE ABREU, daughter of Roque Fernandes˙ de Abreu N8, though in NFP Corte Real it is stated that this Isabel Nunes de Abreu was the daughter of the one we consider here her grandfather. She succeeded to her father's house and married Gaspar Dias da Costa, son of another Gaspar Dias da Costa and his wife Margarida Jorge, grandson of Francisco˙ da Costa and Maria˙ Dias, and great grandson of Manoel˙ da Costa Corte Real, who was from Braga and in 1517 married (in Arganil) (...) de Figueiredo˙ [NFP Corte Real §11 N3][iii]

10 Roque Fernandes˙ de Abreu

---

[i] In NFP Moura §16 N14, Pedro Castanheda de Moura's wife is called Agueda *Nunes de Figueiredo˙*, and not Agueda de Abreu. (T. N.)

[ii] Section §122, which is supposed to refer to the same daughter of Roque Fernandes de Abreu mentioned here, has several differences from the present section. To begin with, the name mentioned in §122 is Elena *de Abreu* (and not Elena Madeira); her husband is said to be Pedro *Madeira* (and not Pedro Moreira), and there is not a single similarity between the names of her three children given here and those of her five children mentioned in §122. (T. N.)

[iii] In NFP Corte Real §11 N3, Izabel Nunes de Abreu N9 is said to be the daughter of Roque Fernandes˙ de Abreu and Izabel *Nunes* (and not Isabel Francisca˙ de Figueiredo˙). According to what is stated at the beginning of the present section, this seems to be a mistake, for in N7 and N8 it is stated that Roque Fernandes˙ de Abreu and Izabel Nunes were the parents of another Roque Fernandes˙ de Abreu, who in turn was the husband of Izabel Francisca˙ de Figueiredo˙ and the father of the said Izabel Nunes de Abreu N9. (T. N.)

N10 ROQUE FERNANDES˙ DE ABREU, son of Isabel Nunes de Abreu N9, married Anna de Figueiredo˙, daughter of Sebastião Alvares˙ de Figueiredo˙ and Domingas Affonso˙

        11 Luis de Abreu §116

        11 Maria˙ de Abreu de Figueiredo˙

        11 Dr. Pedro da Costa de Abreu, a university graduate and Public Prosecutor

        11 Isabel, a nun in the convent of Saint Anne in Coimbra

Roque Fernandes˙ de Abreu's second marriage was to Maria˙ de Sequeira˙ Castello Branco˙, by whom he had

        11 Manoel˙ de Sequeira˙ de Abreu §117

        11 Roque de Abreu, a clergyman

        11 D. Luiza de Abreu §118

        11 D. Marianna, a nun

        11 D. Elena, a nun

N11 MARIA˙ DE ABREU DE FIGUEIREDO˙, daughter of Roque Fernandes˙ de Abreu N10, married Thomé Chixorro Pinheiro of Montemor-o-Velho, son of Manoel˙ Chixorro Pinheiro, Knight of the Order of Christ and his wife D. Violante Lobo da Gama [see NFP Pedigree Charts, Tome 2, *lf.* 41 *rev.*]

        12 Andre Chixorro da Gama

N12 ANDRE CHIXORRO DA GAMA, son of Maria˙ de Abreu de Figueiredo˙ N11, was a Fidalgo of the King's Household and a Knight of the Order of Christ, married D. Catarina˙ Jeronima Jusarte, daughter of Antonio˙ Juzarte Raudano and his third wife D. Catarina˙ Barreto de Simas [NFP Jusarte §32 N10][i]

        13 Thome Chixorro da Gama Lobo, who was still alive in 1774

§80

N5 FERNÃO GOMES DE ABREU or FERNÃO RODRIGUES DE ABREU, son of João Gomes de Abreu §16 N4. According to a justification made by his descendants, he was the son of Bishop João Gomes de Abreu, as stated in a land deed written in 1562 in the manor of Passo de Coucieiro, territory of the village of Regalados, by notary public Thome Francisco˙ by request of Gaspar Rabello. Fernão Rodrigues˙ de Abreu lived in Viseu and, also according to his descendants, was a *Fidalgo*-Squire of the King's Household, by which he was entitled to a 1000-real housing allowance. He married D. Mecia Cardoso or Brites Dias Rabello, daughter

For details about Portuguese ranks of nobility, see p. v

---

[i] In NFP Jusarte §32 N10, Catarina˙ Jeronima Jusarte's husband is called Andre Chichorro da Gama *Lobo.* (T. N.)

of Lopo Dias Rabello and his second wife Maria˙ Affonso˙ Carvalho˙ [NFP Rabelo §1 N8][i]

6 Pedro Rabello de Abreu

6 Gil Fernandes˙ de Abreu, who some consider to have been the bastard son of his grandfather João Gomes de Abreu, who allegedly had him by D. Isabel Sotomayor. He married Isabel Annes de Bouro [with issue in §40 N5][ii]

6 Antonio˙ de Abreu, or João Fernandes˙ de Abreu §81

For details about Portuguese ranks of nobility, see p. v.

N6 PEDRO RABELLO DE ABREU, son of Fernão Gomes de Abreu N5, was a *Fidalgo*-Squire of the King's Household, and married Brites˙ Rodrigues˙ Taveira, daughter of Pedro Rodrigues˙ Taveira, or Pedro Rodrigues˙ Ferreira

7 Gaspar Rabello de Abreu

7 Maria Rabello, who married Pedro Ferreira˙ of Vila Nova da Rainha, near Teixeda

7 Isabel Dias Rabello, wife of Francisco˙ Cardoso de Abreu [§84 N11]

7 Jeronimo Affonso˙ Rabello, who as Prior of Juncais instituted an entail, appointing as grantees the children of his sister Isabel

For details about Portuguese ranks of nobility, see p. v.
King Sebastian r. 1557–1578

King Philip II of Spain r. 1556–1598;
as Philip I of Portugal r. 1580–1598;
King Philip III of Spain (Philip II of Portugal) r. 1598–1621

N7 GASPAR RABELLO DE ABREU N6, succeeded to his father's house, was a *Fidalgo*-Squire of the King's Household and Treasury Clerk of King Sebastian. He married Elena Boto and was buried in his own chapel of Saint Onouphrius of the Trinity in Lisbon

8 Pedro Gomes de Abreu, who was Treasury Clerk of King Philip II

8 Sebastião de Abreu, who was Treasury Clerk of King Philip III and had issueless children

§81

LORDS OF THE MANOR OF BAZELGA

N6 ANTONIO˙ DE ABREU or JOÃO RODRIGUES˙ DE ABREU[iii] was the son of Fernão Gomes de Abreu or Fernão Rodrigues˙ de Abreu §80 N5. Known

---

[i] In NFP Rabelo §1 N8, Brites Rabello's husband is called *Francisco˙* Rodrigues˙ de Abreu, and not Fernão Rodrigues (or Gomes) de Abreu. (T. N.)

[ii] In §40 N5, Gil Fernandes de Abreu is said to have been the son of João Gomes de Abreu §16 N4; in that same passage, the author says he disagrees with the opinion by which this Gil Fernandes was the son of Fernão Gomes de Abreu. (T. N.)

[iii] In §81 N5 Sub6, another version for this person's name is João *Fernandes˙* de Abreu. (T. N.)

as "o Grande" (the Great), he was a Fidalgo of the King's Household, lived in Tomar, married and had

   7 Pedro Alvares' de Abreu

N7 PEDRO ALVARES' DE ABREU, son of Antonio' de Abreu N6, was a Fidalgo of the King's Household, by which he was entitled to a 1600-real housing allowance. He lived in Tomar, was the lord of the entail and manor of Bazelga and married Felipa de Magalhães', daughter of Fernão de Magalhães' and his wife (...), daughter of Antonio' Lopes da Costa, Alcaide General of Tomar

  8 Manoel' de Abreu, who married Maria' Sanches and had
   9 Pedro Alvares' de Abreu, in India, sp
   9 (...)
  8 Antonio' de Abreu (in *Corographia Portuguesa*, Tome 3, p. 178[i], it is stated that this Antonio' de Abreu was the son of João Rodrigues' de Abreu N6, an opinion we do not accept, for we think the latter was Antonio's grandfather)

N8 ANTONIO' DE ABREU, son of Pedro Alvares' de Abreu N7, was a Fidalgo of the King's Household, Knight of the Order of Christ, Captain General of the Fleet of India and the first advowee of the convent of Santa Cita. He is considered by some to have been the son of João Fernandes' de Abreu, the grandson of Fernão Rodrigues' de Abreu and the great grandson of João de Abreu de Sousa, whose parents were the lords of Regalados, though we hold a different opinion. Like his father, he lived in Tomar, where he was, as mentioned above, lord of Bazelgas and advowee of Santa Cita. He married D. Isabel Pimentel, daughter of Diogo Alvares' Ramires [see Frey Manoel' da Esperança, *História Sarafica*, Book 2, Chapter 37 N 30], and his wife D. Maria' Cordovil de Sousa

  9 Pedro Alvares' de Abreu
  9 João da Silva

N9 PEDRO ALVARES' DE ABREU, son of Antonio' de Abreu N8, succeeded to his father's grants and house and was the lord of the entail and manor of Bazelga. He moved to Castile, where he married D. Francisca' de Toledo, daughter of D. Fernando Alvares' de Toledo (Commander of the Galleys of Spain and Governor and Captain General of Perpignan) and his wife D. Izabel Sanguera. Others say D. Francisca' de Toledo was an illegitimate daughter, for her parents were not married. D. Izabel Sanguera was the bastard daughter of D. Ignino de Cordona, who had her by D. Maria' de Mendonça, daughter of the lords of Torrezilha in Aragon. D. Fernando de Toledo was the son of D. Fradique de Toledo, *Claveiro* (*lit.* Keeper of the Keys) of the Order of Alcantara, and his wife

---

[i] *Corographia Portuguesa* (3 vols.), written by Father Antonio Carvalho da Costa (1650-1715) and published for the first time between 1706 and 1712. (T. N.)

D. Maria˙ da Silva˙, and the grandson of D. Fernando de Toledo (Commander of Leon and a descendant of the Dukes of Alva) and his wife D. Maria˙ de Roxas

      10 Antonio˙ de Abreu de Sousa

      10 Fradique Alvares˙ de Toledo, who died young

      10 João da Silva, e Sousa §103

N10 ANTONIO˙ DE ABREU DE SOUSA, son of Pedro Alvares˙ de Abreu N9, succeeded to the house of Bazelga, was a Fidalgo of the King's Household and married D. Joanna de Menezes, daughter of Jeronimo Fragoso de Albuquerque˙ and D. Francisca˙ de Menezes or Ignes de Menezes [NFP Pereira §47 N23][i]

      11 D. Luisa Francisca˙ de Menezes

N11 D. LUISA FRANCISCA˙ DE MENEZES, daughter and heiress of Antonio˙ de Abreu N10, married Colonel Ruy Fernandes˙ de Sequeira˙, son of Luis de Sequeira˙ and his wife D. Felipa de Castro [NFP Sequeira §2 N10]

      12 Luis Antonio˙ de Sequeira˙ e Menezes, who married twice, sp

      12 Antonio˙ Pereira˙, a monk

      12 D. Felipa, a nun

      12 D. Luisa, a nun

      12 D. Leonor de Sequeira˙

N12 D. LEONOR DE SEQUEIRA˙, daughter of D. Luisa Francisca˙ de Menezes N11, succeeded to the estates of the Sequeiras in the village of Moura, an entail that was instituted in 1439 by Nuno Affonso˙ de Sequeira˙ and which assigned to its grantees the duty of offering dinner to the King on the occasions His Majesty visited São Vicente da Beira. She married Simão Pereira˙ de Brito, with issue

§82

King Dinis r. 1279–1325

N6 NUNO GONÇALVES˙ DE ABREU, son of Gonçallo Rodrigues de Abreu §3 N5, lived in the time of King Dinis. In the convention signed between the villages of Valadares and Melgaço in 1317, he and his brother Lopo Gonçalves˙ were the representatives of the latter. He married D. Maria˙ Rodrigues˙ da Silva, daughter of Martim Gomes da Silva, called "O Moço" (the Younger), and his second wife D. Theresa Garcia˙ de Seabra [see NFP Silva §1 N6 and *Corographia Portuguesa*, Tome 3, *If.* 367. Count D. Pedro (title 39 N4) does not inform the name of the father of this Nuno Gonçalves˙; instead he only mentions his son (below) and says he married D. Mecia Rodrigues˙][ii]

---

[i] In NFP Pereira §47 N23, Joanna de Menezes's mother's name is *Ignez de Menezes*. (T. N.)

[ii] In NFP Silva §1 N6, Martim Gomes da Silva's daughter (and Nuno Gonçalves de Abreu's wife) is called *Mecia* or *Branca* da Silva, and not Maria˙ Rodrigues˙ da Silva. (T. N.)

7 Gil Nunes de Abreu

7 D. Joanna Nunes de Abreu, who some say was the wife of Vasco Gil Bacellar, though according to Monterroio, it was his aunt that he married [see Bacelar NFP §1 N3][i]

King Peter I r. 1357–1367

N7 GIL NUNES DE ABREU, son of Nuno Gonçalves' N6, was the Alcaide General of Castro Laboreiro, an office granted to him by King Peter I, to whom he paid homage for the said castle on June 24, 1358, as stated in the Book of Records of this King, *lf.* 24. He married D. Theresa de Novaes, daughter of Ruy de Novaes and his wife D. Maria' Pires Cerveira [NFP Novaes §12 N9]

§83

N6 LOPO GONÇALVES' DE ABREU. According to Count D. Pedro [title 39, *lf.* 217], Lopo Gonçalves' was the son of Gonçallo Rodrigues' de Abreu §3 N5, an opinion we also support (see the comments about Lopo Gonçalves' de Abreu made by Alvaro Ferreira' de Vera in his additions to Count D. Pedro's *Livro de Linhagens, lf.* 217). In 1301, Lopo Gonçalves de Abreu was the leader and captain of the Abreus in the dispute this family had with the Novais and Quintelas, led by Fernão Affonso' de Quintella. This rivalry ran so high that King Dinis, fearing the danger these turmoils could bring to the kingdom, managed with great effort to assemble them on April 5 of the said year, and made them swear friendship [Ref.: Count D. Pedro, title 39 §2; Brandão, *Monarquia Lusitana*, Part 4, Book 14, Chapter 24]. He married Aldonça Rodrigues', daughter of Rodrigo Annes Gafo of Galicia, and his wife D. Mecia Pires de Cerveira

7 Nuno Gonçalves' de Abreu

7 Gonçallo Rodrigues' de Abreu

7 D. Leonor Lopes

Lopo Gonçalves' de Abreu also had by his mistress Maria' Alvares'

King Afonso IV r. 1325–1357

7 B. Diogo Lopes de Abreu, who was legitimated by King Afonso IV and obtained from this monarch the grant of enjoying all the honours of his family as though he was a legitimate son

N7 NUNO GONÇALVES' DE ABREU, lord of Melgaço, son of Lopo Gonçalves' de Abreu N6, was called "O Moço" (the Younger). His wife's name was mistaken by Count D. Pedro for that of Nuno Gonçalves' de Abreu, the

---

[i] Obscure part in the original text, in which the information about the chapter of Bacelar is missing (having been included here by guesswork). In Bacelar NFP §1 N3, Joanna Nunes de Abreu's mother (and Nuno Gonçalves de Abreu's wife) is said to be *Mecia* Rodrigues' *de Vasconcellos*, and not Maria' Rodrigues' da Silva. (T. N.)

Elder's [§82 N6]. Count D. Pedro [title 30, *ff.* 217] gives him the same parents we do. He married D. Joanna or Maria Rodrigues˙ de Vasconcellos, daughter of Ruy Pires de Vasconcellos and his wife D. Mayor Martins [NFP Vasconcellos §3 N11][i]

    8 Gonçallo Rodrigues˙ de Abreu

    8 Joanna Nunes de Abreu, who others say was the wife of Vasco Gil Bacellar [*see also* §82 N6][ii]

N8 GONÇALLO RODRIGUES˙ DE ABREU, son of Nuno Gonçalves˙ de Abreu N7, was the Alcaide General of Elvas, married D. Theresa Alvares˙ Pereira˙, sister of Constable D. Nuno Alvares˙ Pereira˙ and bastard daughter of D. Alvaro Pereira˙ [NFP Pereira §1 N13]

For Constable Nuno Alvares Pereira, see box on p. 9

    9 Nuno Gonçalves˙ de Abreu

    9 João Gonçalves˙ de Abreu §109

    9 Lopo Gonçalves˙ de Abreu

    9 D. Ignes Pereira˙ de Abreu, second wife of Diogo Lopes de Azevedo˙, lord of São João del Rei [with issue in NFP Azevedo §19 N18]

    9 D. Genebra de Abreu, wife of Mem Rodrigues˙ de Vasconcellos, son of Joanne Mendes de Vasconcellos and his wife D. Maria˙ de Goes [NFP Vasconcelos §68 N15][iii]

    9 Diogo de Abreu §95

N9 LOPO RODRIGUES˙ DE ABREU, son of Gonçallo Rodrigues˙ de Abreu N8. He moved from Entre Douro and Minho to Beira Province and was a *Fidalgo* of the Household of Infante Ferdinand, the father of King Manuel I. Lopo Rodrigues de Abreu was General Accountant of the provinces of Beira and Trás-os-Montes and by his wife he acquired the lordship of Arcuzelo, not far from Gouvea, and that of Pega in the territory of the city of of Guarda. He

Infante Ferdinand (1433-1470)

---

[i] In NFP Vasconcellos §3 N11, Nunes Gonçalves de Abreu's wife's first name is said to be *Joanna* or *Mecia* (and not Maria), and her surname is not given. There is also an obscure part saying that "according to the other book (or chapter), this Joanna or Mecia was the wife of João Martins˙, son of João Martins˙ de Soalhães". In NFP Soalhães §3 N11, it is said that a "João Martins˙ de Soalhães was married to (…), daughter of Ruy Pires de Vasconcellos in NFP Vasconcelos §(…)". However, according to this second version, this lady was João Martins de Soalhães's wife, not his daughter-in-law. (T. N.)

[ii] However, in §82 N6 Joanna Nunes de Abreu is said to be the daughter of Nuno Gonçalves de Abreu, the Elder. (T. N.)

[iii] In NFP Vasconcelos §68 N15, it is said that Mem Rodrigues˙ de Vasconcellos's wife was "Aldonça or Genebra de Abreu", whose parentage is the same given here. However, the author also mentions another version, stating that he had seen in a chronicle that this Mem Rodrigues˙ de Vasconcellos˙ was married to Izabel Pereira˙. (T. N.)

lived in the village of Fornos near Algodres, Bishopric of Viseu, in the parish of Pinhel, nowadays Linhares. He married D. Brites Vaz˙ Cardoso, daughter of Vasco Paes Cardoso do Amaral and his wife D. Isabel Vaz˙ de Castello Branco˙. (However, in NFP Cardoso §1 N5 Sub6, D. Brites Vaz˙ Cardoso is given as the daughter of the ones we consider here her grandparents, Vasco Paes Cardoso and D. Brites Annes do Amaral (§1 N5), though the first parentage we mention above is more probable (sic)][i]

    10 Pedro Lopes de Abreu
    10 Francisco˙ Lopes de Abreu §94
    10 Lourenço Lopes de Abreu Castello Branco˙
    10 Gonçallo Rodrigues˙ de Abreu, sp
    10 Lopo de Abreu, sp
    10 D. Maria˙ Lopes de Castello Branco˙

N10 PEDRO LOPES DE ABREU CASTELLO BRANCO[ii], son of Lopo Rodrigues˙ de Abreu N9, succeeded to his father's house, was the lord of Fornos de Algodres and had the lordships of Arcuzelo and Pega. He was a page and towel-bearer to Queen D. Leonor, and a *Fidalgo* of the King's Household . His nobility charter, which grants privileges to all his caretakers and servants, is recorded in the Council Chamber of Viseu. He married (1) Catarina˙ Fernandes˙ Albuquerque˙, daughter of Fernão Annes de Albuquerque, lord of Algodres, an estate in which he resided in 1491

    11 Lopo de Abreu Castello Branco
    11 Jorge de Abreu Castello Branco §88
    11 D. Maria˙ Lopes Castello Branco, wife of Ruy Barreiros of Viseu
        (who presumably married D. Maria˙ de Barros as his second wife
        [NFP Barros §101]). D. Maria˙ Lopes Castello Branco and her
        husband were the parents of
        12 D. Francisca˙ Barreiros, who was the wife of Antonio˙ Godinho
        and had
        13 Gaspar Barreiros, the Canon of Viseu
        13 D. Isabel Barreiros
        13 D. Elena Barreiros, wife of Manoel˙ Pessanha

As a widower, Pedro Lopes de Abreu had a bastard son

    11 B. Francisco˙ Lopes de Abreu §89

---

[i] However, contrary to what is stated here, in NFP Cardoso §2 N6 Sub7 the author says he *also disagrees* with the version by which Brites Vaz˙ Cardoso is the daughter of Vasco Paes Cardoso and D. Izabel Vaz Castello Branco. (T. N.)

[ii] In N9 Sub10, his surname *Castello Branco* is omitted. (T. N.)

Pedro Lopes de Abreu's second wife was D. Isabel Cardoso, daughter of Gonçallo Cardoso Homem de Vasconcellos and his wife Maria˙ Rodrigues˙ Soares, lords of the entail of Taipa in Lamego

      11 Francisco˙ Cardoso de Abreu §84

      11 D. Elena Cardoso §85

      11 D. Anna Cardoso §86

      11 D. Francisca˙ Lopes Cardoso §87[i]

N11 LOPO DE ABREU CASTELLO BRANCO, born in Fornos, was the son of Pedro Lopes N10 and his first wife. He was a *Fidalgo* of the King's Household, lord of Arcuzelo and Pega, and General Collector of Ransom Funds in the city of Viseu He did not succeeded to the house of Fornos, which was inherited by his half brother Francisco˙ Cardoso (son of his father's second marriage). He lived in the city of Guarda, where he married D. Catarina˙ Borges, daughter of (...)

      12 Luis de Abreu Castello Branco, who succeeded to the house and the entail of Arcuzelo and Pega, and married D. Francisca˙ de Mello, daughter of Fernão de Pina, Chief Chronicler, sp. In the See of Guarda he and his wife built a chapel which they liberally endowed and where they were buried. His nephew succeeded to the entail

      12 D. Brites de Abreu

N12 D. BRITES DE ABREU, daughter of Lopo de Abreu N11, succeeded to the house and entail of Arcuzelo and Pega, married Fernão Neto da Silva˙, a very distinghished nobleman from Ciudad Rodrigo, who after his wife's decease held the office of Chief Treasurer of the See of Ciudad Rodrigo, upon the renunciation of his uncle João da Silva˙

      13 D. Antonio˙ da Silva

      13 D. Luis da Silva, Chief Treasurer of the See of Ciudad Rodrigo, upon the renunciation of his father

      13 D. (...), wife of Manoel˙ Carveiro de Carvalho, a Fidalgo of the King's Household, sp

      13 D. (...)

N13 D. ANTONIO˙ DA SILVA, son of D. Brites de Abreu N12, succeeded to his father's house and married D. Joanna Teixeira˙ of Pinhel, who after her husband's decease, became the first wife of D. Felipe de Aragão, a Castilian nobleman

In the battle of Alcazarquivir in Morocco (August 4ᵗʰ, 1578) a Portuguese army of nearly 15.000 men led by King Sebastian was completely routed by the Moors and the King himself was killed. Many Portuguese survivors were taken prisoner and later released after a massive payment of ransoms, and this explains the office of General Collector of Ransom Funds, held by Lopo de Abreu Castello Branco §83 N11 and his nephew Pedro Lopes de Abreu §90 N12.

---

[i] In §87, this lady is called Francisca˙ Lopes *de Castello Branco*. (T. N.)

14 D. Antonio˙ da Silva, who succeeded to his father's house and married (...), daughter of D. Felix de Aragão, sp

14 D. Isabel da Silva, who succeeded to the house and entails of her brother. She married (by an arrangement made between the couple's families) D. Antonio de Aragão, son of D. Felix de Aragão and his first wife

14 D. Branca de Menezes, lady-in-waiting to her ladyship (sic)[i], married D. João de Mello, lord of Povolide

§84

LORDS OF FORNOS DE ALGODRES

Cardinal-Infante Afonso (1509-1540), son of King Manuel I

N11 FRANCISCO˙ CARDOSO DE ABREU, son of Pedro Lopes de Abreu §83 N10 and his second wife, succeeded his father to the house of Fornos de Algodres and to all the estates the latter possessed in the said region. He was a *Fidalgo* of the King's Household and held the offices of Chief Collector and Distributor of the alms of the Cardinal-Infante D. Afonso's estates. He married D. Isabel Dias Rabello, daughter of Pedro Rabello de Abreu, Fidalgo of the King's Household, and his wife D. Brites Rodrigues˙ Ferreira˙ [§80 N6]. On March 2, 1551, D. Isabel Dias Rabello made her will, in which she mentioned the names of all the children she had by her husband. After his wife's decease, Francisco˙ Cardoso de Abreu became the Abbot of Fornos; this is the reason why some consider his children bastards, though it is a mistake, for in his will dated February 14, 1572, it is stated that his children were legitimate. Some have also commited the mistake of considering that the mother of his legitimate issue was Isabel Domingues, by whom Francisco Cardoso de Abreu actually had bastard children after having become an abbot, as mentioned below. His legitimate issue was

12 Francisco˙ Cardoso, who died young, sp

12 Lopo de Abreu Castello Branco

12 Gaspar de Abreu, Appellate Judge in Oporto, who married D. Francisca˙ Castanhedo, with issueless children. On April 8, 1616, Gaspar de Abreu and his wife enfeoffed the lands of Anunciada with their seat in the manor of Costa, excluding from the heritage of the said entail any of their descendants who married anyone with plebeian ancestry until the 5th generation

12 D. Isabel Abreu Castello Branco˙, who married Dr. Domingos˙ Borges da Costa, a Royal Appellate Judge, and had

13 Domingos˙ Borges Castello Branco, who married in Lamego and was the grantee of the entail mentioned above

---

[i] Obscure passage in the original text. (T. N.)

13 Jose Borges Castello Branco˙, a clergyman

13 Francisco˙ Borges Castello Branco, who served in India, from where he returned with the rank of Admiral of the Fleet. He married (in Tarouca) D. Felipa de Gouvea, and had

14 Baltazar Borges de Carvalho˙

As said above, after his wife's decease Francisco˙ Cardoso de Abreu became the Abbot of Fornos and had an illegitimate relationship with Isabel Domingues˙, by whom he had

12 B. Francisco Cardoso, a Jesuit

12 B. D. Elena, a nun in Louvão

12 B. D. Paulla, *ditto*

N12 LOPO DE ABREU CASTELLO BRANCO, son of Francisco˙ Cardoso de Abreu N11, was a *Fidalgo* of the King's Household, lord of the house of Fornos and Purveyor of Algarve, Guarda and Viseu, where he died. He married (in Mondim) D. Maria Proença, daughter of Gonçallo do Valle, Fidalgo of the King's Household, and his wife D. Maria Proença Botelho

13 Manoel˙ Botelho de Abreu

13 Francisco˙ Cardoso de Abreu, Vicar of Santa Maria of Varzea de Gois

13 Gaspar de Abreu, whose children were stabbed to death while they were sleeping in bed on January 10, 1625, in revenge for his having attacked an eminent person of the Village of Fornos with a bull's horn

13 D. Maria˙, a nun in Pinhel

N13 MANOEL˙ BOTELHO DE ABREU, son of Lopo de Abreu N12, was a *Fidalgo* of the King's Household, succeeded to his parents' house and the entail of Anunciada and Juncais. He married D. Julliana Cabral de Mello, daughter of Francisco˙ Cabral de Távora and his wife D. Maria˙ do Campo e Sampaio˙. The latter couple lived in Trancoso and owned the house of Minhocal, which they bestowed in dowry upon their daughter. According to information provided by the said D. Maria˙ do Campo, she inherited from her father these estates, which have remained in the house of Fornos. Francisco˙ Cabral was the son of Domingos˙ Cabral [NFP Melo §72 N14][i]

14 Francisco˙ de Abreu Castello Branco

14 Luis de Abreu Castello Branco, who died young

---

[i] In NFP Melo §72 N14, Juliana Cabral's husband is called Manoel Botelho de Abreu *Castello Branco*, and her mother's name is Maria *de Campos de* Sampaio. (T. N.)

N14 FRANCISCO˙ DE ABREU CASTELLO BRANCO˙, son of Manoel˙ Botelho de Abreu N13, was a *Fidalgo* of the King's Household and succeeded to his father's house. In the charter by which he was appointed the Captain General of the Village of Fornos, it was also stated that his powers extended to the villages of Figueiró da Granja and Matança. He was the first to hold this office, but did not have successors for it, so these villages were separated, Fornos being vested in the *Infante* of Portugal. Francisco de Abreu Castello Branco married twice; his first marriage (in 1653) was to D. Maria˙ de Sampaio˙ Pereira˙, from the village of Assumar, for which union he had to obtain a dispensation due to the kinship between him and his bride. By his wife's dowry he received the manor of Torgal in Armamar, and other estates. D. Maria˙ de Sampaio˙ Pereira˙ was the daughter of Manoel˙ Rabello Teixeira˙ and his wife D. Marianna Pereira˙ de Sampaio˙, daughter of Simão Saraiva de Sampaio˙ and his wife D. Catarina˙ Coelho of Cáceres [NFP Coutinho §98 N10], though in that chapter he is not mentioned as being her father (sic)[i]. Manoel˙ Rabello Teixeira˙ was the son of Gaspar Rabello Teixeira˙, from the house of Poço de Lamego [see Carvalho §15 N11][ii] and his wife Marta de Gouvea

> 15 João de Abreu Castello Branco, who succeeded to his father's house, was the Captain General of Penela and married D. Maria˙ Luisa de Lemos, sp. He enfeoffed the estates of São Francisco (with their seat in the manor of the same name, near Penela) in the successors of the house of Fornos
>
> 15 Francisco Cabral de Abreu
>
> 15 Manoel˙ de Sampaio˙ Cardoso, who died young sp
>
> 15 D. Luisa, a nun in Santa Clara

Francisco de Abreu's second wife was D. Marianna da Costa Pacheco, sp

N15 FRANCISCO˙ CABRAL DE ABREU CASTELLO BRANCO˙, son of Francisco˙ de Abreu Castello Branco˙ N14 and his first wife, succeeded to his father's house and to the estates enfeoffed by his brother in São Francisco of Penela. In 1689 he married D. Anna Mendes de Andrade of Goes, daughter and heiress of Manoel˙ Bayão de Andrade (who after his wife's decease entered upon a religious life and became the vicar of the parish of Goes) and his wife D. Maria˙ Feyo Mansa, daughter of Fulgencio Dias Manso de Magalhães, a distinguished person of Lousão and Goes, and his wife D. Catarina˙ Feya, a descendant of the Chief Alcaides of Sortelha Soares, lords of the entail of Monte Redondo. Manoel˙ Bayão was the son of another Manoel˙ Bayão, Captain General of Goes and a descendant of the Baiões

---

[i] Contrary to what is stated here, in NFP Coutinho §98 N9 and N10, Maria de Sampaio Pereira is indeed said to be the the daughter of Manoel˙ Rabello Teixeira˙ and his wife D. Marianna Pereira˙ de Sampaio˙, and the maternal granddaughter of Simão Saraiva de Sampaio˙ and his wife Catarina Coelho. (T. N.)

[ii] This reference is not Gaio's NFP Carvalho, but a chronicle about the Carvalho family written by António Peixoto de Queirós. (T. N.)

Velleses of Lousão and Goes, and his wife D, Maria˙ Mendes Correa˙ Pereira˙, daughter of Antonio˙ Mendes, Captain General of Gouvea

> 16 Jose Antonio˙ de Abreu
>
> 16 Francisco˙ Cabral, sp
>
> 16 D. (...), in whose will it is stated that she married Francisco˙ da Costa Mombaça and had issueless children

N16 JOSE ANTONIO˙ DE ABREU, son of Francisco˙ Cabral de Abreu N15, succeeded to his father's house, married (in 1774 in the village of Marim, territory of Mesãofrio) D. Catarina˙ Matilde Sotomayor Ledesma, e Medeiros, daughter of Miguel Guedes de Figueiredo˙ Sotomayor, from the village of Mesãofrio, and his wife D. Maria de Carvalho Lousada of the house of Barreiro in Vila Marim, daughter of Domingos Medeiros Pinto, of the house of Mechinhos in Vila Marim, and his wife D. Isabel da Rocha Coutinho, of the house of Outeiro de Cima, also in Vila Marim

> 17 D. Magdalena Thomasia, who married her relative João de Mello Figueiredo˙, sp
>
> 17 D. Jose de Nossa Senhora da Porta, a monk of the Order of the Holy Cross of Coimbra, born in 1725
>
> 17 Francisco˙ de Abreu Castello Branco
>
> 17 Antonio˙ de Abreu, who died as a novice of the Order of the Holy Cross of Coimbra
>
> 17 Fray João de Mello, a Bernardine monk, *b*. 1732
>
> 17 Caetano de Abreu Castello Branco˙, *b*. 1734, Prior of São João da Manta, in Covilhã
>
> 17 Fray Bernardo, a Bernardine monk
>
> 17 Alexandre de Mello de Abreu, Prior of Figueiró dos Vinhos, *b*. 1739
>
> 17 D. Bernarda Narcisa Benevenuta de Abreu Saraiva, who married (in Covilhã) Luis de Macedo Feyo de Castello Branco˙

LORDS OF THE ENTAILS OF ANUNCIADA AND JUNCAES AND THE ENTAILS OF SÃO FRANCISCO OF PENELA

N17 FRANCISCO˙ DE ABREU CASTELLO BRANCO˙, son of Jose Antonio˙ de Abreu N16, was born in 1728, succeeded to his father's house of Fornos de Algrodes and to the entails of Anunciada, Juncaes and São Francisco of Penela. He was also the lord of the house of Barrreiro in Vila Marim, and the owner of the taxes on the yokes of oxen in Pinheiro and Fragoselas near Viseu. He married his relative D. Maria Delfina Osorio Sarmento˙ de Vasconcellos, daughter of Manoel˙ Ozorio do Amaral (lord of the house of Almeida and the entail of Espirito Santo, Captain General of Azurara da Beira) and his second wife and relative D. Anna Isabel Sarmento˙ de Vasconcellos, e Castro, daughter of Jose

Sarmento de Vasconcellos of Algoso (Fidalgo of the King's Household and Captain General of Moimenta da Beira) and his wife D. Maria Josefa de Carvalho˙ e Castro, of Paradinha, daughter and heiress of João de Andrade de Carvalho, Knight of the Order of Christ, and his wife D. Maria˙ Luisa da Silva, e Castro, of Pinhel

   18 João de Abreu Castello Branco˙
   18 D. Bernarda
   18 Pedro Lopes de Abreu
   18 D. Auta

<h2 style="text-align:center">§85</h2>

MINHOCAL

N11 D. ELENA CARDOSO, daughter of the second wife of Pedro Lopes de Abreu §83 N10, married (1) Affonço Gonçalves˙ or Diogo Gonçalves˙, a university graduate from Celorico de Basto, lord of an entail which previously was part of Minhocal

   12 Dr. Jose de Abreu, Dean of Lisbon
   12 Antonio˙.de Abreu, who went to India
   12 Francisco˙ Cardoso, who went to India
   12 Pedro de Abreu Castello Branco˙, lord of the house of Minhocal,
     who married D (...), daughter of Manoel˙ Dias Maldonado

Elena Cardoso married as her second husband Appellate Judge Fernão Gil, and had

   12 João Gil de Abreu
    12 Luis de Abreu, who married (in Celorico) Catarina˙ de Pina, daugh-
     ter of Rodrigo Mendes of Cerolico de Basto and his wife D. Vio-
     lante de Pina of Guarda, and had
     13 Manoel˙ de Abreu, who married (...) and had
      14 Vallerio de Abreu

N12 JOÃO GIL DE ABREU, son of D. Elena Cardoso N11 and her second husband, was a Judge of the Appeal Court in Lisbon, where he died. He married Maria˙ Cabral

   13 D. Isabel, a nun in Viana
   13 D (...), ditto
   13 Gonçallo de Abreu, a Jesuit
   13 Dr. Antonio˙ Cabral Castello Branco˙, who lived in Celorico

<h2 style="text-align:center">§86</h2>

N11 D. ANNA CARDOSO DE ABREU, daughter of Pedro Lopes de Abreu §83 N10 and his second wife, married Pedro de Almeida of Alenquer

12 Dr. Jorge de Almeida, Abbot of Ribafeita in Viseu §134

12 D. Anna de Almeida

12 D. Isabel Cardoso de Abreu, wife of Gaspar de Gouvea Cardoso, son of Nuno de Gouvea [with issue in NFP Gouvea §73 N10]. Another author states that she was the wife of Simão Rodrigues˙ de Abreu, with issue [as in §94 N11]. She probably married twice

12 D. Mecia de Almeida Castello Branco˙, who married Manoel˙ Antunes, a university graduate

12 D. Elena Cardoso Castello Branco˙

N12 D. MECIA DE ALMEIDA, daughter of D. Anna Cardoso de Abreu N11, married Manoel˙ Antunes de Seixas

13 Father Manoel˙ de Almeida, a Jesuit who visited the Court of Prester John and Ethiopia, where he preached to the Barbarians

13 Anna Cardoso de Abreu, who married Antonio˙ Rodrigues˙ Loureiro, son of Francisco˙ de Almeida and his wife D. Joanna Lourenço [NFP Loureiro §29 N8][i]

13 Father Jorge de Almeida, a Jesuit who died in India

13 Pedro de Almeida Castello˙ Branco˙

13 D. Luisa de Castello Branco §135

N13 PEDRO DE ALMEIDA CASTELLO BRANCO, son of D. Mecia de Almeida N12, married Maria˙ de Figueiredo˙, daughter of Pedro Rabello, a university graduate

14 Francisco˙ de Almeida, a university graduate and canon in the See of Viseu

14 D. Maria˙ de Figueiredo˙, who married Bernardo Pereira˙, a Knight of the Order of Christ, from Cerolico, and had

15 D. Umbelina de Castello Branco˙, who married Paullo de Vasconcellos˙, a Knight of the Order of Christ, with issue

14 D. Mecia de Castello Branco, who married Paullo Cabral, sp. She later married Fernando de Almeida de Vasconcellos˙, son of Manoel˙ Pereira˙ de Vasconcellos˙, lord of Mosamades, and D. Elena de Barros, in the chapter of [sic][ii]

Prester John was a legendary Christian sovereign in the Middle Ages who was said to rule over an Eastern kingdom, surrounded by Pagan and Muslim countries. Many European explorers tried to find his kingdom in the hope of establishing commercial and military alliances with him. Eventually his name was used in a general and imprecise way to refer to Christian kings ruling over Eastern and African countries.

---

[i] In NFP Loureiro §29 N8, Francisco˙ de Almeida's wife is called Joanna *Loureiro*, and not Joanna Lourenço. (T. N.)

[ii] Though in this passage the name of the cross-referenced chapter is omitted, in NFP Almeida §20 N15 there is mention of a Manuel˙ Pereira˙ *de Almeida* (instead of Manuel Pereira de Vasconcellos), who married Elena de Barros and had by her several children who were given the surname Vasconcellos. Yet none of them is given the name Fernando˙ de Almeida de Vasconcellos; one of the children is called *Fernão* de Almeida, who is said to have married Maria de Almeida (and not Mecia de Castello Branco˙), and is said to have had no issue by her. (T. N.)

§87

N11 D. FRANCISCA˙ LOPES DE CASTELLO BRANCO[i], daughter of Pedro Lopes de Abreu §83 N10 and his second wife. She married Cristovão de Unhão of Torrezelo, with whom she lived in Santa Marinha, near Ceia
> 12 João de Abreu de Castello Branco
> 12 D. Felipa de Carvalho˙ Castello Branco
> 12 D. Maria˙ de Unhão Castello Branco

N12 JOÃO DE ABREU CASTELLO BRANCO, son of D. Francisca˙ Lopes Castello Branco N11, married D. Ignes de Carvalho, daughter of Gomes de Carvalho Maldonado and D. Branca Ferrão
> 13 Cristovão de Abreu Castello Branco, a representative of the Royal Treasury in Lisbon

§88

N11 JORGE DE ABREU CASTELLO BRANCO˙, son of Pedro Lopes de Abreu §83 N10 and his first wife, married D. Felipa Varella, daughter of Pedro Rodrigues˙ Ferreira. He and his wife enfeoffed the Chapel of the Holy Spirit in the See of Viseu, with daily masses
> 12 Pedro de Abreu, who went to India, sp
> 12 Lopo de Abreu, a Jesuit
> 12 D. Elena Ferreira˙, who married (in Vila Nova da Rainha) Antonio˙ Ferreira˙, sp
> 12 D. Brites de Abreu, a nun in the convent of Madre de Deus in Lisbon
> 12 D. Anna de Abreu, below
> 12 B. Jorge de Abreu, who enfeoffed the Chapel of the Holy Spirit in his nephew Manoel˙ de Abreu N(...) below (this version seems to be more probable than the one by which Manoel's lands were inherited from his father)

N12 D. ANNA DE ABREU, daughter of Jorge de Abreu N11, succeeded to her father's house, married her relative Luis Loureiro de Figueiredo, a Knight-*Fidalgo*, lord of the entail of Possessão da Boa Aldea, son of Luis Annes Loureiro and his wife D. Catarina˙ de Figueiredo˙ [with issue in NFP Loureiro §3 N7, though in that source Luis Loureiro is not said to have the parents we mention here, being instead considered the son of Antonio˙ Loureiro and his wife Antonia˙ de Gouvea]

For details about Portuguese ranks of nobility, see p. v

---

[i] In §83 N10 Sub11, this lady is called Francisca˙ Lopes *Cardoso*. (T. N.)

N11 FRANCISCO˙ LOPES DE ABREU, bastard son of Pedro Lopes de Abreu §83 N10. According to some he was a legitimate son, although the most common opinion is that he was a bastard, which is stated by his grandnephew Manoel Botelho de Abreu in his chronicle about the Castelo Branco family, in which it is said that Pedro Lopes de Abreu had Francisco Lopes de Abreu when he was a widower. Francisco Lopes de Abreu married Agueda de Figueiredo˙, daughter of Luis Annes Loureiro (a *Fidalgo* of the King's Household, lord of Possessão da Boa Aldea) and his wife Catarina˙, or Anna de Figueiredo˙ [NFP Loureiro §2 N5][i]

> 12 Antonio˙ Lopes de Castello Branco, a Canon in Viseu, abbot of Santa Maria de Sergueiros and São Cipriano
> 12 Luis de Abreu de Figueiredo˙
> 12 Pedro Lopes de Abreu §90
> 12 Miguel de Figueiredo˙ §93
> 12 João de Figueiredo˙, a Canon in Viseu, Abbot of Sequeiros, who had an illicit relationship with Maria˙ Teixeira˙, a single woman, who afterwards got married; he had
>> 13 Agueda de Figueiredo˙, who married Francisco˙ Mendes, son of Pedro Mendes, lord of the estates of Silvares
> 12 Nicolao de Figueiredo˙, who married Joanna de Almeida, and had
>> 13 Agueda de Figueiredo˙, who married Jorge Tenreiro, son of Francisco˙ Vieira, a university graduate
>> 13 Francisco˙ Lopes, a clergyman
>> 13 João de Figueiredo˙, a Canon in Viseu
> 12 D. Anna de Figueiredo˙, who married Nuno Rabello, son of Gonçallo Rabello [with issue in NFP Rebelo §47 N12]

N12 LUIS DE ABREU DE FIGUEIREDO, son of Francisco˙ Lopes de Abreu N11, owned the estates of Lagoa and Carvalhal and others inherited from his father. He married (in Espinhal, in the municipality of Penela) D. Isabel Queimada, a descendant of the Queimados of this Kingdom, great granddaughter of Vasco Queimado, the Elder, of Setúbal, a very distinguished nobleman in the time of *Infante* Peter, to whom he was the first Chief Guard

Infante Peter (1392-1449), son of King John I of Portugal and Queen Philippa of Lancaster

---

[i] In NFP Loureiro §2 N5, Agueda de Figueiredo˙ is called Agueda de Figueiredo *de Loureiro*. Her husband is called Francisco˙ Lopes de *Castello Branco*˙ (and not Francisco Lopes de Abreu) and her mother's name is given as Catarina˙ de Figueiredo. (T. N.)

13 Francisco˙ de Abreu, a university graduate, who lived in Viseu and owned Lagoa and the estates enfeoffed by Antonio˙ Gomes Coimbra. In 1594 he made a justification of his nobility based on his connections with the families of Abreu, Loureiro, Castello Branco and Figueiredo

13 Fray Antonio˙, a monk of the Third Order of St. Francis of Assisi

13 Luis de Abreu, who married in Vousela, with issue

13 Manoel˙ de Abreu, who died at the battle of Alcazarquivir

13 Maria˙ de Figueiredo˙, who married (in Redinha) Fernão Lopes, a very wealthy scholar

In the battle of Alcazarquivir in Morocco (August 4ᵗʰ, 1578) a Portuguese army of nearly 15.000 men led by King Sebastian was completely routed by the Moors and the King himself was killed (see also box on p. 93)

§90

N12 PEDRO LOPES DE ABREU, son of Francisco˙ Lopes de Abreu §89 N11. Like his father's brother, he was General Collector of Ransom Funds in the city of Viseu[i]. He was a Knight of the Order of Santiago, and married (in Oliveira do Hospital) Paulla de Faria Cabral, daughter of Vasco de Faria and his wife Isabel Velloso Cabral, granddaughter of Fernão Cabral, lord of Belmonte. Vasco de Faria˙ was a *Fidalgo* of the King's Household, and served in Africa and Italy, sustaining his own troops

13 Francisco˙ de Figueiredo˙ Castello Branco

13 Pedro de Abreu Castello Branco §91

13 Antonio˙ de Abreu Castello Branco §92

13 Manoel˙ de Abreu, sp

N13 FRANCISCO˙ DE FIGUEIREDO˙ CASTELLO BRANCO, son of Pedro Lopes de Abreu N12, known as "O Racha", was a Fidalgo of the King's Household and General Trial Judge in the estates of the Duke of Aveiro, He married twice, the first time to D. Maria˙ de Almeida, daughter of Diogo Coelho de Almeida

14 D. Maria˙ de Abreu Castello Branco, who married Roque de Mello Francisco de Figueiredo married as his second wife D. Francisca˙ de Figueiredo˙ Castello Branco, daughter of João, or Jeronimo Loureiro de Castello Branco and his wife D. Maria˙ Cardoso

14 Francisco˙ de Figueiredo˙

N14 FRANCISCO˙ DE FIGUEIREDO, son of Francisco˙ de Figueiredo˙ N13, called "o Moço" (the Younger) in order to distinguish him from his father. He owned the estate of Outeiro, succeeded to the entail of Alvaro Vaz de Castello

---

[i] In the original text it is said that this Pedro Lopes de Abreu held this office *like his father*. Yet the only member of this family who is said to have been a General Collector of Ransom Funds was his father's brother, Lopo de Abreu Castello Branco §83 N11, so we have changed this passage on the assumption that the author committed a mistake. (T. N.)

Branco, and of João or Jeronimo Loureiro, his mother's grandfathers, and also owned the estate of Escouros. He was a General Trial Judge of the Infante's estates, and married D. Anna de Gouvea, daughter of Domingos˙ de Figueiredo˙, known as "O Rosa", and his wife D. Maria Coelho

> 15 Manoel de Abreu Castello Branco

N15 MANOEL˙ DE ABREU CASTELLO BRANCO, son of Francisco˙ de Figueiredo˙ Castello Branco N14, inherited his parents' house, married D. Isabel Rabello, daughter of Nuno Leitão Pereira˙ and D. Suzana Soeiro de Albergaria, paternal granddaughter of Dr. Andre Leitão de Sequeira˙ and D. Joanna Rabello, and maternal granddaughter of Manoel˙ Soeiro de Albergaria and his wife Maria Nunes de Carvalho˙

> 16 Manoel˙ de Abreu Castello Branco

LORDS OF THE ENTAILS OF OUTEIRO AND LADARIO

N16 MANOEL˙ DE ABREU CASTELLO BRANCO, son of Manoel˙ de Abreu N15, was the lord of the entail of Outeiro, and married D. Leonor de Macedo, e Mendonça, daughter and heiress of Manoel˙ Nunes de Carvalho, lord of the entail of Ladario, and his wife D. Marcellina de Mendonça [NFP Macedo §50 N4]

> 17 Sebastião de Abreu Castello Branco

N17 SEBASTIÃO DE ABREU CASTELLO BRANCO, son of Manoel˙ de Abreu N16 [see NFP Pedigree Charts, Tome 4, *ff.* 91], inherited his father's house and married his cousin D. Maria Theresa de Gusmão, daughter of Pedro de Chaves, e Gusmão, lord of the honor of Cergas, Commendatory of São Martinho de Amoreira, son of D. Diogo de Chaves, e Gusmão, Commendatory of Calatrava, and D. Ignes de Zuniga [NFP Macedo §26 N5][i]

> 18 Manoel˙ de Abreu Castello Branco

N18 MANOEL˙ DE ABREU CASTELLO BRANCO, son of Sebastião˙ de Abreu N17, was the lord of the entail of Outeiro and Ladario, married D. Joanna de Figueiredo˙ Pimentel, daughter of Carlos Correa˙ Pimentel, a Knight of the Order of Christ in Sanhoane and Commendatory of Penaguião

> 19 Francisco˙ de Abreu Castello Branco, Fidalgo of the King's Household

---

[i] In NFP Macedo §26 N5, Sebastião de Abreu Castello Branco's wife is called Maria˙ *Zuniga e* Gusmão. (T. N.)

§91

N13 PEDRO DE ABREU CASTELLO BRANCO˙, son of Pedro Lopes de Abreu §90 N12, married D. Anna Cardoso, daughter of Antonio Cardoso and his wife Catarina˙ Cardoso, of Viseu

    14 Manoel˙ de Abreu Castello Branco

    14 Pedro de Abreu Castello Branco

    14 Roque de Abreu

He married (in Besteiros) as his second wife D. Isabel de Macedo or D. Isabel de Figueiredo˙ de Barros, daughter and heiress of Simão de Figueiredo˙, lord of the house of Carvalhiços near Viseu, and Brites da Fonseca˙, daughter of Francisco˙ da Fonseca˙

    14 D. Maria˙ Castello Branco, who married Antonio˙ de Gouvea de Vasconcellos, son of Francisco˙ da Gouvea de Vasconcellos and his second wife D. Maria˙ de Figueiredo˙ [with issue in NFP Gouveia §24 N15]

§92

LORDS OF THE HOUSE OF CHARNECA

N13 ANTONIO˙ DE ABREU CASTELLO BRANCO, son of Pedro Lopes de Abreu §90 N12, married (in Viseu) D. Joanna de Barros, daughter of Antonio˙ de Figueiredo˙ and his wife Maria de Barros [NFP Figueiredo §19 N11]

    14 Duarte de Abreu

    14 Jorge de Abreu, who was, together with his sisters, advowee of the Church of Silgueiros, a title which they received as descendants of João Annes Loureiro, son of Daniel Loureiro, but to which they renounced in favor of Simão de Barros. He married D. Isabel Ximenes, a descendant of the original family of Ximenes, and had

        15 Antonio˙ de Abreu, sp

        15 Francisco˙ de Figueiredo˙, who died in the War of Acclamation, sp

        15 D. Elena de Figueiredo˙, wife of Dr. Felipe da Silva Pereira˙, with issue

    14 D. Joanna

    14 D. Maria˙, unmarried

    14 (...), wife of Manoel˙ Saraiva, in Penalva

    14 D. Elena de Abreu, wife of Diogo de Lemos

    14 D. Paulla de Faria, who married (in Penelva) (...), and had

        15 Pedro de Albuquerque

The War of Acclamation (upon the acclamation of King John IV of Portugal) was fought between Portugal and Spain and lasted from 1640 to 1668. Also known as the War of Restoration, it began when a revolution in Portugal ended the Iberian Union under the rule of King Philip IV of Spain (Philip III of Portugal), and gave the Portuguese throne to the Duke of Bragança (see also box on p. 93)

N14 DUARTE DE ABREU CASTELLO BRANCO, son of Antonio˙ de Abreu N13, was the lord of the entail and manor of Charneca in the territory of Lisbon, and married Brites Teixeira˙

>>15 Miguel de Abreu Castello Branco
>>15 Fray Bartolomeu, a Provincial of the *Gracianos*[i]
>>15 Lopo de Abreu, who married D. Isabel de Vasconcellos and had
>>>16 Duarte da Cunha de Abreu
>>15 D. Isabel de Abreu, wife of Fernão Figueira de Azevedo˙, lord of the manor of São Gemil and the entail of Grajal [with issue in §127]

N15 MIGUEL DE ABREU CASTELLO BRANCO, son of Duarte de Abreu (Castello Branco) N14, succeeded to the house of Charneca, where he lived. He married Antonia Leitão, daughter of Francisco˙ Lopes Leitão and his wife Guiomar Carvalhosa

>>16 Diogo de Abreu
>>16 Fray Lopo de Abreu, a Carmelite monk
>>16 Fray Luis, a Trinitarian monk

N16 DIOGO DE ABREU CASTELLO BRANCO, son of Miguel de Abreu (Castello Branco) N15, succeeded to the house of Charneca, married D. Guiomar Borges de Mesauita, daughter of Fernão Borges de Castro and his wife D. Isabel do Rego, daughter of Feleciano do Rego, lord of the entails of Calvana and Metela

>>17 Antonio˙ de Abreu Castello Branco

N17 ANTONIO˙ DE ABREU CASTELLO BRANCO, son of Diogo de Abreu (Castello Branco) N16, was the lord of the house of Charneca, married D. Maria˙ Antonia˙ Castello Branco, daughter of Appellate Judge Sebastião de Abreu Serrão and his wife D. Maria˙ Castello Branco, paternal granddaughter of Manoel˙ Soares de Abreu and his wife and cousin D. Isabel Serrão, daughter of Diogo Serrão de Abreu and D. Maria˙ de Castello Branco, daughter of Bartolomeu Sanches Brariel Saboiano[ii] and his wife Branca de Castello Branco, daughter of Luis de Castello Branco

>>18 D. Maria˙ de Castello Branco do Rego

---

[i] Name of a religious order in Portugal. (T. N.)

[ii] As the omission of commas in the original text is more a rule than an exception, it is not clear if "Saboiano" is part of this gentleman's name (Bartolomeu Sanches Brariel Saboiano) or if the author meant he was from Savoy, France: Bartolomeu Sanches Brariel, Saboiano (Savoyan). We have opted for the first version. (T. N.)

N18 D. MARIA˙ DE CASTELLO BRANCO DO REGO, daughter of Antonio˙ de Abreu N17, succeeded to her father's house and married Pedro Vaz Soares, Fidalgo of the King's Household, owner of the taxes on the yokes of oxen in Penelva and the harvests in Sulfar, Commendatory of Santa Maria de Monção and son of João Soares Rabello

> 19 Antonio˙ de Abreu Rego, Fidalgo of the King's Household, lord of the entail of Charneca, etc.
>
> 19 Francisco˙ Soares de Macedo, Monsignor of the Patriarchal See in Lisbon

§93

N12 MIGUEL DE FIGUEIREDO˙, son of Francisco˙ Lopes de Abreu §89 N11, was a Fidalgo of the King's Household and married Mecia Pinto, daughter of Lopo Pinto, and granddaughter of Alvaro Pinto, Bailiff of Leça [NFP Pinto §239 N1 and §343 N2]

> 13 Francisco˙ Pinto, who went to India
>
> 13 Lopo Pinto, who went to India
>
> 13 Manoel˙ Pinto, who lived in Brazil
>
> 13 D. Isabel Pinto

N13 D. ISABEL PINTO, daughter of Miguel de Figueiredo˙ N12, was married twice, the first time to Antonio˙ Salgado, son of Pedro Salgado, a university graduate, and his wife Maria˙ de Beça of Tentugal

> 14 Jose Pinto, grandson of Miguel de Figueiredo˙ N12 and his wife, married D. Lourença da Fonseca˙ and had
>
> > 15 Jose Pinto, who married D. Maria˙ de Tavora and had
> >
> > > 16 Jose Pinto de Abreu, who married D. Maria˙ Sanches and had
> > >
> > > > 17 Manoel˙ Munhos de Abreu, who married D. Verissima de Figueiredo˙ and had
> > > >
> > > > > 18 D. Francisca˙ Caetana, who married Francisco˙ Barbosa Canaes [NFP Amado §49 N15][i]

D. Isabel Pinto married as her second husband Jeronimo de Mendanha or Mendonça Tavares of Tavarede, son of Antonia˙ de Mendanha and her husband Thome Dias de Almeida [NFP Mendanha §74 N5]

§94

N10 FRANCISCO˙ LOPES DE ABREU, son of Lopo Rodrigues˙ de Abreu §83 N9, married D. (...)

> 11 Simão Rodrigues˙ de Abreu

---

[i] In NFP Amado §49 N15, Francisco˙ Barbosa Canaes's wife is called Francisca˙ Caetana *do Rosario de Figueiredo˙ Castello Branco*. (T. N.)

N11 SIMÃO RODRIGUES˙ DE ABREU, son of Francisco˙ Lopes de Abreu N10, lived in Alenquer and was married twice, the second time to his relative Isabel Cardoso de Abreu, daughter of Pedro de Almeida and his wife Anna Cardoso de Abreu [§86 N11]
      12 João Rodrigues˙ de Abreu

N12 JOÃO RODRIGUES˙ DE ABREU, son of Simão Rodrigues˙ de Abreu N11, married Valeria Ramos de Sá
        13 Simão Rodrigues˙ de Abreu
        13 Brother Paullo, a Trinitarian monk

N13 SIMÃO RODRIGUES˙ DE ABREU, son of João Rodrigues˙ de Abreu N12, lived in Alenquer, where he married Joanna Maria˙ Pereira˙ da Silva, daughter of Francisco˙ Pereira˙ da Mota, of Torres Vedras, and Leonor da Silva
      14 Francisco˙ de Abreu

N14 FRANCISCO˙ DE ABREU PEREIRA˙ DE FIGUEIREDO˙, son of Simão Rodrigues˙ de Abreu N13, was a Fidalgo of the King's Household, Captain of the Militia and Judge of the Royal Rights of the Village of Azambuja. He married D. Maria˙ de Gusmão, of Lisbon, daughter of Gomes Dias da Costa, and his first wife D. Brites Valasques de Gusmão
        15 Bernardo Pereira˙ de Gusmão
        15 João de Gusmão Pereira˙, Captain of the Militia in the parish of
            Torres Vedras
        15 D. Joanna, a nun in Alenquer

N15 BERNARDO PEREIRA˙ DE GUSMÃO, son of Francisco˙ de Abreu N14, was a Criminal Judge in Lisbon, and a General Trial Judge of Minas, with office in Bahia (Brazil) in 1716, and married (...)
      16 Raymundo Jose de Gusmão

N16 RAYMUNDO JOSE DE GUSMÃO, son of Bernardo Pereira˙ de Gusmão N15. On Abril 9, 1749, he was made a Fidalgo of the King's Household for the services rendered by his uncle and father-in-law. He married his cousin D. Theresa Maria˙ Leonor de Vasconcellos, e Lugo, daughter and heiress of João de Seixas de Vasconcellos (numerary Chamber Valet and Knight of the Order of Christ) and his wife D. Maria Leonor de Vasconcellos

For details about Portuguese ranks of nobility, see p. v

§95

N9 DIOGO DE ABREU, son of Gonçallo Rodrigues de Abreu §83 N8, married D. Isabel Mendes de Vasconcellos, daughter of Joanne Mendes de Vasconcellos and his wife D. Maria˙ Goes [NFP Vasconcelos §60 N14]

  10 Alvaro de Abreu
  10 Luis de Abreu
  10 Ruy de Abreu §96

N10 ALVARO DIAS DE ABREU, son of Diogo de Abreu N9, succeeded to his father's entail in Elvas. He married D. Maria˙ Vaz˙ da Silva, daughter of João da Silva

  11 Manoel˙ de Abreu

Amado states that Alvaro Dias de Abreu married as his second wife D. Luisa de Abreu

N11 MANOEL˙ DE ABREU, son of Alvaro Dias de Abreu N10, succeeded to his father's entail and house. He lived in Elvas around 1550, and was married twice, the first time to D. Catarina˙ Ponte, daughter of Ruy Cordeiro, who was buried near the cross of Saint Dominic's Church in Elvas

  12 D. Isabel de Abreu

He married as his second wife D. Ignes Lobão, with whom he lived in Badajoz around 1555

N12 D. ISABEL DE ABREU, daughter of Manoel˙ de Abreu N11 and his first wife, married D. Miguel da Silva [NFP Silva][i]

§96

N10 RUY DE ABREU, son of Diogo de Abreu §95 N9, married D. Florença da Ponte

  11 Mem Rodrigues˙ de Abreu, e Vasconcellos
  11 Sebastião de Abreu §97
  11 D. Leonor de Abreu §98
  11 Diogo de Abreu

N11 MEM RODRIGUES˙ DE ABREU DE VASCONCELLOS[ii], son of Ruy de Abreu N10, went to India when he was 25 years old. He married D. Felipa de Mascarenhas, daughter of Sancho Sanches da Gama and his wife D. Isabel da Silva

---

[i] We have not found in the chapter of Silva any cross-reference showing these names, though in NFP Silva §36 N12 it is said that a Miguel da Silva was the husband of Izabel *Pessanha* (and not Izabel de Abreu), daughter of *Alvaro Pessanha de Abreu* (and not Manoel de Abreu). (T. N.)

[ii] As can be illustrated by this case, it is relatively common in this work to have variations (sometimes slight, sometimes not so small) in the name of the same person. As can be seen here, Mem Rodrigues de Abreu *de* Vasconcellos N11 was called a few lines above (N10 Sub11) Mem Rodrigues de Abreu, *e* Vasconcellos. (T. N.)

12 Ruy de Abreu, e Vasconcellos

12 Garcia˙ Sanches, who married D. Violante Pegado, sp

12 Florença de Mascarenhas, wife of Mem Rodrigues˙ de Vasconcellos

12 Guiomar, a nun in the convent of Santa Clara in Elvas

N12 RUY DE ABREU E VASCONCELLOS, son of Mem Rodrigues˙ de Abreu (de Vasconcellos) N11, married (in Portel) D. Maria˙ Barbosa, daughter of Lourenço Paes and D. Catarina˙ Mendes Barbosa

        13 Francisco˙ de Abreu, who married D. Marianna de Brito, daughter of Francisco˙ Mendes de Azevedo˙, sp

        13 D. Catarina˙ de Abreu, who was married twice, the first time to Martim Affonso˙ de Lucena, sp, and the second time to Damião de Castro, of Castelo de Vide

        13 Antonio˙ de Abreu, a notary public in Elvas, who married sp

§97

N11 SEBASTIÃO DE ABREU, son of Ruy de Abreu §96 N10, married Ignes Pereira˙, daughter of Antonio˙ Pereira˙ of Elvas and his wife Maria˙ Nunes

        12 Ruy de Abreu, who married (in Lisbon) D. Theresa de Seixas, sp

        12 Mem Rodrigues˙ de Abreu, who married, sp

        12 João Pereira˙ de Abreu

        12 Antonio˙ Pereira˙, who died as a student

        12 Gonçallo Rodrigues˙, a Jesuit and later a Carmelite monk

        12 D. Florença, a nun in Elvas

        12 D. Ignes, *ditto*

N12 JOÃO PEREIRA˙ DE ABREU, son of Sebastião de Abreu N11, married as his first wife Brites Coelho, sp, and as his second wife Elena do Couto, daughter of Bento Sardinha and Ignes do Couto of Elvas

        13 Sebastião de Abreu Pereira˙, who married (in Lisbon) D. Marianna de Gusmão, sp

        13 D. Brites, wife of Estevão Pegado of Valadares

§98

N11 D. LEONOR DE ABREU, daughter of Ruy de Abreu §96 N10, married João Lourenço, son of (...) and his wife Isabel Martins˙ Caçada

        12 Manoel˙ de Abreu

N12 MANOEL˙ DE ABREU, son of D. Leonor de Abreu N11, married Brites Amado, daughter of Diogo Amado and his wife Ignes Varella
  13 Constança de Abreu

N13 CONSTANÇA DE ABREU, daughter of Manoel˙ de Abreu N12, married Diogo da Fonseca˙, son of Bernardo da Fonseca˙, of Portalegre, and his wife Isabel Juzarte
  14 D. Luiza de Abreu

N14 D. LUIZA DE ABREU, daughter of Constança de Abreu N13, married (in Vila Viçosa) Estevão Mendes da Silveira, Cavalry Captain and Commander of the Cavalry of Alentejo, and had issue

§99

N2 GOMES GONÇALVES˙ DE ABREU, considered by some the son of Lourenço Gomes de Abreu and D. Theresa Correa˙ [§2 N1], which opinion we uphold. Others state that he was the son of Gonçallo˙ Rodrigues˙ de Abreu and his wife D. Mecia Rodrigues˙ [§3 N5], with which we disagree, for it is not natural that two sons should have the same name.[i] He was a contemporary of King Dinis and King Afonso IV, and Alcaide General of Melgaço, and married D. Maria˙ Soares Tangil

King Dinis r. 1279–1325
King Afonso IV r. 1325–1357

  3 Vasco Gomes de Abreu §101
  3 João Gomes de Abreu, below
  3 Ruy Gomes de Abreu §100

N3 JOÃO GOMES DE ABREU, son of Gomes Gonçalves˙ de Abreu N2, lived in the time of King Peter I and King Ferdinand, who bestowed upon him the office of Chief Alcaide of Torres Vedras in 1369, and of Tomar in 1373, and also granted to him the royal rights of a quarter of the taxes on the fruit harvests, which had been obtained from the Crown by his father-in-law Estevão Visente, through an instrument dated January 19, 1417, in Sabugueiro, recorded in Book 2, *lf.* 84. He married (…), daughter of Estevão Visente

King Peter I r. 1357–1367
King Ferdinand r. 1367–1383

  4 Gonçalo Annes de Abreu

N4 GONÇALO ANNES DE ABREU, son of João Gomes de Abreu N3, was Chief Alcaide of Alter do Chão by donation of Constable D. Nuno Alvares Pereira. He was also by right and inheritance the lord of Castelo de Vide, Povoas and Meadas, and the lord of the royal lands of Coimbra and the lands of São Marcos and Armenta in Sacavem. He married D. Antonia˙ Falcão, daughter of Lourenço Annes Falcão and his wife Mor Gonçalves˙. In 1363 and 1365, King Peter I enfeoffed in this Gonçallo Annes de Abreu, in his parents-in-law Lourenço Annes Falcão and Mor Gonçalves˙ and in Nuno Fernandes˙, all nephews of the Bishop of Évora,

For Constable Nuno Alvares Pereira, see box on p. 9

their manors called Alvarandeo in the territory of Évora, these grants being confirmed by El Rey D. Ferdinand in 1367, as better informed in NFP Falcão Introduction. Gonçallo Annes de Abreu had

> 5 Gonçallo Annes de Abreu, who was the lord of the said lands, and married Lady Isabel, daughter of Mozem João Folcho and his wife Lady Charina de Estamberg, from which union the family of Falcão originates [NFP Falcão §1 N1]
>
> 5 D. Catarina· de Abreu, who according to some (which we do not agree with), was the wife of Monsignor João Falcão (...)

§100

N3 RUY GOMES DE ABREU, son of Gonçallo Gomes de Abreu §99 N2[i]; married (...) and lived in Arronches

> 4 Martim Rodrigues· de Abreu
>
> 4 Gonçallo Rodrigues· de Abreu, with issue in §83 N8, though we do not agree with this information[ii]

N4 MARTIM RODRIGUES· DE ABREU, son of Ruy Gomes de Abreu N3. King John I bestowed upon him the Royal Rights of Arronches. He married (...)

> 5 D. Maria· de Abreu

N5 D. MARIA· DE ABREU, daughter of Martim Rodrigues· de Abreu N4, married (in Elvas) Manoel· Pessanha

> 6 D. Senhorinha de Abreu, who married Henrique de Mello, son of João Mendes de Oliveira and his first wife D. Brites de Mello [with issue in NFP Melo §71 N11 Sub12][iii]

§101

N3 VASCO GOMES DE ABREU, son of Gomes Gonçalves· de Abreu §99 N2 (some say this Vasco Gomes de Abreu was the son of Gomes Lourenço de Abreu §64 N1, with which we disagree). Vasco Gomes de Abreu succeeded to his father's

King John I r. 1385–1433

---

[i] In §99 N2, Ruy Gomes de Abreu's father is called Gomes *Gonçalves* de Abreu, and not Gonçallo Gomes de Abreu. (T. N.)

[ii] In §83 N8, there is a Gonçallo Rodrigues· de Abreu N8, son of Nuno Gonçalves· de Abreu N7, who cannot be the same person mentioned here. (T. N.)

[iii] In NFP Melo §71 N11 Sub12, Senhorinha de Abreu's husband is called Henrique de Mello *de Oliveira*. (T. N.)

For Deuladeo Martins and these events, see box on the next page

house and married Deuladeo Martins, who defended the siege of Monção in the time of Henry II of Castile, by which reason and in memory of this feat the said town has her portrait in its coat of arms and flag [see *Corographia Portuguesa*, Tome 1, Chapter 3, *ff.* 210 §2]. Deuladeo Martins was buried in the chapel of the parochial church of this town

    4 Alvaro de Abreu

King Ferdinand r. 1367–1383
King John I r. 1385–1433
King Edward r. 1433–1438

N4 ALVARO DE ABREU, son of Vasco Gomes de Abreu N3, succeeded to his father's house in the time of Kings Ferdinand, John I and Edward. He lived inMonção and married Guiomar Alvares˙

    5 Constança de Abreu, who married Rodrigo Annes de Araujo˙, Alcaide General of Alharis [with issue in NFP Araujo §173 N19]

§102

N8 LUIS DA SILVA˙ DA CUNHA, son of Ignacio Soares de Abreu §26 N7, Rector of the Church of Pinheiro da Ermida, had bastard issue

    9 D. Jeronima da Silva˙

N9 D. JERONIMA DA SILVA˙, bastard daughter of Luis da Silva˙ N8, had

    10 D. Catarina˙ Cardoso or D. Cecilia Cardoso, wife of Pedro Pereira˙ de Vasconcellos, with issue, no further details

§103

N10 JOÃO DA SILVA, E SOUSA, son of Pedro Alvares˙ de Abreu §81 N9, was in the Army in Alentejo and held the ranks of Infantry Captain and Cavalry Captain. In the Cavalry he also served as a Commander General and Lieutenant General. He was also a Brigade General and an Artillery General, and was nicknamed "Ladrão Gaião" (*lit.* Clever Thief) due to the amount of pillaging that his enemies suffered from him. He was Governor of Rio de Janeiro (Brazil), and had bastard issue

    11 Pedro Alvares˙ de Abreu, who served with his father and went to India, where he died sp

João da Silva˙ had bastard children by Maria˙ Pereira˙, a noble woman from Campo Maior

    11 João Jose da Silva˙
    11 Fradique Alvares˙ de Toledo, who was with his father in Angola and fled to Castile, with no further details

DEULADEO MARTINS

In 1369, the army of King Peter I of Castile was defeated by that of his illegitimate half-brother Henry of Trastamara, and the sovereign was slain by Henry, who proclaimed himself King Henry II of Castile. The new sovereign was not recognized by King Ferdinand of Portugal, who claimed the Castilian throne on the grounds that Peter had left no heirs and that he, Ferdinand, was the legitimate great grandson of King Sancho IV of Castile, and Peter's cousin. This dispute led to three wars between the Portuguese and the Castilian sovereigns, all of them won by Henry, who consolidated his claim to the Kingdom of Castile.

On one of the occasions Portugal was invaded by King Henry's armies, the Portuguese city of Monção, in the northernmost part of the country, withstood a long siege imposed by the Castilian forces. When famine within the besieged city menaced to break its resistance, Deuladeo Martins, the wife of Chief Alcaide Vasco Gomes de Abreu [§101 N3], in a shrewd and desperate act, climbed the battlements and began throwing the city's last provisions upon the enemies. This made the Spanish army, which was also starving, believe there was plenty of food in the city, which weakened its morale and caused its retreat. In honor of this lady, the inhabitants of Monção included her portrait in the city's flag and coat of arms, with a motto that was a corruption of her name, Deuladeo: "Deus o deu, Deus o ha dado" (lit. Port.: "God gave it, God has given it").

Arms of the City of Monção

125

N11 JOÃO JOSE DA SILVA˙, bastard son of João da Silva˙ N10, was a Doctor in Canon Law and a Judge in Lisbon[i]. Afterwards he served in the Regiment of Cascais and was Second Lieutenant in the 3rd Regiment of Setúbal. He died in 1699, having married D. Maria˙ de Almeida˙, daughter of D. Antonio˙ de Almeida

       12 D. Francisca˙ de Almeida

§104

N8 RUY GOMES DE ABREU, son of Antonio˙ de Abreu Lima §28 N7, was a Fidalgo of the King's Household, married D. Isabel de Araujo˙ de Azevedo, daughter of Fernão Velho de Araujo˙, lord of the fief of Refoios, and his wife Ignes de Amorim [NFP Araujo §35 N24][ii]

       9 Leonel de Abreu Lima

       9 João Gomes de Abreu Lima §106

       9 D. Sebastianna de Lima §107

       9 D. Anna, wife of Jeronimo de Sousa Machado, lord of the house of Lage, sp

       9 Diogo Gomes de Abreu, Rector of Fornelos

       9 Fernando de Abreu Lima, Knight of Malta

       9 D. Brites

       9 D. Ignes, unmarried

N9 LEONEL DE ABREU LIMA, son of Ruy Gomes de Abreu N8, was a Fidalgo of the King's Household and the lord of the house of Paço Vedro, which he acquired through his wife D. Joanna Barreto da Cunha, daughter of Payo Velho Barreto and his wife Anna Coelho Velloso [NFP Costa §71 N7][iii]

       10 Ruy Gomes de Abreu

       10 Fray Payo, Commendatory of Vila Cova in the Order of Malta and Commendatory of Távora

       10 D. Marianna de Noronha §105

N10 RUY GOMES DE ABREU, son of Leonel de Abreu N9, was a Fidalgo of the King's Household, the lord of Paço Vedro and an Infantry Colonel of the Militia. He married (in Barca) D. Benta de Castro Correa˙, daughter of Gonçallo da Costa Correa˙ and his wife Isabel de Castro Soares˙, lords of the entail of Riba Feita [NFP

---

[i] Obscure part in the original text: "e Juis da teguria in Lx.ᵃ". (T. N.)

[ii] In NFP Araujo §35 N24, it is said that Ignes de Amorim was also known by a longer name: Ignes de Amorim *Antas Fernandes˙ Ledo*. (T. N.)

[iii] In NFP Costa §71 N7, Joanna Barreto da Cunha's father is called Payo Velho *de Araújo˙*, and not Payo Velho Barreto. (T. N.)

Costa §41 N7][i]

> 11 Leonel de Abreu Lima
> 11 Gonçallo de Abreu, Commendatory of Cerveira in the Order of Malta
> 11 Antonio˙ de Abreu, who made an enfeoffment of his lands. He held the Grand Cross, and was a Lieutenant General and Commander of the Fleet of the Order of Malta, and was appointed envoy to King Joseph I by the Great Master of his Order
> 11 D. Gabriel, a priest of the Order of the Holy Cross of Coimbra
> 11 Bento de Abreu, sp
> 11 D. Maria˙ Isabel de Noronha

King Joseph I r. 1750 –1777

N11 LEONEL DE ABREU LIMA, son of Ruy Gomes de Abreu N10, was a Fidalgo of the King's Household, the lord of the house of Paço Vedro and Riba Feita, and inherited his father's house. He married for the first time in Galicia, but had no issue. Afterwards he married as his second wife (also in Galicia) D. Anna Josefa de Flores e Hespanha, e Mosquera, daughter of D. Benito Ozores Sotomayor and D. Anna Josefa Romay, e Hespanha, lords of the ancient house of Real in the Kingdom of Galicia (D. Anna Josefa de Romay was a descendant of the Galician house of Quadro)

> 12 D. Rosalia Manoel de Abreu Lima, who inherited her father's estates, married (in Anquião) Francisco˙ Joaquim˙ de Abreu Lima, a Page-*Fidalgo* of the King's Household, son of Antonio˙ Jose de Abreu Lima, Fidalgo of the King's Household, and his wife D. Francisca˙ Xavier˙ de Lara [§28 N14][ii]
> 12 D. (...), sp

For details about Portuguese ranks of nobility, see p. v

§105

N10 D. MARIANNA DE NORONHA, daughter of Leonel de Abreu Lima §104 N9, married (in Lisbon) Andre Lopes de Oliveira, Page-Fidalgo of the King's Household and Purveyor of the Tobacco Customhouse, son of Dr. Manoel˙ Lopes de Oliveira˙ (Royal Appellate Judge, Royal Solicitor and Chief Chancellor) and his wife Elena Esquivel [NFP Oliveira §37 N9]

For details about Portuguese ranks of nobility, see p. v

---

[i] In NFP Costa §41 N7, Gonçallo da Costa (the surname Correa is omitted) is said to have married his relative Izabel de Castro *da Costa* (and not Izabel de Castro Soares) and to have had, among other children, Benta *da Costa* (and not Benta de Castro Correa), wife of Ruy *Lopes* de Abreu (and not Ruy Gomes de Abreu). (T. N.)

[ii] In §28 N14, Antonio Jose de Abreu Lima's wife is said to have a longer name: Francisca˙ *Antonia˙* Xavier de *Moraes* Lara, e *Souza.* (T. N.)

11 Manoel˙ de Oliveira˙ de Abreu Lima

11 Bernardo

11 Antonio˙ de Oliveira˙ de Abreu

11 Jose

11 D. Elena, unmarried

11 Leonel

11 Jacinto de Oliveira˙, an Envoy or Minister to Rome, where some say
he made an enfeoffment of lands [see NFP Pedigree Charts, Tome
1, *ff.* 157 and *ff.* 158)

*For details about Portuguese
ranks of nobility, see p. v*

N11 MANOEL˙ DE OLIVEIRA˙ DE ABREU LIMA, son of D. Marianna de
Noronha N10, was baptized in January, 1693, in the Parish of Our Lady of Pena in
Lisbon. He was Commendatory of Sampaio in Oliveira de Frades in the Order of
Christ, an office he held despite the protests of his family. He lived in his house in
Campo de Santana in Lisbon, was a Page-Fidalgo of the King's Household, Alcaide
General of Ourém and Purveyor of the Tobacco Customhouse. He married (in
Galicia) D. Maria˙ Theresa de Abraldes de Azevedo Portocarreiro, of the house of
Romiraens, daughter of D. Jose de Azevedo˙ Ribeiro˙, lord of the fief of Romiraens,
and his wife D. Belchiora Manoella de Abraldes Portocarreiro, daughter of D. João
Antonio˙ de Abraldes, lord of Guimaraens, São Mamede, São Cristovão and other
estates, and his wife D. Theresa Paulla da Veiga Portocarreiro˙. D. Maria Theresa
was the granddaughter of D. Diogo Abraldes de Mendonça, lord of Guimaraens,
and his wife D. Antonia˙ de Azevedo˙ Camanho, of the house of the Counts of
Altamira

12 Jose Manoel˙ de Oliveira˙ de Abreu de Azevedo˙, who enlisted in
the army as a cadet in the Regiment of Michelemburgo (sic), and
received from the Crown all the estates and offices of his father, sp

12 Andre de Oliveira˙, a Second Lieutenant

12 João Francisco˙ Borges de Oliveira˙, a Knight of Malta, in which
Order he was the Commendatory of Aguas Santas

12 D. Antonia˙, married (with issue) her cousin Bernardo Ramires
Esquivel, a Navy Colonel (see NFP Pedigree Charts, Tome 4, *ff.* 07
rev.) Bernardo Ramires is the 1st Baron of Arruda, Admiral of the
Royal Fleet, President of the Admiralty and Commendatory of the
Order of Christ [with issue in NFP Oliveira §38 N11][i]

12 D. Marianna de Azevedo˙ e Noronha, who retired to the convent of
Encarnação in Lisbon

---

[i] In NFP Oliveira §38 N11, Bernardo Ramires is called Bernardo Ramires *Esquivel,* and is also said to be
the 1st Viscount of Estremoz (besides being the Baron of Arruda); his wife is called Antonia˙ *de
Azevedo˙ e Noronha.* (T. N.)

N12 ANDRE DE OLIVEIRA, or ANDRE FRANCISCO˙ DE OLIVEIRA DE ABREU, second son of Manoel˙ de Oliveira˙ N11, succeeded his brother to their family's house, was Commendatory of Sampaio de Oliveira, Alcaide General of the Village of Outeiro, and served in a Royal Regiment

§106

For details about Portuguese ranks of nobility, see p. v

N9 JOÃO GOMES DE ABREU LIMA, son of Ruy Gomes de Abreu §104 N8, was the lord of the fief of Refoios in Ponte de Lima, which he inherited from his mother. He married D. Marianna de Vasconcellos˙, daughter of D. Isabel Coelho and her husband Gaspar de Amorim [NFP Costa §126 N7]*i*, according to records dated August 10, 1672 made in Refoios by notary public Gabriel Pereira˙ Barbosa. He was a Page-Fidalgo of the King's Household and lived in Refoios do Lima

       10 Tristão Gomes §131*ii*
       10 Gaspar de Abreu Lima
       10 Manoel˙ de Abreu Lima §108
       10 D. Anna de Abreu, who married Luis de Mesquita Bezerra [with
          issue in NFP Bezerra §8 N5]*iii*
       10 B. D. Paulla de Abreu de Lima §142

For details about Portuguese ranks of nobility, see p. v

N10 GASPAR DE ABREU LIMA, son of João Gomes de Abreu N9, was a Page-Fidalgo of the King's Household and an eminent genealogist. He married D. Maria˙ Josefa Vieira, daughter of Antonio˙ Alvares˙ Maciel, lord of the house and entail of Outeiro, near Ponte do Lima, and his wife D. Anna Pinto Vieira, who inherited her father's estates [NFP Maciel §1 N7]*iv*

       11 Manoel˙ de Abreu, unmarried
       11 Francisco˙ de Abreu Lima
       11 D. Francisca˙
       11 D. Joanna, a nun in the convent of Vale de Pereiros
       11 D. Josefa
       11 D. Josefa Anna, a nun in the convent of Vale de Pereiros

---

i In NFP Costa §126 N7, Marianna de Vasconcellos's father is called Gaspar de Amorim *de Araujo˙*. (T. N.)

ii In the original text, this passage (§106 N9 Sub10) gives Tristão Gomes's descendency until his great grandchildren, and is repeated (seemingly by mistake) in §131. In order to avoid repetition, we have opted to omit the first reference, leaving it to §131, in which he is called Tristão Gomes *de Abreu Lima*. (T. N.)

iii In NFP Bezerra §8 N5, Luiz de Mesquita˙ Bezerra's wife (and João Gomes de Abreu's daughter) is called Anna de *Noronha*, and not Anna de Abreu. (T. N.)

iv In NFP Maciel §1 N7, Maria Josefa Vieira's father is called Antonio˙ *Gonçalves˙* Maciel, and not Antonio Alvares Maciel. (T. N.)

For details about Portuguese ranks of nobility, see p. v

11 João de Abreu Lima

11 Antonio˙ de Abreu Lima

11 B. Miguel de Abreu de Sousa, who went to America[i]

N11 FRANCISCO˙ DE ABREU LIMA, son of Gaspar de Abreu N10, was the lord of the house of Outeiro, a Page-Fidalgo of the King's Household and served as an Infantry Captain in the Minho Army. He married D. Anna Margarida Cardoso de Menezes Alpoim, bastard daughter of Bruno Antonio˙ Cardoso de Menezes (a Knight of the Order of Christ and Appellate Judge of the Oporto Region) and his mistress D. Caetana de Alpoim, who had this daughter when she was single and later married the lord of the house of Andorinha [NFP Barreto §44 N12[ii]; NFP Felgueiras §19 N8; NFP Cardoso §49 N 7; see also *Estrangeiros no Lima* §244[iii]]

12 D. Maria˙ Gertrudes

12 João Gomes de Abreu

12 Felipe de Abreu Lima §129

12 D. Rosa de Menezes

12 D. Caetana Josefa de Lima Vasconcellos˙, wife of Antonio˙ Joaquim˙ Bezerra Rego e Lima, son of Ignacio Bezerra Rego Lima e Melo, captain of Albergaria and advowee of Brandar

13 Francisco˙ de Abreu Bezerra

13 D. Maria˙ Jose de Mello

N12 JOÃO GOMES DE ABREU LIMA PINTO CARDOSO, son of Francisco˙ de Abreu Lima N11, is a Fidalgo of the King's Household, inherited his father's house and married his cousin D. Marianna Victoria de Lencastre e Queiroz˙, first daughter of Joaquim˙ de Queiroz˙ Ribeiro˙ Botelho Camanho (of the village of Amarante, a Fidalgo of the King's Household and Knight of the Order of Malta, though not professed) and his wife D. Margarida Antonia de Lencastre Barros de Portugal [NFP Queiroz §60 N20][iv]

13 Gaspar de Abreu Lima, who was two years old according to a document dated 1808. He was born on November 12, 1807 (sic)[v] and baptized on December 8 of the same year in the Chapel of Our Lady of the Imaculate Conception in his family's house in Outeiro

---

[i] Of course, *America* here means the American Continent, not the United States of America. (T. N.)

[ii] In NFP Barreto §44 N12, the lord of the house of Andorinha is said to be João Antonio Pereira de Castro Gomes. (T. N.)

[iii] *Estrangeiros no Lima* (2 Vols.) was written by Manuel Gomes de Lima Bezerra and published for the first time in 1785-1791. (T. N.)

[iv] In NFP Queiroz §60 N20, João Gomes de Abreu's father-in-law is called Joaquim˙ de Queiros de Vasconcellos˙ Coimbra Camanho. (T. N.)

[v] There seems to be a small error in this passage, for if Gaspar de Abreu Lima was born on November 12, 1807, he could not have been two years old in the next year. (T. N.)

13 D. Maria˙ Jose de Sousa de Lencastre, who was born on December
    23, 1808, and baptized in January 1809

13 D. Maria Margarida Antonia˙ de Lencastre, who was born on
    September 4, 1810, and died in infancy

13 D. Maria˙ Romana de Menezes Camanho, born on September 13,
    1811 and baptized on December 8 of the same year

13 Francisco˙ de Abreu Lima Telles, *b*. August 5, 1814

13 Antonio˙ de Abreu Lima, *b*. May 21, 1817

13 Ruy Gomes de Abreu de Sousa, *b*. October 30, 1818

13 Bruno Antonio˙ Cardoso de Menezes, *b*. February 28, 1820

13 Francisco˙ Pinto Pereira˙ de Maciel, *b*. October 17, 1823

13 D. Maria˙ Margarida Antonia˙ da Conceipção Noronha, *b*. October,
    1821

    (all the above children were baptized in the chapels of the house
    of Outeiro)

13 D. Maria˙ Leonor Teles de Menezes, who was baptized on October
    17, 1827 in the Parish Church

§107

N9 D. SEBASTIANNA DE LIMA, daughter of Ruy Gomes de Abreu §104 N8,
married Luis de Meireles Borges, son of Luis de Meireles de Brito and his wife
Anna Borges [NFP Amorim §71 N7][i]

    10 Luis de Meireles, grandfather of Alberto de Seabra

    10 Ruy Gomes de Abreu, who married D. Leonor de Macedo, bastard
        daughter of Luis Palhares de Brito, Abbot of Vale, and his mistress
        Angela Aranha [NFP Barros §23 N12]

    10 D. Suzana

    10 D. Paulla

    10 D. Isabel

    all three daughters were nuns

N10 LUIS DE MEIRELES, son of D. Sebastianna de Lima N9, married D.
Maria˙ de Amorim, daughter of Pedro de Amorim (of Ponte de Lima), brother
of Fray Antonio˙ de Barros Magalhães˙

    11 D. Luisa Xavier˙ de Lima, who married Pantaleão de Ceabra

---

[i] In NFP Amorim §71 N7, Luiz de Meirelles Borges's mother is called Anna Borges *Pacheco*. (T. N.)

§108

N10 MANOEL˙ DE ABREU LIMA, son of João Gomes de Abreu (Lima) §106 N9, married D. Joanna Coutinho˙ sp, and had bastard issue

      11 B. D. Anna Theresa de Abreu, wife of Santos Luis Barreto, Knight of the Order of Christ

      11 B. D. Josefa Anna de Abreu

N11 D. ANNA THEREZA DE ABREU, bastard daughter of Manoel de Abreu Lima N10, married Santos Luis Barreto de Lima, son of Santos Barreto de Lima de Antas and his wife D. Maria˙ da Cunha Pereira˙ de Araujo˙, of Coura. Santos Luis was the paternal grandson of Jacome Barreto de Antas and his wife D. Anna Barreto de Lima, and the maternal grandson of Antonio˙ da Cunha Pereira˙ and his wife Maria˙ de Araujo [NFP Barbosa §218 N28]*i*

      12 Manoel˙ de Abreu Barreto de Lima

      12 Fray Antonio˙, a Bernardine monk

      12 Fray Francisco˙, *ditto*

      12 Rev. Lourenço de Abreu Barreto, Vicar of the Church of Feitosa

      12 Gaspar de Abreu Barreto Lima

      12 D. Anna Matilde de Abreu Lima, who married Jose de Sousa Pereira˙ Marinho Brandão de Amorim, second son of Francisco˙ Jose de Sousa, lord of the manor of Cazaes, and his wife D. Maria˙ Vitoria da Gama, e Castro [NFP (...) (sic); see NFP Araujo §52 N28, §97 N30 and §305 N28; NFP Barreto §87 N12; NFP Amorim §6 N11]*ii*, and had

         13 Francisco˙ de Sousa Pereira˙ de Amorim, who married his cousin D. Marianna de Sousa e Menezes, daughter of Manoel˙ de Sousa Pereira˙ de Amorim and D. Maria˙ do Caŕmo Sousa, e Menezes [NFP Barreto §87 N13 and NFP Amorim §6 N13]*iii*

            14 Luis de Sousa Pereira˙ Marinho

         13 D. Anna

         13 Antonio˙

         13 Jose

         13 D. Maria

---

i There are several small differences between the names presented here and the names given in NFP Barbosa §218 N27-N28, in which Santos Luis Barreto de Antas (and not Santos Luis Barreto de Lima) is said to have married Anna *de Abreu Lima* (and not Anna Thereza de Abreu) and to have been the son of Maria˙ da Cunha (and not Maria de Araujo). (T. N.)

ii In NFP Araujo §52 N28 and NFP Araujo §97 N30, Francisco Jose de Souza de Amorim's wife is said to be Maria˙ Vitoria *Falcão Marinho* (and not Maria Vitoria da Gama, e Castro). In NFP Amorim §6 N11, she is called Maria Vitoria *Marinho Falcão*. (T. N.)

iii In NFP Amorim §6 N13, Francisco de Souza Pereira de Amorim is called Francisco˙ Jose de Souza *de Amorim*. (T. N.)

N12 GASPAR DE ABREU BARRETO, son of D. Anna Theresa N11, married D. (...), daughter of Manoel˙ de Sousa de Amorim, lord of the house of Cazaes in Gemieira, and his wife D. Maria˙ do Castro de Sousa, e Menezes [NFP Costa §(...) N(...) (sic)]ⁱ

§109

N9 JOÃO GONÇALVES˙ DE ABREU, son of Gonçallo Rodrigues˙ de Abreu §83 N8. He was a very distinguished nobleman, lived in Elvas and was a steward of Queen Philippa, King John I's wife. He was the lord of the entail of Serra by grant of Martim Vaz Serra, the former owner of these estates. He married D. Brites Barbudo, of Calatrava, Castile, by whom he acquired the entail of Salina, which was instituted by his wife
    10 Fernão de Abreu

Queen Philippa (1359-1415), daughter of John of Gant, Duke of Lancaster, and wife of King John I of Portugal

N10 FERNÃO DE ABREU, son of João Gonçalves˙ de Abreu N9, was the lord of the entail of Serra and Salina, the Chapel of Trindade de São Francisco de Xabregas in Lisbon, Albergaria das Portas de São Pedro in Alfama, and the entail of Sempre Noiva in Arraiolos. He was a member of the King's council, and married D. Isabel Gonçalves˙ Neto, daughter of Affonso Martins˙ Albernos
    11 Pedro de Abreu
    11 João Fernandes˙ de Abreu, a Fidalgo of the King's Household, who married D. Joanna de Castro, daughter of Alvaro de Castro, and had
        12 Estevão de Abreu
        12 D. Catarina˙ de Castro, wife of Ruy Dias Pereira˙
        12 D. Maria˙ de Castro, a nun in the Convent of Jesus in Aveiro
    11 Lopo de Abreu, no further details
    11 Fernão Lopes de Abreu, no further details
    11 D. Mayor de Abreu, who married Fernão da Silva, e Menezes, of Elvas
    11 D. Felipa de Abreu

N11 PEDRO DE ABREU, son of Fernão de Abreu N10, owned the entails of his house and was a very distinguished nobleman, who had a notable participation in the celebration in Évora of the marriage of Prince Afonso, the son of King John II. He married D. Elena de Aguiar, a Castilian lady-in-waiting to the Princess, wife of the said Infante
    12 Duarte de Abreu

Prince Afonso (d. 1491) was the sole legitimate son of King John II, and married Isabella, daughter of the Catholic Monarchs Isabella I of Castile and Ferdinand II of Aragon.

ⁱ We have not found these people referred to in NFP Costa. (T. N.)

For details about Portuguese ranks of nobility, see p. v

N12 DUARTE DE ABREU, son of Pedro de Abreu N11, succeeded to his father's house, was the lord of the entail of Sempre Noiva, and married D. Catarina˙ Bayão, daughter of Gonçallo Pires Bayão, Page-*Fidalgo* of the King's Household, granddaughter of Pedro Bayão (Chamber Valet and Chief Guard to Prince Afonso) and his wife Germineza Rosa, or da Roza [as recorded in NFP Baião §5 N4][i]

      13 Pedro de Abreu

      13 Gaspar de Abreu, who went to India

      13 Francisco˙ de Abreu, *ditto*

      13 Onofre de Abreu, *ditto*

N13 PEDRO DE ABREU, son of Duarte de Abreu N12, inherited his father's house, was a Fidalgo of the King's Household and married D. Antonia˙ da Gama, daughter of Estevão da Gama, Captain of Mina, and his wife D. Catarina˙ Juzarte

      14 Duarte de Abreu

      14 João Fernandes˙ de Abreu, who died at the battle of Alcazarquivir, sp

      14 Estevão da Gama, who served in Mazagan, sp

      14 Pedro de Abreu, who died in Africa

      14 Manoel˙ de Abreu, *ditto*

      14 D. Maria˙, who died unmarried

In the battle of Alcazarquivir in Morocco (August 4ᵗʰ, 1578) a Portuguese army of nearly 15.000 men led by King Sebastian was completely routed by the Moors and the King himself was killed (see also box on p. 93)

N14 DUARTE DE ABREU, son of Pedro de Abreu N13, was a Fidalgo of the King's Household and married D. Anna de Almeida

      15 Pedro de Almeida, who married D. Luisa de Mello, sp

Duarte de Abreu married as his second wife D. Francisca˙ Coutinho˙, sp, and married as his third wife D. Maria˙ de Mello, daughter of Jaime de Mello Pereira˙ and lady-in-waiting to D. Catarina˙[ii]

      15 Luis de Abreu de Mello

      15 Duarte de Mello, who married D. Luisa Soares, sp

      15 João de Mello, a Jesuit

N15 LUIS DE ABREU DE MELLO, son of Duarte de Abreu N14 and his third wife, inherited his father's house and was a Fidalgo of the King's Household. He served D. Theodosio, Duke of Bragança, and his son King John IV, to whom he was Lord Steward. He was also the Alcaide of Melgaço and was granted two commendams in the Order of Christ. He was married four times, the first time to D. Clara Soares

King John IV r. 1640–1656

      16 Duarte de Abreu Mello

---

[i] In NFP Baião §5 N4, Catarina Bayão is said to be the daughter of the one we consider here her paternal grandfather, Pedro Bayão, and his wife *Genebra* Rosa (and not Germineza Rosa). (T. N.)

[ii] Perhaps Queen Catherine, wife of King John III [r. 1521-1557]. (T. N.)

Luis de Abreu married as his second wife D. Anna de Mello, sp. He married as his third wife D. Mayor Maria de Vargas, daughter of D. Luis de Vargas and his wife D. Mayor de Ulhoa, daughter of Vicente Vaz and his wife D. Constança de Ulhoa

    16 Duarte de Mello Pereira˙, sp

    16 João de Mello, who was executed (by having his throat cut) in Rossio, Lisbon, in 1674, for having taken part in a conspiration together with Gaspar Maldonado

Luis de Abreu's fourth wife was D. Elena de Velhano, by whom he had no issue

N16 DUARTE DE ABREU E MELLO, son of Luis de Abreu (de Mello) N15 and his first wife, inherited his father's house and was a Fidalgo of the King's Household. He married D. Anna Pinheiro, daughter of Visente Vaz Pinheiro

    17 Luis de Abreu de Mello

N17 LUIS DE ABREU DE MELLO, son of Duarte de Abreu N16, inherited his father's house, married D. Violante de Meza, a New Christian[i], daughter of Gaspar Fernandes˙, brother of Cristovão Rodrigues˙, Marquiss of Elvas, as a result of which marriage he went to India

§110

N10 MATHEUS PEGADO DE ABREU, son of Lourenço Mendes de Abreu §73 N9, married in Vimiozo

    11 Garcia˙ Mendes de Abreu

    11 Antonio˙ Pegado, who had issue in Trás-os-Montes

N11 GARCIA˙ MENDES DE ABREU, son of Matheus Pegado N10, lived in Pombal, where he married Joanna Mascarenhas, daughter of Domingos˙ Lopes Nobre and his wife (...) Pinheiro, sister of João Pinheiro, Clerk of the Writs of Pombal

    12 Antonia˙ de Lemos Mascarenhas

N12 ANTONIA˙ DE LEMOS MASCARENHAS, daughter of Garcia˙ Mendes N11, married (in Leiria) Antonio˙ Gomes de Lemos, probate court officer of that city, son of Manoel˙ de Lemos Cardoso and his wife Pantaliana Rabello

    13 João de Lemos de Abreu, who married D. Isabel Maria˙ de Sousa, widow of Bartolomeu˙ Mendes de Abreu [§(...) N(...)] (sic)[ii], sp

---

[i] New Christians were the Jews converted to Christianism, a relatively common fact in the Iberian Peninsula. (T. N.)

[ii] The name Bartolomeu Mendes de Abreu also appears in §48 N10 and §74, referring to a grandfather and his grandson. However, none of them is said to have had a wife called Isabel Maria de Sousa, as given here. (T. N.)

13 D. Joanna Mascarenhas, wife of Antonio˙ da Fonseca˙ Mancellos, Clerk of the Writs of Pombal

13 D. Maria˙ Lemos

N13 D. MARIA˙ LEMOS, daughter of Antonia˙ de Lemos N12, received in dowry the office of Probate Court Officer of the town of Leiria, where she married João de Mello de Andrade˙, son of Placido de Araujo˙, e Mello, who held the office of Clerk of Pinhaes in Leiria, and his wife Margarida da Rosa, sister of Simão da Rosa Guerra, Dean of Leiria

> 14 Plácido de Araujo˙, Probate Court Officer of Leiria, married (...), daughter of Pedro Gomes Rosa and D. Brites de Albuquerque˙, with issue

§111

LORDS OF THE MANOR OF ORÃO

N10 MIGUEL MENDES DE ABREU, son of Lourenço Mendes de Abreu §73 N9, lived in Pombal, where he was Master of the Stores. He married (in Cortes, in the territory of Leiria) Maria˙ da Fonseca˙, daughter of João de Azambuja and his wife Isabel da Fonseca˙

> 11 João Mendes de Abreu
> 11 D. Maria˙ de Abreu, who married her cousin Lourenço Mendes de Abreu [§74 N11]

N11 JOÃO MENDES DE ABREU, son of Miguel Mendes N10, married (in Traveira) D. Marianna, daughter of Francisco˙ Varella and his wife Anna Sarenha

> 12 Francisco˙ Mendes de Abreu

João Mendes de Abreu married again in Redinha, sp

N12 FRANCISCO˙ MENDES DE ABREU, son of João Mendes N11, lived in his manor of Traveira and was the lord of the manor of Orão. He married D. Antonia˙ de Amorim, daughter of Jorge Pessoa de Amorim, of Rabaçal and D. Marianna de Gouvea [see NFP Pedigree Charts ff. 118 rev, in Tome 2, and NFP Faria §135 N12]

> 13 Antonio de Abreu Amorim Pessoa
> 13 D. Marianna de Amorim Pessoa e Gouvea, who married Adrião Pereira˙ de Sampaio˙, lord of the manor of Geria, son of Diogo Pereira˙ de Sampaio˙
> 13 D. Josefa
> 13 D. Antonia˙
> 13 D. Maria˙
> 13 B. Thomaz Mendes

N13 ANTONIO˙ DE ABREU DE AMORIM PESSOA, son of Francisco˙ Mendes de Abreu N12, inherited his father's house and the manor of Orão, and married D. Catarina Joaquina Mauricia de Machado Pimentel Baracho
    14 Alberto de Abreu de Amorim Pessoa §137

§112

N10 FELIPA MENDES DE ABREU, daughter of Lourenço Mendes de Abreu §73 N9, married (in Arcos de Valdevez) Agostinho Gonçalves˙
    11 Antonio˙ Gonçalves˙

N11 ANTONIO˙ GONÇALVES˙ DE ABREU, son of Felipa Mendes N10, was born in Couceiro, territory of Regalados, and married (in Valença do Minho) Isabel Bacellar, daughter of João Vaz, of Couceiro and Isabel Gonçalves˙ Bacellar, of Valença do Minho
    12 Pedro Gonçalves˙ Bacellar

N12 PEDRO GONÇALVES˙ DE ABREU BACELLAR, son of Antonio˙ Gonçalves˙ N11, lived in Figueira, near Buarcos, and held the office of Clerk of Public Records
        13 (...), his heiress, who married Matheus Rabello, with whom she lived in Coimbra, with issue

§113

THE ABREUS CURADOS OF CINCO VILAS

N1 PEDRO DE ABREU, of Leiria, was the son of (...) and a servant to the Duke of Caminha, whom he accompanied to Cinco Vilas, becoming the Clerk of Transfer Taxes of this place by the Duke's grant. He married Jeronima Carvalho, a native of Águeda
        2 Manoel˙ de Abreu
        2 Maria˙ de Abreu, wife of Antonio˙ Dias of Casal

N2 MANOEL˙ DE ABREU, son of Pedro de Abreu N1, held his father's office and married (in Águeda) Maria Curado, daughter of Baltazar˙ Godinho
        3 Bras Curado
        3 Manoel˙ de Abreu, who lived in Ribeira de Alge, married Anna Curado, daughter of Felipe Curado and his wife Catarina˙ Antunes, and had
        4 Manoel˙ de Abreu
        4 Maria˙ Curado

3 Maria˙ de Abreu §114
3 Isabel de Abreu

N 3 BRAZ CURADO, son of Manoel˙ de Abreu N2, married Isabel Themudo, daughter of Baltazar˙ Godinho and Maria Themudo
    4 João Corado

§114

N3 MARIA˙ DE ABREU, daughter of Manoel˙ de Abreu §113 N2, married Felipe Gomes of Ribeira de Alge, who received as his wife's dowry the office of Clerk of the Transfer Taxes
    4 Manoel˙ de Abreu

N4 MANOEL˙ DE ABREU, son of Maria˙ de Abreu N3, married Isabel Themuda, daughter of Simão Temudo and his wife Maria˙ Lopes
    5 Manoel˙ de Abreu
    5 Francisco˙ de Abreu
    5
    5
    (sic)

§115

OTHER BRANCHES OF THE ABREUS: ABREU TOSCANO (*see also* §40)

N1 RAFAEL DE ABREU, son of (...), married Leonor Toscano, daughter of Dr. Francisco˙ Toscano, who was the Chief Chancellor of India and was mentioned by Jacinto Freire de Andrade˙ in his *Vida de D. João de Castro* (The Life of D. João de Castro), Book 4 §128 N1
    2 Rafael Toscano de Abreu
    2 Dr. João Toscano, a Corregidor in India, with issue, no further details

N2 RAFAEL TOSCANO DE ABREU, son of Rafael de Abreu N1, married D. Isabel de Abreu de Mello, daughter of Antonio˙ de Abreu
    3 Francisco˙ de Abreu Toscano
    3 Dr. Manoel˙ Toscano de Abreu, a Corregidor of Beja, married twice, but had no issue by either marriage. However, he had a bastard daughter, Leonor, who was a nun in Beja
    3 Aleixo de Abreu, unmarried, in India, sp

3 Dr. João Toscano, an Appellate Judge and Criminal Corregidor in India, who married D. Maria˙ Camelo Castello Branco, by whom he had

4 Baltazar˙ Camelo Castello Branco

3 João Toscano de Abreu, who married in São Tomé, sp

3 (...), Fray Graciano

N3 FRANCISCO˙ DE ABREU TOSCANO DE MELLO, son of Rafael Toscano (de Abreu) N2, married D. Antonia˙ Dias Lobo, daughter of Jorge Dias Cavaleiro[i] and D. Anna de Oliveira˙ Freire

4 Antonio˙ de Abreu Toscano, a Knight of the Order of Christ, who died in India

4 Rafael Toscano, who died in India

4 Manoel˙ Lobo

4 Braz Lobo, who died in India

4 D. Barbara de Mello, who married Manoel˙ Peixoto Cirne for love [with issue in NFP Vilarinho §5 N7][ii]

§116

N11 LUIS DE ABREU, son of Roque Fernandes˙ de Abreu §79 N10, married (in the village of Sandomil) Maria˙ do Amaral

12 Roque Fernandes˙ de Abreu

N12 ROQUE FERNANDES˙ DE ABREU, son of Luis de Abreu N11, an Officer of the Inquisition, married D. Josefa de Magalhães˙, daughter of Manoel˙ de Magalhães˙

13 Luis de Abreu

13 D. Antonia˙

13 D. (...)

§117

N11 MANOEL˙ DE SEQUEIRA˙ DE ABREU, son of Roque Fernandes˙ de Abreu §79 N10 and his second wife [NFP Pedigree Charts, Tome 4, *ff.* 124], was Captain General of Loriga and Vila Pouca in Beira, where he lives. He married

---

[i] In this passage, it is not clear if "Cavaleiro" is part of this gentleman's name (Jorge Dias Cavaleiro) or if it was a possible reference to his nobility rank (Jorge Dias, Cavaleiro (a Knight)). Anyway, we have preferred to adopt the first version. (T. N.)

[ii] In NFP Vilarinho §5 N7, it is said that Manoel Peixoto Cirne married his brother Cristovão Peixoto's maid, who was presumably Barbara de Mello, though her name is not explicitly given. (T. N.)

his relative D. Francisca· de Abreu, daughter of Pedro Madeira and his wife D. Maria· de Figueiredo· Brandão [§122 N10]

        12 Roque Fernandes· de Abreu

        12 D. Maria·

        12 D. Elena

§118

N 11 D. LUIZA DE ABREU, daughter of Roque Fernandes· de Abreu §79 N10 and his second wife, married (in Beijos, near Viseu) João Ornelas da Fonseca·, a Fidalgo of the King's Household

        12 João Ornellas Rolim de Abreu

        12 Antonio· da Fonseca· Ornellas

        12 Roque de Ornellas de Abreu

        12 Pedro de Ornellas de Abreu

        12 Jose Caetano

        12 Bento de Ornellas

        12 D. Barbara Jacinta de Abreu

        12 D. Maria·, who died young

        12 D. Joanna

        12 D. Clara

        12 D. Isabel Engracia

N12 JOÃO DE ORNELLAS ROLIM DE ABREU, son of D. Luiza de Abreu N11, inherited his father's house and was unmarried in 1710 [see NFP Gouveia §57][i]

§119

N9 ANNA DE ABREU, daughter of Roque Fernandes de Abreu §79 N8, married her relative João Madeira Arraes, a resident of Vila Cova, and had

        10 Maria· Madeira

N10 MARIA MADEIRA, daughter of Anna de Abreu N9, married Pedro Borges de Castro, son of Alvaro Borges de Castro da Silva· Gil, grandson of Ruy Borges, who lived in Lapa, near Tourais

        11 Pedro Borges de Castro

        11 João Borges §120

        11 Catarina· Borges de Abreu [see §121], who married Manoel· de Brito

---

[i] In NFP Gouveia §57 N15 Sub16, it is said that Luiza de Abreu (NFP Abreu §110 N11) was the wife of *Joze* de Ornellas da Fonseca· (and not João de Ornellas da Fonseca), and there is no reference to a son of this couple called João de Ornellas Rolim de Abreu. (T. N.)

N11 PEDRO BORGES DE CASTRO, son of Maria Madeira N10, married his cousin Antonia˙ Borges Tavares, daughter of João Borges of Anceriz, nephew of Pedro Borges Tavares, Inquisitor of the General Council of the Holy Office of Coimbra

      12 Rodrigo Borges de Castro
      12 D. Umbelina, a nun in Lorvão

N12 RODRIGO BORGES DE CASTRO, son of Pedro Borges N11, succeeded to his father's house, was an officer of the Inquisition, lived in Galizes and was unmarried in 1712

§120

N11 JOÃO BORGES, son of Maria Madeira §119 N10, married (in Vila Cova) Anna Barreto de Brito

      12 Manoel˙ de Brito, sp
      12 Simão, a canon in Coimbra
      12 Fray Rodrigo, a Bernardine monk
      12 Fray Manoel˙, a Capuchin monk
      12 Maria˙ da Esperança, a nun in Campos
      12 Theresa, a nun in Sendelgas, who died in 1710
      12 Catarina˙ Borges de Abreu

§121[i]

N11 CATARINA˙ BORGES DE ABREU, daughter of D. Maria˙ Madeira de Mendonça and her husband Pedro Borges de Castro [§119 N10 above]. This lady should not be confused with her namesake, mentioned in §120 N11 Sub12, who was the daughter of her brother João Borges §120 N11. She married (in Pomares) her relative Manoel˙ de Brito Barreto, Captain General of the village of Avô, son of Antonio˙ Madeira da Costa and Maria de Brito. The said Manoel˙ de Brito and his wife enfeoffed their lands by an instrument dated March 24, 1694, written by notary public Antonio˙ Pereira˙ da Silva in the village of Avô, region of Pomares, territory of the village of the same name, in the District of

---

[i] In the original text, there is not a section beginning (§) separating this Catarina Borges de Abreu from the previous subsection (João Borges N11), though this omission is clearly a mistake for, as said above, the Catarina Borges de Abreu given here (§121) is João Borges's sister, not his daughter (who had the same name as her aunt, being mentioned in §121 N11 Sub12). (T. N.)

Guarda. This instrument imposed on the grantees the condition that they should yearly observe a date verbally informed by the grantors, and that they should also adopt the surnames of Brito Barreto, Costa and Castro. It was a highly profitable entail, as can be seen in the partition that Dean Manoel de Brito, the grantors' grandson, made among his children in 1764 [see NFP Costa Corte Real §15 N5, and also NFP Pedigree Charts, Tome 2, *ff. 93 rev.* and N109 *rev.*][i]

> 12 Bento Madeira de Castro
> 12 Manoel˙ de Brito Barreto, a canon in Coimbra
> 12 Fray Luis, a Bernardine monk
> 12 D. Paulino, a priest of the Order of the Holy Cross of Coimbra
> 12 Father Jose, a Jesuit
> 12 D. Maria Barreto Borges, who married (in Gois) Antonio˙ Barreto Perdigão, son of D. Marianna do Rego Villas Boas and Antonio˙ Barreto Perdigão [with issue in NFP Vilas Boas §20 N14][ii]

N12 BENTO (or BERNARDO) MADEIRA DE CASTRO, son of Catarina˙ Borges de Abreu N11, inherited his father's house, was an officer of the Inquisition and married (...), daughter of Agostinho Juzarte Maldonado, Chief Courier of Coimbra, and his wife D. Anna Baptista da Silva [see NFP Pedigree Charts, Tome 1, Chart 96]

> 13 Manoel˙ de Brito Barreto
> 13 D. Anna de Castro, who married (in Celorico) Bernardo de Almeida de Eça, her stepmother's brother
> 13 D. Catarina˙ de Castro

Bento Madeira de Castro's second wife was D. Maria˙ da Trindade (whom he married in Celorico da Beira), daughter of Manoel˙ de Almeida de Eça, of Cerolico da Beira, and his first wife (...)

§122

N9 ELENA DE ABREU, daughter of Roque Fernandes˙ de Abreu §79 N8, married her relative Dr. Pedro Madeira, corregidor of the district of Viseu, where he died[iiii]

---

[i] In NFP Costa Corte Real §15 N5, Catarina Borges de Abreu is said to be the daughter of João Borges and Maria˙ Madeira, contrary to what is stated at the beginning of this section, according to which she was the daughter of Alvaro Borges de Castro da Silva˙ Gil and (another) Maria˙ Madeira, this last version also appearing in NFP Pedigree Charts, Tome 2, *ff. 93 rev.* and N109 *rev.* (T. N.)

[ii] In NFP Vilas Boas §20 N14, Antonio Barreto Perdigão's wife is called *Maria˙ de Brito* (and not Marianna Barreto Borges), and her mother is Catarina˙ Borges *de Castro* (and not Catarina Borges de Abreu). (T. N.)

[iii] There are several differences between this section and §79 N8 Sub9 concerning the names related to this daughter of Roque Fernandes de Abreu. For more details, see footnote *ii* on p. 97. (T. N.)

    10 João Madeira, who died as a probate court judge in Santarém

    10 Pedro Madeira

    10 Fray Manoel˙ Madeira, a Bernardine monk

    10 Fray Roque, a Capuchin monk

    10 D. Elena, who died young

    10 D. Paulla

N10 PEDRO MADEIRA, son of Elena de Abreu N9, married his second cousin Maria de Figueiredo˙ Brandão, daughter of João Martins˙ Brandão of Sameice and D. Maria˙ Affonso˙ de Castro, paternal granddaughter of Marcos Brandão de Abrantes and D. Isabel de Figueiredo˙, and maternal granddaughter of Aleixo Affonso˙ Madeira and Cecilia Madeira da Costa

    11 Manoel˙ Madeira

    11 D. Patornilha, who died young

    11 D. Francisca˙ de Abreu, who married her relative Manoel˙ de Sequeira˙ de Abreu [with issue in this chapter §117 N11]

    11 D. Elena, a nun in Lorvão

    11 D. Rosa

§123

ABREU QUENTAL OF POMBAL

N1 MANOEL˙ DE ABREU DE MACEDO DE ALEMQUER [see §21 N8 in this chapter and NFP Macedo §32][i], married (in Pombal) Maria de Oliveira, daughter of Gonçallo Carvalho Denis and Elena de Soveral de Oliveira

    2 Manoel˙ do Quental de Abreu

    2 Catarina˙ de Carvalho Denis, wife of Diogo Jorge de Medeiros, Chamber Valet to Infante D. Duarte, with issue

    2 Elena de Abreu de Carvalho, wife of Manoel˙ Lobo do Casal

Infante Duarte of Portugal (1515-1540), son of King Manuel I

N2 MANOEL˙ DO QUENTAL DE ABREU, son of Manoel˙ de Abreu N1, was one of the first Army Captains in the time of King Sebastian. He lived in the village of Pombal, where he married Luisa de Mattos Pessoa, sp. He married as his second wife (in Lisbon) Luisa Alemão, daughter of Diogo Fernandes˙ Alemão

King Sebastian r. 1557–1578

    3 Luis do Quental de Abreu

---

[i] We have not found any unquestionable reference to this Manoel de Abreu de Macedo de Alenquer, neither in §21 N8 of this chapter nor in NFP Macedo §32. In the latter reference, a Manoel de Macedo is mentioned (whose paternal grandfather did indeed make a grant to the convent of St. Clara de Alenquer, and whose wife was called Maria˙), though it is also said that he married in India (and not in Pombal) and did not have issue. (T. N.)

*John IV was acclaimed
King of Portugal in 1640.*

N3 LUIS DO QUENTAL DE ABREU, son of Manoel' do Quental N2, was an Army Captain in Lisbon before the acclamation of King John IV. He was the lord of the manor of Fapenno in the territory of Redinha, and married (...) Arnão of Louriçal, sp. His second wife was D. Luisa de Andrade' or D. Brites de Lara e Muge, a native of Aveiro, daughter of Antonio' Monteiro de Abreu, of Ourém, and D. Maria' de Andrade', daughter of Antonio' de Andrade' da Gama and D. Genebra Teixeira' [NFP Monteiro §58 N5]*i*

> 4 Carlos de Abreu do Quental, who went several times to India but eventually came back to Portugal, and fortune took him to side with Castile, which he served as a Cavalry Captain, taking the side of Portugal at the end of the war. Some say he left legitimate issue in Castile
>
> 4 Fray Feleciano, a friar in the Monastery of Christ
>
> 4 Lucas de Abreu da Gama
>
> 4 (daughters who became nuns)

N4 LUCAS DE ABREU DA GAMA, son of Luis do Quental N3, was a Fidalgo of the King's Household [see NFP Pedigree Charts, Tome 3, *ff. 58, rev.* and *ff.* 134]. He inherited the manor of Tapeos, where he lived, was a captain of the Cavalry and the Militia in Leiria and married (at the foot of the Estrela Mountains) D. Anna Theresa de Castro, niece of João da Costa, of Oliveirinha, daughter of Gaspar' da Costa Brandão, also of Oliveirinha and D. Anna Borges de Castro. Gaspar da Costa was the son of Gaspar Nunes Brandão and Maria Nunes Godinho, daughter of Gaspar Nunes de Figueiredo'. D. Anna Borges was the daughter of Alvaro Borges and Maria' Deniz

> 5 Antonio' de Abreu da Gama
>
> 5 D. Felecianna

N5 ANTONIO' DE ABREU DA GAMA, son of Lucas de Abreu N4, was a Fidalgo of the King's Household and lived in his manor in Canas de Senhorim, where he was Captain General. He was alive in 1722, and was married to D. Eugenia Maria de Sobral, daughter and heiress of João Sobral de Figueiredo', of Canas de Senhorim, and D. Antonia' Maria' da Fonseca' [see NFP Pedigree Charts, Tome 3, *ff.* 58 *rev.*]. Through this marriage to D. Eugenia he acquired the lands enfeoffed by Simão Coelho do Amaral, which had belonged to João do Sobral, the Elder, her 6th generation ancestor, who was married to Maria Deniz

> 6 Custodio Luis de Abreu da Gama §136

---

i In NFP Monteiro §58 N5, Luis do Quental de Abreu is said to have married Beatriz de Andrade, whose mother was Maria' de Andrade' *da Gama*, and whose maternal grandmother was Genebra Teixeira' *de Queiros*. (T. N.)

§124

N5 RUY GOMES DE ABREU, son of Pedro Gomes de Abreu, lord of Regalados (in §2 N4), lived in Valença do Minho, where he died shortly before 1487. He is mentioned in the *Historia Genealogica da Casa Real* [Book14, Tome 12 §4 *ff.* 427] and in many other genealogical chronicles of the Portuguese nobility. His name also appears in a land partition instrument, written on July 10, 1487 by notary public Ruy Vaz de Valença and made by João Esteves, Abbot of São Lourenço da Capela, on behalf of João Rodrigues*, a servant of the said Ruy Gomes. Ruy Gomes married D. Isabel de Barros, daughter of D. Gonçallo de Barros, Commendatory of the Monasteries of Rendufe [see NFP Barros §1 N5 Sub6 and NFP Barros §90]

§125

THE ABREUS OF ESPINHEL

N1 FRANCISCO* DE ABREU is said to be a descendant of the original Abreus, as was proved by his grandson in his plea to gain the right to bear the coat of arms of that family. There is no information about whether he was married
   2 Joanna de Abreu

N2 JOANNA DE ABREU, daughter of Francisco* de Abreu N1, lived in Ancão and married Manoel* Fernandes
   3 Antonio* de Abreu

N3 ANTONIO* DE ABREU, son of Joanna de Abreu N2. On December 17, 1604, he was granted the right to bear the coat of arms of his family. He lived in the village of Ancão and got married
   4 Damião de Abreu
   4 Father Manoel* de Abreu
   4 Luis de Abreu, Registrar for the missing and the deceased

N4 DAMIÃO DE ABREU, son of Antonio* de Abreu N3, married Magdalena Viegas Franco
   5 Antonio* de Abreu

N5 ANTONIO* DE ABREU, son of Damião de Abreu N4, lived in Espinhel, where he owned a splendid residence, which he shared among his children. He married D. Leonor Corte Real, daughter of Fernão Rodrigues* Bacellar, a servant of the Duke of Caminha, and his wife Leonor da Costa of Parada

6 Damião de Abreu, who died young

6 Jose de Abreu Bacellar

6 Fray Fernando, a monk of the Order of Christ

6 Antonio˙ de Abreu Bacellar §126[i]

N6 JOSE DE ABREU BACELLAR, son of Antonio˙ de Abreu Bacellar N5, lived in Espinhel, married D. Elena de Mendonça, daughter of Cipriano Moniz and D. Maria˙ de Mendonça, e Vasconcellos

7 Antonio˙ de Abreu Corte Real

§126

N6 ANTONIO DE ABREU CORTE REAL, son of Antonio˙ de Abreu §125 N5[ii], married his sister-in-law D. Theresa de Mendonça e Vasconcellos, daughter of Cipriano Moniz and his wife D. Maria˙ Mendonça, e Vasconcellos

7 Joaquim˙ de Abreu Corte Real

7 Thomaz Moniz Ribeiro˙

7 Cepriano Moniz

7 D. Leonarda

§127

N15 D. ISABEL DE ABREU, daughter of Duarte de Abreu (Castello Branco) §92 N14, married Fernão or Francisco˙ Figueira de Azevedo˙[12], lord of the manor of Gomil and the entail of Grajal, son of Agostinho Figueira de Azevedo (who held a commendam in Tangier, where he was slain by the Moors) and his wife D. Luisa de Mendonça, daughter of Jorge de Mendonça Adail, who lived in Tangier. Fernão or Francisco˙ Figueira de Azevedo˙ was the paternal grandson of Francisco˙ Figueira de Azevedo˙, Purveyor of the Fleet, who followed King Sebastian to Africa, and his wife (...), daughter of Duarte de Albuquerque˙, who bestowed in dowry upon his daughter the captainship of Ceylon. Francisco˙ Figueira de Azevedo˙ was the

King Sebastian r. 1557–1578. For more details about these events, see box on p. 93 and margin on p. 105.

---

[i] In §126, he is called Antonio de Abreu *Corte Real.* (T. N.)

[ii] In §125 N5, he is called Antonio de Abreu *Bacellar.* (T. N.)

[12] Nevertheless, in NFP Figueira §11 N6, it is stated that Francisco˙ Figueira married D. Maria˙ da Silva˙, that his second wife was D. Maria˙ or Izabel da Silva, daughter of Lourenço Soares de Albergaria [see NFP Soares de Albergaria §11 N11 Sub12], and that he had[iii]

16 Lourenço Figueira˙ de Azevedo, N16 below

[iii] Unlike what is stated here, in NFP Figueira §11 N6 it is said that Francisco˙ Figueira married Isabel de Abreu, and that he was also found to have been the husband of Maria˙ da Silva˙, daughter of Lourenço Soares de Albergaria. (T. N.)

son of João Figueira de Azevedo (who lived in Évora and was a Purveyor and Accountant of the parishes of Alentejo Province) and his wife Catarina de Sá; he was the paternal grandson of Diogo Figueira and his wife (...) de Azevedo˙, and the great grandson of Affonço Figueira [NFP Figueira §11 N1 and §12]

   16 Lourenço Figueira de Azevedo˙

N16 LOURENÇO FIGUEIRA DE AZEVEDO˙, son of D. Isabel de Abreu N15. (It is most probable that this Lourenço Figueira de Azevedo˙ was the son of Francisco˙ Figueira de Azevedo and his second wife D. Isabel or Maria da Silva˙, daughter of Lourenço Soares de Albergaria and his wife Ignes de La Barrera [NFP Soares de Albergaria §11 N12 Sub13], for according to §92 above, D. Isabel de Abreu was the first wife of Francisco˙ Figueira[i] [see NFP Pedigree Charts, Tome 1, *lf.* 4 *rev.*]). He was a Page-*Fidalgo* of the King's Household, lived in Lisbon and had by his mistress Antonia de Oliveira (whom, according to some, he abducted from the Court), or by D. Antonia˙ de Mendonça

   17 B. Francisco Figueira de Azevedo˙

N17 FRANCISCO˙ FIGUEIRA DE AZEVEDO˙, bastard son of Lourenço Figueira N16, was made a Fidalgo of the King's Household, was the lord of the manor of São Gomil and married D. Luisa de Amaral, who, according to a chronicle, was the lady of the house of Grajal, daughter of Antonio˙ Ferreira Leitão, lord of the house of Grajal, and his wife D. Catarina˙ de Lemos. D. Luisa de Amaral was the paternal granddaughter of Cristovão Ferreira˙ Freire, an Appellate Judge in Bahia, Brazil, and his wife D. Violante Rabello, and great granddaughter of Vasco Fernandes˙ Freire, Captain General of Fonte Arcada. D. Catarina˙ de Lemos was the daughter of Francisco˙ da Costa and his wife Maria˙ de Lemos [NFP Amado §34 N13; see also NFP Pedigree Charts, Tome 1, *lf.* 4, *rev.*][ii]

   18 Luis Ferreira˙ de Mendonça
   18 D. Maria˙ Antonia˙ Corte Real, second wife of Nicolao de Tovar
     de Vasconcellos [NFP Figueiredo §32 N5; see also NFP Pedigree
     Charts, Tome 1, *lf.* 4][iii]

For details about Portuguese ranks of nobility, see p. v

---

[i] Contrary to what is stated here, in §92 it is said that Isabel de Abreu was married to *Fernão* Figueira *de Azevedo*˙, (and not to Francisco˙ Figueira), and it is not informed that she was her husband's second wife. (T. N.)

[ii] In NFP Amado §34 N13, Luisa do Amaral's husband is called Francisco Figueira de *Andrade* (and not Francisco Figueira de Azevedo), and her mother's name is given as Catarina˙ *da Costa* de Lemos. (T. N.)

[iii] In NFP Figueiredo §32 N5, Maria Antonia Corte Real's parents are said to be Francisco˙ *Figueiredo*˙ de Azevedo˙ (and not Francisco Figueira de Azevedo) and Luisa *Magdalena* do Amaral. (T. N.)

N18 LUIS FERREIRA˙ DE MENDONÇA, son of Francisco˙ Figueira de Azevedo˙ N17, was a Fidalgo of the King's Household, lived in Grajal and married D. Violante Clara da Silva, daughter and heiress of Manoel˙ Cardoso Madeira, of Armamar, lord of the entail of Guadalupe, and his wife Marianna de Sá da Fonseca˙, daughter of Jeronimo Rodrigues da Fonseca˙, of Castelo (...), paternal granddaughter of Domingos˙ Cardoso Madeira and his wife D. Marianna da Silva

> 19 Francisco˙ Jose de Mendonça Madeira, Fidalgo of the King's Household, married D. Francisca˙ Micaella de Castro, e Menezes, daughter of Luis Cardoso de Menezes (Fidalgo of the King's Household and Captain General of São Cosmado) and his wife D. Elena de Castro [with issue in NFP Cardoso §30 N11]

§128

N7 ANTONIO˙ FERNANDES DE ABREU, son of Luis de Abreu §79 N6
> 8 Anna Fernandes de Abreu

N8 ANNA FERNANDES˙ DE ABREU, daughter of Antonio˙ Fernandes˙ de Abreu N7, married Bartolomeu Dias, of Travanca de Lagos
> 9 Roque Fernandes˙ de Abreu

N9 ROQUE FERNANDES˙ DE ABREU, son of Anna Fernandes˙ de Abreu N8, married Anna Affonso da Costa, daughter of Manoel˙ Dias da Costa and Maria˙ Affonso
> 10 Manoel Roque de Abreu

N10 MANOEL˙ ROQUE DE ABREU, son of Roque Fernandes˙ de Abreu N9, married D. Brites Monteiro, daughter of Pedro Ribeiro˙ Furtado and D. Isabel Godinho. D. Brites was the paternal granddaughter of Antonio˙ Feyo and Brites Monteiro, and the maternal granddaughter of Simão da Costa Godinho [see NFP Pedigree Charts, Book 4, ff. 87, rev.]
> 11 D. Brites Monteiro

N11 D. BRITES MONTEIRO, daughter of Manoel˙ Roque de Abreu N10, married João de Abranches de Abreu Castello Branco˙, lord of the entail of Nossa Senhora da Piedade. The latter was the son of Manoel˙ de Figueiredo˙ Castello Branco˙ and his wife D. Leonor de Abranches; the paternal grandson of Manoel˙ Fernandes˙ de Figueiredo and his wife Antonia˙ de Almeida, and the maternal grandson of Antonio˙ de Abranches and his wife Luisa Gomes. Antonio˙ de Abranches was the son of João Antunes and Leonor de Abranches, daughter of Manoel˙ Affonso˙ and Isabel Alvares˙ de Abranches. Manoel˙ Fernandes˙ de Figueiredo˙ was the son of his namesake and his wife Felipa Gonçalves˙ de Figueiredo˙; his wife Anna de Almeida (sic)[i] was the daughter of Salvador Ribeiro˙ Pinto and Salvadora de Castello Branco

> 12 Felipa de Abranches Castello˙ Branco [NFP Pedigree Charts, Tome 2, *ff.* 65, *rev.*]
> 12 Roque Ribeiro˙ de Abreu [NFP Pedigree Charts, Tome 2, *ff.* 174]

§129

N12 FELIPE DE ABREU LIMA, son of Francisco˙ de Abreu Lima §106 N11, is a Fidalgo of the King's Household, was a traveling judge, an office he no longer holds, and married D. Maria˙ Adelaide de Abreu Lima, though this marriage was at first held to be invalid on the grounds that the proxies were not empowered or that she withdrew hers; however, it was later legitimated after she had them corrected. She was the daughter and heiress of Manoel˙ Joaquim Coelho da Costa Maya (Lecturer in Mathematics, Knight of the Order of Christ and lord of the house of Prosello in Ponte do Porto) and his wife D. Maria˙ Jeronima de Passos de Probem [NFP Araujo §465 N30][ii]

§130

BARBEITA

King Sancho II r. 1223–1248
King Afonso III r. 1248–1279

N6 GARCIA˙ DE ABREU, son of Gonçallo Rodrigues˙ de Abreu §3 N5, lived in the time of King Sancho II and King Afonso II, was the lord of the fief of Barbeita and married (...)
> 7 João Garcia˙ de Abreu

King Dinis r. 1279–1325

N7 JOÃO GARCIA˙ DE ABREU, son of Garcia de Abreu N6. In the records of King Dinis's survey of Portugal, he is mentioned as the lord of the fief of Barbeita in the district of Fraião, nowadays in the municipality of Coura, in Santa Marta de Coixos, where in Crioins a son of João Garcia's was raised by Durão Pires. He had
> 8 Pedro Annes de Abreu

---

[i] A few lines above, Manoel˙ Fernandes˙ de Figueiredo's wife is called Antonia de Almeida, and not Anna de Almeida. (T. N.)

[ii] In NFP Araujo §465 N30, Manoel Joaquim Coelho da Costa's wife is called Maria˙ Jeronima de Barboza Paços de Probem, and their daughter's name is Maria˙ Adelaide de Abreu Lima *de Vasconcellos˙*. (T. N.)

N8 PEDRO ANNES DE ABREU, son of João Garcia de Abreu N7, was the lord of Barbeita, which was confirmed by King Afonso III on December 19, 1263
>9 Garcia Pires de Abreu

King Dinis r. 1279–1325. For details about this conflict, see §83 N6

N9 GARCIA PIRES DE ABREU, son of Pedro Annes N8, was one of the noblemen assembled in the agreement made by King Dinis between the Abreus and the Quintelas. He married D. Mor Giraldes, widow of Affonso˙ Martins˙, who, in 1346 bestowed many estates upon her granddaughter
>10 Affonço Giraldes de Abreu

King Afonso IV r. 1325–1357
King Peter I r. 1357–1367
King Ferdinand r. 1367–1383

N10 AFFONÇO˙ GIRALDES DE ABREU, son of Garcia Pires N9, was the lord of the fief of Barbeita in the time of Kings Afonso IV and Peter I. On August 17, 1379, King Ferdinand bestowed upon him the royal estates of Toxar in Lisbon
>>11 D. Violante Affonso˙, who married Diogo Gomes de Abreu, son of Lourenço Gomes [§49 N2]
>>11 Mor Giraldes de Abreu

N11 MOR GIRALDES DE ABREU, daughter of Affonço˙ Giraldes N10, was the lady of the manor and fief of Barbeita by her grandmother's grant, and married Estevão Rodrigues˙ de Carvalho˙
>>12 Luis Affonso˙ de Carvalho˙
>>12 Alvaro Affonso˙ de Carvalho˙, who married Guiomar Pereira˙ [NFP Araujo §340 N21][i]. As the said Alvaro Affonso had no issue, together with his brother Luis Affonso˙ he enfeoffed the entail of Barbeita in 1547 (Alvaro Affonso˙ was tenant of D. Vasco Marinho's estates, in which office he accumulated much wealth)

N12 LUIS AFFONSO˙ DE CARVALHO˙, son of Mor Giraldes N11, was the lord of Barbeita and married Rosa Fernandes˙ Bacellar. Some say he had no issue by this marriage, and had the daughter below by a mistress called Carvalha. After his wife's decease, Luis Affonso˙ became a clergyman and was the curate of the church of Taboia, of which he obtained the advowson and whose lands he leased to his parishioners. Together with his brother he enfeoffed the lands of Barbeita, which he bestowed upon his daughter as a dowry
>>13 D. Genebra Fernandes˙ de Carvalho˙, who married Pedro de Castro or Pedro Vaz Pereira˙ de Castro [with issue in NFP Araujo §340 N22][ii]

---

[i] In NFP Araujo §340 N21, Alvaro Affonso de Carvalho's wife is called *Germineza* Pereira˙, and not Guiomar Pereira. (T. N.)

[ii] In NFP Araujo §340 N22, Pedro Vaz Pereira˙ de Castro's wife is called Genebra *Affonso˙* de Carvalho˙, and not Genebra Fernandes de Carvalho. (T. N.)

§131

THE ABREUS OF REGALADOS

N10 TRISTÃO GOMES DE ABREU LIMA, son of João Gomes de Abreu §106 N9[i], was a Fidalgo of the King's Household and married D. Anna de Faria˙, daughter of Matheus Felgueira˙ and Isabel de Faria˙, but with whom he never had a marital life, sp. He had a bastard daughter by D. Catarina˙ de Sena de Brito Malheiro, sister of Luis de Brito Malheiro, lord of the house of Abobreira, near Ponte de Lima [see this chapter §70 (sic)][ii]

   11 Maria Luiza de Abreu Lima

N11 MARIA LUIZA DE ABREU LIMA, bastard daughter of Tristão Gomes de Abreu N10, according to a justification supported by witnesses and made by her descendants. She was abducted by Manoel˙ Rodrigues˙ Pereira, whom she married. However, in a petition submitted by Manoel˙ Rodrigues˙ Pereira's grandchildren in order to be granted a nobility charter, she is not mentioned as his wife. Her husband was the son of João Rodrigues˙ de Lima, a native of Coura, and his wife Marianna Gomes, and the grandson of Gaspar Rodrigues˙ Lima and Maria˙ Rodrigues˙

   12 Rodrigo Antonio˙ de Abreu Lima

N12 RODRIGO ANTONIO˙ DE ABREU LIMA, son of Maria˙ Luisa de Abreu N11. According to the information we have received, he is the lord of the emphyteutic lands of Casal da Lage in Beiral do Lima, which he obtained through his grandmother D. Catarina˙ de Sena, of the house of Abobreira. He is a Knight of the Order of Christ and was a Judge of the Customhouse in Oporto in 1816. He married D. Anna Catarina˙ de Almeida, e Silva, sister of Antonio˙ Thomas de Almeida, e Silva˙ (who was the Chief Treasurer of the Northern Forces, a Fidalgo of the King's Household and a Knight of the Order of Christ, and was apparently from Lisbon, and the husband of D. Anna Margarida˙ Vieira da Cunha, e Silva). D. Anna Catarina˙ de Almeida˙ was the daughter of Mauricio de Almeida da Silva˙ (clerk of the Commerce Union register office) and his wife Anna Theresa Rosa. The said Anna Catarina˙ was the paternal granddaughter of Diogo de Almeida da Silva˙ and his wife Theresa Maria˙, and the maternal granddaughter of Jose Pereira˙ and his wife Maria˙ Theresa of Nossa Senhora da Enxara

---

[i] See fn. *ii* on p. 129. (T. N.)

[ii] In §70 it is said that a Catarina de Brito *Pimenta* (and not Catarina de Brito Malheiro) had a bastard son by *Francisco de Brito Malheiro* (and not Tristão Gomes de Abreu Lima), and that she was the maternal granddaughter of the lord of the house of Abobreira. Yet there is no explicit mention of any name given in the present section. (T. N.)

For details about Portuguese ranks of nobility, see p. v

13 D. Marianna, wife of Jose Vicente Taveira [with issue in NFP Amado §12 N17][i]

13 Jose Mauricio de Abreu Lima §140[ii]

13 Rodrigo Luciano, who was an aide-de-camp of D. Diogo de Sousa. On May 4, 1830, he was granted a charter of *Fidalgo*-Knight for services rendered in the Peninsula War in Portugal, and also for his services as a Colonel of an Infantry Regiment in Luanda, Angola, and in India

13 Pedro Alexandre de Abreu Lima, who held the office of Clerk of the Council Board in the Oporto Customs, a professed Knight of the Order of Christ and the Order of the Immaculate Conception, and a Knight-*Fidalgo* of the King's Household by a charter dated March 11, 1831. In June 1831 he had his name registered in the General Records of grants, in which his grandfather is also mentioned (a document which we have had the opportunity to see)

§132

N9 GARCIA˙ MENDES DE ABREU, son of Antão Mendes de Abreu §73 N8. He was a university graduate and married D. Joanna de Mascarenhas de Lemos

　　10 D. Antonia˙ de Lemos de Abreu Mascarenhas

N10 D. ANTONIA˙ DE LEMOS DE ABREU, daughter of Garcia Mendes de Abreu N9, married Antonio˙ Gomes de Lemos, son of Manoel˙ de Lemos and his wife Pantaleana Rabello, paternal grandson of Diogo Gonçalves˙, or Diogo Gomes, of Canal and D. Guiomar de Lemos, and maternal grandson of Antonio˙ Rabello and D. Camilia de Moura

　　11 D. Joanna de Mascarenhas de Abreu, e Lemos

N11 D. JOANNA DE MASCARENHAS DE ABREU, daughter of D. Antonia˙ de Lemos N10, married Antonio˙ da Fonseca˙ Mancellos, Fidalgo of the King's

---

[i] In NFP Amado §12 N17 (in which this couple's issue is not given, unlike what is stated here), she is called Marianna *de Abreu Lima*, and her husband is Jose Taveira *de Magalhães*˙ (and not Jose Vicente Taveira). (T. N.)

[ii] In the original text, Jose Mauricio de Abreu Lima's wife and grandparents are mentioned in this passage, and their names appear again in §140, a section with much more details about the said Jose Mauricio and his relatives. In order to avoid repetition, we have opted to suppress this first reference. However, there are some small differences between the names mentioned in these two sections. Here, her wife's name was Joaquina Rita de Almeida, whereas in §140 she is called Joaquina de Almeida, e Silva. Her father's name is given here as Antonio Thomas de Almeida, whereas in §140 he has a longer name: Antonio˙ Thomas de Almeida˙, e Silva. (T. N.)

Household of Pombal, son of Paullo da Fonseca˙ Mancellos, Fidalgo of the King's Household and his wife D. Catarina˙ de Carvalho˙ [NFP Mancellos §1 N6; see also NFP Pedigree Charts, Tome 2, *ff.* 80, *rev.*]

§133

N7 GIL FERNANDES DE ABREU, son of Duarte Gil Bouro de Abreu §40 N6[i], married Guiomar Lourenço de Lima, bastard daughter of Dr. Fernão Lourenço de Lima, bastard son of Bartolomeu Lourenço de Lima, commendatory of São Tirso, for whom the abbeystead of Refoios, Campello, Vermelho, Reimonde, São João do Souto and Cerdal was legally reserved, according to a confirmation dated October 2, 1450. In the records he was called the Abbot of Carvoeiro and Archpriest of the See of Braga, and was the bastard son of D. Leonel Lima, 1st Viscount of Villa Nova [NFP Lima §4 N12]

       8 João Fernandes˙ de Lima, of Braga

       8 D. Catarina˙ Fernandes˙ Lima˙

       8 Maria˙ Lourenço de Lima

       8 Bartolomeu˙ Fernandes˙ de Lima

       8 Theresa Fernandes˙ de Lima

       8 Pedro Fernandes˙ Lima

N8 MARIA˙ LOURENÇO DE LIMA, daughter of Gil Fernandes˙ de Abreu N7, married Antonio˙ Vaz, who came from Cabreira, son of Antonio Vaz

       9 Bartolomeu˙ de Lima, who married Isabel da Rocha §143

       9 Ignes Vaz, who married Antonio˙ Fernandes˙ Baldreo, a farmer, with issue

       9 Guiomar Lourenço de Lima

       9 João

       9 (...), who married Gregorio˙ Soares, son of Antonio˙ Vivas

       9 Domingas˙, who married Gaspar Soares

       9 Catarina Antunes, who married Antonio˙ da Rocha, a farmer

       9 Anna Vaz, who married Manoel˙ Ledo [with issue in NFP Ledo §1 N3][ii]

       9 Antonio˙ Toscano, who married Isabel da Costa Velloso [with issue in NFP Costa §42 N6][iii]

---

[i] This reference footnote gives some differences between the information provided by §40 N6 and the present section. (T. N.)

[ii] In NFP Ledo §1 N3, he is called Manoel Ledo *de Campos*, and his (second) wife is called Anna Vaz *de Lima*. (T. N.)

[iii] In NFP Costa §42 N6, Isabel da Costa Velloso's husband is called Antonio˙ Toscano *de Lima*. (T. N.)

N9 GUIOMAR LOURENÇO DE LIMA, daughter of Maria˙ Lourenço N8, married Baltazar˙ Mendes, son of Mendo Affonso˙ de Gondiacas, and Anna Fernandes
        10 Gaspar Mendes de Lima

N10 GASPAR MENDES DE LIMA, son of Guiomar Lourenço N9, was the abbot of Penascaes and had bastard issue by Maria˙ Gomes
        11 Guiomar Lourenço de Lima, who married Manoel˙ da Silva˙ Tinoco, lord of the manor of Portela in São Pris, Barca, son of Domingos˙ da Silva˙ Tinoco, lord of the said manor, and his wife Maria˙ Ledo de Lima [with issue in NFP Aranha §74 N14]

§134

N12 JORGE DE ALMEIDA CASTELLO˙ BRANCO, son of D. Anna Cardoso de Abreu §86 N11, was the abbot of Ribafeita near Viseu and had bastard children
        13 Francisco˙ de Almeida Castello Branco
        13 Maria˙ da Assumpção, a nun in the convent of Jesus in Viseu

N13 FRANCISCO˙ DE ALMEIDA CASTELLO˙ BRANCO, son of Jorge de Almeida N12, married his second cousin Mecia de Almeida Castello˙ Branco, daughter of Gaspar Loureiro, and his wife Luisa de Castello Branco, daughter of Mecia de Almeida Castello˙ Branco, who was Francisco's aunt, the sister of his father Jorge de Almeida [§135 N13]
        14 Jorge de Almeida
        14 João de Abreu Castello˙ Branco, who married (...)

N14 JORGE DE ALMEIDA CASTELLO˙ BRANCO, son of Francisco˙ de Almeida N13, married (in Faia, just beyond Senhora da Lapa) D. Bernarda de Abreu
        15 Jorge de Almeida
        15 Isabel Cardoso de (...)

§135

N13 LUISA DE CASTELLO BRANCO, daughter of D. Mecia de Almeida §86 N12, married Gaspar Loureiro, son of Antonio˙ Rodrigues˙ de Figueiredo˙, known as Penedo[i]

---

[i] Obscure fragment in the original text: "Gaspar Loureiro fº de An.to Rz de Figd.º, e o Penedo", the latter piece of information being translated by guesswork. (T. N.)

14 Antonio˙ Rodrigues˙ de Figueiredo

14 Fray Gaspar, a Capuchin monk

14 Genebra de Figueiredo˙

14 Francisca˙, who died in infancy[i]

14 Mecia de Almeida Castello Branco, who married Francisco˙ de Almeida˙, son of Dr. Jorge de Almeida Castello Branco [§134 N12]

14 Maria˙ Loureiro, who married Manoel˙ Ferras Castello Branco, son of Francisco˙ de Carvalho˙, with issue

N14 ANTONIO˙ RODRIGUES˙ DE FIGUEIREDO˙, son of Luisa Castello Branco N13. He married (of his own will but against that of all his relatives) Archangella Machado, only daughter of Thomaz Machado de Andrade, lord of the entail of Alcofra and Maria˙ de Lemos, daughter of Antonio˙ de Lemos, o Velho (the Elder), a resident of Viseu

15 Gaspar de Loureiro, the Younger

15 Miguel de Loureiro

15 (sic)

§136

THE ABREUS OF CANAS DE SENHORIM

N6 CUSTODIO LUIS DE ABREU DA GAMA, son of Antonio˙ de Abreu da Gama §123 N5, was a Fidalgo of the King's Household, a Knight of the Order of Christ, the Captain General of Canas de Senhorim and the lord of the manor of Tapaios in the territory of Redinha. He married D. Maria˙ Luisa de Mello, e Castro, daughter of João Lobo da Costa Borges, Fidalgo of the King's Household, lord of the entail of São Miguel do Outeiro, and his wife D. Elena Maria˙ de Mello, e Mendonça of Selorico [see NFP Pedigree Charts, Tome 3, *ff.* 58, *rev.* and *ff.* 134]

7 Antonio˙ de Abreu da Gama

7 D. Francisca˙ Theresa de Castro, e Mello

---

[i] Obscure fragment: "14 Genebra de Figd.º 15 Fran.ca mor. meninas". The change of number (14-15) suggests that Francisca was the daughter of Genebra de Figueiredo, but the plural form in "mor. meninas" shows that they both died in infancy, which contradicts the first statement. We have opted to consider that they were sisters, and inform that Francisca died in infancy (with the probably wrong information about Genebra de Figueiredo's premature death being caused by a transcription error. (T. N.)

N7 ANTONIO˙ DE ABREU DA GAMA, son of Custodio Luis de Abreu N6, was a Fidalgo of the King's Household, married D. Joanna Rita de Almeida˙ Castello Branco, daughter of Dionizio de Almeida˙ Castello Branco, Fidalgo of the King's Household, and D. Anna Leonor Ferreira˙, paternal granddaughter of Fernão de Almeida˙ Castello Branco, Fidalgo of the King's Household and D. Isabel Loureiro, and maternal granddaughter of Dr. Antonio˙ Francisco˙ Duarte and D. Maria˙ Leonor Ferreira˙

8 Antonio˙ Maria˙ de Abreu da Gama

N8 ANTONIO˙ MARIA˙ DE ABREU DA GAMA, son of Antonio˙ de Abreu da Gama N7, Fidalgo of the King's Household, married D. Maria˙ Maxima Osorio Machuca de Vilhena, daughter of Jose de Sousa da Cunha Preto and D. Antonia˙ Osorio Machuca de Vilhena [NFP Coutinho §325 N17]

9 Antonio˙ Maria˙ de Abreu da Gama do Amaral Osorio, who was unmarried in 1828

§137

LORDS OF THE MANOR OF ORÃO

N14 ALBERTO DE ABREU DE AMORIM PESSOA, son of Antonio˙ de Abreu de Amorim Pessoa §111 N13, became the lord of the house of his father and of the manor of Orão, and married D. Luisa Felizarda da Cunha Coutinho

15 Francisco˙ Antonio˙ de Abreu de Amorim Pessoa

§138

LORDS OF THE HOUSE OF ALEVIADA

N14 LUIS DA CUNHA COUTINHO˙, son of Luis da Cunha Coutinho˙ §30 N13 and his second wife D. Maria˙ de Mello. He had (by his niece (...), daughter of his sister D. Vitoria, second wife of Gonçallo Pinto de Magalhães˙, son of Diogo Pinto de Magalhães˙, lord of the manor of Capella in Fregim near Amarante), the son below [NFP Magalhães §89 N17][i]

15 B. Luis da Cunha Coutinho˙

---

[i] In NFP Magalhães §89 N17-N18, this Vitoria is said to have the surname "*da Cunha*", and her husband is called Gonçallo Pinto *Leite Pereira˙ de Magalhães˙*. (T. N.)

N15 LUIS DA CUNHA COUTINHO˙ MACHADO, E MELLO, bastard son of Luis da Cunha N14, was legitimated by his father and married D. Maria˙ Augusta Guedes, daughter of Manoel˙ Bernardo Guedes Carvalho˙ de Menezes, lord of the house of Bairro in Lobrigos [NFP Pinto §185[i] and NFP Pedigree Charts, Tome 2, *ff.* 203 *rev.*]

§139

N10 COSME DE ABREU DE LIMA, bastard son of Manoel˙ de Abreu Lima §25 N9, married Serafina de Palma Alcoforado, daughter of Gonçallo˙ Correa˙ Barba de Mesquita˙ and Luisa de Palma
      11 Bento˙ de Mesquita˙ Alcoforado

N11 BENTO MESQUITA ALCOFORADO, son of Cosme de Abreu N10, married D. Marianna de Teive de Macedo, daughter of Sebastião˙ Ribeiro˙ de Teive, Keeper of the Victuals, and his wife D. Maria˙ Pereira˙ Ferreira˙
      12 João de Mesquita˙ Alcoforado

N12 JOÃO DE MESQUITA˙ ALCOFORADO, son of Bento de Mesquita˙ N11, married D. Felipa Maria˙ de Almada, e Mello, daughter of Affonso˙ Luis de Mello de Gouvea and his wife D. Joanna Pereira˙ de Aguillar Pantoja

§140[ii]

N13 JOSE MAURÍCIO DE ABREU LIMA, son of Rodrigo Antonio˙ de Abreu Lima §131 N12, is a Knight of the Order of Christ and a Fidalgo and Knight of the King's Household (by a charter dated May 4, 1830), Judge of the Customhouse in Oporto, lord of the emphyteutic lands of Casal da Lage in

---

[i] NFP Pinto §185 N17 refers to Manoel˙ Bernardo Guedes *Pereira˙* (and not Carvalho˙) de Menezes, and does not make any mention of his daughter given here. (T. N.)

[ii] In the original text, there were three sections before this one about Jose Mauricio de Abreu Lima, which we have preferred to omit. The first of them (§138 in the original) refers to Lopo Gomes de Abreu and his descendency, a text which is already given in §63 (q. v.), so we have suppressed it here in order to avoid repetition. The other two sections (§139 and §140 in the original) were strangely blank, with only the information that the people who were supposed to be there are mentioned in the chapter of Abreu of Grade. The next section (which is the one presented here, about Jose Mauricio de Abreu Lima), received the number §141 in the original text, but appears here as §140 due to these and other changes that we have been forced to make in order to have a more coherent numeration pattern. In the original text, part of the information presented here was also given in §131 N12 Sub13, in which a footnote shows some details about the differences between these two passages. (T. N.)

King John VI r. 1816–1826

Beiral do Lima and of the manor of Nossa Senhora de Guadalupe in Souto de Rebordoins. He married his first cousin D. Joaquina de Almeida, e Silva, daughter of Antonio˙ Thomas de Almeida, e Silva˙, (Knight of the Order of Christ, Fidalgo of the King's Household by grant of King John VI, and Chief Treasurer of the Northern Forces), and his wife D. Anna Margarida Vieira da Cunha, e Silva, heiress and paternal granddaughter of Mauricio de Almeida, e Silva, clerk of the Commerce Union register office, and his wife Anna Theresa Pereira˙; and maternal granddaughter of Jacinto Gomes de Carvalho (Knight of the Order of Saint James, chief forest keeper of the village of Meires, and lord of the manor of Sereijinhas in the same village) and D. Maria˙ Vieira da Cunha

> 14 Rodrigo Antonio˙ de Abreu Lima
> 14 Jose Luciano de Abreu Lima
> 14 D(...)
> 14 D(...)
> 14 D(...) (sic)

§141

N15 D. MARIA CLARA BARBOSA DA CUNHA, daughter of Francisco˙ Barbosa da Cunha §47 N14, married Martinho Luis Marques do Couto, lord of the house of Fontinha in Estarreja

> 16 Manoel˙ Bernardo da Cunha Couto, e Mello
> 16 Francisco˙ Barbosa, a university graduate and canon in Braga
> 16 Pedro Barbosa, a canon in Braga
> 16 Joaquim˙ Calisto Barbosa
> 16 Jose Luis Barbosa

§142

For details about Portuguese ranks of nobility, see p. v

N10 D. PAULA DE ABREU LIMA, bastard daughter of João Gomes de Abreu Lima §106 N9, lord of the fief of Refoios and Page-*Fidalgo* of the King's Household [§105 N9], who fathered her by D. Isabel Maciel, a noble woman descended from the original family of Maciel. Though D. Paula was not legitimated, she was acknowledged by her father. She married Luis Pereira˙ de Brito, lord of the manor of Reris and Gericó in Refoios do Lima, son of (...)

> 11 D. Ventura de Abreu Lima

N11 D. VENTURA DE ABREU LIMA DE BRITO, daughter of D. Paulla de Abreu N10, inherited her father's house and married Marcos Antonio˙ da Silva da Costa Borges, lord of the entail of Bonhadouro in Besteiros and Chief Courier of Ponte de Lima, bastard son of Cristovão da Silva˙ da Costa (Fidalgo of the King's

Household and lord of the entail of Bonhadouro) and his mistress Maria˙ da Rocha. Cristovão da Silva˙ da Costa, who legitimated his son, was the son of Bento da Silva˙ Borges and D. Agueda da Costa

    12 D. Antonia˙ Leonor Maria˙ da Silva˙ de Abreu Lima, who inherited her father's estates, married João Marcos de Sá Sotomayor, lord of the manor of Quinzo, son of Favião de Brito, e Sousa, lord of the said manor and his wife D. Maria˙ de Sá Sotomayor [with issue in NFP Maciel §32 N5][i]

§143

N9 BARTOLOMEU DE LIMA, son of Maria˙ Lourenço de Lima §133 N8, married Isabel da Rocha, daughter of Baltazar˙ da Rocha, a cloth merchant, and his wife Joanna Lopes, daughter of Garcia Lopes and his wife Isabel Lopes [NFP Lopes da Barca §11 N5]

    10 Joanna de Lima, who married João Barbosa, son of João Mendes and Anna Beatriz de Ferreira˙ in Arcos

    10 Anna da Rocha, who married Baltazar˙ de Araujo˙, Law Officer of Arcos, etc.

        11 Antonia˙ de Araujo˙, who married João de Almeida of Santa Eulalia de Ruivos

        11 Baltazar˙ de Araujo˙, who married (...), daughter of Bento da Fonseca˙

    10 Maria˙ da Rocha, who married Antonio˙ da Costa Aranha of Arcos, and had

        11 Pedro de Caldas, who married Isabel da Costa, with issue

§144

N10 JOÃO GOMES DE ABREU, son of Leonel de Abreu §2 N9, a clergyman, had bastard children

    11 B. Antonia˙ de Abreu

    11 B. Pedro Gomes de Abreu, who served in India

    11 B. Leonel de Abreu, who studied in Coimbra, no further details

---

[i] In NFP Maciel §32 N5, D. Ventura de Abreu Lima de Brito's daughter is called Antonia *de Abreu e Lima* (and not Antonia Leonor Maria da Silva de Abreu Lima, as stated here), who was the wife of João Marcos de *Brito e Souza* (and not João Marcos de Sá Sotomayor), son of Favião de Brito, e Souza and his wife Maria˙ de Sá *de Amorim* (and not Maria de Sá Sotomayor). (T. N.)

THE ABREUS OF GRADE

There are many different opinions about the origin of this family. Some say it stems from Garcia Vaz Aranha de Azevedo, son of Martim or Mem Vaz Aranha [NFP Aranha §52 N7]. This Garcia Vaz obtained from his uncle João Gonçalves˙ Aranha the Tower of Grade, which was under the command of Azere. This tower had belonged to D. Maria˙ Dias, daughter of Diogo Annes Aranha, who lived around 1590. Others say that João Gonçalves˙ Aranha, Commendatory of Azere, did not grant the Tower of Grade to Garcia Vaz Aranha, but that the tower instead had belonged to Garcia's father, Martim or Mem Vaz Aranha, as is stated in NFP Aranha §52 N7. Some say Garcia married D. Mecia Gomes de Abreu, daughter of Vasco Gomes de Abreu, lord of Regalados, and his wife D. Maria˙ Annes Portocarreiro [NFP Abreus of Regalados §2 N2]. Others say this family descends from Garcia Vaz de Abreu, father of D. Sancha Gracia, who married Gil Vasques Bacellar [NFP Bacelar §1 N4], and that Garcia Vaz descended from Gonçallo˙ Rodrigues˙ de Abreu, who won the battle of Veiga da Matança with the idea of digging pits on the battlefield which were then covered with grating and branches, and into which the enemies fell, and that is the reason why the members of this family have in their coat of arms the figure of a grating besides the symbols of the Abreus, in memory of this deed.[i] Others state that the said Mecia Gomes de Abreu was the daughter of Alvaro Vaz de Abreu, a resident in the parish of São João da Ribeira, son of Vasco Gomes de Abreu, though, according to what we have stated above, Vasco was Mecia's father, and not her grandfather. Finally, others say that Mecia Gomes de Abreu was the daughter of Gomes Lourenço de Abreu [NFP §1 N6]; however,

---

[i] *Grade: Port.* grating. For this episode, see NFP Abreu of Regalados §1 N1. However, the ancestor of the Abreus in this reference is called Gonçallo *Martins* de Abreu, and not Gonçallo Rodrigues de Abreu. (T. N.)

King Manuel I (b. 1469; d.1521)

in spite of the long tradition reputing these Abreus as being from Regalados, this has never been proved to be true. Some sources say Garcia˙ Vaz Aranha, lord of the house of Grade and honor of Paredes in the suburbs of Viana, was very well acquainted with Infanta D. Brites, the mother of King Manuel I, and that D. Brites, just before her death at Grade, wrote to D. Mecia Gomes, requesting that all D. Mecia's children and husband be sent to her. So D. Mecia dispatched to the Queen her four children, two sons and two daughters, with two trunks on a beast of burden, and according to the Infanta's wish they were all sent to become monks and nuns, with the exception of the eldest son, Alvaro Vaz de Abreu, mentioned below in N1[i]

Yet in an instrument we have seen dated 1723, by which João Bento de Abreu was granted the right to bear a coat of arms, it is proved that the said Alvaro Vaz de Abreu was the son of João de Abreu and the grandson of Alvaro de Abreu[ii]. There is also a justification dated April 25, 1505, made by Ruy de Abreu (son of the same Alvaro de Abreu and husband of Senhorinha Gomes Pereira˙) [NFP Soares Tangil §19 N7][iii], in which Ruy de Abreu states that he was the son of Alvaro de Abreu of the village of Caminha, and the grandson of João de Abreu, a very distinguished nobleman of the said village, and first cousin to Pedro Gomes de Abreu, the Elder, lord of Regalados. In this same instrument it is stated that this João de Abreu was married to D. Ignes Dias de Sousa, daughter of D. Lopo Dias de Sousa, Master of the Order of Christ [NFP Sousa §4 N17]. This João de Abreu is the person to whom we attribute the origin of this family, an interpretation which is also in accordance with a chronicle we have seen.

So we think it is a mistake to consider that the stem of these Abreus was Garcia Vaz Aranha, son of Martim Vaz Aranha, lord of Grade, and husband of Mecia Gomes de Abreu, sister of Pedro Gomes, the Elder, for had this been true, his descendants would have adopted the same surname inherited by the male line. So, if it is true that Garcia Vaz Aranha was the lord of Grade (whether because of his Abreu ascendancy or because he was granted this office by the Commendatory of Azere), it is supposed that he did not have issue by his wife, so the Tower of Grade later passed to his brother and brother-in-law Alvaro Vaz N1, or to his nephew, and in either case the Tower of Grade went back to bearers of the name Abreu, and that is why they are called "Grade"

---

[i] Yet in §1 N1 it is said that Alvaro Vaz de Abreu was the son of Vasco Gomes de Abreu and Maria (or Mayor) Annes Portocarreiro, and not of Garcia Vaz Aranha and Mecia Gomes de Abreu. (T. N.)

[ii] However, according to what is stated in §1 N1-N3, it was *Alvaro de Abreu* who was the son of João de Abreu and the grandson of Alvaro *Vaz* de Abreu. (T. N.)

[iii] In Soares Tangil §19 N7, Senhorinha Gomes Pereira's husband is called Alvaro *Vaz* de Abreu. (T. N.)

§1

N1 ALVARO VAZ DE ABREU was the son of Vasco Gomes de Abreu, lord of Regalados, and his wife D. Maria˙ Annes Portocarreiro [NFP Abreus of Regalados §2 N2]ⁱ . He lived in the manor of Talhavezes, near Ponte de Lima, and married D. Maria˙ Rodrigues˙ Pacheco, or according to others, D. Theresa de Escovar

> 2 João de Abreu
>
> 2 Brites or Beatriz de (sic), who married Martim Gonçalves˙ de Sequeira, lord of the manor of Torre and the manor-house of the family of Sequeira˙ [with issue in NFP Sequeiros §3 N4]
>
> 2 Theresa Gomes de Abreu §31

N2 JOÃO DE ABREU, son of Alvaro Vaz de Abreu N1, was a very distinguished nobleman in Caminha and first cousin to Pedro Gomes de Abreu. In a justification dated April 25, 1505 and presented by his grandson Ruy de Abreu, it is stated that he was the lord of Regalados and married D. Ignes Dias de Sousa, daughter of D. Lopo Dias de Sousa, Master of the Order of Christ [NFP Sousa §4 N17]

> 3 Alvaro de Abreu

N3 ALVARO DE ABREU. In a instrument dated 1723 by which João Bento de Abreu was granted the right to bear a coat of arms, it is stated that Alvaro de Abreu was the son of João de Abreu N2 and the grandson of the above-mentioned ancestors. Alvaro de Abreu, who was dubbed "the one from Fonte de Monção", was the lord of the Tower of Grade and Alcaide General of Lapela, and married Guiomar Affonso˙ Villarinho, daughter of Affonso˙ Rodrigues˙ Villarinho and Constança Lourenço [NFP Vilarinho §1 N3]ⁱⁱ

> 4 Pedro de Abreu
>
> 4 Affonso˙ de Abreu, who married Anna do Valle de Passos, daughter of Germinesa do Valle [NFP Passos §15 N15]
>
> 4 Manoel˙ de Abreu, sp
>
> 4 Ignes de Abreu §2
>
> 4 Mecia de Abreu §3
>
> 4 Anna de Abreu, who married Lopo de Lira [NFP (...)] (sic)
>
> 4 Constança de Abreu §19
>
> 4 Ruy de Abreu, who presented the above-mentioned justification. He married Senhorinha Gomes Pereira˙ [with issue in NFP Soares Tangil §19 N7]

ⁱ In NFP Abreus of Regalados §2 N2, Alvaro Vaz de Abreu's mother is called *Mayor* Annes Portocarreiro, and not Maria˙ Annes Portocarreiro. (T. N.)

ⁱⁱ In NFP Vilarinho §1 N3, Guiomar Affonso˙ Villarinho's mother is called Constança Lourenço *de Abreu*. (T. N.)

4 Guiomar Affonso˙ de Abreu, who married João Rodrigues˙ Bacellar
[with issue in NFP Bacelar §1 N10]

N4 PEDRO DE ABREU, son of Alvaro de Abreu [§1 N3], was a very
distinguished nobleman and married Aldonça Vaz Soares, daughter of Ruy
Palhares and his wife Senhorinha Gomes do Lago [NFP Palhares §5 N6]. This
information was extracted from an instrument dated 1723 by which Jose Bento
de Abreu was granted the right to bear a coat of arms
> 5 Affonço de Abreu §11
> 5 Martim de Abreu
> 5 Anna de Abreu §12
> 5 Ignes de Abreu (yet some say she is the Ignes de Abreu mentioned
> > in §2, an opinion with which we and many others agree)
> 5 Mecia de Abreu §14
> 5 Maria de Abreu §13
> 5 Francisco˙ de Abreu Soares (who, according to some, is the one
> > mentioned in §6, an opinion we do not uphold)
> 5 Antonio˙ de Abreu, who had by Maria˙ Barbosa of Coura
> > 6 Alvaro de Abreu Soares, no further details
> 5 Guiomar Vaz de Abreu, in §10

N5 MARTIM DE ABREU, son of Pedro de Abreu N4, married in Ceuta, where
he was a captain, sp

§2

N4 IGNES DE ABREU, daughter of Alvaro Vaz de Abreu §1 N3[i]. (According
to others, this Ignes de Abreu was the daughter of Pedro de Abreu §1 N4, an
opinion supported by most authors). She married Pedro Gonçalves˙ Zuniga, a
Galician nobleman who lived in the manor of Arguello, in the territory of Monção,
where he moved after having committed crimes in Castile. He was the son of D.
Gonçallo de Zuniga, lord of the entail of Pesqueira in Galicia, and his wife D.
Elvira de Zuniga, of the house of Monte Rei, and daughter of D. Pedro de
Zuniga, Count of Monte Rey
> 5 Constança de Abreu
> 5 Genebra de Abreu §5
> 5 Francisco˙ de Abreu §6[ii]

---

[i] In §1 N3, her father is called Alvaro de Abreu, and not Alvaro Vaz de Abreu. On the other hand, in
§1 N4 Sub5, it is said that this Ignes de Abreu was the daughter of Pedro de Abreu §1 N4, though
the author says explicitly that he and many others disagree with this latter version. (T. N.)

[ii] In §6, he is called Francisco˙ de Abreu *Zuniga*. (T. N.)

N5 CONSTANÇA DE ABREU, daughter of Ignes de Abreu N4, married (in Val de Milher, Galicia) Alvaro Pires de Ceta, a noble knight, or Estevão Pires de Cepta
        6 Alvaro Pires de Ceta

N6 ALVARO PIRES DE CETA, son of Constança de Abreu N5, married (in Monção) Maria˙ Soares de Brito, daughter of Gomes Correa˙ and his wife Ignes Rodrigues˙, who were members of the nobility

§3

N4 MECIA DE ABREU, daughter of Alvaro Vaz de Abreu §1 N3, married Francisco˙ Rabello, son of Alvaro Rabello, who was the son of Affonso˙ Vieira and his wife Catarina Rabello, daughter of João Alvares˙ Rabello and his wife Ignes Fernandes [NFP Rabelo §70 N12]
        5 Manoel˙ de Abreu Rabello
        5 Cristovão Rabello §9
        5 Antonio˙ de Abreu, who married Catarina˙ de Almeida, daughter of
                Alvaro Fernandes˙ Ledo [NFP Ponte Ledo §1 N3][i]
        5 Pedro de Abreu, who married (in the municipality of Penela) Anna
                do Vale

N5 MANOEL˙ DE ABREU RABELLO, son of Mecia de Abreu N4, married D. Brites de Antas, daughter of Vasco de Antas
        6 Alvaro de Abreu §4
Manoel de Abreu Rabello's second wife was Isabel de Sá Sotomayor, daughter of Bernardo Quinteiro and his wife Guiomar de Sá Sotomayor, daughter of Duarte de Sá [NFP Jacome §20 N5 and N6][ii]
        6 Francisco˙ Rabello Sotomayor

N6 FRANCISCO˙ RABELLO SOTOMAYOR, son of Manoel˙ Rabello de Abreu N5, married Anna Borges Pacheco, daughter of Belchior Borges Pacheco and Leonor de Amorim, daughter of Pedro de Amorim Calheiros [NFP Amorim §60 N7]
        7 João de Sá Sotomayor §23
        7 Leonor de Sá Sotomayor
        7 Brites da Rocha, unmarried
        7 Marianna de Sá, a nun
        7 Manoel˙ de Abreu Rabello, a clergyman

---

[i] In the original text, this cross-reference was NFP Ledo §27 N9, which is a mistake, for that section does not even exist. (T. N.)

[ii] In NFP Jacome §20 N6, Isabel de Sá Sotomayor's father is called Bernardo Quinteiro *Baldaia*. (T. N.)

N7 LEONOR DE SÁ SOTOMAYOR, daughter of Francisco· Rabello N6, second wife of Pedro Barbosa [with issue in NFP Barbosa §51 N26][i]

§4

N6 ALVARO DE ABREU, son of Manoel· de Abreu Rabello §3 N5 and his first wife, married Guiomar de Sá Sotomayor, daughter of Bernardo Quinteiro and his wife Guiomar de Sá Sotomayor [NFP Jacome §20 N6][ii]
> 7 Isabel de Sá Sotomayor
> 7 Maria de Sá Sotomayor, wife of Francisco· de São Miguel Mogeimas, son of Francisco· de São Miguel [NFP Amorim §22 N7]
> 7 Leonor de Sá Sotomayor, who married Gaspar Pinto Correa·, son of Sebastião Pinto and his wife [NFP Correia §71 N7][iii]

N7 ISABEL DE SÁ SOTOMAYOR, daughter of Alvaro de Abreu N6, married Francisco· Borges of Ponte de Lima, son of Nuno Borges Soares and his wife Maria dos Guimaraens (or Brites dos Guimaraens), and grandson of Gregorio de Lançoens and Margarida de Barros
> 8 Father Manoel· de Abreu
> 8 Nuno Borges, who married D. Isabel de Mesquita Brandão, daughter of Miguel Brandão de Mesquita· and Maria Malheiro [with issue in NFP Malheiro §7 N9][iv]
> 8 Father Pedro de Abreu
> 8 D. Mecia, wife of Francisco· Borges de Lançoens, sp
> 8 Guiomar de Sá Sotomayor

N8 GUIOMAR DE SÁ SOTOMAYOR, daughter of Isabel de Sá N7, married Francisco· Barbosa Aranha, son of Baltazar Barbosa Aranha and Genebra Soares de Brito [NFP Aranha §41 N10-N11][v]
> 9 D. Genebra de Brito Sotomayor, sp
> 9 João de Sá Sotomayor, a priest of the Order of the Holy Cross of Coimbra, sp

---

[i] In NFP Barbosa §51 N26, Leonor de Sá Sotomayor's husband is called Pedro Barbosa *Pereira*. (T. N.)

[ii] In NFP Jacome §20 N6, Isabel de Sá Sotomayor's father is called Bernardo Quinteiro *Baldaia*. (T. N.)

[iii] In NFP Correia §71 N7, Leonor de Sá Sotomayor's father is called Alvaro de Abreu *Rebello*. (T. N.)

[iv] In NFP Malheiro §7 N9, the first couple mentioned here is called Nuno Borges *Soares* and Isabel de Mesquita. (T. N.)

[v] In NFP Aranha §41 N10, the latter lady's surnames are inverted: Genebra *de Brito Soares*. (T. N.)

9 D. Ignocensia de Sá Sotomayor, who was the wife of Baltazar˙ de Matos Cerqueira˙ of Oporto, and had

10 Pedro

10 Paullo

10 D. Mecia, who was unmarried in 1703

9 D. Isabel de Sá Sotomayor

N9 D. ISABEL DE SÁ SOTOMAYOR, daughter of D. Guiomar de Sá N8, married Antonio˙ Falcão Marinho, son of Braz Falcão Marinho, a Knight of the Order of Christ, and D. Isabel de Abreu de Faria [NFP Araujo §196 N30 and NFP Barreto §86 N9]

10 Francisco˙ Barbosa, who died young

10 Fray Antonio˙, an Augustinian monk

10 Jose Falcão Marinho, who married D. Theresa Maria˙ Malheiro, daughter of Francisco˙ de Moura Maris [with issue in NFP Faria §31 N13]

10 Father Manoel˙, a priest of the Order of St. John the Evangelist

10 Fray Bento, a Bernardine monk

10 Visente

§5

N5 GENEBRA DE ABREU, daughter of Ignes de Abreu §2 N4, married Francisco˙ Affonso˙, a Fidalgo of the King's Household of the village of Moreira, in the territory of Monção

6 Jorge de Abreu Zuniga, who married (in Arcos) Catarina˙ de Brito [NFP Cerqueira §88 N7]

6 Salvador de Azevedo Zuniga §22[i]

6 Manoel˙ de Abreu, who married in Peru

6 Pedro de Abreu, Abbot of Mei, with issue

6 Francisco˙ de Abreu §8

6 Maria de Abreu Zuniga

6 Jeronimo de Abreu, who married in Lisbon

N6 MARIA˙ DE ABREU ZUNIGA, daughter of Genebra de Abreu N5, married Diogo Soares Falcão, nicknamed Bigodes (*lit.* Moustache), who lived in the parish of Moreira, territory of Monção and was the son of Pedro Falcão Marinho and Catarina˙ Soares de Lençoins [NFP Soares Tangil §10 N10][ii]

---

[i] In §22, he is called Salvador de *Abreu* Zuniga. (T. N.)

[ii] In NFP Soares Tangil §10 N10 Sub11, Maria de Abreu Zuniga's husband is called Diogo Soares *de Abreu*, and not Diogo Soares Falcão. (T. N.)

7 Fray Braz, a Trinitarian monk

7 Leão Soares Falcão

7 Braz de Abreu Zuniga §7

7 Catarina· Soares, who married (in the village of Monção) João
   Rodrigues· de Araujo·, and had issue. She and her husband
   enfeoffed their lands, imposing several conditions on the grantee,
   who was their nephew Diogo Soares, son of Braz de Abreu

N7 LEÃO SOARES FALCÃO, son of Maria· de Abreu Zuniga N6, married (in
Arcos) Anna de Brito Barbosa, daughter of Gaspar de Cerqueira· de Novaes,
lord of the tower of Real (manor-house of the Cerqueiras), and Ignes de Brito
Barbosa [NFP Cerqueira §89 N8], and maternal granddaughter of Pedro Gil
Barbosa

8 Simão Soares Falcão, a clergyman

8 Mathias de Brito Marinho, sp

8 Gaspar Cerqueira· Barbosa

N8 GASPAR CERQUEIRA· BARBOSA, son of Leão Soares N7, married Anna
de Lira de Brito, daughter of João de Araujo· and Rufina de Lira de Brito. The
latter was the daughter of Baltazar· Vaz Rabello and Ignes de Lira, who lived in
their manor of Rabello in Santa Ovaia of Redemoinhos, in the territory of Arcos.
Baltazar Vaz Rabello was the son of Baltazar· Vaz de Brito and Anna Mendes,
daughter of Belchior Mendes, o Velho (the Elder), of Arcos [see NFP Aranha
§59 N11][i]

9 D. Rufina de Abreu Soares, who married Manoel· de Araujo· e
   Vasconcellos, son of Francisco· de Araujo· de Azevedo· and D.
   Angella Coelho [with issue in NFP Araujo §264 N26][ii]

9 Leão Soares, Abbot of São Jorge

9 Braz de Abreu, a canon in Braga

9 D. Elena de Abreu, who married Agostinho da Costa Barreto (an
   officer of the Inquisition, an Army Captain in Barca and the lord
   of the house of Terreiro do Espirito Santo), son of Catarina· da
   Costa Cardoso and Pedro Fernandes Rodrigues [with issue in NFP
   Costa §78 N8][iii]

9 D. Joanna, a nun in Barcelos

9 D. Antonia·, unmarried

9 Ignes de Lira, who married Braz de Faria· Marinho, with issue

---

[i] In NFP Aranha §59 N11, Baltazar Vaz de Brito's mother is called Anna Mendes *Aranha*. (T. N.)

[ii] In NFP Araujo §264 N25, Francisco· de Araujo· de Azevedo·'s wife's name is Angella *Pacheco* (and
not Angella Coelho), the Pacheco version seeming to be the correct one, for she is said to be the
daughter of Jacome Pacheco. (T. N.)

[iii] In NFP Costa §78 N8, Agostinho da Costa Barreto's wife is called Elena *Gomes* de Abreu. (T. N.)

N5 Captain FRANCISCO˙ DE ABREU ZUNIGA, called "cabeças de Mocinho", son of Ignes de Abreu §2 N4. According to Francisco Ventura Maciel in his genealogical works on the city of Braga, this Francisco de Abreu was the son of Pedro de Abreu and his wife Aldonça Soares [§1 N4], an opinion we do not uphold and against which there is the evidence that if Francisco˙ de Abreu had this second parentage, there would be no reason why he should also adopt the family name of Zuniga. Francisco married Maria˙ Soares, daughter of Diogo Soares, called "Tato" (*lit.* Stammerer), and his wife Magdalena Folgueira˙ Correa [NFP Soares Tangil §6 N9 Sub10]

> 6 Alvaro Soares de Brito, who married (in Arcos) Joanna de Neiva Feyo, daughter of Isabel de Neiva and Antonio˙ Feyo [with issue in NFP Costa §139 N5][i]
> 6 Ambrozio de Abreu Zuniga, below
> 6 Ignes de Lencoins, sp
> 6 Catarina˙ de Lencoins, sp
> 6 Jose de Brito Soares, sp
> 6 Joanna de Brito, sp
> 6 Magdalena Correa˙, wife of Paullo Pereira˙

N6 AMBROZIO DE ABREU ZUNIGA, son of Francisco˙ de Abreu Zuniga N5, was a Judge of the Customhouse in Valença and married Anna Velloso de Sousa Bacellar, daughter of Gomes Velloso Bacellar and Francisca˙ Cardoso Folgueira˙ [NFP Bacelar §22 N11 and NFP Soares §27][ii]

> 7 Diogo Soares de Brito
> 7 Francisco˙ de Abreu, who married (in the manor of Bouças, Galicia) Isabel de Benevides, daughter of Rodrigo Benevides and Theresa de Sequeiros˙ Sotomaior, and had
>> 8 Anna de Abreu, wife of Manoel˙ Soares de Brito, son of Andre de Barros Falcão and Anna de Abreu [NFP Soares Tangil §11 N13]

In a deed dated 1625 in Valença it is recorded that Ambrozio de Abreu was married to D. Maria˙ de Prado. This leads us to believe that the said Ambrozio married twice. In another instrument written in the same town in 1633, it is stated that he had the following children

> 7 Maria˙ de Prado, who married Cosme de Brito [with issue in NFP Soares Tangil §45 N10]

---

[i] In NFP Costa §139 N4, Isabel de Neiva's parents are called Antonio˙ *Feijo* (and not Antonio Feyo) and Isabel de Neiva *Taveira*. (T. N.)

[ii] However, we have not found either in NFP Soares Tangil §27 or in NFP Soares de Algergaria §27 any direct reference to the family mentioned here. (T. N.)

7 Damião de Lençoins, an Infantry Major in Bahia, Brazil, where he married D. Ignes as his first wife, sp. His second wife was D. Francisca˙ Pereira˙ do Lago, daughter of Colonel Francisco˙ Pereira˙ do Lago, sp

N7 DIOGO SOARES DE BRITO, son of Ambrozio de Abreu Zuniga N6, was a Judge of the Customhouse in Valença, and married Maria˙ do Valle as his first wife, with no further details

   8 Anna da Conceipção, a nun in Valença

Diogo Soares de Brito's second wife was Luisa de Araujo˙ e Sousa, daughter of Margarida da Rocha and her husband Gonçallo Lopes de Aguião [NFP Araújo §124 N23]*i*, by whom he had

   8 Theotonio Soares de Brito

   8 Antonio˙ Soares, Knight of the Order of Christ

   8 Damião de Lençoens de Azevedo˙, who married (in Viana) D. Marianna de Sá Sotomayor, daughter of Manoel˙ da Rocha de Sá Tourinho and his wife Isabel Ferraz [with issue in NFP Faria §90 N10]

   8 D. Margarida, a nun in the convent of the Imaculate Conception in Braga

   8 D. Maria˙, *ditto*

   8 D. Francisca˙, *ditto*

N8 THEOTONIO SOARES DE BRITO, son of Diogo Soares de Brito N7, was a Knight of the Order of Christ and lived in Bahia, Brazil, where he married D. Magdalena Pereira˙, daughter of Colonel Francisco˙ Pereira˙ do Lago, institutor of the entail of Santa Barbara in the Brazilian Province of Bahia de Todos os Santos, and his wife D. Andresa de Araujo˙ e Mello, who was the daughter of Domingos Aranha de Araujo˙ and D. Francisca˙ Dias de Magalhães˙. The said D. Magdalena Pereira˙ was the paternal granddaughter of Salvador Pereira˙ do Lago, lord of the entail of Santa Barbara, and D. Maria˙ de Caldas, daughter of Payo Velloso. Francisco˙ Pereira˙ do Lago was, as it was stated, a Colonel in Bahia and a Lieutenant General. According to the Rector of Morufe, Francisco˙ Pereira˙ do Lago was from Ponte de Lima, in the parish of Souto, near the said village, like his parents Salvador and Magdalena. In this same source it is stated that Domingos˙ Aranha de Araujo˙ was also from Ponte de Lima, his wife Francisca˙ Dias de Magalhães˙ being from Bahia

   9 Jose Soares de Brito

   9 D. Luisa, a nun in the Convent of the Imaculate Conception in Braga

---

i In NFP Araújo §124 N23, Gonçallo Lopes de Aguião's wife is called Margarida da Rocha *de Souza*, and their daughter's surnames are inverted: Luisa de *Sousa de Araujo*. (T. N.)

9 Damião de Lançoins, sp
9 Francisco˙ Soares, sp
9 D. Antonia˙ Pereira˙, sp
9 D. Ursulla de Brito, sp
9 D. Andresa, sp
9 D. Catarina˙, sp
9 D. Maria, sp

N9 JOSE SOARES DE BRITO, son of Theotonio Soares N8, was a Fidalgo of the King's Household, a Knight of the Order of Christ and the lord of the entail of Santa Barbara in Bahia. He married D. Ignes Maldonado, daughter of D. João Maldonado de Azevedo and his wife D. Brites da Gama Lobo. D. João Maldonado was an Appellate Judge and a Judge of the Appeal Court of Oporto. D. Ignes Maldonado was the paternal granddaughter of D. Francisco˙ Maldonado, Knight of the Order of Christ, and D. Olaya da Silva˙ e Mello, daughter of João Nunes Rogado. D. Ignes was the maternal granddaughter of Affonço Mendes Lobo, Knight of the Order of Christ and Governor of Olivença, and D. Maria˙ de Chaves Lobo, daughter of Affonso˙ Pestana da Gama [NFP Maldonado §7 N6][i]

10 Manoel˙ Jose Soares de Brito
10 D. Magdalena (or Margarida) Maldonado §24
10 Francisco˙ Xavier Maldonado, sp

N10 MANOEL˙ JOSE SOARES DE BRITO, son of Jose Soares de Brito N9, was a Knight of the Order of Christ, a Fidalgo of the King's Household and the lord of the entail of Santa Barbara. He lived in his manor of Lamarosa near Coimbra, and married (in Olivença, in the Province of Alentejo) D. Anna de Avilla Pereira˙ da Gama, daughter of Francisco˙ Mexia Migueis, Lieutenant Governor of the Castle of Olivença, and D. Leonor de Avilla Pereira˙ [NFP Lobo §63 N13][ii]

11 Francisco˙ Xavier Soares de Brito, who was alive in 1745, sp
11 D. Damaso, a monk of the Order of the Holy Cross of Coimbra
11 D. Leonor Getrudes da Gama, e Brito, who married Marçal de Macedo Valasques de Sá de Oliveira˙ (Fidalgo of the King's Household and lord of the house of Macedo in Coimbra and others), son of Jorge de Macedo Valasques (Fidalgo of the King's Household

---

[i] In NFP Maldonado §7 N6, Affonço Mendes Lobo's wife is called Maria˙ *da Rocha* Lobo, and not Maria de Chaves Lobo. (T. N.)

[ii] In NFP Lobo §63 N13, Francisco Mexia Migueis's wife is called Leonor Pereira˙ *de Abreu* (and not Leonor de Avilla Pereira), and their daughter is called Anna *Mexia* de Avilla (and not Anna de Avilla Pereira da Gama). (T. N.)

and lord of the said entails), and D. Monica da Parada, who inherited her father's lands [mentioned in NFP Macedo §53 N17][i]. D. Leonor had

12 D. Joaquina Xavier Libania de Macedo Valasques[ii], who inherited her father's lands and married Carlos de Cordes Brandão, a resident in Sardoal, with issue

11 João Ignacio, who died unmarried

§7

N7 BRAZ DE ABREU ZUNIGA, son of Maria˙ de Abreu Zuniga §5 N6, was an Army Major and married (in Arcos) D. Francisca˙ dos Guimaraens, daughter of Gaspar Barbosa[13], of Caminha, and his wife Agueda de Brito, daughter of Gaspar or Antonio˙ Mendes Aranha and his wife D. Elena de Guimaraens˙ de Brito, who was the daughter of Andre Barbosa Coelho and Francisca˙ dos Guimaraens˙ de Brito [see NFP Prado §6 N5 (sic)[iii] and NFP Passos de Probem §45 N17]

8 Diogo Soares Falcão
8 Bento Aranha de Brito, Abbot of (...)
8 D. Maria˙, sp
8 Bartolomeu, sp
8 D. Catarina˙, a nun in the convent of Monção
8 D. Elena, *ditto*

---

[i] In NFP Macedo §53 N17, Jorge de Macedo Valasques's wife is called Monica de Parada *e Oliveira*. Besides that, in NFP Macedo §53 N18, the author is not sure about the first name of this couple's son, who is called Manoel (or Marçal) de Macedo Valasques de Sá de Oliveira˙ (T. N.)

[ii] This lady's name is omitted in the original version, but can be found in NFP Macedo §53 N18, where her husband's surnames appear inverted: Carlos *Brandão de Cordes*. (T. N.).

[13] Gaspar Barbosa was the son of João Barbosa and his wife Maria˙ de Antas[iv] [see NFP Prado §6 N5 and NFP Aranha §61 N10][v].

[iii] As regards the cross-reference NFP Prado §6 N5, see footnote *v* below. (T. N.)

[iv] In NFP Passos de Probem §45 N17, Gaspar Barbosa's mother is called Maria˙ de Antas *de Mesquita*. (T. N.).

[v] We have not found any mention about these people in NFP Prado, and the cross-reference NFP Prado §6 N5 does not even exist. In NFP Aranha §61 N10, it is said that Gaspar Barbosa was married to Angella or Agueda de Brito. (T. N.).

N8 DIOGO SOARES FALCÃO, son of Braz de Abreu Zuniga N7, was an Infantry Captain, a Knight of the Order of Christ and the lord of the manor and lands of Moreira, which were enfeoffed by his aunt. He married D. Anna de Sousa, daughter of Paullo Vaz Bayão, a rich merchant of the village of Arcos, and his wife Maria˙ de Sousa, paternal granddaughter of João Vaz Bayão, a businessman in Arcos [mentioned in NFP Araujo §309 N26 and NFP Araujo §311][i]

    9 Theodosio de Abreu Soares, sp

    9 D. Brites Josefa de Abreu, who married D. Garcia de Noronha de Mesquita˙ [with issue in NFP Machado §27 N25][ii]

    9 D. Maria˙ Josefa dos Guimaraens, who married João da Rocha Brito de Aguião, son of Jacome de Brito da Rocha [with issue in NFP Costa §79 N10][iii]

    9 D. Francisca˙, a nun in Barcelos like her sisters below

    9 D. Anna

    9 D. Joanna

    9 D. Felipa

    9 D. Luiza

§8

N6 FRANCISCO˙ DE ABREU, son of Genebra de Abreu §5 N5, married (in Arcos) Leonor de Évora, who descended from the family of Évora according to the justification presented by his grandson Pedro de Araujo˙ Aranha N8 below

    7 Margarida de Abreu

N7 MARGARIDA DE ABREU, daughter of Francisco˙ de Abreu N6, married Pedro de Araujo˙ Aranha, son of Pedro Fernandes˙ Aranha and his wife Joanna de Araujo˙ [NFP Aranha §108 N10][iv]

    8 Luis de Araujo˙, who married in Lisbon

    8 Francisco˙ de Abreu, who married in Brazil

    8 Pedro de Araujo˙ Aranha

---

[i] In NFP Araujo §309 N26, Paullo Vaz Bayão's wife is called Maria˙ de Souza *Pacheco*, and their daughter is called Anna *de Magalhães˙ de Souza*, who in NFP Araujo §311 is said to have married Diogo Soares *de Brito* (and not Diogo Soares Falcão). (T. N.)

[ii] In NFP Machado §27 N25, D. Garcia de Noronha's wife is called Brites Josefa de Abreu *Soares*. (T. N.)

[iii] In NFP Costa §79 N10, João da Rocha de Brito's wife's name is Maria˙ Josefa *de Magalhães˙ de Brito*, and not Maria Josefa dos Guimaraens. (T. N.)

[iv] In NFP Aranha §108 N10, Pedro de Araujo˙ Aranha's wife is called Margarida *Gomes* de Abreu. (T. N.)

For details about Portuguese ranks of nobility, see p. v

N8 PEDRO DE ARAUJO˙ ARANHA, son of Margarida de Abreu N6, married (in Rebordeões) Maria Lobato. This Pedro de Araujo˙ was made a Knight-Fidalgo by an instrument dated May 20, 1692, as recorded in Book #16, *ff.* 145, for the services he rendered in the wars in America as well as in Portugal, by furnishing horses for these campaigns, and also for the services of his father Pedro de Araujo˙ Aranha, who performed military duties, and the services of his uncle Domingos˙ Rodrigues˙. Pedro de Araujo˙ Aranha N8 presented a justification stating that he was the son of another Pedro de Araujo˙ Aranha and the grandson of Pedro Fernandes˙ Aranha, who was the grandson of João Gonçalves˙ Aranha, Commendatory of Azere. He also declared that his grandmother was Joanna de Araujo˙, granddaughter of Alvaro Rodrigues˙ de Araujo˙, Commendatory of Rio Frio. The instrument of this justification is dated March 8, 1660, and was written in Arcos by notary public Matheus da Costa, and witnessed by Manoel˙ de Abreu Lima, Fidalgo of the King's Household and resident in Arcos; by Reverend Luis de Brito, of the same place; by Francisco˙ Pereira˙ de Castro of the manor of Faquello; by Alexandre de Brito Brandão, by Francisco˙ Borges Pacheco and others, all of the witnesses having declared under oath that the said Pedro descended from the families of Araujo, Aranha, Zuniga, Évora and Pacheco. To this instrument were also added other attestations made by Sebastião˙ Pereira˙ do Lago, of Braga, Fidalgo of the King's Household; by Bento da Silva˙ de Menezes, Fidalgo of the King's Household; by Pedro de Araujo˙, lord of the manor-house of Lobeos and by the Viscount of Ponte de Lima, which were all dated 1660, and another dated 1684, made by João Pereira˙ do Lago, of Braga, Fidalgo of the King's Household. We have seen all these documents in this year of 1807

> 9 Ambrosio Gomes de Abreu, who married D. Luisa Pereira˙ de Abreu, daughter of Manoel˙ de Sousa de Abreu [with issue in NFP Costa §18 N10][i]

§9

N5 CRISTOVÃO DE ABREU[ii], son of Mecia de Abreu §3 N4, married (...) in Regalados

> 6 Belchior da Fonseca˙
>
> 6 Gaspar da Fonseca˙
>
> 6 Dr. Gregorio˙ Rabello, Vicar General of Valença and Abbot of Santa Eulália, had bastard issue
>
>> 7 Cristovão Rabello, who married (in the municipality of Penela) Anna do Vale

---

[i] In NFP Costa §18 N10, Ambrosio Gomes de Abreu's wife is called Luiza *do Rego Barboza* Pereira˙ de Abreu. (T. N.)

[ii] In §3 N4 Sub5, he is called Cristovão *Rabello*, and not Cristovão de Abreu. (T. N.)

N6 BELCHIOR˙ DA FONSECA˙, son of Cristovão de Abreu N5, married in Regalados

> 7 Maria˙ de Barros
> 7 Maria˙ da Silva
> 7 Francisca˙ da Fonseca˙, who married and had issueless children
> 7 Jeronima da Silva, who married (in Regalados) Antonio˙ de Abreu Folgueira˙

§10

N5 GUIOMAR VAZ DE ABREU, daughter of Pedro de Abreu §1 N4. A charter by which Jose Bento de Abreu, one of her descendants, was granted the right to bear a coat of arms, states that she was the daughter of the parents mentioned above, which is in accordance with the information presented in NFP Magalhães §58 N8, in which it is stated that she married Gomes Rodrigues˙ de Magalhães˙, son of Payo de Rodrigues˙ de Magalhães˙ and D. Maria˙ de Sequeira˙, and had the issue mentioned in that chapter, information we suppose to be true[i]

§11

N5 AFFONÇO DE ABREU, son of Pedro de Abreu and his wife Aldonça Vaz Soares §1 N4, had bastard issue by Maria˙ Barbosa of Coura

> 6 Alvaro de Abreu Soares

N6 ALVARO DE ABREU SOARES, bastard son of Affonço de Abreu N5, was a Probate Court Judge in Monção, and married D. Felipa de Abreu, bastard daughter of Pedro Gomes de Abreu, lord of Regalados [NFP Abreu of Regalados §2 N7] (sic)[ii]. Some state that this D. Felipa was a nun; maybe she was so after her husband's decease. Another possibility is the occurence of the mistake of confusing this D. Felipa de Abreu with a nun who had the same name, though this does not seem to be correct. Another error is to confuse this Felipa de Abreu with a nun of the same name who was the legitimate daughter of Leonel de Lima, (this D. Felipa de Abreu was the bastard daughter of Leonel de Abreu [see NFP Abreu §2 N7]) (sic)[iii]

> 7 Pedro Gomes de Abreu, sp
> 7 Maria de Abreu

---

[i] In NFP Magalhães §58 N8, Payo de Rodrigues de Magalhães's wife is called D. Maria˙ de Sequeira˙ *Sotomayor.* (T. N.)

[ii] Contrary to what is stated here, NFP Abreu of Regalados §2 N7 does not refer to Pedro Gomes de Abreu, but to Leonel de Abreu, who is said to be the son of Pedro Gomes de Abreu N6 and the father of Felipa de Abreu N7 Sub8. Thus, according to what is stated in NFP Abreu of Regalados, Pedro Gomes de Abreu is not Felipa de Abreu's father, but her paternal grandfather. (T. N.)

[iii] The sentence in parentheses is obscure and clearly contradicts what is stated immediately before; actually, in NFP Abreu §2 N7, it is said that Felipa de Abreu was the *legitimate* daughter of Leonel de Lima. (T. N.)

174

N7 MARIA DE ABREU, daughter of Alvaro de Abreu Soares N6, married (in Monção) Sebastião Barbosa Soares, son of Gaspar Barbosa, a university graduate, and his wife Isabel Soares de Moscoso, and grandson of another Gaspar Barbosa and his wife Isabel Soares [NFP Barbosa §96 N24][i]

    8 D. Felipa de Abreu Noronha

N8 D. FELIPA DE ABREU NORONHA, daughter of Maria˙ de Abreu N7, married Francisco˙ de Castro, Governor of Monção, son of Diogo Soares and his wife Catarina˙ Velho, daughter of Manoel˙ Pereira˙ de Lira and Joanna Mogueimas. Manoel˙ Pereira˙ de Lira was the son of Pacivel de Lira, o Velho (the Elder) and D. Isabel da Costa

       9 Diogo de Abreu de Lima, sp, Governor of Diu in India
       9 Manoel Pereira˙, sp, a Captain of the Navy in India
       9 Francisco˙ Soares, sp, *ditto*
       9 Sebastião de Castro de Abreu de Noronha
       9 D. Felipa, a nun in the convent of St. Benedict in Viana, like her sisters below
       9 D. Paulla
       9 D. Maria˙

Diu, or Dio, an Indian town which was conquered by Portugal in 1535 and remained as a Portuguese colony until 1961

N9 SEBASTIÃO DE CASTRO DE ABREU, son of D. Felipa de Abreu N8, was a Knight of the Order of Christ, a remunerated Army Colonel and a Probate Court Judge in Monção. He married D. Maria˙ Sotomayor, daughter of (...) de Sousa and D. Maria˙ das Neves Sotomayor, lords of the house of Tora. However, in the books of Toris, Sebastião is said to have married D. Isabel de Sousa, daughter of João de Araujo˙ e Sousa of Tora and D. Maria˙ das Neves Sotomayor

       10 Francisco˙ de Castro Soares de Abreu, who married of his own free will
       10 (...), a nun in Monção

§12

N5 ANNA DE ABREU, daughter of Pedro de Abreu §1 N4, married Gonçallo de Barros, this couple being the lords of the manor of Lomba in the territory of Monção, in the parish of Moreira

      6 Jeronimo Soares, who married in Ponte de Lima, sp. He had bastard issue by Isabel Violante
      7 João Soares

---

[i] In NFP Barbosa §96 N23, Gaspar Barbosa the Elder is called Gaspar Barbosa *de Lima*, and his wife's name is Isabel *Lopes*, and not Isabel Soares. (T. N.)

N5 MARIA DE ABREU, daughter of Pedro de Abreu §1 N4. This parentage, with which we agree, seems to be more probable than the one by which she is given as the daughter of Pedro de Abreu de Barros and Joanna da Rocha [§14 N6]. She married Manoel˙ de Araujo˙ Bacellar (Fidalgo of the King's Household, Page to *Infanta* D. Isabel and lord of the house of Agrelo), son of Gabriel Casco de Lira and his wife Maria˙ Affonço Bacellar, lords of the manor of Agrelo and house of Grade [NFP Bacelar §24 N12 and NFP Araujo §(...) (sic)][i]. According to the Rector of Morufe, Maria˙ de Abreu was the daughter of Pedro de Abreu §1 N4, information that seems to be correct, and which we uphold

  6 Francisca˙ de Araujo˙
  6 Maria˙ de Abreu Soares §17
  6 Catarina˙, a nun
  6 Anna, a nun
  6 Anna de Abreu, who according to another author was married in Grade

N6 FRANCISCA˙ DE ARAUJO˙, daughter of Maria˙ de Abreu Soares N5, was the lady of the manor of Agrelo and married Antonio˙ de Passos Figueiroa, a Fidalgo Knight of the King's Household, son of Diogo de Passos and his wife D. Rita de Amorim of the town of Caminha. D. Rita de Amorim was the daughter of Sebastião de Amorim and Maria˙ Mendes de Carvalho, of the town of Monção [NFP Passos §5 N14][ii]. There is a chronicle stating that Antonio Passos was a Knight-Fidalgo, a professant of the Order of Christ and an executor of the Royal Treasury in Vila Real and Guimaraens

For details about Portuguese ranks of nobility, see p. v

  7 Bartolomeu de Passos Figueiroa
  7 Manoel˙ de Passos Figueiroa §15
  7 Maria˙ de Abreu de Passos §18
  7 D. Anna de Abreu de Passos §16
  7 Isabel de Passos, sp

N7 BARTOLOMEU DE PASSOS FIGUEIROA, son of Francisco˙ de Araujo˙ N6. He was the lord of the house of Agrello and married Brites Barbosa, daughter of Marcos Malheiro Pereira˙ and his wife Violante Barbosa de Antas, lord of the entail of Antas. Brites Barbosa was the paternal granddaughter of Antonio˙ Dias Malheiro of Ponte de Lima and his wife Senhorinha Pereira˙, residents of São Miguel de Fontouro [NFP Barbosa §95 N23 and §87 N22; NFP Antas §1 N10 and NFP Malheiro §13 N5]

---

[i] In NFP Bacelar §24 N12, Maria Afonso's husband is called Gabriel Casco *de Araujo˙* (and not Gabriel Casco de Lira). Contrary to what is stated here, we have not found any direct reference to this family in NFP Araujo. (T. N.)

[ii] In NFP Passos §5 N14, Antonio de Passos Figueiroa's father is called Diogo de Passos *Figueiroa*. (T. N.)

8 Cristovão de Passos, Abbot of Cosourado
8 Agostinho Pereira˙
8 Antonio˙ de Passos
8 Marcos Malheiro
8 D. (...)
8 D. (...)

N8 AGOSTINHO PEREIRA˙, son of Bartolomeu de Passos Figueiroa N7, married (in Viana) Paulla Mendes, sp. He had bastard issue by his maid (whom he later married in order to legitimate his children) D. Anna Esteves, known as Anna of São Miguel de Fontoura, daughter of Estevão Mendes de Brito and his wife Anna de Matos, a native of Beiral do Lima, paternal granddaughter of Antonio˙ de Brito and his wife Paulla Mendes, from Viana

> 9 Antonia˙ Pereira˙ de Antas, who married her cousin Antonio˙ Pereira˙ Sotomayor, sp
> 9 Antonio˙ Pereira˙ de Antas
> 9 D. Marta Pereira˙, who married Antonio˙ Pereira˙ Sotomayor, the same person who married her sister

N9 ANTONIO PEREIRA˙ DE ANTAS, son of Agostinho Pereira˙ N8. He did not inherit his father's house for he granted his inheritance to D. Marianna de Figueiroa, daughter of Francisco˙ Barbosa Figueira, his cousin and Governor of Caminha, upon this lady's marriage to Antonio˙ de Amorim Pereira [NFP Amorim §11 N8]. The said Antonio˙ Pereira˙ de Antas married (in the parish of São João de Longos Vales, territory of Monção) D. Maria˙ Angelica de Sá Marinho Falcão, daughter of Antonio˙ de Sá da Rocha, an Army Captain, and his wife Angelica Marinho Falcão, daughter of Antonio Falcão and his wife D. Isabel Soares Marinho

> 10 Antonio˙ Jose Pereira˙ de Antas
> 10 D. Maria˙ Pereira˙ de Antas §25
> 10 D. Arcangella Micaella, who had by Fray Jose da Natividade, a monk in the monastery of São João and Prior of the Hospital of Valença
>> 11 Rosa Angelica Pereira˙ de Antas, who married Alexandre Machado Pais de Araujo˙ Gayo [NFP Gaio §65 N11][i]
> 10 D. Joanna Maria˙ Pereira˙ de Antas §26

---

[i] In NFP Gaio §65 N11, Alexandre Machado's wife is called Rosa Angelica *Germana*, and it is said that she was baptized with the name Archangella Rosa. These people are also referred to in NFP Faria §91 N14. (T. N.)

N10 ANTONIO˙ JOSE PEREIRA˙ DE DANTAS, son of Antonio˙ Pereira˙ de Antas N9, married (in the village of Arcos) his relative Marcelina Rosa Falcão, daughter of Ignacio Falcão Marinho, an apothecary in the said village, and his wife Maria˙ de Antas

  11 Antonio˙ Luis Pereira˙ de Antas Sotomayor

§14

N5 MECIA DE ABREU, daughter of Pedro de Abreu §1 N4, was the lady of the entail of Pia in Ponte de Lima and succeeded to her father's house. Some say she married Francisco˙ de Barros, son of Denis de Barros and his wife Brites Fernandes Ledo [NFP Barros §59 N7 and NFP Araujo §416 N23 (sic)]*i*

  6 Pedro de Abreu de Barros
  6 João de Abreu, who died in infancy

N6 PEDRO DE ABREU DE BARROS, son of Mecia de Barros N5, lived in Viana, where he married Joanna da Rocha, of noble ancestry, daughter of Diogo Soares Pereira˙ and Brites Bezerra Barbosa. Pedro de Abreu and his wife enfeoffed their lands of the house of Grade. Others say that Pedro de Abreu de Barros was the son of Mecia de Abreu [§3 N4]*ii*, which we do not agree with, for this Pedro was appointed the grantee of the lands entailed by his grandmother Brites Fernandes˙ [as mentioned in NFP Barros §59; see also NFP Ponte Ledo §12 N3]. Upon the extinction of this line, the entail passed to Jacome Pereira˙ Soares [NFP Bacelar §10 N17 Sub18]

  7 Magdalena de Abreu
  7 Diogo Soares, sp
  7 Pedro Gomes de Abreu, who got married, sp
  7 Brites Bezerra, with deceased issue
  7 Maria˙ de Abreu Soares, who, according to some, was the wife of Manoel˙ de Araujo˙ Bacellar [in §13 N5], though this seems to us to be a mistake

N7 MAGDALENA DE ABREU, daughter of Pedro de Abreu N6, married Luis Palhares, son of Antonio de Macedo de Brito and his wife Anna Cação de Brito [with issue in NFP Barros §23 N12]*iii*

---

i There is no subsection N23 in NFP Araujo §416, nor have we been able to find any explicit reference to the members of this family in the chapter of Araujo. (T. N.)

ii In the original text it is said that this Mecia de Abreu is mentioned in §13 N4 (which corresponds to §13 N5 in this version), though that section is about Maria de Abreu, and not Mecia de Abreu. By guesswork we have identified this Mecia de Abreu with the one given in §3 N4, who actually had a son called Pedro de Abreu. (T. N.)

iii In NFP Barros §23 N12, Magdalena de Abreu's husband is called Luis Palhares *de Brito*. (T. N.)

8 D. Isabel, who cohabited with one of her father's servants. The couple fled to Galicia, where he was slain and she became a nun

§15

N7 MANOEL˙ DE PASSOS FIGUEIROA, son of Francisca˙ de Araujo˙ §13 N6, was a Fidalgo of the King's Household and the lord of the entail of Agrelo. He married (in Caminha) D. Anna de Lima, daughter of Catarina˙ de Lima and her husband Andre Velho [NFP Barbosa §38 N23]*i*

       8 Francisco˙ Barbosa Figueira
       8 Francisca˙ de Araujo˙
       8 Jeronima
       8 Antonio˙ Velho

N8 FRANCISCO˙ BARBOSA FIGUEIRA˙, son of Manoel˙ de Passos N7, was a Fidalgo of the King's Household, the lord of the entail of Agrelo, an Infantry Major and Lieutenant General, Commendatory of the Order of Christ and a distinguished Knight. He married (in Arcos) D. Ignes de Seabra, or Ignes de Saraiva, daughter of Payo da Rocha (officer of the Inquisition, who later became the Abbot of Sebadim and a Commissary of the Inquisition), and his wife Ignes de Seabra de Brito; paternal granddaughter of Cosme de Barros de Brito and D. Isabel de Araujo˙, or Isabel da Rocha, e Sousa, daughter of Alvaro da Rocha, lord of the house of Casal Soeiro [NFP Barros §20 N11]

       9 D. Marianna Figueira de Sousa, who married D. Antonio˙ de Amorim Pereira˙, son of D. Lourenço de Amorim (Governor of the Castle of Viana and Commendatory of the Order of Christ), and his wife D. Anna da Rocha Trancoso [with issue in NFP Amorim §11 N8]

§16

N7 ANNA DE ABREU DE PASSOS, daughter of Francisca˙ de Araujo˙ §13 N6, married (in Rey) D. Francisco˙ de Passos

       8 D. Jacinto de Passos
       8 D. Benta de Passos, who married in Val de Melhor, Bayona

§17

N6 MARIA˙ DE ABREU SOARES, daughter of Maria de Abreu §13 N5, married Affonso˙ Pereira˙ de Castro of Monção, lord of the house of Faquello, son of João Gomes Pereira˙, o Velho (the Elder), and his wife Anna Pereira˙ Soares [NFP Araujo §358 N23]

---

i In NFP Barbosa §38 N23, Anna de Lima's mother is called Catarina de Lima *Barbosa*. (T. N.)

7 Francisco' Pereira' de Castro, a university graduate
7 João Gomes, Abbot of Santa Maria de Souto, who had bastard children
    8 Affonso' Pereira'
    8 Antonio'
    8 Manoel'
7 Manoel' de Araujo', who was a university graduate, commissioner of the Inquisition and a distinguished genealogist; he had bastard issue
    8 Fray Estevão, a Carmelite monk
7 D. Antonia' Pereira' de Castro
7 Bartolomeu Pereira' de Castro, who married D. Antonia' Pereira' de Castro, daughter of Felix Pereira' de Castro and his wife D. Maria' Folgueira [with issue in NFP Araujo §329 N27]
7 Gaspar Pereira', Rector of Pias
7 João Gomes Pereira', who lived in Bahia[i] and married Maria' de Almeida, daughter of Adão Francisco' Rabello and his wife Brites de Almeida. Adão Francisco' was the son of Ceprião Francisco' Rabello and his wife Maria' Thomas, of Penso, in the territory of Caria, in the Bishopric of Lamego. Beatriz de Almeida[ii] was the daughter of Andre Ribeiro', a native of Povoa de Baixo, and Felipa de Almeida. João Gomes Pereira had
    8 Marianna
    8 Vitoria
    8 Antonia' Maria

N7 FRANCISCO' PEREIRA' DE CASTRO, a university graduate, son of Maria' Abreu Soares N6, married (in Arcos) Brites Barbosa Pereira', daughter of Lucas Gomes Pereira' and his wife Germineza Pereira' de Castro [NFP Araujo §376 N25]. They lived in the manor of Faquello
    8 Francisco Pereira' de Castro
    8 Reverend Alexandre Pereira', Abbot of Carvalheira
    8 Maria' Pereira', a nun
    8 Germineza Pereira', a nun
    8 Brites Barbosa, a nun
    8 Francisca', a nun
    8 B. Manoel' Pereira', nicknamed "o Canhoto" (the Left-Hander)

---

[i] Bahia: a province in Brazil. (T. N.)

[ii] The name *Beatriz* is a more modern version of *Brites*. Almost always in the text the author used the name Brites, but in this case, seemingly by mistake, he wrote first that this lady was called Brites, and a few lines below said that her name was Beatriz. (T. N.)

N8 FRANCISCO˙ PEREIRA˙ DE CASTRO, son of Dr. Francisco˙ Pereira˙ N7, was a Knight of the Order of Christ and married D. Maria˙ Pereira˙ de Castro, daughter and heiress of Pedro Marinho Sotomayor, Knight of the Order of Christ, and his wife Felipa de Almeida [NFP Marinho §12 N17][i]

    9 Affonço Pereira˙ de Castro

    9 Pedro Marinho, who went to India

    9 Alexandre Pereira˙, Abbot of Carvalheira

    9 D. Maria˙, a nun in the monastery of Salvador in Braga

    9 D. Felipa, *ditto*

    9 D. Francisco˙, a priest of the Order of the Holy Cross of Coimbra

N9 AFFONÇO PEREIRA˙ DE CASTRO, son of Francisco˙ Pereira˙ de Castro N8, was a Fidalgo of the King's Household, the lord of the entail of Faquello and Grade, and married D. Antonia˙ Maria˙ de Castro, daughter of D. Antonia˙ Pereira˙ de Castro and her husband and relative Bartolomeu Pereira˙ de Castro [NFP Araujo §330 N28, where this generation is described][ii]

§18

THE ENTAIL OF ROSAL

N7 MARIA DE ABREU DE PASSOS, daughter of Francisca˙ de Araujo˙ §13 N6, married João Gomes Pereira˙ Barbosa, son of João Gomes Barbosa Pereira˙ and his wife Felipa Barbosa [NFP Araujo §358 N24]

    8 Felix Pereira˙ de Castro

    8 Francisca˙ de São João, a nun

    8 Anna Pereira˙, a nun in the convent of St. Francis in Monção

    8 Martim Pereira˙, who died in infancy

N8 FELIX PEREIRA˙ DE CASTRO, son of Maria˙ de Abreu de Passos N7, was a Fidalgo of the King's Household, a Knight of the Order of Christ, the Captain General of Monção and the lord of the entail of Rosal and Sago. He was married twice, the first time to D. Maria˙ Felgueira, daughter of Anna de Araujo˙ e Castro, and her husband Antonio˙ Rabello Soares [with issue in NFP Araujo §329 N26][iii]. His second wife was D. Margarida Pereira˙ Sotomayor, daughter of

---

[i] In NFP Marinho §12 N17, Pedro Marinho Sotomayor's daughter (and Francisco Pereira de Castro's wife) is called *Filipa de Almeida*, and not Maria Pereira de Castro. (T. N.)

[ii] In NFP Araujo §330 N28, Affonço Pereira de Castro's wife, like her mother, is called Antonia˙ *Pereira˙* de Castro, and not Antonia Maria de Castro. (T. N.)

[iii] In NFP· Araujo §329 N26, Felix Pereira˙ de Castro wife's name is said to be Maria, *or Antonia* Felgueira *de Castro*. (T. N.)

Marcos Malheiro Pereira and his wife D. Elena de Meireles [NFP Bacelar §1 N14][i]

    9 D. Maria˙ Pereira˙ Sotomayor, who married (in Ponte de Lima) her relative Gaspar Marinho Pereira˙, lord of the entail of Barreiros, son of Gaspar Marinho Pereira˙ and Mecia Pereira˙ Ferraz [with issue in NFP Costa §124 N8]

§19

N4 CONSTANÇA DE ABREU, daughter of Alvaro Vaz de Abreu §1 N3, married as her first husband João Rodrigues˙, nicknamed "o Seitil" after he was sentenced to pay a libel indemnity in *seitis*.[ii] This João Rodrigues˙, who was also called by some João Rodrigues˙ de Abreu, "o Velho" (the Elder), is said to have been a Fidalgo-Squire (according to documents possessed by Marcos Pereira˙ Bacellar), and was the son of Fernão Rodrigues˙ de Miranda and his wife Francisca˙ da Cunha

For details about Portuguese ranks of nobility, see p. v

    5 João Rodrigues˙ de Abreu, from whom descend the Soares of the entail of Santa Luzia in Valença §28
    5 Guiomar Affonço de Abreu
    5 Anna de Abreu, who married in Troporis
    5 Antonia˙ de Abreu

We have found a reference of Constança de Abreu or Constança Lourenço de Abreu married to Gil Velho, Alcaide General of Valença

    5 Brites Velho
    5 Catarina˙ de Santo Antonio˙
    5 Anna de Abreu

N5 GUIOMAR AFFONÇO DE ABREU, daughter of Constança de Abreu N4, married João Soares Pereira˙, son of Pedro Vaz Soares Bacellar and his wife Mecia Pereira˙ [NFP Soares Tangil §4 N7][iii]

    6 Alvaro Pereira˙, who married (in Ponte de Lima) Maria de Araujo, daughter of Martim Soares
    6 Sebastião Pereira˙ §27[iv]
    6 Antonio˙ Pereira˙ de Castro, or Soares[v]
    6 Francisco˙ Pereira˙, who married in Porrinho, sp

---

[i] In NFP Bacelar §1 N14, Margarida Pereira Sotomayor's father is called Marcos Malheiro Pereira˙ *Bacelar*. (T. N.)

[ii] Seitil or ceitil was a Portuguese monetary unit in the reign of King John I (1385-1433). (T. N.)

[iii] In NFP Soares Tangil §4 N7, Guiomar Affonço de Abreu's husband is called João *Pereira˙ Soares Bacellar*, and not João Soares Pereira. (T. N.)

[iv] In §27, he is called Sebastião Pereira˙ *Soares*. (T. N.)

[v] In N6 below he is given a different name: Antonio˙ Pereira˙ *Bacellar*. (T. N.)

6 Manoel Pereira˙, who married (in Monção) Maria˙ Pereira˙, daughter of Ignacio de Araujo˙, sp

6 Constança Pereira˙, who married Rodrigo Rabello, son of Braz Rabello [NFP Marinho §15 N15][i]

6 Ignes Pereira˙ Soares, wife of Vasco Rodrigues˙ Bacellar [NFP Bacelar §1 N12][ii]

N6 ANTONIO˙ PEREIRA˙ BACELLAR,[14] son of Guiomar Affonso˙ de Abreu N5. His parentage is unclear, for some consider him the son of Senhorinha Pereira˙ and her husband Bento Vellozo Bacellar [as mentioned in NFP Bacelar §23 N13], though the information we present here is probably more correct.[iii] The said Antonio˙ Pereira˙ died at the entrance of Lages in Valença, where he was a Court Probate Judge, according to some. He married D. Catarina˙ de Castro (who was reputed to be a new Christian (Jew)), daughter of Alvaro de Castro, Fidalgo of the King's Household

7 Francisco˙ Pereira˙ de Castro

7 Constança Pereira˙, who married Gregorio de Lençoens [with issue in NFP Lanços §3 N5][iv]

7 Antão Pereira˙ §21

N7 FRANCISCO˙ PEREIRA DE CASTRO, was the son of Antonio˙ Pereira˙ Bacellar[15], and his wife Catarina˙ de Castro, or the son of Antonio˙ Pereira˙ de

---

[i] In NFP Marinho §15 N15, Rodrigo Rabello's wife is called Constança *de Abreu*, and not Constança Pereira. (T. N.)

[ii] In NFP Bacelar §1 N12, it is said that Vasco Rodrigues Bacellar "married his cousin Giomara Affonso˙ de Abreu or D. Ignes Pereira Soares (…)". (T. N.)

[14] Gabriel Pereira˙ de Castro of Valença, a descendant of this António Pereira Bacellar, says he has authentic documents showing that Antonio was the son of Guiomar Affonso de Abreu and her husband João Soares Pereira N4 above, a parentage which is also supported by Fray João˙ da Madre˙ de Deus˙, though it differs from the one presented in NFP Bacelar §23 N13.[v]

[iii] Actually in a footnote in NFP Bacelar §23 N13, the author says that he indeed agrees with the version presented here in NFP Abreu of Grade. (T. N.)

[iv] In NFP Lanços §3 N5, Constança Pereira, Gregorio de Lençoens's wife, is called Constança *de Abreu Soares*. (T. N.)

[v] In N5 Sub6, this Antonio Pereira Bacellar is called Antonio˙ Pereira˙ *de Castro*, or *Soares*. In NFP Bacelar §23 N13, he is called Antonio˙ Pereira˙ de Castro, and his only mentioned child is Francisco˙ Pereira˙ de Castro, unlike the information presented here, which says that he was also the father of Constança Pereira˙ and Antão Pereira˙. (T. N.)

[15] Others consider this Francisco Pereira de Castro to be the son of António˙ Pereira˙ de Castro and his wife Catarina˙ de Castro [NFP Bacelar §23 N13], though the first parentage seems to be more probable, in favor of which we have already certified. So we consider to be a mistake what is said in the chapter of Bacelar regarding the parentage of this Francisco Pereira de Castro. His descendant Gabriel Pereira˙ de Castro says he has authentic documents proving that António Pereira Bacellar N5 above was the son of João Soares Pereira˙ and his wife Guiomar Affonso˙ de Abreu.

Castro. He was a Probate Court Judge in Valença and married Maria Barbosa Bacellar, who, according to some, was the daughter of Lourenço or Leonardo Barbosa, a physician, and his wife Isabel Coronel Arelano of the city of Tui, daughter of João Coronel [see also the comments on these names in NFP Bacelar §23 N14 and NFP Barbosa §150 N24 and NFP Barbosa §29 N24][i]. However, according to Maria Barbosa Bacellar's descendants, she was the daughter of Chancellor Francisco˙ Barbosa and his wife Maria˙ Fernandes˙ Bacellar, and the said Leonardo Barbosa was her brother, not her father. This seems to us to be more probable, and is given in NFP Barbosa §29 N23[16]

> 8 Gabriel Pereira˙ de Castro
> 8 Father Luis, a canon in Valença
> 8 Fernão Pereira˙ de Castro §20
> 8 Catarina˙ de Castro

N8 GABRIEL PEREIRA˙ DE CASTRO, son of Francisco˙ Pereira˙ de Castro N7, was a Knight of the Order of Christ, a Probate Court Judge in Valença, and married Mecia de Brito, having received in dowry the office of Captain General of Valença. This marriage, recorded in the books of the parish of Santo Estevão, *fl.* 90 *rev.*, was dated December 24, 1769. The bride's parents were Cosme de Brito and his wife Maria˙ de Prado [NFP Soares Tangil §45 N11][ii]

> 9 Francisco˙ Pereira˙ de Castro
> 9 Antonio˙ Pereira˙, a canon in Valença and Abbot of Santa Marinha, who made an enfeoffment of his lands
> 9 Violante, a Carmelite nun in Valença
> 9 Maria˙ de São Francisco, a nun in Valença

---

[i] In NFP Barbosa §150 N24, Francisco Pereira de Castro's wife is called Maria˙ Barbosa, and her parents are said to be Leonardo (or Lourenço) Barbosa *Bacellar* and Isabel Coronel *Arnada* (and not Isabel Coronel Arelano). Yet in NFP Barbosa §29 N24, it is said that this parentage is wrong (the reason for this conclusion is given in fn. 16 below), and that her parents were Francisco Barbosa Leite and his wife Maria Fernandes Bacellar. (T. N.)

[16] If Francisco Pereira de Castro's wife, Maria Barbosa, were the daughter of Dr. Lourenço or Leonardo Barbosa, it would have been nearly impossible for her alleged grandson Luis to be a canon, or for her alleged great grandson Antonio (Pereira) to have become the Abbot of Santa Marinha.[iii]

[ii] In NFP Soares Tangil §45 N10 Sub11, Gabriel Pereira de Castro's wife is called *Maria* de Brito, but this seems to be a mistake, for a few lines below (in N11), she is called Mecia de Brito. (T. N.)

[iii] The reason why the author says that [found in NFP Barbosa §29 N24] is the fact that Dr. Leonardo Barbosa was burned by the Inquisition for being an unrepentant Jew, which would have prevented his alleged descendants (Luis and Antonio) from receiving holy orders and promotion within the Church. (T. N.)

N9 FRANCISCO PEREIRA˙ DE CASTRO, son of Gabriel Pereira˙ de Castro N8, was a Knight of the Order of Christ, an officer of the Inquisition, a Probate Court Judge in Valença and a beneficiary of the tithes in São Pedro da Torre. He served in the Militia as a remunerated captain, being later advanced to major (as recorded in 1683 in the Book of the Council Chamber of Valença, *ff.* 213 *rev.*). He married (in Ponte de Lima) D. Catarina˙ de São Miguel, daughter of Baltazar˙ Leitão and his wife Brites de Antas, of Jewish ascent [NFP Leitão §76 N5][i]

         10 Gabriel Pereira˙ de Castro

         10 Antonio˙ Pereira˙, sp

         10 Francisco˙ Pereira˙, Abbot of Santa Marinha

         10 Gaspar de São Miguel

         10 D. Brites, a nun in Valença, like her sisters below

         10 D. Mecia

         10 D. Micaella

N10 GABRIEL PEREIRA˙ DE CASTRO, son of Francisco˙ Pereira˙ de Castro N9, married D. Maria˙ Xavier Pacheco Marinho, daughter of Francisco˙ Pereira˙ Marinho and D. Marianna de Castro [NFP Araujo §44 N28][ii]

         11 Francisco˙ Pereira˙ de Castro, who married D. Rosa Luisa de Lima, e Mello, daughter of Gaspar da Rocha Pereira˙, a university graduate, and D. Leonor Pereira˙ de Castro [with issue in NFP Soares Tangil §41 N13]

§20

N8 FERNÃO PEREIRA˙ DE CASTRO, son of Francisco˙ Pereira˙ de Castro §19 N7, married as his first wife (in Torres Novas) a girl who was on pilgrimage to Santiago de Compostela, and had by her

         9 (...), who remained in Torres Novas

---

[i] Obscure fragment: "casou em Ponte do Lima com D. Catª de S. Miguel fª de Baltezar Leitão, e sua m.er Brites de Antas no ttº de Leitoins § 76 N 5 X. N.". The abbreviation X. N. stands for cristão-novo (or cristã-nova), i. e. a New Christian (Jew), but it is not clear about whom the reference is made. We have opted to assume that the information is about D. Catarina (though in NFP Leitão §76 N5 it is not informed that this family was of Jewish ancestry). (T. N.)

[ii] In NFP Araujo §44 N28, Maria Xavier (Pacheco Marinho)'s parents are called Francisco˙ *Pacheco* Marinho (and not Francisco Pereira Marinho) and *Maria˙*, or Marianna *Luiza Pereira˙* de Castro. (T. N.)

Fernão Pereira''s second wife was Joanna de Mello, daughter of Gonçallo˙ Teixeira˙ Coelho and widow of Francisco˙ Pereira˙ [NFP Teixeira §1 N17; see also this chapter §27 N7][i]

>9 Gabriel Teixeira˙ Coelho

N9 GABRIEL TEIXEIRA˙ COELHO, son of Fernão Pereira˙ N8 and his second wife, was a Fidalgo of the King's Household, the Captain General of Valença and a military stud farm superintendent. He married D. Maria˙ Teixeira˙ do Amaral, daughter of Mathias Pereira˙ and his wife Maria˙ Cerqueira˙ [NFP Teixeira §1 N17 Sub18][ii], and had bastard issue

>>10 Sebastianna de Mello, who married (in the parish of Silva) Carlos Osorio Coutinho˙, a Knight of the Order of Christ

§21

N7 ANTÃO PEREIRA˙, son of Antão Pereira˙ Bacellar §19 N6[iii], married (in Braga) Maria˙ de Lima, who was the daughter of João de Lima and sister of Carrilho (who was arrested by the Inquisition in Coimbra) and whose aunts were known as the Oliveiras

>8 Francisco˙ Pereira˙ Aranha

N8 FRANCISCO PEREIRA˙ ARANHA, son of Antão Pereira N7, was a prosecutor in Valença, married Maria Pereira˙ Lobato, daughter of Payo Rodrigues˙ and his wife Maria˙ Pereira˙ Queiros, daughter of Antonio˙ de Queiros Marinho and his wife Maria˙ Pereira˙ Lobato, daughter of Antonio˙ Pereira˙ Lobato and his wife Anna de Caceres, daughter of Jorge de Caceres of Rial near Monção. Antonio˙ Pereira˙ Lobato was the son of João Vaz Lobato of Juste and his wife Mecia Lopes Pereira˙, daughter of Lopo de Lira and Germineza Pereira˙ de Castro [NFP Lira §14 N8][iv]

>9 Antão Pereira˙
>9 Miguel Pereira˙
>9 Natalia de Castro

---

[i] In the original text, Joanna de Mello's father's name is abbreviated as "G.es Teixᵃ", which could mean "Gonçalves" or "Guimarães" Teixeira˙. Yet in NFP Teixeira §1 N17 and in NFP Abreu of Grade §27 N7 he is called Gonçallo Teixeira Coelho, a version we have preferred to adopt. (T. N.)

[ii] In NFP Teixeira §1 N17 Sub18, Maria˙ Teixeira˙ do Amaral's husband is called *Gonçallo* Teixeira Coelho, seemingly by mistake, for this is her father's name, whereas her husband is called here *Gabriel* Teixeira Coelho. (T. N.)

[iii] In this passage of the original text, it is said that Antão Pereira's father was Francisco Pereira, though this contradicts the information given in §19 N6, in which his father's name is Antão Pereira˙ Bacellar, a version we have preferred to adopt. (T. N.)

[iv] In NFP Lira §14 N8, Maria Pereira Lobato is said to be the daughter of Payo Rodrigues˙ and another Maria˙ Pereira˙ *Lobato*, and not Maria˙ Pereira˙ Queiros. (T. N.)

N6 SALVADOR DE ABREU ZUNIGA, son of Genebra de Abreu §5 N5*i*, was the lord of the entail of Vilar and married (in Ponte de Lima) Elena Cerqueira˙, grantee of the lands enfeoffed by her uncle Gaspar Pires Machado

>7 Cristovão de Abreu Zuniga
>
>7 Francisco˙ de Abreu Zuniga, a priest
>
>7 Maria˙ da Visitação, a nun

N7 CRISTOVÃO DE ABREU ZUNIGA, son of Salvador de Abreu N6, inherited his father's entail and married Francisca˙ Barbosa de Amorim, daughter of João Barbosa Calheiros, lord of the entail of Caldelas, and Isabel de Amorim Pacheco [NFP Amorim §3 N9 and NFP Amorim §54 N7]

>8 D. Elena de Abreu Zuniga

N8 D. ELENA DE ABREU ZUNIGA, daughter and heiress of Cristovão de Abreu N7, married Xisto de Fraga Botelho, son and heir of Francisco˙ de Fraga Botelho and D. Maria˙ de Miranda Botelho, of the house of Ermida da Vila Real. Francisco˙ de Fraga was a Fidalgo of the King's Household, and is mistakenly referred to as Antonio˙ da Fraga in NFP Fraga §1 N3*ii*

>9 D. Anna Maria˙ Botelho, wife and heiress of Carlos Malheiro Bacellar, Knight of the Order of Christ, son of Marcos Malheiro Bacellar (Fidalgo of the King's Household and lord of the entail of Fontoura) and his wife D. Elena de Meirelles [with issue in NFP Bacelar §2 N15]*iii*
>
>9 D. Isabel, a nun in the convent of Salvador in Braga
>
>9 D. Josefa, a nun
>
>9 D. Francisca˙, a nun

§23

N7 JOÃO DE SÁ SOTOMAYOR, son of Francisco˙ Rabello Sotomayor §3 N6, married Ignes de Amorim, daughter of Gonçallo Coelho de Araujo˙ and his wife Catarina˙ Barbosa de Araujo˙ [NFP Araujo §172 N25]

---

i In §5 N5, he is called Salvador de *Azevedo* Zuniga. (T. N.)

ii Actually in NFP Fraga §1 N3 it is said that Xisto de Fraga Botelho's parents are Antonio de Fraga Botelho and his wife Maria Borges de Miranda, and not Francisco˙ de Fraga Botelho and D. Maria˙ de Miranda Botelho. (T. N.)

iii In NFP Bacelar §2 N15, Anna Maria˙ Botelho's husband's name is given as Carlos Malheiro Pereira˙ Bacellar, and his father as Marcos Malheiro Pereira˙ Bacellar. (T. N.)

8 João de Sá Sotomayor, who pursued an academic career in humanities, and married D. Maria˙ Joanna Barreto, daughter of D. Sebastianna de Lima and her husband Felix Barreto da Gama [with issue in NFP Barros §23 N13]*i*

8 D. Manoel˙, a canon in Santo Agostinho

8 Fray Gonçallo, a Benedictine monk

8 Antonio˙ de Azevedo˙, Abbot of Gandra

8 D. Maria˙, a nun in the convent of Vale

8 D. Micaella, *ditto*

8 Francisco˙ Rabello de Sá, who died as an appellate judge in Braga

8 Jeronimo

8 D. Anna

§24

N10 D. MAGDALENA or D. MARGARIDA MALDONADO, daughter of Jose Soares de Brito §6 N9, married Bartolomeu Pinto Botelho, lord of the house of Rede, near Mesãofrio, and Fidalgo of the King's Household, who was alive in 1742 and was the son of Rodrigo Vaz Pinto, lord of the house of Rede and D. Mecia Isabel de Sousa of the house of Bordonhos [NFP Monteiro §46 N15; see also NFP Pedigree Charts, Tome 1, N 154]*ii*

11 D. Mecia Maldonado, who married D. João Maldonado de Azevedo, sp

11 D. Anna, a nun in Lamego

11 Rodrigo Pinto de Sousa

N11 RODRIGO PINTO DE SOUSA, son of D. Magdalena Maldonado N10, married (in Oporto) D. Luisa de Mello, e Sousa, daughter of Martim Affonso˙ de Mello, Fidalgo of the King's Household and D. Jeronima de Sousa Alcoforado [NFP Gaio §30 N11]*iii*

12 D. Maria˙ do Carmo Pinto˙, who inherited her father's lands and married Francisco˙ Pinto Peixoto (Fidalgo of the King's Household and lord of the house of Felgueiras and Fermedo), son of Gonçallo Peixoto da Silva˙ and D. Anna Pinto [NFP Machado §38 N26]*iv*

---

i In NFP Barros §23 N14, Maria˙ Joanna Barreto's father is called Felix Barreto da Gama e Castro. (T. N.)

ii In NFP Monteiro §46 N15, Magdalena Teresa Maldonado's husband is called Bartolomeu Pinto *de Souza*, and not Bartolomeu Pinto Botelho. (T. N.)

iii In NFP Gaio §30 N11, Rodrigo Pinto de Souza's wife is called Luiza *Rita* de Mello, and not Luiza de Mello, e Sousa. (T. N.)

iv In NFP Machado §38 N26, Gonçallo Peixoto da Silva˙'s wife is called D. Anna *Benedita* Pinto *de Vilhena*, and they are said to be the parents of Francisco *Peixoto Pinto Pereira da Fonseca Coelho*. (T. N.)

12 B. Jose Manoel˙ Pinto, whose mother was a distinguished lady. He was a member of the College of São Paulo, a professor in Lisbon and an envoy to Russia

12 B. Joaquim˙ Pinto, who pursues an academic career in humanities

§25

N10 D. MARIA˙ PEREIRA˙ DE ANTAS, daughter of Antonio˙ Pereira˙ de Antas §13 N9, married (in Valença) Antonio˙ Jose de Brito, a lawyer in the said village, son of (...), a native of Moura

    11 Jose Ignacio de Brito, e Antas

    11 D. Maria˙ (...) Pereira˙ de Antas, who married Dr. Manoel Pinto. They live in Lisbon and had

        12 D. Anna

        12 Simão, a Second Lieutenant in the Navy

§26

N10 D. JOANNA MARIA˙ PEREIRA˙ DE ANTAS, daughter of Antonio˙ Pereira˙ de Antas §13 N9, married Antonio˙ Jose Pereira˙ de Mello, chief forest keeper of the territory of Valença, son of Manoel˙ Pereira˙ dos Santos and D. Joanna Maria˙ de Mello, and grandson of Gaspar Pereira˙ da Rocha and his wife Paulla Maria˙ da Costa Silva˙, daughter of Domingos˙ Fernandes˙, of the parish of Parada, and his wife Maria˙ Fernandes˙, of Esteve, parish of Vico [NFP Barbosa §210 N26][i]. Manoel˙ Pereira dos Santos was Brazilian; he was an officer of the Inquisition, a councilman and an *ex officio* judge in Valença [see NFP Soares Tangil §41 N12][ii]

    11 Manoel˙ Antonio˙ Pereira˙ de Castro

    11 D. Maria˙ Thomasia

    11 D. Antonia˙ Joaquinna

    11 Jose Antonio˙

    11 Antonio˙ Lourenço

    11 D. Joanna Antonia˙ Maria˙ Pereira˙ de Antas §30

    11 Francisco˙ Ignacio

§27

N6 SEBASTIÃO PEREIRA˙ SOARES, son of Guiomar Affonso˙ de Abreu §19 N5, married (in the parish of Silva, territory of Valença) D. Maria˙ de Castro, daughter of Baltazar˙ de Castro and D. Ignes da Costa

---

[i] In NFP Barbosa §210 N26, Manoel Pereira dos Santos's wife is called Joanna *Antonia*˙ de *Lima*, e Mello, and not Joanna Maria de Mello. (T. N.)

[ii] In NFP Soares Tangil §41 N12, Manoel˙ Pereira˙ dos Santos's father is called Gaspar *da Rocha Pereira*, and not Gaspar Pereira da Rocha. (T. N.)

7 Francisco˙ Pereira˙ de Castro

7 Pedro Soares de Castro, Chief Treasurer of Valença

7 João Pereira˙ de Castro §29

7 D. Isabel Pereira˙ de Castro, who married Baltazar˙ Marinho Sotomayor, lord of the entail of Marinhos, with deceased issue [NFP Marinho §19 N15]

N7 FRANCISCO˙ PEREIRA˙ DE CASTRO, son of Sebastião Pereira˙ Soares N6, married D. Joanna de Mello (who later joined the convent of Vila do Conde as a nun), daughter of Gonçallo Teixeira˙ Coelho, lord of Sergude, and D. Maria˙ de Noronha. (This Joanna de Mello married Fernão Pereira˙ de Castro [§20 N8] as her second husband) [NFP Teixeira §1 N17]

8 Sebastião Pereira˙ de Mello, who married D. Marianna da Cunha, daughter of Manoel˙ da Cunha Sotomayor and D. Isabel Malheiro Brandão [with issue in NFP Malheiro §6 N10]

§28

N5 JOÃO RODRIGUES˙ DE ABREU, son of Constança de Abreu §19 N4, married Anna de Sá, daughter of Guiomar de Sá Sotomayor and Bernardo Quinteiro Baldaia, Fidalgo of the King's Household [NFP Jacome §20 N6]

6 Constança de Abreu, wife of Gaspar Araujo˙ de Azevedo˙, son of Tristão de Araujo• de Azevedo˙ and his wife Isabel de Aguiar [with issue in NFP Araujo §37 N24]*i*

§29

N7 JOÃO PEREIRA DE CASTRO, son of Sebastião Pereira˙ §27 N6, married (in Porrinho, Galicia) D. Ursulla Vaz de Castro, daughter of Gregorio˙ Vaz de Castro

8 D. Pedro de Castro

8 D. Sebastião de Castro, sp, who died in the War of Catalonia

8 D. Gregorio˙ de Castro, who married D. Francisca˙ Ozores, daughter of Affonso˙ Pereira˙ Soares and Paulla˙ Pereira of Galicia. D. Gregorio˙ de Castro was a heavy cavalry captain and a General Commissary of the Cavalry. He had

9 D. Faustina, no further details

9 D. Germineza, no further details

9 D. Ursulla, no further details

---

i In NFP Araujo §35 N23, Tristão de Araújo e Azevedo's wife is called Isabel de Aguiar *da Gama*. (T. N.)

8 D. Isabel de Castro, who married (in Vigo) her cousin D. Francisco˙ Soares, son of D. Francisco˙ Vasques Ozores

9 D. Diogo, no further details

9 D. Josefa, no further details

N8 D. PEDRO DE CASTRO, son of João Pereira˙ de Castro N7, married D. Pascoa Soares, daughter of João Soares and D. Anna Cabral of Vila Nova de (...), in the Archbishopric of Santiago

9 D. Joaquina

9 D. Maria˙, no further details

§30

N11 D. JOANNA ANTONIA˙ MARIA˙ PEREIRA˙ DE ANTAS, daughter of Joanna Maria˙ Pereira˙ de Antas §26 N10, married (...), nephew of the Abbot of Cerdal Manoel˙ João Ribeiro˙, from this town of Barcelos[i], son of Jacinto Ribeiro˙ and (...), who was the bastard daughter of Father João da Silva and his mistress (...), daughter of Manoel˙ Gomes de (...) and Jacinta Ribeiro˙, daughter of (...)

12 Antonio Jose Pereira˙ de Mello, born in October, 1804

§31

N2 THERESA GOMES DE ABREU, daughter of Alvaro Vaz de Abreu §1 N1, married (...)

3 Gonçallo Gomes de Abreu

N3 GONÇALLO GOMES DE ABREU, son of Theresa Gomes N2, married (...)

4 Maria˙ Gomes de Abreu

N4 MARIA˙ GOMES DE ABREU, son of Gonçallo˙ Gomes N3, married Andre Rodrigues˙ Mogueimas, son of Ruy Gonçalves˙ Mogueimas

5 Alexandre de Abreu, who lived in his manor of Monte Redondo, in the territory of Arcos, and married Magdalena Barbosa, daughter of Maria˙ Barbosa de Sousa and Antonio˙ Vaz Taboada [with issue in NFP Caldas §36 N5]

---

[i] "This town of Barcelos": Felgueiras Gaio was from Barcelos. (T. N.)

CREDITS LIST

Figure (p. 1): from *Corografia Portugueza* by Antonio Carvalho da Costa (1706). Valentim da Costa Deslandes: Lisbon.

Arms of Count Henry (p. 4); arms of the Queens of Portugal (p. 9); arms of the Princes of Portugal (p. 93): by Antonio Soares Albergaria (1632) in *Tropheus Lusitanos.* Jorge Rodrigues: Lisbon.

Figures (foldout; arms of Monção, p. 125): by Ubirajara Magalhães.

NAME INDEX

Introduction

People's names are located in the text by 2 numbers, the first indicating the section § and the second the subsection N in which they are found (v. g., 15-2 means §15 N2). When the two numbers are preceded by a "G", it means that the name is found in the Chapter of the Abreus of *Grade*. In most cases there is not this "G", which means that the reference is about the *Abreus of Regalados*, the first and biggest chapter of this book.

Two useful notes (and also two caveats) about this system are:

1. It is very common to find people referred to by different names in different passages of Gaio's work. For instance, there are two passages in this book in which the names Maria *da Silva* and Maria *de Roxas* refer to a same woman, and similarly in other two passages the names Manuel de Abreu *Castelo Branco* and Manuel de Abreu also indicate the same person. So if you do not find a specific name, you should try a variant, by omitting, adding or changing names and surnames.

2. Conversely to what is said above, it also occurs sometimes that a single name refers to different people in a same section and subsection. For instance, in 28-10 (i. e., in the Chapter of the Abreus of Regalados, §28 N10), there are two men, father and son, who have the same name *Antonio de Abreu Lima*, and sometimes there are even three namesakes with the same two numbers. So it is recommendable to read the entire reference (i. e., the subsection) in order to make sure about the occurrence or not of namesakes.

Abbreviations Used in This Index

d.: daughter	f.: father
G: Abreu of Grade (Chapter)	h.: husband
m.: mother	ref.: reference
s.: son	w. wife

AGUIAR, Matheus Ferreira de: 38-3
AGUILLAR, Joanna de: 57-8
ALBERGARIA, Antonio Soares de: 44-8; 69-9
ALBERGARIA, Diogo Soares de: 12-5; 12-6
ALBERGARIA, Fernão Soares de: 10-4
ALBERGARIA, Gomes Soares de: 12-5
ALBERGARIA, Isabel de Mello de: 10-4
ALBERGARIA, Lopo Soares de: 12-6
ALBERGARIA, Lourenço Soares de: 12-5; 12-6; 127-15; 127-16
ALBERGARIA, Manoel Soeiro de: 90-15
ALBERGARIA, Suzana Soeiro de: 90-15
ALBERNOS, Affonso Martins: 109-10
ALBERNOS, Thomas Feleciano de: 5-10
ALBUQUERQUE, Brites de: 110-13
ALBUQUERQUE, Catarina Fernandes: 83-10
ALBUQUERQUE, Duarte de: 127-15
ALBUQUERQUE, Fernão Annes de: 83-10
ALBUQUERQUE, Jeronimo Fragoso de: 81-10
ALBUQUERQUE, Pedro de: 92-13
ALCOFORADO, Bento de Mesquita: 139-10; 139-11
ALCOFORADO, João de Mesquita: 139-11; 139-12
ALCOFORADO, Pedro Martins: 3-5
ALCOFORADO, Severina de Palma: 139-10
ALCOFORADO, Thereza Pires: 3-5
ALEMÃO, Diogo Fernandes: 123-2
ALEMÃO, Luisa: 123-2
ALEMQUER, Manoel de Abreu de Macedo de: 123-1
ALMADA, Antonio de: 21-6
ALMADA, Salvador de Abreu de: 48-10
ALMEIDA, Anna de: 86-11; 109-14; 128-11
ALMEIDA, Antonia de: 128-11
ALMEIDA, Antonio de: 47-14; 69-10; 103-11
ALMEIDA, Catarina de: G 3-4
ALMEIDA, Diogo Coelho de: 90-13
ALMEIDA, Felipa de: 77-9; 77-10
ALMEIDA, Francisca de: 28-9; 28-10; 103-11
ALMEIDA, Francisco de: 86-12; 86-13; 134-14; 135-13
ALMEIDA, Gervasio de: 34-15
ALMEIDA, Guiomar Freire de: 47-12
ALMEIDA, Henrique Henriques de: 73-12
ALMEIDA, Isabel de: 2-7
ALMEIDA, Joanna de: 34-15; 89-11
ALMEIDA, João de: 2-7; 143-9
ALMEIDA, João Pinto de: 69-10
ALMEIDA, João Rabello de: 47-14
ALMEIDA, Jorge de: 134-13; 86-11; 86-12; 134-14
ALMEIDA, Josefa de: 34-15
ALMEIDA, Luis Correa de: 43-14
ALMEIDA, Manoel de: 86-12
ALMEIDA, Manoel Henrique de: 76-8
ALMEIDA, Maria de: 77-9; 90-13; 103-11
ALMEIDA, Mecia de: 86-12; 86-13; 135-13
ALMEIDA, Pedro de: 94-11; 17-9; 86-11; 109-14
ALMEIDA, Sebastianna de: 47-12; 78-8
ALMEIDA, Serafina de: 48-11
ALMEIDA, Theresa Henriques de: 73-12
ALMEIDA, Thome Dias de: 93-13
ALPOIM, Anna Margarida Cardoso de Menezes: 106-11
ALPOIM, Caetana de: 106-11
ALPOIM, Francisco Xavier de: 7-10; 25-14
ALPOIM, João de: 7-10
ALVARES, Antonio: 53-11
ALVARES, Catarina: 25-13
ALVARES, Francisco: 32-10

ALVARES, Guiomar: 101-4
ALVARES, Ignes: 31-10
ALVARES, João: 31-10
ALVARES, Leonor: 31-10
ALVARES, Manoel: 27-11
ALVARES, Maria: 83-6
ALVARES, Theresa: 49-3
ALVIM, Felipa de: 61-11
ALVIM, Maria de Barros de: 61-11
ALVIM, Pedro de Mello e: 51-9
AMADO, (ref): 95-10
AMADO, Annes (ref): 23-3; 73-5
AMADO, Brites: 98-12
AMADO, Diogo: 98-12
AMARAL, Arcangella Micaella Josefa de: 47-14
AMARAL, Brites Annes do: 83-9
AMARAL, Francisco da Fonseca do: 47-14
AMARAL, Isabel do: 14-6
AMARAL, João Paes do: 14-6
AMARAL, Luisa de: 127-17
AMARAL, Manoel Ozorio do: 84-17
AMARAL, Maria do: 116-11
AMARAL, Paulla Rabello do: 47-14
AMARAL, Simão Coelho do: 123-5
AMARAL, Theobaldo de Lemos do: 15-7
AMARAL, Vasco Paes Cardoso do: 83-9
AMAURY V, Count of Évreux: 1-1
AMORIM, Antonia de: 111-12
AMORIM, Beatriz de: 28-7
AMORIM, Francisco de Sousa Pereira de: 108-11
AMORIM, Gaspar de: 106-9
AMORIM, Ignes de: 104-8
AMORIM, Jorge Pessoa de: 111-12
AMORIM, Jose de Sousa Pereira Marinho Brandão de: 108-11
AMORIM, Leonor de: G 3-6
AMORIM, Manoel de Sousa de: 108-12
AMORIM, Manoel de Sousa Pereira de: 108-11
AMORIM, Maria de: 107-10
AMORIM, Pedro de: 107-10
AMORIM, Victoria de: 51-9
ANA, (d. of Antonio de Abreu Lima): 28-11
ANA, (d. of Diogo da Cunha de Azevedo): 44-11
ANDRADE, Alvaro de Meyreles de: 55-11
ANDRADE, Anna Mendes de: 84-15
ANDRADE, Antonia Maria Gama de: 28-11
ANDRADE, Felipa de: 16-6
ANDRADE, Francisca de Payva, e: 39-5
ANDRADE, Francisco de: 50-9
ANDRADE, Jacinto Freire de (ref): 115-1
ANDRADE, João de Mello de: 110-13
ANDRADE, João Freire de: 50-7
ANDRADE, Lourenço da Gama de: 28-11
ANDRADE, Luisa de: 123-3
ANDRADE, Manoel Bayão de: 84-15
ANDRADE, Manoel Leitão de: 39-5
ANDRADE, Manoel Tenreiro de: 78-7
ANDRADE, Maria de: 39-5; 123-3
ANDRADE, Thomaz Machado de: 135-14
ANGELA LUIZA, (d. of Rafael de Abreu Lima): 52-10
ANGELICA, (d. of Antonia Perestrello): 48-10
ANGELLA, (d. of Rozaria da Cunha): 33-11
ANNA, (d. of Anna Matilde de Abreu Lima): 108-11
ANNA, (d. of Bartolomeu Mendes de Abreu): 74-10
ANNA, (d. of Felipa da Cunha de Azevedo): 45-11

ANNA, (d. of João Gomes de Abreu): 2-11
ANNA, (d. of Luisa da Silva): 65-11
ANNA, (d. of Pedro Gomes de Abreu): 28-8; 75-10
ANNA, (d. of Ruy Gomes de Abreu): 104-8
ANNA, (d. of Vicente de Macedo da Cunha): 34-15
ANNA JOAQUINA, (d. of Antonio Teixeira de
    Mello, e Castro): 68-14
ANNA LEONOR, (d. of Leopoldo Luis de Sousa):
    36-15
ANNES, Catarina: 40-5
ANNES, Isabel: 12-6
ANNES, Maria: 30-9
ANNES, Pedro: 130-9
ANTÃO, (s. of Lourenço Mendes de Abreu): 73-9
ANTÃO, (s. of Pedro Gomes de Abreu): 75-10
ANTAS, Amaro da Rocha Pita de: 25-10
ANTAS, Brites de: G 3-5
ANTAS, Catarina de: 61-11
ANTAS, Cecilia Gonçalves de: 64-6
ANTAS, Elena de: 61-11
ANTAS, Ignes Vas de: 4-10
ANTAS, Isabel Mendes de: 4-10
ANTAS, Jacome Barreto de: 108-11
ANTAS, João Teixeira de: 27-8
ANTAS, Martim Teixeira de: 27-8
ANTAS, Rodrigo Alvares de: 64-6
ANTAS, Santos Barreto de Lima de: 108-11
ANTAS, Vasco de: G 3-5
ANTHONY, Prior of Crato: 76-6
ANTONIA, (d. of Felipa da Cunha de Azevedo):
    45-11
ANTONIA, (d. of Francisco Mendes de Abreu):
    111-12
ANTONIA, (d. of Manoel de Oliveira de Abreu
    Lima): 105-11
ANTONIA, (d. of Roque Fernandes de Abreu):
    116-12
ANTONIO, (s. of Anna Matilde de Abreu Lima):
    108-11
ANTONIO, (s. of Anna Thereza de Abreu): 108-11
ANTONIO, (s. of Jeronimo Pereira de Mello): 68-12
ANTONIO, (s. of Luis de Abreu de Figueiredo):
    89-12
ANTUNES, Catarina: 113-2; 133-8
ANTUNES, Guiomar: 69-10
ANTUNES, João: 128-11
ANTUNES, Manoel: 63-12; 86-11
ARAGÃO, Antonio de: 83-13
ARAGÃO, Felipe de: 83-13
ARAGÃO, Felix de: 83-13
ARANHA, Angela: 52-9; 107-9
ARANHA, Antonio da Costa: 143-9
ARANHA, Francisco Barbosa: 28-5
ARANHA, Garcia Vaz: 1-6; 2-2
ARANHA, João Burgueira: 52-9
ARANHA, Sebastião Burgueira: 52-9
ARAUJO, Antonia de: 143-9
ARAUJO, Baltazar de: 143-9
ARAUJO, Beatris Bravo de: 7-8
ARAUJO, Fernão Velho de: 6-11; 104-8
ARAUJO, Francisco de: 61-11
ARAUJO, Gaspar de: 2-10
ARAUJO, Gaspar Franco de: 64-7; 64-8
ARAUJO, Isabel de: 25-9
ARAUJO, João Pereira de: 28-9

ARAUJO, Maria da Cunha Pereira de: 108-11
ARAUJO, Maria de: 10-5; 70-11; 108-11
ARAUJO, Paschoa de: 59-11
ARAUJO, Paullo Carneiro de: 77-11
ARAUJO, Payo Rodrigues de: 2-4
ARAUJO, Placido de: 110-13
ARAUJO, Rodrigo Annes de: 101-4
ARCANGELLA, (d. of Jose Manoel Barbosa da
    Cunha, e Mello): 47-15
ARNÃO, (...) (w. of Luis do Quental de Abreu):
    123-3
ARRAES, João Madeira: 119-9
AUTA, (d. of Francisco de Abreu Castello
    Branco): 84-17
AVAL, Sebastião de: 40-7
AVEIRO, Duke of: 90-13
AZAMBUJA, Fernão Rodrigues de: 74-12
AZAMBUJA, João de: 74-11; 74-12; 111-10
AZAMBUJA, Luis Galvão de: 74-12
AZEVEDO, (,,,) (w. of Diogo Figueira): 127-15
AZEVEDO, Agostinho Figueira de: 127-15
AZEVEDO, Antonio da Cunha de: 44-10; 68-11;
    68-12
AZEVEDO, Antonio de Araujo de: 64-8
AZEVEDO, Briolanja de: 7-7
AZEVEDO, Diogo da Cunha de: 44-10; 44-11
AZEVEDO, Diogo de: 19-5
AZEVEDO, Diogo Lopes de: 83-8
AZEVEDO, Estevão Paes de: 2-1
AZEVEDO, Felipa da Cunha de: 45-11
AZEVEDO, Fernão Figueira de: 92-14; 127-15
AZEVEDO, Francisco Barbosa da Cunha de: 47-14
AZEVEDO, Francisco Figueira de: 12-6;
    127-15;127-16;127-17;127-18
AZEVEDO, Francisco Mendes de: 96-12
AZEVEDO, Gaspar Borges de: 21-6
AZEVEDO, Gaspar de: 12-5
AZEVEDO, Isabel de Araujo de: 104-8
AZEVEDO, Jeronima da Cunha de: 68-11
AZEVEDO, Jeronimo da Cunha: 44-9; 44-10
AZEVEDO, João Figueira de: 127-15
AZEVEDO, João Rodrigues de: 10-5
AZEVEDO, Jose Manoel de Oliveira da Abreu de:
    105-11
AZEVEDO, Lourenço Figueira de: 127-15; 127-16
AZEVEDO, Lucas de Barros de: 26-9
AZEVEDO, Maria da Cunha de: 44-11; 44-12
AZEVEDO, Maria de: 26-8
AZEVEDO, Maria Jeronima de: 44-9
AZEVEDO, Maria Vasques de: 2-2
AZEVEDO, Martim Lopes de: 19-5
AZEVEDO, Pedro Lopes de: 10-6
AZEVEDO, Simão Alvares de: 25-13
AZEVEDO, Simoa de: 26-8
AZEVEDO, Theresa Correa de: 2-1
BACELLAR, Antonio de Abreu: 125-5; 125-6
BACELLAR, Fernão Rodrigues: 125-5
BACELLAR, Ignes Affonço: 1-6
BACELLAR, Isabel: 112-11
BACELLAR, Isabel Gonçalves: 112-11
BACELLAR, João Rodrigues: G 1-3
BACELLAR, Jose de Abreu: 125-5; 125-6
BACELLAR, Leonor Rodrigues: 49-4; 64-2
BACELLAR, Pedro Gonçalves: 112-11
BACELLAR, Pedro Gonçalves de Abreu: 112-12

BACELLAR, Rosa Fernandes: 130-12
BACELLAR, Vasco Gil: 2-2;64-1;64-2;82-6;83-7
BAENA, João de: 40-6
BAENA, Leonor Annes: 40-6
BALDREO, Antonio Fernandes: 133-8
BALIEIRO, Gomes: 73-8
BARACHO, Catarina Joaquina Mauricia de Machado
    Pimentel: 111-13
BARBOSA, Catarina Mendes: 96-12
BARBOSA, Diogo: 18-7
BARBOSA, Feliciana: 26-9
BARBOSA, Francisco: 28-5; 47-15; 141-15
BARBOSA, Gabriel Pereira (ref): 106-9
BARBOSA, João: 47-12; 143-9
BARBOSA, Joaquim Calisto: 141-15
BARBOSA, Jose Luis: 141-15
BARBOSA, Maria: 96-12; G 1-4
BARBOSA, Miguel: 60-9
BARBOSA, Pedro: 18-7; 141-15; G 3-7
BARBOSA, Pedro de Barros: 28-10
BARBUDO, Brites: 109-9
BARCELLOS, Count of: 2-1; 2-3
BARRADAS, Guiomar Moniz: 76-8
BARREIRO, Maria: 77-12
BARREIROS, Elena: 83-10
BARREIROS, Francisca: 83-10
BARREIROS, Gaspar: 83-10
BARREIROS, Isabel: 83-10
BARREIROS, Ruy: 83-10
BARRERA, Ignes de la: 12-6; 127-16
BARRETO, Brites Velho: 6-11
BARRETO, Fernão Velho: 6-11; 51-7
BARRETO, Gaspar de Abreu: 108-12
BARRETO, Lourenço de Abreu: 108-11
BARRETO, Manoel de Brito: 121-11; 121-12
BARRETO, Payo Velho: 104-9
BARRETO, Santos Luis: 108-10
BARRIGA, Pedro Annes: 31-10
BARROS, Anna de: 7-7; 7-8
BARROS, Barnabe Vieira de: 43-12
BARROS, Briolanja de: 28-8
BARROS, Diogo de: 26-9; 28-8
BARROS, Elena de: 86-13
BARROS, Genebra: 6-11; 51-7
BARROS, Gonçallo de: 124-5
BARROS, Gonçallo Esteves de: 28-8
BARROS, Heitor de: 64-3
BARROS, Isabel de: 28-8; 124-5
BARROS, Isabel de Figueiredo de: 91-13
BARROS, Joanna de: 92-13
BARROS, João de Barros (ref.): 16-10
BARROS, Leonel de: 43-12
BARROS, Lopo de: 7-7; 7-8
BARROS, Manoel Vieira de: 43-12; 43-13; 43-14
BARROS, Maria de: 21-7;25-9;52-10;83-10;92-13
BARROS, Pedro de: 18-7
BARROS, Quiteria Maria Vieira de: 43-13; 43-14
BARROS, Simão de: 92-13
BARROS, Simão de Magalhães de: 29-11
BARROS, Violante de: 27-8
BARROSO, Baltazar Alvares Vieira: 4-10; 7-8
BARTOLOMEU, (s. of Duarte de Abreu Castello
    Branco): 92-14
BASTO, Alvaro Meirelles de: 63-10
BASTO, Barbara de: 33-12

BASTO, Gonçallo de: 33-12
BASTO, João Esteves de: 30-10; 33-11
BASTO, Maria de: 33-12
BASTO, Thome de: 33-11; 36-14
BAYÃO, Catarina: 109-12
BAYÃO, Gonçallo Pires: 109-12
BAYÃO, Manoel: 84-15
BAYÃO, Pedro: 109-12
BEATRIZ or BRITES, (d. of Alvaro Vaz de Abreu):
    G 1-1
BEÇA, Maria de: 93-13
BEINA, João Rodrigues: 40-6
BEJA, Duke of: 73-5
BERNARDA, (d. of Francisco de Abreu Castello
    Branco): 84-17
BERNARDA, Angelica: 47-15
BERNARDO, Brother (s. of Jose Antonio de
    Abreu): 84-16
BERNARDO, (s. of Marianna de Noronha): 105-10
BEZERRA, Francisco de Abreu: 106-11
BEZERRA, Luis de Mesquita: 106-9
BEZERRA, Manuel Gomes de Lima: 1-1
BORDONHOS, Abbot of: 77-9
BORGES, Alvaro: 123-4
BORGES, Anna: 107-9
BORGES, Bento da Silva: 142-11
BORGES, Catarina: 21-7; 83-11
BORGES, Diogo: 21-8
BORGES, Francisco: G 4-7
BORGES, João: 119-10; 119-11; 120-11
BORGES, João Lobo da Costa: 136-6
BORGES, Luis de Meireles: 107-9
BORGES, Marcos Antonio da Silva da Costa: 142-11
BORGES, Maria Barreto: 121-11
BORGES, Maria: 76-9
BORGES, Marta: 73-11
BORGES, Nuno: G 4-7
BORGES, Payo: 61-10
BORGES, Pedro: 21-6; 21-9; 119-12
BORGES, Ruy: 119-10
BOTELHO, Diogo: 66-6
BOTELHO, Fernão de Horta: 18-10
BOTELHO, Francisco: 18-10; 74-12
BOTELHO, Jose Lourenço: 73-15
BOTELHO, Manoel Martins: 17-7
BOTELHO, Maria: 18-10
BOTELHO, Maria Proença: 84-12
BOTELHO, Pedro Paes: 44-8
BOTO, Angella Figueira: 17-9
BOTO, Antonio Rodrigues: 45-11
BOTO, Elena: 80-7
BOTO, Francisco: 45-11
BOTO, Francisco Figueira: 17-9
BOURO, Affonso Martins: 40-5
BOURO, Duarte Gil: 40-5
BOURO, Isabel Annes de: 40-5; 80-5
BOURO, João Affonso de: 40-5
BRAGANÇA, 2nd Duke of: 51-7
BRAGANÇA, Duchess of: 30-9
BRAGANÇA, Duke of: 6-11; 10-7
BRANDÃO, Antonio: 30-13
BRANDÃO, Antonio Sanches: 12-5
BRANDÃO, Domingos: 18-9
BRANDÃO, Fernão: 2-6
BRANDÃO, Gaspar da Costa: 123-4

BRANDÃO, Gaspar Nunes: 123-4
BRANDÃO, Ignes: 2-6; 52-7
BRANDÃO, Isabel de Mesquita: G 4-7
BRANDÃO, João Alves: 18-9
BRANDÃO, João Martins: 122-10
BRANDÃO, Lourenço Ferreira: 51-10
BRANDÃO, Luis: 12-5
BRANDÃO, Maria: 18-9; 18-10
BRANDÃO, Maria de Figueiredo: 117-11; 122-10
BRANDÃO, Marianna: 51-10
BRANDÃO, Paulla: 30-13
BRANDÃO, Pedro Alves: 18-9
BRAVO, (...) (w. of Leonardo da Cunha): 17-8
BRIOLANJA, (d. of Jorge de Abreu): 7-7
BRITES, (d. of Antonio de Abreu Lima): 28-7
BRITES, (d. of João Gomes de Abreu): 28-5
BRITES, (d. of João Pereira de Abreu): 97-12
BRITES, (d. of Leonel de Abreu Lima): 51-8
BRITES, (d. of Ruy Gomes de Abreu): 2-6; 104-8
BRITES, (d. of Ruy or Rodrigo Gomes de
       Abreu): 52-7
BRITES, (w. of Gil de Castro): 21-6
BRITES, (w. of Luis de Abreu da Cunha): 48-11
BRITES or BEATRIZ, (d. of Alvaro Vaz de
       Abreu): G 1-1
BRITES, Queen of Castile: 49-2
BRITO, Anna de: 2-10
BRITO, Anna Barreto de: 120-11
BRITO, Baltazar Pimenta de: 70-11
BRITO, Fernão Tavares de: 10-7
BRITO, Frutuozo Pimenta de: 70-11
BRITO, Giraldo de: 4-10
BRITO, Gonçallo de Araujo: 59-11
BRITO, Jacome de Araujo e: 59-11
BRITO, João de: 2-5
BRITO, Luis de: 2-5
BRITO, Luis de Meireles de: 107-9
BRITO, Luis Palhares de: 107-9
BRITO, Luis Pereira de: 142-10
BRITO, Manoel de: 119-10; 120-11; 121-11
BRITO, Maria de: 121-11
BRITO, Maria Soares de: G 2-6
BRITO, Marianna de: 96-12
BRITO, Simão Pereira de: 81-12
BRITO, Ventura de Abreu Lima de: 142-11
BROCHADO, (...) (h. of Maria de Abreu): 72-8
BULHÕES, Luisa de: 16-11
BULHÕES, Maria Coutinho de Eça e: 16-11
BULHÕES, Pascoella de: 16-11
CABRAL, Antonio: 76-8
CABRAL, Diogo Fernandes: 27-6
CABRAL, Domingos: 84-13
CABRAL, Fernão: 90-12
CABRAL, Francisca Dias: 27-6
CABRAL, Francisca Moniz: 76-8
CABRAL, Francisco: 84-15
CABRAL, Gonçallo de Azevedo: 77-9
CABRAL, Gonçallo Fernandes: 26-8
CABRAL, Isabel de Almeida: 47-12
CABRAL, Isabel Velloso: 90-12
CABRAL, Jorge Dias: 27-6
CABRAL, Maria: 85-12
CABRAL, Paulla de Faria: 90-12
CABRAL, Paullo: 86-13
CABRAL, Pedro Alvares: 76-8
CABRAL, Simão de Azevedo: 26-8; 77-9

CABREIRA, Luis da Costa: 17-9
CAÇADA, Isabel Martins: 98-11
CAÇÃO, Maria de Brito: 5-10
CAETANO, (s. of Luís da Cunha Coutinho):
       30-13
CALDAS, Francisco de: 28-5
CALDAS, Gomes Rodrigues de: 49-4
CALDAS, Pedro de: 143-9
CALHEIROS, Garcia Lopes: 52-9
CALHEIROS, Isabel Lopes: 70-11
CALHEIROS, Manoel Coelho: 70-11
CALHEIROS, Pedro de Amorim: G 3-6
CALVA, Leonor Gonçalves: 38-3
CAMANHO, Antonia de Azevedo: 105-11
CAMANHO, Joaquim de Queiroz Ribeiro Botelho:
       106-12
CAMANHO, Maria Romana de Menezes: 106-12
CAMARAÇA, Marquis of: 54-9
CAMELO, João de Moura: 30-12
CAMINHA, Count of: 16-4; 40-5
CAMINHA, Duke of: 113-1; 125-5
CAMPELLO, Francisco: 34-13
CAMPELLO, Ignes: 32-10
CAMPELLO, Joanna: 30-12
CAMPELLO, João: 34-13
CAMPELLO, Vicente Vaz: 43-11
CAMPOS, Elena de: 15-7
CAMPOS, Henrique de Lemos de: 15-7
CAMPOS, Joanna de: 36-13
CAMPOS, Maria de: 26-8
CAMPOS, Theobaldo de Lemos de: 15-7
CANAES, Francisco Barbosa: 93-13
CANERA, Marquis of: 8-11
CARDOSO, Andre Coelho: 44-11
CARDOSO, Anna: 83-10; 91-13
CARDOSO, Antão: 15-6
CARDOSO, Antonio: 15-6; 91-13
CARDOSO, Brites Vaz: 83-9
CARDOSO, Catarina: 91-13; 102-9
CARDOSO, Cecilia: 102-9
CARDOSO, Elena: 83-10; 85-11; 85-12
CARDOSO, Felippa Pacheco: 44-11
CARDOSO, Francisca Lopes: 83-10
CARDOSO, Francisco: 83-11; 84-11; 85-11
CARDOSO, Gaspar de Gouvea: 86-11
CARDOSO, Isabel: 83-10; 134-14
CARDOSO, Jeronima: 15-6; 19-6
CARDOSO, João Gomes de Abreu Lima Pinto:
       106-12
CARDOSO, Manoel de Lemos: 110-12
CARDOSO, Manoel de Sampaio: 84-14
CARDOSO, Maria: 15-7; 90-13
CARDOSO, Maria Dias: 44-12
CARDOSO, Mecia: 40-5; 80-5
CARDOSO, Vasco Paes: 83-9
CARLOS, (s. of Antonio de Lima de Abreu): 51-9
CARNEIRO, Antonia: 30-10
CARNEIRO, Manoel Vieira: 43-13
CARNEIRO, Maria: 30-10; 33-11
CARVALHA, (mistress of Luis Affonso de Carvalho):
       130-12
CARVALHO, Alvaro Affonso de: 130-11
CARVALHO, Anna de Mello de: 15-7
CARVALHO, Antonio Teixeira de: 33-13
CARVALHO, Baltazar Borges de: 84-11
CARVALHO, Catarina Coelho de: 78-8

CARVALHO, Catarina de: 132-11
CARVALHO, Clara: 30-11
CARVALHO, Diogo Lopes de: 28-10
CARVALHO, Elena de Abreu de: 123-1
CARVALHO, Estevão Rodrigues de: 130-11
CARVALHO, Fernão de: 30-8
CARVALHO, Francisco de: 135-13
CARVALHO, Genebra Fernandes de: 130-12
CARVALHO, Ignes de: 87-12
CARVALHO, Jacinto Gomes de: 140-13
CARVALHO, Jeronima: 113-1
CARVALHO, Joanna Barros de: 15-7
CARVALHO, João de Andrade de: 84-17
CARVALHO, João Mendes de: 17-9
CARVALHO, Luis Affonso de: 130-11; 130-12
CARVALHO, Luisa de: 30-8
CARVALHO, Manoel Carveiro de: 83-12
CARVALHO, Manoel de: 30-11; 69-10
CARVALHO, Manoel Nunes de: 90-16
CARVALHO, Manoel Peixoto de: 28-10
CARVALHO, Maria Affonso: 80-5
CARVALHO, Maria de: 27-7; 44-8; 69-10
CARVALHO, Maria Nunes de: 90-15
CARVALHO, Paullo Teixeira de: 33-13
CARVALHO, Ruy Lourenço de: 27-7
CARVALHO, Simão de: 27-7
CARVALHOSA, Guiomar: 92-15
CARVOEIRO, Abbot of: 133-7
CARVOEIROS, Cosme Denis Freire de: 16-11
CASAL, Manoel Lobo do: 123-1
CASTANHEDO, Francisca: 84-11
CASTELLO BRANCO, Alvaro Vaz de: 90-14
CASTELLO BRANCO, Antonio Cabral: 85-12
CASTELLO BRANCO, Antonio de Abreu: 90-12;
    92-13; 92-16; 92-17
CASTELLO BRANCO, Antonio de Abreu Rego:
    73-14
CASTELLO BRANCO, Antonio Lopes de: 89-11
CASTELLO BRANCO, Antonio Rodrigues de:
    13-6
CASTELLO BRANCO, Baltazar Camelo: 115-2
CASTELLO BRANCO, Branca de: 92-17
CASTELLO BRANCO, Bras de Figueiredo: 77-10
CASTELLO BRANCO, Brites Balieira: 73-8
CASTELLO BRANCO, Caetano de Abreu: 84-16
CASTELLO BRANCO, Cristovão de Abreu: 87-12
CASTELLO BRANCO, Diogo de Abreu: 92-16
CASTELLO BRANCO, Dionizio de Almeida: 136-7
CASTELLO BRANCO, Domingos Borges: 84-11
CASTELLO BRANCO, Duarte de Abreu: 92-14
CASTELLO BRANCO, Elena Cardoso: 86-11
CASTELLO BRANCO, Eulalia Vaz de: 13-6
CASTELLO BRANCO, Felipa de Abranches:
    128-11
CASTELLO BRANCO, Felipa de Carvalho: 87-11
CASTELLO BRANCO, Fernão de Almeida: 136-7
CASTELLO BRANCO, Francisca de Fiqueiredo:
    90-13
CASTELLO BRANCO, Francisca Lopes de: 87-11;
    87-12
CASTELLO BRANCO, Francisco Borges: 84-11
CASTELLO BRANCO, Francisco Cabral de Abreu:
    84-15
CASTELLO BRANCO, Francisco de Abreu: 84-13;
    84-14; 84-15; 84-16; 84-17; 90-18
CASTELLO BRANCO, Francisco de Almeida:

134-12; 134-13
CASTELLO BRANCO, Francisco de Figueiredo:
    90-12; 90-13; 90-15
CASTELLO BRANCO, Isabel Abreu: 84-11
CASTELLO BRANCO, Isabel Vaz de: 83-9
CASTELLO BRANCO, Jeronimo Loureiro de:
    90-13
CASTELLO BRANCO, Joanna Felicia de: 31-14
CASTELLO BRANCO, Joanna Luisa de: 73-14;
    73-15
CASTELLO BRANCO, Joanna Rita de Almeida:
    136-7
CASTELLO BRANCO, João de Abranches de
    Abreu: 128-11
CASTELLO BRANCO, João de Abreu: 84-14; 84-17;
    134-13
CASTELLO BRANCO, João de Abreu de: 87-11;
    87-12
CASTELLO BRANCO, João Loureiro de: 90-13
CASTELLO BRANCO, Jorge de Abreu: 83-10; 88-11
CASTELLO BRANCO, Jorge de Almeida: 134-12;
    134-14; 135-13
CASTELLO BRANCO, Jose Borges: 84-11
CASTELLO BRANCO, Lopo de Abreu: 83-11; 83-10;
    84-11; 84-12
CASTELLO BRANCO, Lourenço Lopes de Abreu:
    83-9
CASTELLO BRANCO, Luis de: 92-17
CASTELLO BRANCO, Luis de Abreu: 83-11; 84-13
CASTELLO BRANCO, Luis de Macedo Feyo de:
    84-16
CASTELLO BRANCO, Luisa de: 86-12; 134-13;
    135-13; 135-14
CASTELLO BRANCO, Manoel de Abreu: 13-6;
    90-14; 90-15; 90-16; 90-17; 90-18; 91-13
CASTELLO BRANCO, Manoel de Figueiredo:
    128-11
CASTELLO BRANCO, Manoel Ferras: 135-13
CASTELLO BRANCO, Manoel Godinho de: 10-6;
    10-8
CASTELLO BRANCO, Maria: 91-13; 92-17
CASTELLO BRANCO, Maria Antonia: 92-17
CASTELLO BRANCO, Maria Camelo: 115-2
CASTELLO BRANCO, Maria de Abreu: 90-13
CASTELLO BRANCO, Maria de Sequeira: 79-10
CASTELLO BRANCO, Maria de Unhão: 87-11
CASTELLO BRANCO, Maria Lopes de: 83-9; 83-10
CASTELLO BRANCO, Mecia de: 86-13
CASTELLO BRANCO, Mecia de Almeida: 86-11;
    134-13; 135-13
CASTELLO BRANCO, Miguel de Abreu: 92-14;
    92-15
CASTELLO BRANCO, Pedro de Abreu: 85-11;
    90-12; 91-13
CASTELLO BRANCO, Pedro de Almeida: 86-12;
    86-13
CASTELLO BRANCO, Pedro Lopes de Abreu:
    83-10
CASTELLO BRANCO, Pedro Vaz Soares: 73-14
CASTELLO BRANCO, Salvadora de: 128-11
CASTELLO BRANCO, Sebastião de Abreu: 90-16;
    90-17
CASTELLO BRANCO, Umbelina de: 86-13
CASTRO, Afonso de: 49-4
CASTRO, Alvaro de: 57-10; 109-10
CASTRO, Angela de: 62-9

FARYA, Ignes Tenorio de: 73-12
FEIRA, Gomes Lourenço da: 49-2
FELECIANO, (s. of Luis do Quental de Abreu): 123-3
FELGUEIRA, Matheus: 131-10
FELGUEIRAS, Alvaro: 28-9
FELICIANNA, (d. of Lucas de Abreu da Gama): 123-4
FELIPA, (d. of Jorge de Abreu): 7-7
FELIPA, (d. of Leonel de Abreu): 2-7
FELIPA, (d. of Lopo Gomes de Abreu): 2-5
FELIPA, (d. of Luis Fradique da Cunha, e Mello): 77-12
FELIPA, (d. of Luisa Francisca de Menezes): 81-11
FELIPA, (d. of Maria da Cunha de Azevedo): 44-12
FELIPA, (w. of Luis de Abreu): 16-4
FELIPA, Joanna: 34-13
FERDINAND III, Holy Roman Emperor: 8-11
FERDINAND, King of Portugal: 2-2; 2-3; 2-4; 49-2; 99-3; 99-4; 101-4; 130-10
FERNANDES, Anna: 133-9
FERNANDES, Antonio: 34-13
FERNANDES, Gaspar: 109-17
FERNANDES, Ignes: G 3-4
FERNANDES, Luis: 48-10
FERNANDES, Manoel: 43-12; 125-2
FERNANDES, Margarida: 48-10
FERNANDES, Maria: 19-6
FERNANDES, Nuno: 99-4
FERNANDES, Thome: 16-4
FERNANDO, Infante of Portugal: 83-9
FERNANDO, (s. of Antonio de Abreu): 125-5
FERNANDO, (s. of Hipolito de Macedo): 34-14
FERRÃO, Branca: 87-12
FERREIRA, Anna Beatriz de: 143-9
FERREIRA, Anna Leonor: 136-7
FERREIRA, Antonio: 88-11
FERREIRA, Brites: 38-3
FERREIRA, Brites Rodrigues: 84-11
FERREIRA, Catarina: 16-10; 27-8
FERREIRA, Damazia: 31-12
FERREIRA, Elena: 88-11
FERREIRA, Francisco: 48-10
FERREIRA, Leonor: 38-3
FERREIRA, Manoel: 27-10
FERREIRA, Marcos: 33-11
FERREIRA, Maria Leonor: 136-7
FERREIRA, Maria Pereira: 139-11
FERREIRA, Pedro: 80-6
FERREIRA, Pedro Lourenço: 18-6
FERREIRA, Pedro Rodrigues: 80-6; 88-11
FERREIRA, Simão: 31-12
FERREIRO, Margarida de: 34-13
FEYA, Catarina: 84-15
FEYO, Antonio: 128-10
FEYO, Antonio Coutinho: 16-11
FEYO, João de Mello: 18-8
FEYO, Manoel: 18-8
FIALHO, Andre: 66-6
FIALHO, Brites: 73-7
FIALHO, Diogo Paes: 66-6
FIALHO, Gracia Paes: 66-6
FIALHO, Guiomar Paes: 66-6
FIALHO, João Vaz: 66-6
FIALHO, Manoel: 66-6
FIGUEIRA, Affonço: 127-15

FIGUEIRA, Cecilia: 17-9
FIGUEIRA, Diogo: 127-15
FIGUEIRA, Fernão: 127-15
FIGUEIRA, Francisco: 127-15; 127-16
FIGUEIRA, Lourenço: 2-2; 127-17
FIGUEIREDO, (...) de (w. of Manoel da Costa Corte Real): 79-9
FIGUEIREDO, Agueda de: 89-11
FIGUEIREDO, Agueda Fernandes de: 79-6
FIGUEIREDO, Anna de: 79-10; 89-11
FIGUEIREDO, Antonia de Andrade: 39-5
FIGUEIREDO, Antonio de: 21-9; 21-10; 92-13
FIGUEIREDO, Antonio Rodrigues de: 135-13; 135-14
FIGUEIREDO, Bernardo de: 16-12
FIGUEIREDO, Bras da Cunha de: 77-10; 77-11
FIGUEIREDO, Brites Rabello de: 30-9; 33-11
FIGUEIREDO, Catarina de: 88-12; 89-11
FIGUEIREDO, Domingos de: 90-14
FIGUEIREDO, Elena de: 92-13
FIGUEIREDO, Felipa Gonçalves de: 128-11
FIGUEIREDO, Francisca de: 50-9
FIGUEIREDO, Francisco Barbosa de: 73-12
FIGUEIREDO, Francisco de: 90-13; 90-14; 92-13
FIGUEIREDO, Francisco de Abreu Pereira de: 94-14
FIGUEIREDO, Gaspar Nunes de: 123-4
FIGUEIREDO, Genebra de: 135-13
FIGUEIREDO, Isabel de: 122-10
FIGUEIREDO, Isabel Francisca de: 79-8
FIGUEIREDO, João de: 89-11
FIGUEIREDO, João de Mello: 84-16
FIGUEIREDO, João Esteves de: 30-9
FIGUEIREDO, João Sobral de: 123-5
FIGUEIREDO, Leonor Barbosa de: 73-12
FIGUEIREDO, Luis de Abreu de: 89-11; 89-12
FIGUEIREDO, Luis Loureiro de: 88-12
FIGUEIREDO, Manoel Fernandes de: 128-11
FIGUEIREDO, Maria de: 86-13; 89-12; 91-13
FIGUEIREDO, Maria de Abreu de: 79-10; 79-11; 79-12
FIGUEIREDO, Miguel de: 89-11; 93-12; 93-13
FIGUEIREDO, Nicolao de: 89-11
FIGUEIREDO, Pedro Affonso de: 79-8
FIGUEIREDO, Sebastião Alvares de: 79-10
FIGUEIREDO, Sebastião de: 78-7
FIGUEIREDO, Simão de: 91-13
FIGUEIREDO, Theodosio Velloso de: 31-14
FIGUEIREDO, Verissima de: 93-13
FINADINHOS, João Maciel: 52-8
FLORENÇA, (d. of Sebastião de Abreu): 97-11
FOGAÇA, Catarina: 21-6
FOLCHO, Mozem João: 99-4
FOLGUEIRA, Belchior de Abreu: 61-11
FONSECA, Antonia da: 21-10
FONSECA, Antonia Maria da: 123-5
FONSECA, Baltazar de Pina da: 44-8
FONSECA, Bento da: 143-9
FONSECA, Bernardo da: 98-13
FONSECA, Brites da: 91-13
FONSECA, Catarina Pinto da: 43-13
FONSECA, Clara da: 27-11
FONSECA, Diogo da: 47-14; 98-13
FONSECA, Felipa da: 30-8
FONSECA, Francisco da: 91-13

FONSECA, Gaspar da: 17-7
FONSECA, Isabel da: 111-10
FONSECA, Jeronimo Rodrigues da: 127-18
FONSECA, João de Azambuja da: 74-12
FONSECA, João Ornelas da: 118-11
FONSECA, Lourença da: 93-13
FONSECA, Manoel da: 30-11
FONSECA, Manoel Pinto da: 43-13
FONSECA, Maria da: 74-11; 111-10
FONSECA, Maria Ferreira da: 74-12
FONSECA, Marianna de Sá da: 127-18
FONSECA, Marianna Margarida da: 67-16
FONSECA, Paulla da: 74-10
FONSECA, Paullo Velho da: 74-10; 75-10
FONSECA, Perpetua Velho da: 74-10
FORNOS, Abbot of: 84-11
FRANCISCA CAETANA, (d. of Manoel Munhos de
        Abreu): 93-13
FRANCISCA, (d. of Antonio de Abreu Lima): 28-10
FRANCISCA, (d. of Francisco de Abreu Lima): 63-12
FRANCISCA, (d. of Gaspar de Abreu Lima): 106-10
FRANCISCA, (d. of Gaspar Gomes de Abreu): 2-10
FRANCISCA, (d. of João Gomes de Abreu): 28-9
FRANCISCA, (d. of Luisa de Castello Branco): 135-13
FRANCISCO, (s. of Anna Thereza de Abreu): 108-11
FRANCISCO, (s. of Francisco Barbosa da Cunha):
        47-13
FRANCISCO, (s. of Hipolito de Macedo): 34-14
FRANCISCO, (s. of Leonel de Abreu Lima): 51-8
FRANCISCO, (s. of Leonel de Abreu): 2-7
FRANCISCO, (s. of Manoel Baltazar de Noronha):
        25-13
FRANCISCO, Thome (ref): 80-5
FRANCISCO XAVIER, (s. of Antonio de Abreu
        Lima): 28-10
FRANCO, Antonio: 64-5; 64-6; 64-7
FRANCO, Estevão: 64-4; 64-5; 64-6
FRANCO, João: 64-4; 64-8
FRANCO, Magdalena Viegas: 125-4
FREIRE, Anna de Oliveira: 115-3
FREIRE, Cecilia Coelho: 47-11; 47-12
FREIRE, Cristovão Ferreira: 127-17
FREIRE, Manoel: 67-13
FREIRE, Vasco Fernandes: 127-17
FREITAS, Maria de: 33-14
FREITAS, Paulla de: 30-11
FREITAS, Thome de: 76-9
FURTADO, Pedro Ribeiro: 128-10
GABRIEL, (s. of Ruy Gomes de Abreu): 104-10
GAFO, Rodrigo Annes: 83-6
GALVÃO, Luisa Botelho: 74-12
GALVÃO, Maria: 74-12
GAMA, Andre Chixorro da: 79-11; 79-12
GAMA, Antonia da: 109-13
GAMA, Antonio de Abreu da: 123-4; 123-5; 136-6;
        136-7; 136-8
GAMA, Antonio de Andrade da: 123-3
GAMA, Antonio Maria de Abreu da: 136-7; 136-8
GAMA, Custodio Luis de Abreu da: 123-5; 136-6
GAMA, Estevão da: 109-13
GAMA, Lourenço da: 28-11
GAMA, Lucas de Abreu da: 123-3; 123-4
GAMA, Sancho Sanches da: 96-11
GAMA, Violante Lobo da: 79-11
GAMBOA, Antonio Pedro: 16-13
GAMBOA, Catarina: 29-10

GAMBOA, Custodia: 16-13
GAMBOA, Francisco Xavier de: 16-13
GAMBOA, Jose Maria: 16-13
GÁNDARA, (ref): 1-1
GARCIA, (s. of Lourenço Mendes de Abreu): 73-9
GARCIA, Alvaro: 31-10; 42-11
GARCIA, Cristovão: 31-10; 42-11
GARCIA, Isabel: 42-11
GARCIA, Maria: 22-2
GASPAR, (s. of Luisa de Castello Branco): 135-13
GAYO, Anna Maria Pereira: 59-11
GAYO, Jacome Pereira: 59-11
GIL, Alvaro Borges de Castro da Silva: 119-10
GIL, Duarte: 40-7
GIL, Fernão: 85-11
GIRALDES, Affonço: 130-11
GIRALDES, Mor: 130-9; 130-12
GIRALDES, Sancha: 3-5
GODINHO, Antonio: 83-10
GODINHO, Baltazar: 113-2; 113-3
GODINHO, Isabel: 128-10
GODINHO, Manoel: 10-7
GODINHO, Maria Nunes: 123-4
GODINHO, Simão da Costa: 128-10
GODINS, Fafes: 3-5
GOES, Damião de (ref): 51-7
GOES, Ignes de: 16-5
GOES, Maria: 95-9
GOES, Maria de: 83-8
GOLIAS, Agueda: 2-6
GOLIAS, Agueda Gomes: 79-7
GOLIAS, Catarina Annes: 2-6
GOMES, Andre: 75-10
GOMES, Antonia: 60-9
GOMES, Baltazar: 27-11
GOMES, Diogo: 2-1; 2-4; 2-6; 10-4; 19-6; 132-10
GOMES, Elena: 64-1; 64-2; 64-3
GOMES, Felicia: 15-6
GOMES, Felipe: 114-3
GOMES, Gonçallo: 10-4
GOMES, Gonçallo Lourenço: 49-2
GOMES, João: 5-10; 19-5; 28-6; 28-9; 28-10; 51-9
GOMES, Lourenço: 2-1; 22-2; 64-1; 130-10
GOMES, Luisa: 128-11
GOMES, Maria: 1-4; 60-9; 133-10
GOMES, Marianna: 131-11
GOMES, Pedro: 2-5; 2-11; 5-10; 7-7; 21-7; 28-9; 71-10;
        75-11
GOMES, Tristão: 106-9
GOMES, Vasco: 2-1; 12-5; 14-6
GONÇALLO, (s. of Joanna Luisa de Castello
        Branco): 73-15
GONÇALVES, Affonço: 85-11
GONÇALVES, Agostinho: 112-10
GONÇALVES, Antonio: 112-10; 112-12
GONÇALVES, Diogo: 30-9; 85-11; 132-10
GONÇALVES, Domingos: 33-11
GONÇALVES, Francisca: 41-13
GONÇALVES, Gil: 26-8
GONÇALVES, Isabel: 16-4
GONÇALVES, Lopo: 82-6
GONÇALVES, Magdalena: 41-11
GONÇALVES, Maria: 32-10; 34-13; 41-12; 43-10
GONÇALVES, Mor: 99-4
GONÇALVES, Nuno: 82-7
GONDIACAS, Mendo Affonso de: 133-9

LIMA, Jose Mauricio de Abreu: 131-12; 140-13
LIMA, Leonel: 133-7
LIMA, Leonel de: 2-3; 2-5; 9-4; 40-7
LIMA, Leonel de Abreu: 25-9; 25-12; 28-13; 51-7; 51-8;
    51-9; 54-8; 59-9; 60-9; 61-11; 71-10; 104-8;
    104-9; 104-10; 104-11; 105-10
LIMA, Lourenço de: 5-12
LIMA, Luisa Xavier de: 107-10
LIMA, Manoel de: 2-8; 25-9; 25-10; 25-11; 51-9; 60-10;
    63-10
LIMA, Manoel de Abreu: 2-10; 52-10; 58-7; 106-9;
    108-10; 108-11; 139-10
LIMA, Manoel de Abreu Barreto de: 108-11
LIMA, Manoel de Oliveira de Abreu: 105-10; 105-11
LIMA, Margarida de: 61-10
LIMA, Maria Adelaide de Abreu: 129-12
LIMA, Maria de Abreu: 59-10; 59-11
LIMA, Maria de Mello e: 60-10; 51-10; 60-10
LIMA, Maria Gonçalves de: 64-5
LIMA, Maria Ledo de: 133-10
LIMA, Maria Lourenço de: 40-6; 133-7; 133-8; 143-9
LIMA, Maria Luiza de Abreu: 131-10
LIMA, Maria Pereira de Abreu: 25-12
LIMA, Maria Rodrigues de: 64-5
LIMA, Miguel de Abreu: 51-8; 59-9; 59-10
LIMA, Natalia de: 62-9
LIMA, Nicolao de Mello: 28-6
LIMA, Nicolao de Mello, e: 58-7
LIMA, Nuno de: 25-12; 25-13
LIMA, Paula de Abreu: 142-10
LIMA, Paulla de Abreu de: 106-9
LIMA, Pedro Alexandre de Abreu: 131-12
LIMA, Pedro de: 40-7; 58-7
LIMA, Pedro Fernandes: 133-7
LIMA, Rafael de Abreu: 52-9; 52-10
LIMA, Rodrigo Antonio de Abreu: 131-11; 131-12;
    140-13
LIMA, Rodrigo de: 9-4; 64-5
LIMA, Rodrigo de Mello e: 2-5; 28-5
LIMA, Rosalia Manoel de Abreu: 104-11
LIMA, Rosalia Manoela de Abreu: 28-13
LIMA, Ruy de Abreu: 62-9
LIMA, Ruy de Abreu de: 52-8
LIMA, Salvador de Abreu: 7-7
LIMA, Santos Luis Barreto de: 108-11
LIMA, Sebastiana de: 63-11
LIMA, Sebastianna de: 104-8; 107-9; 107-10
LIMA, Theresa Fernandes de: 133-7
LIMA, Tristão Gomes de Abreu: 131-10
LIMA, Ventura de Abreu: 142-10
LIRA, Aldonça Alvares de: 49-3; 49-4; 64-3
LIRA, Isabel Lobato de: 49-4
LIRA, Isabel Lopes de: 49-3
LIRA, Lopo de: G 1-3
LIRA, Lopo Gomes de: 2-2; 24-3; 49-3
LIRA, Maria Pereira de: 25-9
LIRA, Vasco Affonço de: 1-6
LOBÃO, Ignes: 95-11
LOBATO, Anna Vaz: 64-3; 64-4; 64-5
LOBATO, Brites: 28-9
LOBATO, Gaspar: 5-11
LOBATO, Gregorio Vaz: 64-3
LOBATO, Guiomar Martins: 49-4
LOBATO, Isabel Lopes: 64-3
LOBATO, Lourenço: 49-4
LOBATO, Ruy: 49-4; 64-3

LOBATO, Vasco: 49-4
LOBO, Antonia Dias: 115-3
LOBO, Antonio de Sousa: 25-11
LOBO, Antonio Jusarte: 48-11
LOBO, Antonio Rabello: 25-11
LOBO, Bento Rabello: 25-11
LOBO, Braz: 115-3
LOBO, Joanna da Gama: 28-11
LOBO, Manoel: 115-3
LOBO, Sebastião Rabello Leite: 25-11
LOBO, Thome Chixorro da Gama: 79-12
LOMBA, João da: 60-9
LOMBA, Maria: 60-9
LOMBA, Miguel Barbosa: 59-9
LOPES, Andre: 32-10
LOPES, Catarina: 27-11
LOPES, Fernão: 89-12
LOPES, Fernão (ref): 2-2
LOPES, Francisco: 89-11
LOPES, Garcia: 143-9
LOPES, Ignacia: 30-8
LOPES, Isabel: 143-9
LOPES, Joanna: 143-9
LOPES, Leonor: 83-6
LOPES, Maria: 114-4
LOPES, Pedro: 83-11
LOUREIRO, Antonio: 88-12
LOUREIRO, Antonio Rodrigues: 86-12
LOUREIRO, Daniel: 92-13
LOUREIRO, Gaspar: 134-13; 135-13; 135-14
LOUREIRO, Isabel: 136-7
LOUREIRO, Jeronimo: 90-14
LOUREIRO, João: 90-14
LOUREIRO, João Annes: 92-13
LOUREIRO, Luis: 10-6; 13-6
LOUREIRO, Luis Annes: 88-12; 89-11
LOUREIRO, Luis Gomes: 21-10
LOUREIRO, Maria: 14-6; 135-13
LOUREIRO, Maria Gomes: 44-10
LOUREIRO, Miguel de: 135-14
LOUREIRO, Pedro de Mesquita: 77-11
LOURENÇO, Constança: 64-1; G 1-3
LOURENÇO, Gomes: 1-4; 2-1; 3-6
LOURENÇO, Gonçallo: 78-7
LOURENÇO, Guiomar: 133-10
LOURENÇO, Joanna: 86-12
LOURENÇO, João: 78-7; 98-11
LOURENÇO, Maria: 133-9
LOURENÇO, Pedro: 78-7
LOURENÇO, (s. of Lourenço Mendes de Abreu):
    73-9
LOUSADA, Gaspar Alvares: 2-2
LOUSADA, Maria de Carvalho: 84-16
LUCENA, Martim Affonso de: 96-12
LUGO, Theresa Maria Leonor de Vasconcellos, e:
    94-16
LUIS GASPAR, (s. of Hipolito de Macedo): 34-14
LUIS, (s. of Catarina Borges de Abreu): 121-11
LUIS, (s. of Jose de Abreu de Mello): 78-9
LUIS, (s. of Manoel Baltazar de Noronha): 25-13
LUIS, (s. of Miguel de Abreu Castello Branco): 92-15
LUISA, (d. of Diogo da Cunha de Azevedo): 44-11
LUISA, (d. of Francisco de Abreu Castello Branco):
    84-14
LUISA, (d. of Isabel da Silva de Noronha): 25-11
LUISA, (d. of Luisa Francisca de Menezes): 81-11

LUIZ, (s. of Felipa da Cunha): 10-5
LUIZA, (d. of Maria da Cunha de Azevedo): 44-12
MACEDO, Anna de: 27-8
MACEDO, Antonio de: 16-6; 16-7; 30-9; 50-7
MACEDO, Camilla de: 34-11
MACEDO, Diogo de: 41-12
MACEDO, Diogo Gonçalves de: 27-6
MACEDO, Francisca de: 16-7; 27-9; 31-10; 31-11; 41-11; 42-11; 50-7; 67-12
MACEDO, Francisco de: 27-8;27-10;27-11;27-12;37-12
MACEDO, Francisco Soares de: 92-18
MACEDO, Gaspar de: 27-10; 30-10; 34-11; 34-13
MACEDO, Gonçallo de: 27-8; 27-11; 41-12
MACEDO, Guiomar de: 27-8;27-9;27-10;31-10;43-10
MACEDO, Hipolito de: 34-13; 34-14; 34-15; 35-15
MACEDO, Ignacio de: 41-11
MACEDO, Ignes de: 27-8
MACEDO, Isabel de: 27-8; 27-9; 67-12; 91-13
MACEDO, Izabel de: 43-10; 43-11
MACEDO, Joanna de: 34-12; 43-11; 43-12; 43-13
MACEDO, Joanna Martins de: 27-8
MACEDO, João de: 50-7
MACEDO, Jose Pinto de: 34-14; 35-15
MACEDO, Leonor de: 34-12; 34-13; 34-14; 107-9
MACEDO, Lucas de Abreu de: 31-12
MACEDO, Luisa de: 27-11; 27-12
MACEDO, Magdalena de: 27-9; 27-10; 27-11
MACEDO, Maria de: 27-6;33-11;43-10;43-11;43-12
MACEDO, Marianna de Teive de: 139-11
MACEDO, Martim Gonçalves de: 27-6
MACEDO, Miguel de: 27-8
MACEDO, Miguel de Coimbra de: 39-5
MACEDO, Paulla de: 67-12
MACEDO, Paullo de: 27-8
MACEDO, Pedro de: 27-8
MACHADO, Archangella: 135-14
MACHADO, Bernarda: 33-13
MACHADO, Jeronimo de Sousa: 104-8
MACHADO, Luisa de Azevedo: 30-13
MACHADO, Manoel: 2-8
MACHADO, Maria Vaz: 59-10
MACIEL, Antonio Alvares: 106-10
MACIEL, Francisco Pinto Pereira de: 106-12
MACIEL, Isabel: 142-10
MACIEL, João: 52-8
MADEIRA, Aleixo Affonso: 122-10
MADEIRA, Domingos Cardoso: 127-18
MADEIRA, Elena: 79-8
MADEIRA, Francisco Jose de Mendonça: 127-18
MADEIRA, João: 122-9
MADEIRA, Manoel: 122-9; 122-10
MADEIRA, Manoel Cardoso: 127-18
MADEIRA, Maria: 119-9; 119-10; 119-11; 120-11
MADEIRA, Pedro: 117-11; 122-9; 122-10
MADUREIRA, Maria Caetana: 43-13
MAGALHÃES, Anna de: 28-7
MAGALHÃES, Antonia de: 16-7
MAGALHÃES, Antonia de Barros de: 28-8
MAGALHÃES, Antonio de: 28-7
MAGALHÃES, Antonio de Barros: 107-10
MAGALHÃES, Antonio Pires de: 28-8
MAGALHÃES, Brites de: 18-7; 50-7
MAGALHÃES, Diogo Pinto de: 30-13; 138-14
MAGALHÃES, Felipa de: 81-7
MAGALHÃES, Fernando de: 2-6
MAGALHÃES, Fernão de: 7-7; 18-7; 81-7

MAGALHÃES, Francisco de: 2-6; 27-12
MAGALHÃES, Francisco do Couto de: 37-12
MAGALHÃES, Fulgencio Dias Manso de: 84-15
MAGALHÃES, Genebra de: 2-6
MAGALHÃES, Gonçallo Pinto de: 30-13; 138-14
MAGALHÃES, Gonçallo Rodrigues de: 7-7
MAGALHÃES, Isabel de: 18-7
MAGALHÃES, João Antunes de: 28-8
MAGALHÃES, João de: 27-11; 33-12; 37-12; 45-12
MAGALHÃES, João Rabello de: 78-10
MAGALHÃES, Jose de: 27-12
MAGALHÃES, Josefa de: 116-12
MAGALHÃES, Manoel de: 2-7; 116-12
MAGALHÃES, Pedro de: 27-12
MAGALHÃES, Ruy Pires de: 33-12
MAGALHÃES, Theresa Bernarda de: 78-10
MALAFAYA, Jorge Fernandes: 44-8
MALDONADO, Agostinho Juzarte: 121-12
MALDONADO, Alvaro: 27-6
MALDONADO, Gaspar: 109-15
MALDONADO, Gomes de Carvalho: 87-12
MALDONADO, Gonçallo: 27-6
MALDONADO, Manoel Dias: 85-11
MALHEIRO, Catarina: 52-8
MALHEIRO, Catarina de Sena de Brito: 131-10
MALHEIRO, Francisco Cordeiro: 28-9
MALHEIRO, Francisco de Brito: 70-11
MALHEIRO, Luis de Brito: 131-10
MALHEIRO, Magdalena: 70-11
MALHEIRO, Margarida Marinho: 59-11
MALHEIRO, Maria: 28-9; G 4-7
MANCELLOS, Antonio da Fonseca: 110-12; 132-11
MANCELLOS, Paullo da Fonseca: 132-11
MANOEL, Infante of Portugal: 5-10
MANOEL, (s. of Antonio da Mota da Cunha): 33-12
MANOEL, (s. of Antonio de Abreu Lima): 28-10
MANOEL, (s. of Clara da Cunha): 47-11
MANOEL, (s. of Joanna Luisa de Castello Branco): 73-15
MANOEL, (s. of João Borges): 120-11
MANOEL, (s. of Luis Fradique da Cunha, e Mello): 77-12
MANSA, Maria Feyo: 84-15
MANSILHA, Gil Affonço: 30-8
MANSILHA, João Lopes: 30-8
MANUEL I, King of Portugal: 10-4; 10-6; 12-6; 19-5; 28-5; 73-5; 83-9
MARGARIDA, (d. of Manoel de Lima): 25-9
MARGARIDA, (d. of Ruy Gomes de Abreu): 2-6
MARGARIDA, (d. of Ruy or Rodrigo Gomes de Abreu): 52-7
MARGARIDA, (d. of Vicente de Macedo da Cunha): 34-15
MARGARIDA JOSEFA, (d. of Leopoldo Luis de Sousa): 36-15
MARIA, (d. of Anna Matilde de Abreu Lima): 108-11
MARIA, (d. of Antonio de Abreu Castello Branco): 92-13
MARIA, (d. of Felipa da Cunha de Azevedo): 45-11
MARIA, (d. of Francisco Mendes de Abreu): 111-12
MARIA, (d. of Isabel da Silva de Noronha): 25-11
MARIA, (d. of João Gomes de Abreu): 2-11; 28-9; 52-9
MARIA, (d. of Jorge de Abreu): 7-7
MARIA, (d. of Leonel de Abreu): 2-7; 4-10
MARIA, (d. of Leonel de Abreu Lima): 51-8
MARIA, (d. of Lopo de Abreu Castello Branco):

MELLO, Felipa de Sá, e: 26-8
MELLO, Felipa Maria de Almada, e: 139-12
MELLO, Fernão de: 26-6
MELLO, Francisca de: 76-6; 83-11
MELLO, Francisca Theresa de Castro, e: 136-6
MELLO, Francisco de Abreu de: 76-6
MELLO, Francisco de Abreu Toscano de: 115-3
MELLO, Francisco Jose de: 18-6; 18-10
MELLO, Gaspar de: 18-8
MELLO, Gonçallo Pedro de: 73-15
MELLO, Gonçallo Vaz de: 18-6
MELLO, Henrique de: 100-5
MELLO, Isabel de: 10-4
MELLO, Isabel de Abreu de: 115-2
MELLO, Isabel Maria de: 30-13
MELLO, Isabel Soares de: 77-10
MELLO, Jeronimo Pereira de: 47-13; 68-11; 68-12;
    68-13
MELLO, Jeronimo Soares de: 76-6
MELLO, Joanna de: 16-8;28-5;51-9;57-10;78-7
MELLO, João de: 16-10; 18-8; 57-8; 83-13; 84-16;
    109-14; 109-15
MELLO, João Teixeira de: 68-12
MELLO, Jorge de: 10-5
MELLO, Jorge de Abreu de: 78-7; 78-8
MELLO, Jose Correa de (ref): 79-7
MELLO, Jose de: 77-13
MELLO, Jose de Abreu de: 26-8;78-8;78-9;78-10;78-11
MELLO, Jose Manoel Barbosa da Cunha, e: 47-14;
    47-15
MELLO, Josefa Francisca de: 28-10
MELLO, Juliana Cabral de: 84-13
MELLO, Leonor de: 28-9; 28-10
MELLO, Lourenço de: 12-6
MELLO, Lourenço Soares de: 56-7
MELLO, Luis da Cunha Coutinho Machado, e:
    138-15
MELLO, Luis da Cunha, e: 26-8; 78-9
MELLO, Luis de Abreu: 109-14; 109-15; 109-16;
    109-17
MELLO, Luis Fradique da Cunha, e: 77-11; 77-12
MELLO, Luis Pessoa de: 16-10
MELLO, Luisa de: 109-14
MELLO, Manoel Bernardo da Cunha Couto, e:
    141-15
MELLO, Manoel Correa de: 47-15
MELLO, Manoel de: 28-6; 78-9
MELLO, Manoel de Abreu de: 76-6; 76-7; 76-8; 76-9
MELLO, Manoel de Lima e: 51-10
MELLO, Manoel de Sousa, e: 26-6
MELLO, Manoel Feyo de: 18-8
MELLO, Maria Clara Barbosa da Cunha, e: 47-14
MELLO, Maria de: 14-6; 17-7; 30-13; 54-8; 57-7; 76-6;
    78-7; 109-14; 138-14
MELLO, Maria de Abreu de: 76-6; 76-7
MELLO, Maria Jose de: 106-11
MELLO, Maria Pessoa de: 19-6
MELLO, Maria Soares de: 13-6
MELLO, Martim Affonso de: 2-4; 57-8
MELLO, Pedro de: 18-6; 18-10; 73-15
MELLO, Placido de Araujo, e: 110-13
MELLO, Roque da Cunha, e: 26-8; 77-9
MELLO, Roque de: 90-13
MELLO, Theresa de: 77-10
MELLO, Vasco Gomes de: 56-7
MELO, Ignacio Bezerra Rego Lima e: 106-11

MENA, Isabel de: 31-13
MENDANHA, Antonia de: 93-13
MENDES, Alvaro: 27-6
MENDES, Anna: 32-9
MENDES, Anna Luisa: 34-15
MENDES, Antonio: 84-15
MENDES, Baltazar: 133-9
MENDES, Bartolomeu: 74-11
MENDES, Bento Teixeira: 25-13
MENDES, Felipa: 112-11
MENDES, Francisco: 89-11
MENDES, Frutuoso: 67-15
MENDES, Garcia: 110-12
MENDES, João: 111-12; 143-9
MENDES, Lourenço: 73-8; 73-10; 74-12
MENDES, Miguel: 111-11
MENDES, Pedro: 27-11; 89-11
MENDES, Rodrigo: 85-11
MENDES, Ruy: 73-12
MENDES, Thomaz: 111-12
MENDONÇA, Antonia de: 127-16
MENDONÇA, Bento Arraes de: 44-7
MENDONÇA, Diogo Abraldes de: 105-11
MENDONÇA, Elena de: 125-6
MENDONÇA, Elena Maria de Mello, e: 136-6
MENDONÇA, Jacinta de: 17-9
MENDONÇA, Joanna Arraes de: 16-14
MENDONÇA, João Cabreira de: 17-9
MENDONÇA, Leonor de Macedo, e: 90-16
MENDONÇA, Luis Ferreira de: 127-17; 127-18
MENDONÇA, Luisa de: 127-15
MENDONÇA, Marcelina de: 90-16
MENDONÇA, Maria de: 81-9
MENDONÇA, Maria Madeira de: 121-11
MENDONÇA, Maria Margarida de: 18-10
MENDONÇA, Thomasia Arraes de: 44-8
MENEZES, Alexandre de Magalhães de: 4-11
MENEZES, Anna de Alpoim e: 25-14
MENEZES, Antonio Barreto de: 40-8
MENEZES, Antonio de Magalhães de: 4-11
MENEZES, Branca de: 83-13
MENEZES, Bruno Antonio Cardoso de: 106-11;
    106-12
MENEZES, Elena de Moraes de Noronha, e:
    28-13
MENEZES, Fernão da Silva, e: 109-10
MENEZES, Francisca Micaella de Castro, e:
    127-18
MENEZES, Francisca or Ignes de: 81-10
MENEZES, Gil de Magalhães e: 33-12
MENEZES, Ignes or Francisca de: 81-10
MENEZES, Jacinto de Magalhães e: 2-4
MENEZES, Jeronima Theresa de Carvalho, e:
    25-14
MENEZES, Joanna de: 81-10
MENEZES, João Tello de: 9-4
MENEZES, Luis Antonio de Sequeira e: 81-11
MENEZES, Luis Cardoso de: 127-18
MENEZES, Luisa Francisca de: 81-10; 81-11;
    81-12
MENEZES, Manoel Bernardo Guedes Carvalho
    de: 138-15
MENEZES, Maria de: 2-4; 2-7; 40-8
MENEZES, Maria do Carmo Sousa, e: 108-11
MENEZES, Maria do Castro de Sousa, e: 108-12
MENEZES, Maria Leonor Teles de: 106-12

PACHECO, Maria Rodrigues: 2-2; G 1-1
PACHECO, Marianna da Costa: 84-14
PAES, Affonso: 66-6
PAES, Brites: 66-6
PAES, Diogo: 66-6
PAES, Garcia: 1-4
PAES, Guiomar: 66-6
PAES, Lourenço: 96-12
PAES, Margarida: 66-6
PAES, Maria: 18-9
PAES, Sancha: 3-5
PAIVA, Catarina de: 44-7
PALHARES, Ruy: G 1-4
PALMA, Luisa de: 139-10
PANTOJA, Joanna Pereira de Aguillar: 139-12
PARAISO, Manoel Mendes: 34-15
PASCOA, (d. of João Gomes de Abreu): 28-9
PASSOS, Anna do Valle de: G 1-3
PASSOS DE PROBEM, Maria Jeronima de: 129-12
PATORNILHA, (d. of Pedro Madeira): 122-10
PAULINO, (s. of Catarina Borges de Abreu): 121-11
PAULLA, (d. of Elena de Abreu): 122-9
PAULLA, (d. of Francisco Cardoso de Abreu): 84-11
PAULLA, (d. of Gaspar de Mello de Abreu): 18-8
PAULLA, (d. of Sebastianna de Lima): 107-9
PAULLO, (s. of Antonio de Abreu Lima): 28-10
PAULLO, (s. of João Rodrigues de Abreu): 94-12
PAYO, (s. of Leonel de Abreu Lima): 104-9
PAYVA, Francisca de: 38-3
PAYVA, Luisa de: 39-4
PEDRO, (s. of Antão Mendes de Abreu): 73-10
PEDRO, (s. of Leonel de Abreu): 2-7
PEDRO, (s. of Leopoldo Luis de Sousa): 36-15
PEDRO, (s. of Lourenço Mendes de Abreu): 73-9
PEDRO, Count D. (ref): 1-1; 2-1; 3-5; 49-2; 82-6; 83-6; 83-7
PEDRO, Infante of Portugal: 73-8; 89-12
PEGADO, Antonio: 110-10
PEGADO, Estevão: 97-12
PEGADO, Matheus: 110-11
PEGADO, Violante: 96-11
PEIXOTO, Baltazar: 27-10
PEIXOTO, Damião do Valle: 28-6
PEIXOTO, Francisco: 27-10
PEIXOTO, Gonçallo: 27-10
PEIXOTO, Jose de Freitas: 7-8
PEIXOTO, Roque Varella: 44-12
PENASCAES, Abbot of: 133-10
PERDIGÃO, Antonio Barreto: 121-11
PERDIS, Rodrigo Esteves Papo de: 44-8
PEREIRA, (ref): 52-8
PEREIRA, Alvaro: 83-8
PEREIRA, Alvaro de Abreu: 57-9; 57-8; 57-9; 57-10
PEREIRA, Andre: 57-7
PEREIRA, Anna de Abreu: 57-10
PEREIRA, Anna Theresa: 140-13
PEREIRA, Antonio: 30-11;36-13;57-7;81-11;97-11
PEREIRA, Antonio da Cunha: 108-11
PEREIRA, Antonio Machado: 30-13
PEREIRA, Antonio Peixoto: 25-10
PEREIRA, Baltazar: 2-9
PEREIRA, Bernardo: 86-13
PEREIRA, Branca: 64-3
PEREIRA, Brites Paes: 13-5
PEREIRA, Duarte de Mello: 109-15
PEREIRA, Felipa: 27-10

PEREIRA, Felipe da Silva: 92-13
PEREIRA, Fernão Gomes: 49-3
PEREIRA, Francisca: 4-10
PEREIRA, Francisca Maria:: 47-13
PEREIRA, Francisco: 2-9
PEREIRA, Francisco Peixoto: 34-12
PEREIRA, Guiomar: 130-11
PEREIRA, Ignacia: 28-6; 57-7
PEREIRA, Ignes: 2-9; 4-10; 68-11; 97-11
PEREIRA, Jaime de Mello: 109-14
PEREIRA, João de Gusmão: 94-14
PEREIRA, João Pimenta: 28-9
PEREIRA, Jose: 131-12
PEREIRA, Jose Machado: 30-13
PEREIRA, Josefa: 68-14
PEREIRA, Leonor: 28-6
PEREIRA, Manoel Pacheco: 67-12
PEREIRA, Manoel Rodrigues: 131-11
PEREIRA, Marcelino (ref): 40-6
PEREIRA, Maria: 34-12; 103-10
PEREIRA, Maria de Campos: 36-13
PEREIRA, Maria de Sampaio: 84-14
PEREIRA, Maria Mendes Correa: 84-15
PEREIRA, Miguel Borges: 61-10
PEREIRA, Nuno Alvares: 49-3; 83-8; 99-4
PEREIRA, Nuno Leitão: 90-15
PEREIRA, Pantaleão dos Reys: 34-14
PEREIRA, Paulla: 57-7
PEREIRA, Placida: 57-7
PEREIRA, Ruy Dias: 109-10
PEREIRA, Sebastião de Abreu: 57-7; 57-8; 97-12
PEREIRA, Senhorinha Gomes: G 1-3
PEREIRA, Theodosio de Macedo: 34-14
PEREIRA, Theresa Alvares: 83-8
PERESTRELLO, Antonia: 48-9; 48-10; 48-11
PERESTRELLO, Antonio Carlos de Abreu de
    Almada: 48-11
PERESTRELLO, Bento da Cunha: 44-7;44-8;
    44-9;48-9;69-9
PERESTRELLO, Francisco Vaz: 44-7
PERESTRELLO, Ignacio da Cunha: 44-8
PERESTRELLO, Jeronima: 44-7; 66-6
PERESTRELLO, Jeronimo da Cunha: 48-11
PERESTRELLO, Luis da Cunha: 48-9
PERESTRELLO, Luisa: 44-7; 44-8
PERESTRELLO, Luiz da Cunha: 44-8
PERESTRELLO, Luiza: 66-6
PERESTRELLO, Manoel Arraes de Mendonça:
    48-11
PERESTRELLO, Maria: 57-9
PERESTRELLO, Maria da Cunha: 44-8; 69-9
PERESTRELLO, Rodrigo da Cunha: 44-9
PERRE, Abbot of: 51-10
PESSANHA, Manoel: 83-10; 100-5
PESSOA, Alberto de Abreu de Amorim: 111-13;
    137-14
PESSOA, Anna: 34-13
PESSOA, Antonio de Abreu Amorim: 111-12;
    111-13
PESSOA, Antonio de Abreu de Amorim: 137-14
PESSOA, Baltazar: 16-8; 16-10; 34-13
PESSOA, Francisco Antonio de Abreu de
    Amorim: 137-14
PESSOA, Joanna: 16-8
PESSOA, João Gomes: 18-8

PESSOA, João Homem: 16-8; 16-10; 19-6
PESSOA, Luisa de Mattos: 123-2
PESSOA, Maria: 34-12; 34-13
PESTANA, Aldonça Rodrigues: 40-6
PETER I, King of Portugal: 2-2; 2-6; 40-6; 49-2; 82-7; 99-3; 99-4; 130-10
PHILIP I of Portugal or PHILIP II of Spain: 5-10; 80-7
PHILIP II of Spain or PHILIP I of Portugal: 5-10; 80-7
PHILIP III, King of France: 1-1
PHILIP III of Portugal or PHILIP IV of Spain: 39-5; 54-9; 54-10
PHILIP IV of Spain or PHILIP III of Portugal: 39-5; 54-9; 54-10
PHILIPPA, Queen of Portugal: 109-9
PIMENTA, Antonio de Brito: 29-10; 70-11
PIMENTA, Baltazar: 70-11
PIMENTA, Catarina de Brito: 70-11
PIMENTA, Cecilia: 70-11
PIMENTA, Domingos: 61-10
PIMENTA, Ignes: 28-9
PIMENTA, Joanna: 28-9
PIMENTEL, Carlos Correa: 90-18
PIMENTEL, Isabel: 81-8
PIMENTEL, Joanna de Figueiredo: 90-18
PIMENTEL, Martim Gonçalves: 2-6
PIMENTEL, Theresa: 31-10
PINA, Catarina de: 85-11
PINA, Fernão de: 16-5; 16-6; 83-11
PINA, Luisa de: 44-8
PINA, Maria de: 44-8
PINA, Rui de (ref): 2-1
PINA, Violante de: 16-5; 16-6; 85-11
PINHEIRO, (...) (w. of Domingos Lopes Nobre): 110-11
PINHEIRO, Anna: 109-16
PINHEIRO, João: 110-11
PINHEIRO, Manoel Chixorro: 79-11
PINHEIRO, Thomé Chixorro: 79-11
PINHEIRO, Visente Vaz: 109-16
PINHO, Antonia de: 47-14
PINHO, Manoel de: 47-12; 47-14
PINHO, Marianna Nogueira de: 47-14
PINTO, Alvaro: 93-12
PINTO, Belchior: 2-9
PINTO, Brites: 32-9
PINTO, Catarina: 51-9
PINTO, Domingos: 36-15
PINTO, Domingos Medeiros: 84-16
PINTO, Francisco: 93-12
PINTO, Isabel: 93-12; 93-13
PINTO, Jose: 93-13
PINTO, Lopo: 93-12
PINTO, Manoel: 93-12
PINTO, Manoel Teixeira: 31-10
PINTO, Maria: 36-15
PINTO, Mecia: 93-12
PINTO, Salvador Ribeiro: 128-11
PINTO, Sebastião: G 4-6
PIRES, Durão: 130-7
PIRES, Garcia: 130-10
PIRES, João: 11-6

PITA, Bras Rodrigues: 4-10
PITA, Ignes: 4-10; 29-10
PONTE, Catarina: 95-11
PONTE, Florença da: 96-10
PORTA, Jose de Nossa Senhora da: 84-16
PORTALEGRE, Antonio Nunes: 38-2; 38-3; 39-5
PORTALEGRE, Bishop of: 12-6
PORTOCARREIRO, Anna da Rocha: 51-10
PORTOCARREIRO, Belchiora Manoella de Abraldes: 105-11
PORTOCARREIRO, Brites: 9-4
PORTOCARREIRO, Diogo da Rocha: 51-10
PORTOCARREIRO, Fernão Annes: 2-2
PORTOCARREIRO, Joanna da Rocha: 51-10
PORTOCARREIRO, João Rodrigues: 2-2
PORTOCARREIRO, Maria Annes: G 1-1
PORTOCARREIRO, Maria Theresa de Abraldes de Azevedo: 105-11
PORTOCARREIRO, Mayor: 9-4
PORTOCARREIRO, Mayor Annes: 2-2
PORTOCARREIRO, Theresa Paulla da Veiga: 105-11
PORTUGAL, Margarida Antonia de Lencastre Barros de: 106-12
POVOAS, Antonio de: 16-7
PREGO, Isabel Alvares: 62-9
PREGO, Justa: 7-10
PREGO, Margarida: 7-10
PRESTER JOHN, King of Ethiopia: 86-12
PRETO, Jose de Sousa da Cunha: 136-8
PROENÇA, Maria: 84-12
PROZELO, Abbot of: 63-12
PRUDENCIA, (d. of Rafael de Abreu Lima): 52-10
PUGA, João Franco de: 64-6; 64-7
QUARESMA, Anna: 51-9
QUARESMA, Maria: 6-11; 51-7
QUEIMADA, Isabel: 89-12
QUEIMADO, Vasco: 9-4; 89-12
QUEIROS, Gracia de: 34-12
QUEIROS, Manoel Velloso de: 42-12
QUEIROZ, Gracia de: 32-11
QUEIROZ, Isabel de: 30-9
QUEIROZ, João de: 30-9
QUEIROZ, Manoel Teixeira de: 32-10; 32-11
QUEIROZ, Marianna Victoria de Lencastre e: 106-12
QUENTAL, Carlos de Abreu do: 123-3
QUENTAL, Luis do: 123-4
QUENTAL, Manoel do: 123-3
QUINTEIRO, Bernardo: G 3-5; G 4-6
QUINTELLA, Fernão Affonso de: 83-6
QUIRO, Anna Dias de: 27-7
QUIRO, Catarina de: 27-7
QUIRO, Gaspar de: 31-11
QUIRO, Gonçallo de: 31-11
QUIRO, Isabel Francisca de: 30-8
RABELLO, Alvaro: G 3-4
RABELLO, Antonia: 26-8
RABELLO, Antonio: 132-10
RABELLO, Brites Dias: 80-5
RABELLO, Catarina: 47-14; G 3-4
RABELLO, Cristovão: G 3-4
RABELLO, Elena Esteves: 30-9
RABELLO, Francisco: G 3-4; G 3-7
RABELLO, Gaspar: 80-5
RABELLO, Gonçallo: 89-11

RABELLO, Gonçallo Esteves: 30-9
RABELLO, Guiomar: 33-12
RABELLO, Isabel: 26-8; 78-9; 90-15
RABELLO, Isabel Dias: 80-6; 84-11
RABELLO, Jeronimo Affonso: 80-6
RABELLO, Joanna: 90-15
RABELLO, João Alvares: G 3-4
RABELLO, João Soares: 92-18
RABELLO, Lopo Cardoso: 26-7
RABELLO, Lopo Dias: 80-5
RABELLO, Manoel de Abreu: G 3-4; G 3-5; G 3-6; G 4-6
RABELLO, Maria: 61-9; 80-6
RABELLO, Matheus: 112-12
RABELLO, Nuno: 89-11
RABELLO, Pantaleana: 132-10; 110-12
RABELLO, Paulla: 47-14
RABELLO, Pedro: 86-13
RABELLO, Violante: 127-17
RAMALHO, Maria: 37-12
RAMIRES, Diogo Alvares: 81-8
RAPOSO, Isabel Toscano: 40-6
RAUDANO, Antonio Juzarte: 79-12
REBELLO, Guiomar: 33-11
REBELLO, João: 36-13
REGADAS, Antonia: 31-10; 41-11; 41-12
REGADAS, Estevão: 31-10
REGADAS, João: 31-10
REGADAS, Miguel: 31-10
REGALADOS, Count of: 2-10; 2-11
REGO, Andre Lopes de Abreu: 30-8; 32-9
REGO, Antonio de Abreu: 92-18
REGO, Diogo Lopes de Abreu: 30-8
REGO, Elena de Moraes do: 48-11
REGO, Feleciano do: 92-16
REGO, Gregorio Lopes do: 27-7; 30-8
REGO, Ignes Dias do: 2-3
REGO, Isabel do: 92-16
REGO, Justa do: 7-10
REGO, Maria de Castello Branco do: 92-17; 92-18
REGO, Ruy Dias do: 2-3
REIMÃO, João Barbosa: 47-12
REYMÃO, Francisco Barbosa: 47-11
REYMÃO, João Barbosa: 47-11
REYMONDO, Fray (ref): 32-9
REYS, Joanna dos: 34-14
REZENDE, Maria Vasques de: 2-2
RIBA DE AVIA, Count of: 54-9
RIBAFEITA, Abbot of: 86-11; 134-12
RIBEIRO, Camilla: 40-8
RIBEIRO, Francisco: 27-8
RIBEIRO, Gonçallo: 37-12
RIBEIRO, Isabel: 27-9; 43-10
RIBEIRO, João: 41-11; 43-10
RIBEIRO, Jose de Azevedo: 105-11
RIBEIRO, Maria: 10-6; 65-11; 73-8
RIBEIRO, Simão: 27-9; 41-11
RIBEIRO, Thomaz Moniz: 126-6
ROCHA, Anna da: 143-9
ROCHA, Antonio da: 133-8
ROCHA, Baltazar da: 143-9
ROCHA, Brites da: G 3-6
ROCHA, Francisco Gonçalves da: 60-10
ROCHA, Ignes da: 58-7
ROCHA, Isabel da: 133-8; 143-9
ROCHA, João Homem da: 77-12

ROCHA, Maria da: 142-11; 143-9
ROCHA, Maria Felicianna da: 77-12
RODRIGO, (s. of João Borges): 120-11
RODRIGO LUCIANO, (s. of Rodrigo Antonio de Abreu Lima): 131-12
RODRIGUES, Aldonça: 83-6
RODRIGUES, Cristovão: 109-17
RODRIGUES, Domingos: 18-9
RODRIGUES, Gonçallo: 3-6; 97-11
RODRIGUES, Ignes: G 2-6
RODRIGUES, Isabel: 66-6
RODRIGUES, João: 124-5
RODRIGUES, Maria: 131-11
RODRIGUES, Mecia: 3-5; 82-6; 99-2
ROLIM, Leonel de Moura: 10-7; 10-8
ROQUE, (s. of Alexandre da Cunha, e Mello): 77-10
ROQUE, (s. of Elena de Abreu): 122-9
ROSA MARIA, (d. of Leopoldo Luis de Sousa): 36-15
ROSA, (d. of Antonio de Abreu Lima): 28-10
ROSA, (d. of Pedro Madeira): 122-10
ROSA, (d. of Vicente de Macedo da Cunha): 34-15
ROSA, (w. of Alexandre da Cunha, e Mello de Abreu): 77-13
ROSA, Anna Theresa: 131-12
ROSA, Germineza: 109-12
ROSA, Margarida da: 110-13
ROSA, Pedro Gomes: 110-13
ROXAS, Catarina de: 12-6
ROXAS, Fernando de: 12-6
ROXAS, Maria de: 12-6; 81-9
ROZA, Germineza da: 109-12
SÁ, Antonia de: 26-7
SÁ, Catarina de: 127-15
SÁ, Duarte de: G 3-5
SÁ, Gomes de: 9-4
SÁ, Isabel de: 26-7
SÁ, Luis de: 26-8
SÁ, Marianna de: G 3-6
SÁ, Pedro de: 9-4
SÁ, Susana de: 7-7
SÁ, Valeria Ramos de: 94-12
SABOIANO, Bartolomeu Sanches Brariel: 92-17
SALGADO, Antonio: 93-13
SALGADO, Leonor: 51-7
SALGADO, Manoel Pereira: 34-12
SALGADO, Pedro: 93-13
SAMPAIO, Adrião Pereira de: 111-12
SAMPAIO, Diogo Pereira de: 111-12
SAMPAIO, Manoel Fernandes de: 16-6
SAMPAIO, Margarida Nogueira de: 33-12
SAMPAIO, Maria do Campo e: 84-13
SAMPAIO, Marianna Pereira de: 84-14
SAMPAIO, Paullo de Mello: 28-9; 28-10
SAMPAIO, Simão Saraiva de: 84-14
SAMPAIO, Theresa Nogueira de: 33-12
SANCHES, Fernão Brandão: 52-7
SANCHES, Garcia: 96-11
SANCHES, Maria: 81-7; 93-13
SANCHO I, King of Portugal: 1-3; 1-4; 3-5
SANCHO II, King of Portugal: 1-5; 3-5; 130-6
SANDOVAL, Alvaro de: 27-6
SANDOVAL, Diogo Gomes: 2-10

SOARES, Pedro Vaz: 73-14; 92-18
SOARES, Tereja: 5-10
SOARES, Thereza: 3-5; 5-10
SOARES, Thome: 26-6
SOBRAL, Eugenia Maria de: 123-5
SOBRAL, João do: 123-5
SOEIRO, Antonio: 7-10
SOTOMAYOR, Antonia: 54-9
SOTOMAYOR, Antonio Sarmento: 54-9
SOTOMAYOR, Benita: 54-9
SOTOMAYOR, Benito Ozores: 104-11
SOTOMAYOR, Fernando: 5-11
SOTOMAYOR, Fernando Annes: 54-9; 54-10;
   54-11
SOTOMAYOR, Francisca: 54-10
SOTOMAYOR, Francisca de: 5-11; 5-12; 54-9;
   54-11
SOTOMAYOR, Francisco Rabello: G 3-5; G 3-6
SOTOMAYOR, Guiomar de Sá: G 3-5; G 4-6;
   G 4-7
SOTOMAYOR, Isabel: 80-5
SOTOMAYOR, Isabel de Sá: G 3-5; G 4-6; G 4-7
SOTOMAYOR, João de Macedo: 68-12
SOTOMAYOR, João de Sá: G 3-6
SOTOMAYOR, João Marcos de Sá: 142-11
SOTOMAYOR, Leonor de Sá: G 3-6; G 3-7; G 4-6
SOTOMAYOR, Maria: 5-10; 5-11
SOTOMAYOR, Maria de: 5-12
SOTOMAYOR, Maria de Oya: 54-8
SOTOMAYOR, Maria de Sá: 142-11; G 4-6
SOTOMAYOR, Miguel Guedes de Figueiredo:
   84-16
SOTOMAYOR, Patornilha de Chaves Mendonça:
   54-11
SOTOMAYOR, Pedro: 5-11; 54-9
SOTOMAYOR, Pedro Alvares: 16-4; 40-5
SOTOMAYOR, Theresa: 54-9
SOUSA, Aldonça de: 2-4
SOUSA, Alvaro de: 36-14
SOUSA, Alvaro de (ref): 31-10
SOUSA, Alvaro Dias de: 2-4
SOUSA, Antonia Caetana de: 73-13; 73-14; 73-15
SOUSA, Antonia de: 7-9
SOUSA, Antonio Caetano de Sousa (ref): 2-3
SOUSA, Antonio de Abreu de: 81-9; 81-10
SOUSA, Brites de: 2-4; 7-9; 27-6
SOUSA, Diogo de: 131-12
SOUSA, Estevão de Correa de Araujo, e: 76-7
SOUSA, Favião de Brito, e: 142-11
SOUSA, Fernando Affonso de: 27-6
SOUSA, Fernão de: 2-5; 40-5
SOUSA, Francisca Antonia Xavier de Moraes Lara,
   e: 28-12
SOUSA, Francisco de: 2-8
SOUSA, Francisco Jose de: 108-11
SOUSA, Genebra de: 40-5
SOUSA, Gonçallo Pereira de: 57-7
SOUSA, Henrique de: 57-9
SOUSA, Ignes Dias de: 2-2; 23-3; G 1-2
SOUSA, Isabel Maria de: 110-12
SOUSA, Joanna de: 2-8
SOUSA, João da Silva, e: 81-9; 103-10
SOUSA, João de: 10-4; 57-9
SOUSA, João de Abreu de: 81-8
SOUSA, João Gomes de: 2-4; 2-5; 28-5

SOUSA, Leonor Angelica de Lara, e: 28-12
SOUSA, Leopoldo Luis de: 36-14; 36-15
SOUSA, Lopo Dias de: 2-2; 2-4; 23-3
SOUSA, Marcos Ferreira de: 33-11
SOUSA, Maria Cordovil de: 81-8
SOUSA, Maria de: 36-14; 53-11
SOUSA, Maria Lobato de: 28-9
SOUSA, Miguel de Abreu de: 106-10
SOUSA, Mor Fernandes de: 27-6
SOUSA, Pedro Ribeiro de: 2-7
SOUSA, Ruy Gomes de Abreu de: 106-12
SOUSA, Simão Ribeiro de: 43-10
SOUTELLO, Anna Dias: 27-8
SURRACA, Maria: 49-4
SUZANA, (d. of Sebastianna de Lima): 107-9
TANGIL, Maria Soares: 99-2
TANGIL, Soeiro Affonso Soares: 2-1
TARRACA, Maria: 49-4
TAVARES, Antonia Borges: 119-11
TAVARES, Antonio de Brito: 10-8
TAVARES, Jeronimo de Mendanha: 93-13
TAVARES, Jeronimo de Mendonça: 93-13
TAVARES, Pedro Borges: 119-11
TAVEIRA, Brites Rodrigues: 80-6
TAVEIRA, Jose Vicente: 131-12
TAVEIRA, Pedro Rodrigues: 80-6
TAVORA, Anna de Araujo de: 64-7
TÁVORA, Francisco Cabral de: 84-13
TAVORA, Luisa de: 54-10
TAVORA, Luiza de: 5-12
TAVORA, Maria de: 93-13
TAVORA, Simão de: 62-9
TEIVE, Sebastião Ribeiro de: 139-11
TEIXEIRA, Antonio: 25-13
TEIXEIRA, Ayres: 32-9; 32-10; 32-11
TEIXEIRA, Brites: 92-14
TEIXEIRA, Clara: 30-11; 33-13
TEIXEIRA, Domingos (ref): 49-3
TEIXEIRA, Duarte Vaz: 32-9
TEIXEIRA, Felipa: 32-9
TEIXEIRA, Francisca dos Guimaraens: 25-10
TEIXEIRA, Gaspar Rabello: 84-14
TEIXEIRA, Genebra: 123-3
TEIXEIRA, Jacinto: 34-12
TEIXEIRA, Joanna: 83-13
TEIXEIRA, Jose: 68-14
TEIXEIRA, Manoel Rabello: 84-14
TEIXEIRA, Maria: 89-11
TEIXEIRA, Marianna: 27-8; 63-10
TEIXEIRA, Pedro: 27-8
TEIXEIRA, Pelagia: 71-9
TELLES, Francisco de Abreu Lima: 106-12
TEMUDO, Simão: 114-4
TENORIO, Antonio de Farya: 73-12
TENORIO, Marchioness of: 5-12
TENORIO, Marquis of: 5-12; 54-10
TENREIRO, Jorge: 89-11
TERESA, Countess of Portucale: 1-1
THEMUDA, Isabel: 114-4
THEMUDO, Isabel: 113-3
THEMUDO, Maria: 113-3
THEODOSIO, Duke: 2-8
THEODOSIO, Duke of Bragança: 109-15
THEODOZIA, (d. of Roque Fernandes de
   Abreu): 79-8

THEREJA, (d. of Antão Gomes de Abreu): 10-4
THERESA, (d. of Antonio de Abreu Lima): 28-10
THERESA, (d. of Felipa da Cunha de Azevedo): 45-11
THERESA, (d. of João Borges): 120-11
THERESA, (d. of Rafael de Abreu Lima): 52-10
THERESA, (w. of Diogo Gomes de Abreu): 19-5
THERESA, (w. of Leopoldo Luis de Sousa): 36-15
THERESA MARIA, (w. of Diogo de Almeida da Silva):
    131-12
THOAR, Catarina de: 12-6
THOAR, Fernando de: 12-6
THOMASIA, (d. of Antonio de Abreu Lima): 28-10
THOMASIA, Magdalena: 84-16
THOME, Antão: 2-7
TINOCO, Brites Velho: 73-10
TINOCO, Domingos da Silva: 133-10
TINOCO, Elena Lopes: 60-10
TINOCO, Francisco Alvares: 60-10
TINOCO, Jeronimo Fernandes Carneiro: 7-7
TINOCO, João: 60-10
TINOCO, Manoel da Silva: 133-10
TINOCO, Mariana da Rocha: 60-10
TINOCO, Martim Velho: 73-10
TOLEDO, Fernando de: 81-9
TOLEDO, Fernão Alvares de: 81-9
TOLEDO, Fradique Alvares de: 81-9; 103-10
TOLEDO, Fradique de: 81-9
TOLEDO, Francisca de: 81-9
TORIS, Apolonia de: 5-10
TORRAVAL, (father-in-law of Vasco Gomes de Abreu):
    11-6
TORRES, Gonçallo de: 64-5
TOSCANO, Antonio: 133-8
TOSCANO, Antonio de Abreu: 115-3
TOSCANO, Antonio Gil: 40-6
TOSCANO, Fernão Gil: 40-6; 40-7; 40-8
TOSCANO, Francisco: 115-1
TOSCANO, Francisco de Abreu: 115-2
TOSCANO, Giraldo Rodrigues: 40-6
TOSCANO, Gomes Martins: 40-6
TOSCANO, Henrique: 40-7; 40-8
TOSCANO, Jeronima: 40-7
TOSCANO, João: 115-1; 115-2
TOSCANO, Leonor: 115-1
TOSCANO, Leonor Martins: 40-6
TOSCANO, Leonor Rodrigues: 40-6
TOSCANO, Miguel: 40-6
TOSCANO, Rafael: 115-3
TOSCANO, Ruy Martins: 40-6
TRILLAR, Laura de: 54-10
TRINDADE, Maria da: 40-7
TUYA, João de Lima Abreu de: 25-12
ULHOA, Constança de: 109-15
ULHOA, Mayor de: 109-15
UMBELINA, (d. of Pedro Borges de Castro): 119-11
UNHÃO, Cristovão de: 87-11
URSULLA, (d. of Hipolito de Macedo): 34-14
VALE, Abbot of: 107-9
VALE, Anna do: G 3-4
VALENÇA, Ruy Vaz de: 124-5
VALENCIA, João Vicente de: 22-2
VALENCIA, Viceroy of: 54-9
VALENTE, Diogo: 45-12
VALLADARES, Guiomar Lourenço: 1-6
VALLADARES, Guiomar Lourenço de: 2-1

VALLADARES, Lourenço Soares de: 1-6
VALLE, Garcia do: 58-7
VALLE, Germinesa do: G 1-3
VALLE, Gonçallo do: 84-12
VALLENA, João Vicente de: 1-6
VARELLA, Felipa: 44-12; 88-11
VARELLA, Francisco: 111-11
VARELLA, Ignes: 98-12
VARELLA, Ignes Sofia: 44-12
VARELLA, Sebastião Pacheco: 44-12
VARGAS, Luis de: 109-15
VARGAS, Mayor Maria de: 109-15
VAS, Maria: 16-4
VASCONCELLOS, Alvaro Carvalho de: 15-7
VASCONCELLOS, Ambrosia de: 56-7
VASCONCELLOS, Anna de: 13-6
VASCONCELLOS, Antonio de Gouvea de: 91-13
VASCONCELLOS, Antonio Pedro de Gamboa:
    16-13
VASCONCELLOS, Caetana Josefa de Lima: 106-11
VASCONCELLOS, Damião de Almeida, e: 56-7
VASCONCELLOS, Diogo Mendes de: 13-6
VASCONCELLOS, Elena de: 30-12
VASCONCELLOS, Fernando de Almeida: 86-13
VASCONCELLOS, Francisco de Gouvea de: 91-13
VASCONCELLOS, Francisco Pinheiro de: 36-14
VASCONCELLOS, Gonçallo Cardoso Homem de:
    83-10
VASCONCELLOS, Guiomar Rodrigues de: 2-1
VASCONCELLOS, Isabel de: 92-14
VASCONCELLOS, Isabel de Almeida, e: 56-7
VASCONCELLOS, Isabel Mendes de: 95-9
VASCONCELLOS, Joanna or Maria Rodrigues de:
    83-7
VASCONCELLOS, Joanne Mendes de: 83-8; 95-9
VASCONCELLOS, João de Seixas de: 94-16
VASCONCELLOS, João Mendes de: 29-11
VASCONCELLOS, Jose Sarmento de: 84-17
VASCONCELLOS, Luis Mendes de: 13-5
VASCONCELLOS, Manoel de: 39-3
VASCONCELLOS, Manoel Godinho de: 30-13
VASCONCELLOS, Manoel Pereira de: 30-13; 86-13
VASCONCELLOS, Maria de: 30-12
VASCONCELLOS, Maria de Araujo e: 52-10
VASCONCELLOS, Maria Delfina Osorio Sarmento
    de: 84-17
VASCONCELLOS, Maria Leonor de: 94-16
VASCONCELLOS, Maria Mendonça, e: 125-6; 126-6
VASCONCELLOS, Maria or Joanna Rodrigues de:
    83-7
VASCONCELLOS, Marianna de: 106-9
VASCONCELLOS, Martim Mendes de: 32-11
VASCONCELLOS, Mem Rodrigues de: 83-8; 96-11
VASCONCELLOS, Mem Rodrigues de Abreu, e:
    96-10; 96-11
VASCONCELLOS, Nicolao de Tovar de: 127-17
VASCONCELLOS, Paulla de: 16-10
VASCONCELLOS, Paullo de: 86-13
VASCONCELLOS, Pedro Pereira de: 102-9
VASCONCELLOS, Ruy de Abreu, e: 96-11; 96-12
VASCONCELLOS, Ruy Pires de: 83-7
VASCONCELLOS, Serafina de Lima, e: 52-10
VASCONCELLOS, Theresa de Mendonça, e: 126-6
VASQUES, Luis: 16-12
VAZ, Anna: 133-8

Arms of the King of Wessex

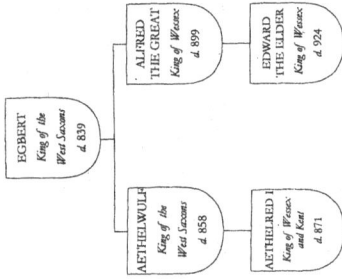

EGBERT
King of the
West Saxons
d. 839

ALFRED
THE GREAT
King of Wessex
d. 899

EDWARD
THE ELDER
King of Wessex
d. 924

AETHELWULF
King of the
West Saxons
d. 858

AETHELRED I
King of Wessex
and Kent
d. 871

ELGIVA
Wife of
Harold Parcus,
King of
Denmark

GORM
THE OLD
King of
Denmark
d. 931

HARALD
BLUETOOTH
King of
Denmark
d. 985

GUNNOR
Duchess of
Normandy

Arms of the Dukes of Normandy

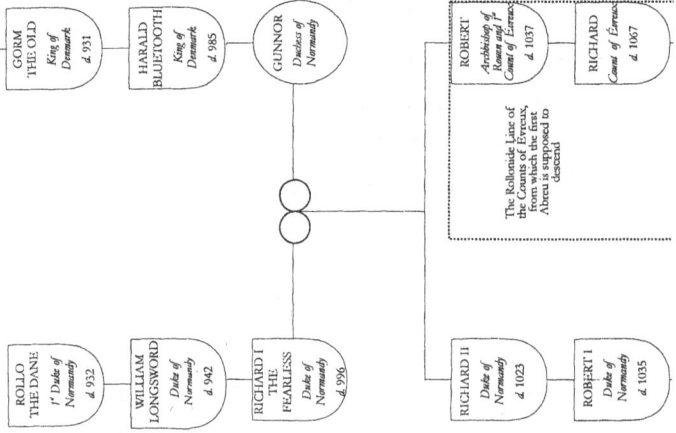

ROLLO
THE DANE
1st Duke of
Normandy
d. 932

WILLIAM
LONGSWORD
Duke of
Normandy
d. 942

RICHARD I
THE
FEARLESS
Duke of
Normandy
d. 996

ROBERT
Archbishop of
Rouen and 1st
Count of Evreux
d. 1037

RICHARD
Count of Evreux
d. 1067

The Rollonide Line of
the Counts of Evreux,
from which the first
Abreu is supposed to
descend

RICHARD II
Duke of
Normandy
d. 1023

ROBERT I
Duke of
Normandy
d. 1035

Arms of the King of France

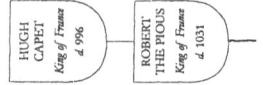

HUGH
CAPET
King of France
d. 996

ROBERT
THE PIOUS
King of France
d. 1031

WILLIAM THE CONQUEROR
Duke of Normandy and King of England
d. 1087

Arms of the Kings of England

GUILLAUME
Count of Évreux
d. 1118

AGNES D'ÉVREUX
Wife of Simon I,
Count of Montfort
l'Amaury

ROBERT
Duke of Burgundy
d. 1076

HENRY I
King of France
d. 1060

missing link

GONÇALLO MARTINS DE ABREU
d. after 1142

Ancient Arms of the Abreu Family

Modern Arms of the Abreu Family

The Gaulish helmet
(a connection with
the wings of the Abreus?)

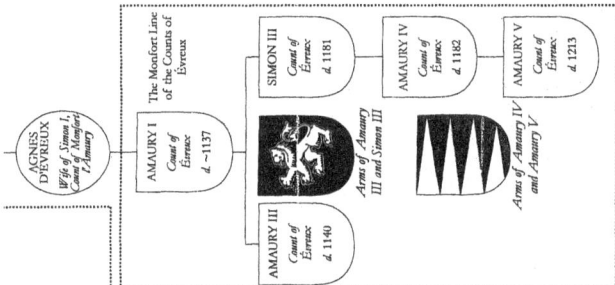

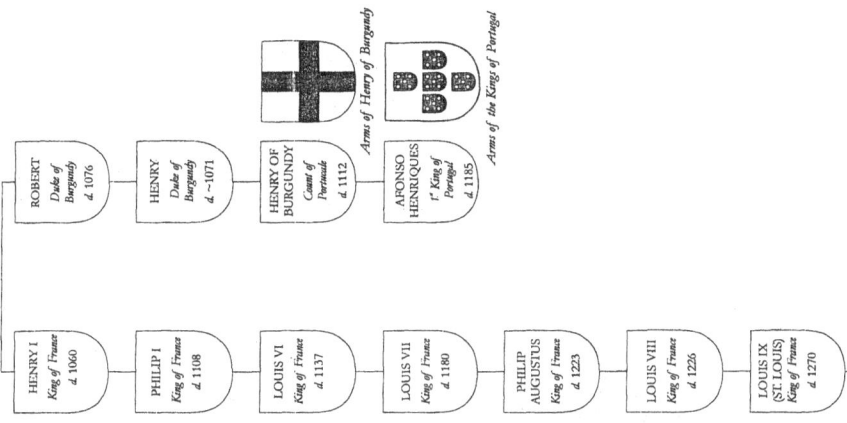

The Montfort Line of the Counts of Évreux

AMAURY I
Count of Évreux
d. ~1137

AMAURY III
Count of Évreux
d. 1140

SIMON III
Count of Évreux
d. 1181

Arms of Amaury III and Simon III

AMAURY IV
Count of Évreux
d. 1182

AMAURY V
Count of Évreux
d. 1213

Arms of Amaury IV and Amaury V

HENRY
Duke of Burgundy
d. ~1071

HENRY OF BURGUNDY
Count of Portucale
d. 1112

AFONSO HENRIQUES
1st King of Portugal
d. 1185

Arms of Henry of Burgundy

Arms of the Kings of Portugal

PHILIP I
King of France
d. 1108

LOUIS VI
King of France
d. 1137

LOUIS VII
King of France
d. 1180

PHILIP AUGUSTUS
King of France
d. 1223

* s death (1172),
the County of
Évreux was vested
in the French Crown

LOUIS VIII
King of France
d. 1226

LOUIS IX
(ST. LOUIS)
King of France
d. 1270

PHILIP III
THE BOLD
King of France
d. 1285

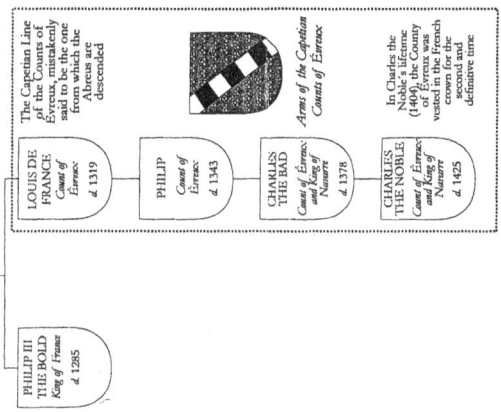

The Capetian Line
of the Counts of
Évreux, mistakenly
said to be the one
from which the
Abreus are
descended

LOUIS DE
FRANCE
Count of
Évreux
d. 1319

PHILIP
Count of
Évreux
d. 1343

Arms of the Capetian
Counts of Évreux

CHARLES
THE BAD
Count of Évreux
and King of
Navarre
d. 1378

CHARLES
THE NOBLE
Count of Évreux
and King of
Navarre
d. 1425

In Charles the
Noble's lifetime
(1404), the County
of Évreux was
vested in the French
crown for the
second and
definitive time

THE COUNTS OF ÉVREUX

As can be seen in the chart shown following, the first line of the Counts of Évreux begins in Robert (d. 1037), Archbishop of Rouen, who was the son of Richard I the Fearless, Duke of Normandy, and Gunnor, a Danish Princess and a fourth-generation descendant of Aethelred I, King of Wessex and Kent, who was the brother of Alfred the Great, the father of Edward the Elder. Gaio states that the Counts of Évreux are descended from Edward, but this connection, although possible, has not been found as far as we are concerned.

Nor does Gaio inform the exact link between Gonçallo Martins de Abreu and his alleged ancestors, the Counts of Évreux. To begin with, the name Gonçallo Martins is clearly not French and if we abide by Gaio's opinion (that the ancestor of the Abreus was a Frenchman from Normandy), we are led to believe that "Gonçallo Martins" is a Portuguese corruption of his original name (perhaps "Gonzales Martin", although this is still an improbable name).

Let us now consider some dates. Gonçallo Martins de Abreu is said to have been a companion to Count Henry of Burgundy (1066-1112) and to have been a general in the battle of Veiga da Matança (1143). The 31-year span between this battle and the Count's decease makes us believe that, at Count Henry's death, Gonçallo was a young man, having been born around 1090. This makes him a contemporary of Guillaume d'Évreux (d. 1118) and his nephews Counts Amaury II (d. 1137), Amaury III (d. 1140) and Simon III (d. 1181). Gonçallo could have been the son of Count Guillaume, who, however, is said to have had no children (at least legitimate), this being the reason why, upon Guillaume's decease, the County was conveyed to the family of the lords of Monfort through the marriage of Simon I of Monfort and Guillaume's sister Agnes d'Évreux. If Gonçallo was not the son of Count Guillaume, he must have been a descendant of Guillaume's ancestors by a male line (according to Gaio). In either case he was a Rollonide, i.e., a descendant by male line of Rollo the Dane, a Viking leader who made several incursions in northern France and, through a deal made with King Charles the Simple (Treaty of Saint-Clair-sur-Epte, 911), accepted to be baptized and became the 1st Duke of Normandy. However, among the Rollonides and their descendants, we have found nobody with a Gonçallo-like name who moved to the Iberian Peninsula in early 12th century.

If this absence of proof weakens Gaio's version, obviously it alone is not evidence that the Évreux connection is false. Maybe further research on ancient documents will clarify these questions some day. On the other hand, and in favor of this French connection, there is a remarkably similarity between the arms of the Abreus and those of the Dukedom of Normandy (and also with the arms of the Kingdom of England, whose sovereigns are also direct descendants of Rollo): the colors are identical (a red shield charged with golden figures) and the general pattern is quite similar, besides the fact that they are also similar to the arms of the Counts of Évreux of the Monfort line (the Abreus' alleged cousins). And we could speculate that the origin of the wings in the arms of the Abreus could be a reminiscence of the French ancestry of this family (the wings of the Gaulish helmet have been since ancient times a typical symbol of France).

There is also a version of Gándara and Lima Bezerra, who claim that the Abreus descend from the Capetian line of the Counts of Évreux. (This line is called the "second" by Gaio, because the first consisted of two successive lines, Rollonide and Monfort, separated by one break in the male line). However, this version is obviously a mistake, for the first Portuguese Abreus (whose names have been recorded in documents dating from the 12th century) could never descend from Louis of France (the first Count of Évreux of the Capetian line), who was born in 1276 and died in 1319.

BIBLIOGRAPHICAL COMMENTS

The data about the Counts of Évreux was found mainly in the article *"Liste des comtes d'Évreux"* in the French Wikipedia (05/17/2007), and in an article entitled *"Normandy, Nobility"*, by Charles Cawley, of the Foundation for Medieval Genealogy (05/17/2007), a study which gives an extensive list of documental sources. The biographical information about the English and Danish kings has been largely taken from Encyclopedia Britannica 2006 Ultimate Reference Suite DVD. The data about the ancestors of Rollo is mainly based on the article *"The Paternal Genealogy of Homer Beers James"* (10/31/2005), which also mentions a great number of documental sources.